Sophistical Practice

Sophistical Practice

Toward a Consistent Relativism

Barbara Cassin

FORDHAM UNIVERSITY PRESS

NEW YORK 2014

Library of Congress Control Number: 2014932516

Printed in the United States of America

16 15 14   5 4 3 2 1

First edition

CONTENTS

IV. Performance and Performative

V. "Enough of the Truth For . . ."

ACKNOWLEDGMENTS

Earlier versions of parts of this book have previously appeared in print. "Toward a New Topology of Philosophy" was first published as "Philosophical Displacements: Interview with Barbara Cassin," in "Three French Philosophers Interviewed by Penelope Deutscher," *Women's Philosophy Review*, no. 24 (2000): 34–56. Penelope Deutscher and I continued and actualized this interview in 2012. "Who's Afraid of the Sophists? Against Ethical Correctness" appeared in *Hypatia* 15, no. 4 (Fall 2000): 102–20. "Speak If You Are a Man, or the Transcendental Exclusion" was published in *Terror and Consensus: Vicissitudes of French Thought*, edited by Jean Joseph Goux and Philip R. Wood (Stanford: Stanford University Press, 1998). "*Topos/Kairos*: Two Modes of Invention" will be published by Michael McDonald on the new Oxford Handbooks website. "Time of Deliberation and Space of Power: Athens and Rome, the First Conflict" appeared in *Javnost—The Public* 12, no. 4 (2005): 39–44. "From Organism to Picnic: Which Consensus for Which City?" was published in *Angelaki* 11, no. 3 (2006): 21–38. "Aristotle with and Against Kant on the Idea of Nature" appeared in *French Women Philosophers: A Contemporary Reader*, edited by Christina Howells (London: Routledge, 2004, pp. 100–121). "Paradigms of the Past in Arendt and Heidegger" appeared in *Comparative Civilizations Review* 22 (Fall 1990): 28–53. "How to Really Do Things with Words: Performance Before the Performative" was first published in French in *Genèse de l'acte de parole*, edited by Barbara Cassin and Carlos Lévy (Turnhout: Brépols, 2011, pp. 113–147). "The Performative Without Condition: A University *sans appel*," which I cowrote with Philippe Büttgen, appeared in *Radical Philosophy* 162

(July/August 2010): 31–37. "Genres and Genders. Woman/Philosopher: Identity as Strategy" was published in *Women Philosophers' Journal*, UNESCO, no. 1 (2011): 25–37. "Philosophising in Languages" appeared in *Nottingham French Studies* 49, no. 2 (Summer 2010): 17–28. "Enough of the Truth For . . ." was originally published in French in *La Vérité*, edited by Bernard Van Meenen (Brussels: Publications des Facultés Universitaires Saint-Louis, 2006, pp. 63–75). "Politics of Memory" appeared in *Javnost—The Public* 8, no. 3 (2001): 9–22. "Google and Cultural Democracy" was first published in French as a chapter in my book *Google-moi: La deuxième mission de l'Amérique* (Paris: Albin-Michel, 2007, pp. 240–251). "The Relativity of Translation and Relativism" appeared in *CR: The New Centennial Review* 12, no. 1 (Spring 2012): 23–45. Permission to reprint is gratefully acknowledged.

I would like to thank Anthony Padgen for his help in revising "Rhetorical Turns in Ancient Greece," Wim van Binsbergen for his revision of the translation of "Politics of Memory," Andrew Goffey as the philosophizing translator, Jennifer Cazenave for her eyes and last hand, Penelope Deutscher, Emily Apter, Jacques Lezra, and Bachir Diagne, who encouraged me to work in English.

Sophistical Practice

Introduction: Toward a New Topology of Philosophy

Barbara Cassin, with Penelope Deutscher

> I don't know how to approach, why not say it, the truth—no more than woman. I have said that the one and the other are the same thing, at least to man.
>
> —JACQUES LACAN, *Encore*[1]

July 1998

PENELOPE DEUTSCHER: In your work, and particularly in *L'effet sophistique* (*The Sophistic Effect*)[2] you have put forward a sophistic history of philosophy. Can you describe this?

BARBARA CASSIN: The sophistic history of philosophy is a history of neglected and repressed traditions, of alternative paths. It is essential to have a plurality instead of a single path. That single, dominant path of ontology goes from Parmenides to Plato via a certain reading of Aristotle up to Heidegger. I'm interested in showing how it goes even up to Habermas, who might seem to be different but belongs to the ontological tradition; he rejects the same things and people as Plato and Aristotle—in particular the sophistic and everything that might look like it. The history of philosophy,

I

the royal road, as history of ontology and phenomenology or as history of communication, cannot be traced or even identified as a path unless one looks, from an outside perspective, at what was, even materially, left to one side.

Sophistic texts are the paradigm of what was not only left to one side but transformed and made unintelligible by their enemies. Imagine you were trying to reconstruct a dinosaur from a few small bones and that these bones had been chewed up by the dinosaur's foes. My work is thus a paleontology of perversion.

To be able to modify the perception we have of the great conceptual history of philosophy and of the royal road of ontology and phenomenology, we have to look elsewhere and even outside philosophy. Philosophy has organized things so that any critique of the royal road is rejected as not being philosophy. And you have to keep working on authors who are difficult to identify, like Anaximander, so praised by Heidegger—but my question is, can one be pre-Socratic in another way?

These "others" have in common another way of speaking, even another conception of *logos*.

I found a very simple model and countermodel, perhaps also a little caricaturish. The model is Parmenides's *Poem* and Platonico-Aristotelian ontology, and the countermodel is the sophistic. Parmenidean ontology is wonderfully analyzed by Heidegger. He shows the connection, the cobelonging between being and speaking: to speak is to speak Being. To be, to think and to say are one and the same. That leads directly to *Unterwegs zur Sprache* (*On the Way to Language*) and to the way in which a human being is entrusted with the "Being There" (*Dasein*) who will speak Being.

The countermodel, I no longer call it ontology but "logology," to take up the term Novalis used to refer to discourse insofar as it is primarily concerned with itself. Sophistics is that second type of *logos*. But one would certainly have to think about the place of atomism, which was appropriated as ontology by Aristotle. But, as Lacan also sniffed, if Democritus is a physicist, the *phusis* he treated was not nature but discourse.[3]

So, sophistics, for me, is a discourse that is primarily and above all performative. It is not a matter of saying what is but of making what one says *be*. One is in a completely different model from that of the physicoontological model, say, where the concern is to account for *physis*, or being, whatever name is used. In the second model, discourse is a "great tyrant"—to use Gorgias's phrase—and creates as it speaks. Now, the first performance is the *polis*. So one finds the opposition between physics and politics reworked.

With sophistics, one passes from physics to politics, from philosophy to literature. All that against the background of a basic discordance, which is the discordance between ontology and logology. I say all this to explain that in my view, one can't work in the mainstream without at the same time working on the countermodels and without working on philosophy's "others."

So obviously, I need numerous traditions, a new geography. I also need the long-term perspective to see what resurgences of antiquity appear in modernity, for example, to see how the regime of discourse forbidden by Aristotle in book *Gamma* of the *Metaphysics* reappears via Freud and Lacan . . . via sophistics, that is, via the possibility of homonymy and the signifier.

The Prostitute's History

PD: What sort of relation is there between the sophistic history of philosophy and the history of philosophy?

BC: Nowadays, what would a sophistic history of philosophy be? It is a history of what was forbidden by the dominant tradition in its efforts to define philosophy and define itself as philosophy. Walter Benjamin used to say: story should be written from the point of view of the prostitute instead of from the point of view of the client. In a certain way, the sophistic history of philosophy writes the history of philosophy from the point of view of the prostitute, that is, from the point of view of the bad "other"—the one whom one has not only the right but also the duty to shun. It's a way of reproblematizing what is inside and outside, interior and exterior.

I showed this, with reference to a precise and crucial point, in *The Decision of Meaning*, when I analyzed the impossible demonstration given by

Aristotle in book *Gamma* of the *Metaphysics*, of the principle of all principles, the law of noncontradiction. Aristotle establishes this first principle, which we all believe and obey, whether we know it or not, through his refutation of sophistics. Aristotle decided that to speak means to say something, that is, to signify something, that is, to signify one and the same thing for oneself and for others. When I say "Good Day," I am not saying "Go to hell," or if I say at the same time "Go to hell," then, according to Aristotle, I am not saying anything at all, I am not even speaking. Outside of the regime of meaning as univocity, there is only "what there is in the sounds of the voice and in the words." To forbid homonymy is as structural as to prohibit incest.

In the course of his demonstration, Aristotle admits that the whole of Greece (Heraclitus and Protagoras, of course, but also Homer and even Parmenides) is in danger of being left out, outside the regime of univocity. But Aristotle works at recouping them and ends up showing that they all speak like him; they all belong to the faithful, they all accept the principle. The only one left outside is the Sophist, who speaks for "the pleasure of speaking," the unrecoupable "speaking plant."

So I am trying to identify a series of philosophical gestures. To each gesture corresponds its "other," which is excluded or sick or mad—and what interests me most is to see how these gestures get reproduced. I'm very interested in seeing how Karl-Otto Apel and Jürgen Habermas reproduce the Aristotelian gesture. How in their work it is the consistent skeptic who becomes the Sophist. Using the same type of argument. What strikes me are the points at which philosophy is impelled to violence. It's what I call "using the stick." When Aristotle says of those "people who are puzzled to know whether one ought to honor the gods and love one's parents" that they "need punishment, while those who are puzzled to know whether snow is white or not need perception,"[4] I want to know at what point philosophy feels it has the right to say that people need punishment . . .

PD: And feels the need to say that people need punishment.

BC: . . . Yes, when does it feel the need to. That comes back to a certain type of problematic that Lyotard had in mind with "the differend." At a certain moment, Habermas excludes certain men, excludes certain types of speech that are actually employed, puts them outside the "communicational community." That is something that interests me a lot.

Philosophy and Its Others

PD: There are also, in your work, reflections on the relation between women and philosophy. In one issue of the *Cahiers du GRIF* published in 1992, "Women-Philosophy," Françoise Collin asks: *From where does one think when one thinks? What are the sources of thought?* You would not refer to "masculine" or "feminine" modes of thought, but in your article in this issue of the *Cahiers*, you say that a woman "makes do with the leftovers, she knows how to make a stew." Apparently, for you there is a relation between being either a man or a woman in contemporary philosophy and the question of how one works as a philosopher, what methodology one chooses, what one's philosophical gestures are. How do you understand this relation?

BC: Perhaps I can begin with the relation between, let's say, the great ontological or phenomenological tradition and its "others." The great ontological or phenomenological tradition is at one and the same time a tradition of submission and a tradition of mastery. It is certainly a submission to being, to the world, to the real. But it is also an absolute mastery in several senses. First, because it defines a straight line, an orthodoxy. And everything which is not within this orthodoxy—either for it or even against it but in a relation which is acceptable because it confirms the rules of the game—is expelled and in a certain way reduced to silence.

All the same, up until now, philosophy has essentially been carried out by men. It is quite natural to assimilate, or to be tempted to assimilate, this philosophical power to power of a masculine kind. So I would say (perhaps one can speak like that without being too simplistic) that the first women I came across in philosophy were the Sophists. They constitute for the Platonico-Aristotelian orthodoxy an unassimilable heterodoxy.

That does not prevent them, in other respects, from returning in force, just as women can overthrow the power of men. The Sophists returned in force, to the point where Hegel called them "the masters of Greece." They returned in force with rhetoric and the Second Sophistic Movement, and they were already there in force in the linguistic constitution of the *polis*. But philosophy as such marginalized them completely.

The philosopher who was mostly responsible for marginalizing them, in this instance, was not so much Plato as Aristotle. Plato fought the Sophists every inch of the way, using, whether he liked it or not, his resemblance to them or the resemblance of Socrates to a Sophist. It was Aristotle who truly classified them as "other," who put them in the index as "other" (in the sense, too, of putting them on the Index) when he demonstrated that their discursive regime, their way of speaking, was not human. They fell outside the principle of noncontradiction, and that made them immediately *homoioi phutôi*—"like plants."

Women did not speak much either, did they? Nor children, nor animals, nor slaves. All of them, they were all a bit on the plant side. In short, I think that philosophy has never been able to prevent itself from being Aristotelian on that level. I'm going very quickly—but there is a persistent position of the "other" which could be thought of as being somewhat feminine. And to occupy that position is "to philosophistisize"—to use Novalis's term. To go on describing the position, showing its genealogy and its effects—that is what is somewhat new.

There is a grand tradition and there is a great orthodoxy, and then there are all the "others." There is philosophical language, and then there is the rest—that is, precisely, rhetoric, literature, a certain type of poetry which is not the great ontological poetry or what is not considered as such, and so on. All these different registers, for me, are analogous, assimilable, adoptable, and adaptable.

That's what I mean by making a stew.

These registers are not accepted as such, and in any case, the passage from one to another is impossible to accept today—at least, impossible to accept in the grand tradition of editorial mastery, which succeeds philosophical mastery.

When I wanted to publish at the same time *The Sophistic Effect* and a collection of short stories (*Avec le plus petit et le plus inapparent des corps*, that's the phrase used by Gorgias to describe the power of *logos* as a small "body" which performs the most divine of acts), it proved impossible. I was told that if I wanted to keep my scholarly reputation, I should not publish the collection of short stories. As far as I was concerned, I thought my reputation would benefit from it. In any event, I published the stories in literary journals. I consider that the stories came out of the same type of work on language and the same type of work on the dominant, orthodox, or again ontological, phenomenological tradition. It is exactly the same type of philosophical work—and I would have been really excited if they could have been accepted at the same time. But as it turned out, they were unable to be.

It makes me absolutely speechless, and I don't feel I can swim against the current, it is too much for me. It is too difficult to swallow. And besides— one final point to explain my relation to, let us say, "masculine" philosophy— of course I have always encountered a lot of goodwill toward my stories or my poems from male philosophers who thought that what I wrote in philosophy was worthless. They have always said to me: "Well, of course, yes, it's brilliant, your writing, when you write stories or poems, it's fantastic." But, you see, for me, there is a kind of social resistance there. It is much easier for a woman to be a novelist than a philosopher. And as soon as she is recognized as a philosopher, she must not be a novelist.

PD: What were the steps, in terms of your training and intellectual development, which led you to the Sophists?

BC: I think the decisive encounter was with Heidegger, whom I met at the *Le Thor* seminar with the poet René Char, and my encounter with French Heideggerianism. That made me want to focus on Greek, and I realized that Greek philosophy was very entangled and twisted. And not only Greek philosophy but Greece, the Greek language, everything that was Hellenic was twisted in a certain way: a grandiose way, but appropriate for only a part of Greece. That really made me want to study the texts again, to understand how the traditions were articulated.

I studied philology, and I realized that viable alternatives existed. They were not always solid enough for my taste, from a philosophical point of view—in other words, I find that Heidegger is, in a certain way, irrefutable. In France, anyway, he has been irrefutable, much more than in Germany, obviously, for a large number of philosophers of the generation preceding mine, but also for my generation and for the one after, even now.

It was Pierre Aubenque who gave me the *Treatise on Non-Being* by Gorgias for my research subject. And from then on, many things crystallized, including the relation between philology and philosophy, between Gorgias and Parmenides. Gorgias put himself forward as a challenger to Parmenides, using other means, and a genuine violence, and above all, a terrifying intelligence, which saw right through ontology. That's how I perceived him, understood him, and that is what set in motion a reflection on the articulation between ontology and its critique. Once again my question is: Can one be pre-Socratic differently? How is there a Greece other than ultra-Heideggerian?

And with those questions, entire sections of Greek culture, not only of philosophy but also of rhetoric and literature, were opened up to being potentially reworked and perceived otherwise. The relation between philosophy and literature itself needs to be worked on—for example, when one begins to juxtapose and understand together the First and Second Sophistic Movements.

My intellectual career was really determined by that encounter with Heidegger. But under the auspices of René Char and of what his presence opened up simultaneously. Char was sufficiently great and even grandiose, sufficiently celestial and terrestrial at the same time, to allow me to question and to put into perspective, let us say, the extraordinary Heideggerian intelligibility. Poetry counts a lot for me—I write poems—but I would say not in a Heideggerian way. I don't sacralize poetry, and I don't think it offers a short path to ontological intuitions. I will always remember the dialogue between Heidegger and Char. Heidegger spoke of the poet and the philosopher as communicating from one mountain peak to another, and Char answered that they were much more like prisoners in an *oubliette* (a dungeon), almost underground prisoners, communicating through very small holes in the walls.

PD: Do you think that philosophers need to rethink the relation to Heidegger . . . ?

BC: Nowadays?

PD: Yes. Is it still a problem for contemporary French philosophy?

BC: I think it is, yes, to a great extent. The only antidote—well, there have been several antidotes. First, there has been more work done on Heidegger, by Derrida, for example, extensive work. But in my view, the real antidote is Deleuze, along with Jean-François Lyotard, who occupied a very complicated position. And Foucault, who certainly died a bit too soon, at least as far as his relation to Greek philosophy is concerned. (His last books, which look directly at Greece, are absolutely conventional; I don't think they come off right.)

PD: Many of your projects provide an occasion for encounters between different domains of philosophy, and the introduction to *Nos Grecs et leurs modernes* (*Our Greeks and Their Moderns*) (1991) explains your interest in getting Anglo-American philosophy and European hermeneutic philosophy to engage in dialogue.

BC: For me, the analytic-hermeneutic difference is very important for Greek philosophy because we are looking at two perceptions of the same texts, which are often difficult to reconcile. But it is not fundamental in philosophy. It gets things out of proportion and leads to conflicts that are sometimes more irritating than really beneficial. I mean that I could get on as well or as badly with someone from the hermeneutic tradition as with someone from the analytic tradition when it comes to Gorgias's *Treatise on Non-Being*. As it happens, I've been involved in scraps with one side as much as the other.

The Spirit of Languages

PD: Could you say something about the question of the spirit of languages? It is connected to your work on untranslatables.

BC: The big project is a dictionary of untranslatable terms in philosophy. It's a bit deceptive to call it that because it's not a dictionary: it won't cover all the terms, and because obviously the untranslatables are translated, and it is their translation that the debates are all about. This is also a way of finally resolving, but certainly not once and for all, my differences with

Heidegger. It's a way of giving another version of the great conceptual tradition which takes us from ancient Greece to modern Germany as though there were only one philosophical language worthy of the name, that of the Greeks and of those who are more Greek than the Greeks, namely the Germans, via, occasionally, a momentary and semiaccidental incursion into a language that one may consider, in a certain period, as interesting; for example, Italian during the Renaissance or Spanish at the time of the Mystics. It's a weapon against "ontological nationalism," which hierarchizes languages and peoples from the point of view of their proximity to being.

What I'm trying to do, by contrast, is understand how each language constitutes an autonomous geography, a net for understanding the world in its own way, a net to catch a world, create its world (something like logology again). A model other than the universality of the *logos* has to be found—Wilhelm von Humboldt offers a conception of language which takes into consideration the plurality of languages.

The *Dictionary of Untranslatables* tries, for example, to reflect on the difference between the words *mind, Geist,* and *esprit*. Or between *logos, ratio,* and *oratio. Mind, Geist,* and *esprit* belong to different semantic networks and give us access to different universes. None of these universes is superior. Then one has to go into enormous detail. One has to see at what point the terms were translated, at what point the bifurcations took place, at what point the superimpositions began to exist. And each time, not only what sort of genealogical arborescence but also what sort of rhizomatic spreading out are at stake.

At the same time as one is interested in discordances between the networks, one is also interested in the singularities. For example, the term *leggiadria*, at a certain point during the Italian Renaissance, was invented for the Mona Lisa's smile, a woman's doelike beauty, that beauty of a wild thing tamed. The term is not well translated by "grace" because "grace" also has a religious meaning that is not truly part of the meaning of *leggiadria*. So each dimension of language has to be perceived in its singularity. So that examples can only be symptoms . . . for example, what's going on when *Istina* and *Pravda* both claim to be translated by "truth" since you absolutely have to refer *Pravda* at least for the domain of justice as well.

My claim is that that we philosophize in languages with words and not with universal concepts—it is also a kind of weapon against a certain type of analytic philosophy. Not that of the linguistic turn or that of Stanley Cavell but the tradition which would see Aristotle as one's best Oxford colleague. That's why the English translation of this dictionary of untranslatable terms is particularly crucial for me.[5] The philosophical point is that languages perform different worlds. The political point is not to see language as a simple means of communication—as when one language (English?) is seen as the universal language of communication. At that point it is no longer a language at all; it's no longer English.[6] We philosophize in words and not in concepts: we have to complicate the universal with languages.

PD: Philosophy tends to deny the spirit of languages?

BC: I think that philosophy tends to turn the spirit of languages into something horrible. I think that the spirit of languages is an absolutely terrifying concept that leads in a straight line to the worst kind of Heideggerianism, that is, Hellenico-Nazism, quite easily identified; although I don't want to caricature too quickly, the caricatures are there.

We have to rethink, set about reconsidering, the possibility that the spirit of languages need not be horrifying. To reflect on, how, at a certain point in Russian history, diglossia, which is the difference between "low" language and "high" language, opens onto two types of perception of the world and could be connected with spiritualism. That sort of phenomenon is on the frontier between linguistics and philosophy.

One gets horrified very quickly when one thinks about a language (*langue*) *qua* language (*langue*), just as when one thinks about a nation *qua* nation. Is there a way of doing it without arousing anxiety (*angoisse*)? The problem has to be rethought, but we have very few instruments at our disposal because, as it happens, the most powerful instruments were or are Graeco-German. So, finding a way of thinking about the problem differently and finding countermodels, real countermodels, gets very difficult. And those are the difficulties I try to confront.

PD: Why did you use the word "anxiety"?

BC: It makes me anxious (it should make everybody anxious!) to suppose the superiority of one language *qua* language in its relation to philosophy, as if Greek, then German, were the languages of being.

To resolve that anxiety requires, on the one hand, rethinking the relation between philosophy and ontology, and that's the reason for the sophistic lever, if you like.

That also means having to rethink the relation—but all in one go—the relation between literature and philosophy and poetry a little differently in order to desacralize all that.

PD: How would you describe your relation to academia, to institutionalized philosophy? You've already touched on the issue when you mentioned the reception of your philological, philosophical work, and literary work.

BC: I have been extremely lucky in that I had the chance to work at the CNRS (National Center for Scientific Research). So I am not answerable to anyone so long as I produce reports explaining, in an acceptable way, how I am working, and so long as I *am* actually working. It was rather unlikely that I would get this position. But it is a generous institution, and as it happened, at a certain point, the people who were involved in the decision were generous, too. I hope we continue to be generous now that I am among the people who decide.

But in the normal course of events, I think that anyone in my position would have given up philosophy. Because after my first doctorate, on *Si Parmenide* (*If Parmenides*) (already something very heavy), I simply couldn't find a job at all, ever. It was understandable because I didn't have the *agrégation* (the highest-level competitive examination). Now, the *agrégation* is something which I couldn't prepare for, I wasn't capable of it, I didn't want to, all of those things, but certainly I wasn't capable of it. It was an obstacle— an *agrégation*, to be "aggregated," and to what?—which I couldn't get past, especially after 1968 and after I'd encountered Heidegger and Char. But there were no other options if I wanted to pursue philosophy. So I had to stick it out for a very long time, financially as well.

I had parents who supported me, I had a research stipend, I worked as a hand model, I painted some portraits, which I was able to sell. I was also asked to write for the *Encyclopaedia Universalis*, and in all these ways I had enough to live on. I led quite a strange life; for a certain time I taught psychotic adolescents in day hospitals, sometimes I taught at the post office, sometimes even at the ENA (the elite university that trains future public administrators). I was able to get by without having to become a philosophy teacher in a provincial *lycée*[7] at a time when I already had a child with someone who worked in Paris. A truly impossible life when one doesn't have parents or a husband or friends to help you or when one doesn't have real enthusiasm for what one is doing.

All this meant that I worked in my own way, according to my own rhythm. I think that teaching psychotic adolescents was the experience from which I learned the most. I did philosophy with them, but obviously not the sort of philosophy that I would teach today to university students. I did ancient philosophy with them; I worked on language in its early stages. I read the *Cratylus* with these adolescents, and seeing Greek words written on the blackboard made them realize that they did have a maternal language, which was far from evident for them. One could even say they realized that the French language was "more of a *mother* tongue," more maternal than any other for them, with an alphabet more familiar than Greek, and that they could play with their language as Plato did with his. They would invent etymologies; we did astonishing, brilliant things.[8] That taught me a lot.

So I was fortunate that I didn't have to deal with institutions until I could do so effectively. That is, until I'd completed enough work for it to be legitimated. But it was enormous luck that I didn't remain on the margins— as a nonagrégée, as a sophist, as a woman. Once I was at the CNRS, things started sorting themselves out without trouble, I really worked hard, and now I feel—and that surprises me a lot—I have a sort of power.

I've just finished retranslating Parmenides's *Poem*; it's not at all intended as a definitive translation but as the exploration of a real question: Greek, *qua* Greek, is it or is it not the language of being? That's the subtitle, by the way: "The Language of Being?" with a question mark.

I perceived in or perhaps projected into Parmenides's *Poem* two main lines of interpretation. The first, suggested to me by Gorgias, is about how being is created by language. Parmenides's *Poem* is first and foremost the

story of Greek, which, following the path of the "is," makes language it-
self into the plot. It deploys syntax and semantics, the whole grammar:
starting from the first "*esti*," from the verb conjugated as "is," it produces
the subject, "*to on*," the being, *l'étant*, substantive, substantified participle as
noun. One can see how, through what linguistic changes, one gets from
verb to subject, from being to substance: that's what I call the ontology of
grammar.

The second thread is how the poem is in itself the narrative of all the
grand narratives. This ontology, which is so new, is in fact a palimpsest
which rearticulates all the previous discourses, from myth to physics via
epic. A sign of that: when being, *to on*, appears in the poem (in fragment
seven), Parmenides uses the words that Homer used to describe Ulysses
when he sails past the Sirens—it (the Being)/he (Ulysses) remains "solidly
rooted there." All Greek texts possess an extraordinary palimpsestic depth,
so we can understand how philosophy and literature are linked together.

PD: In *The Sophistic Effect*, you say specifically that yours is not an interest
"in the margins"; you are not "making a plea for *penseurs maudits* (accursed
thinkers)[9] against vetoes and exclusion." You say also that you are not con-
cerned with "rehabilitating" sophistic thought.

BC: What I'm trying to say is: "Don't get things mixed up." I'm not in-
terested in those who are "rehabilitating sophistics" because rehabilitating
sophistics consists in making Sophists into philosophers after all. They are
welcomed back into the flock ("*agrégés*"!). For example, thinking about the
Anglo-Saxon tradition, G. B. Kerferd thinks that the Sophists are hyper-
rationalists and congratulates them: they want even the formless, even
sensation, to be subject to reason. That type of rehabilitation, which merely
reverses the Platonic judgment about the Sophists while maintaining his
scale of values, doesn't interest me at all.

We are told that they are serious thinkers because they fit perfectly into
the traditional schema of Greek philosophy. One could say the same thing
about the Skeptics. There is a big rehabilitation of the Skeptics, according
to which they are rigorous philosophers, and there is also a rehabilitation of
the Skeptics, according to which they are disturbing philosophers who dis-

rupt philosophy. Obviously, it's the second kind that I'm interested in. But they can't be separated so easily, and the second kind is continually overlapped by the first. The inside always absorbs the outside—that's how it is.

Don't think that I am going to rehabilitate the Sophists by claiming that they are good philosophers. On the contrary, in a pinch I would say that it is the philosophers, insofar as they have excluded the Sophists, who interest me. At the same time, what interests me is the light that sophistics can shed on philosophy. Anyway, it's not because the Sophists are outside that I'm interested in them.

PD: It's because they are excluded?

BC: You've got it. It's the gestures and the strategies. And it might also be said, after all, that I am largely rehabilitating the Sophists as philosophers to the extent to which I make of them, roughly speaking, models for the critique of ontology. As Jean Beaufret used to say—and it's a comment with frightening implications—"A destroyer of torpedo boats [*contre-torpilleur*] is first and foremost a torpedo boat [*torpilleur*]." How can you manage not to get recaptured by the inside? What interests me are the gestures of recapture and the gestures forbidding that recapture.

I am one of the few, in France at any rate, who has really tried to think together the First and the Second Sophistic Movements. There is one Anglo-Saxon tradition, more on the side of analytic philosophers, concerned with the First Sophistic Movement, another Anglo-Saxon tradition, more on the side of the literary classicists, which is concerned with the Second Sophistic Movement. But both together—not really. What interests me is what emerges from all that history. Which connections does Philostratus make? What are the new relations between sophistics, rhetoric, literature, philosophy, politics, and so on?

Paris, 2012

PD: Barbara, here we are some fourteen years later, on the occasion of the English publication of a collection of articles from a great many projects that you have pursued since we first spoke in 1998. There have been a number of political events with which you've engaged since that time. How have they engendered in you new ways of thinking about performance and performativity?

BC: One commitment was to the South African Truth and Reconciliation Commission (TRC). I had a visiting position teaching rhetoric at the University of Cape Town—I was there when Mandela came to power and at the beginning of the TRC. A student of mine who had wanted to do a doctorate on Plato and sophistics became the head of the NGO *Khululekani* (Freedom). That's how it happened that ANC leaders asked me to help think about bringing parliament closer to the people.

I became aware that what was happening with the TRC process was a kind of political sophistry, or sophistical politics. The parallel was the attention given to speech and to the way speech can build things in the world. In this case what was to be built was the "Rainbow People," so suddenly I was on a real political stage.

Another thing that struck me at the time was the number of national languages that were part of the constitution. The constitution itself has to be written in all eleven national languages. Some words were impossible to translate from English (for example, there's no word for "freedom" in every language, and the distinction between *freedom* and *liberty* is certainly not in use everywhere), and conversely a Zulu word such as *ubuntu*—said to mean something like *fellowship* or *reconciliation* ("we are, therefore I am")—cannot be translated into English.

So I spoke with the new government's leaders. We tried to see to what extent speech could help, so that one would not fear the tongue of the other—such as the specific, juridical tongue (for example, that of the parliament, that whole context—which is a tongue in itself). And a few years later I was asked to begin to think about a dictionary of the "untranslatable" terms in the different laws and constitutions in order to try to make the different languages communicate—not only the tongues but also the types of speech, locutions, interlocutions.

And . . . that was a great experience. There was no real solution beyond being more aware that language does things and that there are different languages which are different ways of seizing the world. It was on the basis of those two perceptions that I undertook the research that followed.

PD: Before that you had long been working on a project on untranslatability, but I think in a largely European context? And the founding of the European Union was an important factor there?

BC: As a result, we were talking much more about Europe, and I believed that the only way I could help build a "livable" Europe (if at all) was to focus on the problem of tongues. It was the only political means that I could find, within my own abilities, to hold on to difference. It was the only political path that didn't disgust me.

PD: Why was there a risk of disgust?

BC: The socioeconomic direction of Europe can appear disgusting. I agree that Europe is also desirable if it really does manage to take diversity into account rather than just paying lip service to it—and in many ways, not just socioeconomically.

One of the main dangers concerns languages and a too easy leveling of them. Two possible solutions confronted us, a choice between two possible directions. Either the ideal of one tongue for everybody, the ideal of a "language of mere communication" or a "universal language of communication," a "ULC," but there the ideal was just "communication." And what does that mean exactly: to "just communicate"? Or else, the departure point had to be the problems of communication, and one would start exploring from there on in.

PD: It seemed to you very likely that the problems of communication would be minimized?

BC: No, I think it was that either we were only going to focus on "communication," and then the best way to communicate was going to be a kind of basic global English—Globish—or else we had to focus on the difficulties. Not only word difficulties, of course, but those, too. For me, words and grammars play the role of symptoms—symptoms of differences, of different "worldviews," as the German Romantics used to say. The question was how to explore and dig deeper into these difficulties: with the idea that it is only in making them deeper that we could work through them rather than try to escape them. And that's how I began to conceive the dictionary of untranslatable terms as a European vocabulary of philosophies.

PD: Europe and South Africa provided very different contexts for work on the politics of communication and translation. How did those differences impact the projects?

BC: In South Africa there wasn't a choice between one or many tongues. There were many tongues, and that was the point. There were the "rainbow people." In Europe, we could aspire to be one, or a certain type of "One."

Of course, you encounter the problem of multiculturalism: how to articulate the one and the plural. But it's complicated . . . in South Africa, there was a result. The slogan was "one man, one vote," the end of apartheid took place without bloodshed, there *were* rainbow people, they'd made it happen. But Europe can implode at any moment. It has not yet been accomplished, and we don't know how it could be. It's not a historical necessity. Maybe it is a political or an economic necessity, but nothing ensures that.

I should also say about the European context that we want to hold on to the richness of the plurality of languages as a plurality of cultures and ways of life and so on. Translation imposes itself. We need to communicate through translation and to grasp this new paradigm of translation as our paradigm. What always struck me as very shortsighted in Habermasian consensus is that there is no place for something like translation (we agree, we want to agree, and insofar as we do—we're done). But in translation it really is endless. We build ourselves through translation, not through consensus, and we build a "we" much more through translation than through consensus.

PD: And what projects have followed on from the *Vocabulaire européen des philosophies* (*European Vocabulary of Philosophies*)?

BC: The first has been to "intranslate" (*intraduire*) (the term *intradução* is used by the Brazilian poet Augusto de Campos, and in French it also draws on "introduction," "to introduce") the *Vocabulaire* into other languages—as Emily Apter, Jacques Lezra, and Michael Wood have done for the Anglo-American audience (*Dictionary of Untranslatables: A Philosophical Lexicon*)—that is to say, to rebuild something new inside another language.

Intranslation is a completely philosophical act because it is at once theoretical, poetical, and political. It gives birth to new things as a total performance inside languages and cultures. I am very happy that the first Arabic volume and a Ukrainian version of the project have also been published—I think this conjunction is very important.

And the second new project—again to be pursued with colleagues and friends—concerns the untranslatables of the three monotheisms. At one point I was invited by the Prince of Jordan to Amman to explore the possibility of working on a "concordance of values" (*valeurs*), that's to say of ethical values, between the three monotheisms. And I suggested not that we try to find equivalents—as if we ever could—but that we dig for differences. I proposed beginning to work with about twenty words through which the Torah, the Bible, and the Koran each unfolds and around which they intertwine. This is a very precarious project—we need to pursue it very carefully. And it may be worth noting that the woman who would try to undertake it is Jewish, a baptized Catholic—and as pagan as it gets.

PD: And the *Appel des appels* (*Call of Calls*)?

BC: During the Sarkozy years, many of us (without my knowing exactly who "us" is, perhaps it is a new type of "us" who responded to the *Call of Calls*) were scared—and scandalized—by what we saw as the dismantling of the possibility of professional work (*la casse des métiers*). Professionals such as judges, doctors in hospitals, social workers, teachers and researchers could no longer do their work well. They could no longer take the time they needed. They no longer had the possibility to do what they knew they had to do and what they were able, trained, and professionally committed to do. Of course, it was partly a question of money and the economic crisis. But it wasn't only that. There were also questions of "performance," of evaluation, and of competition that "Europe" had also provoked—that was one of the bad sides of Europeanization. And globalization—and in fact . . . there are many things that come from Canada! For example, the term *impact factor* is used in a specific Canadian context for a bibliometric medical index. Then, suddenly having an "impact factor" became the first, or the only, doorway to obtaining European funds. If we look further, we see that this mode of accounting and accountability of performance is also not far from the rankings that prevail in search engines like Google.

PD: So you've both published on the "schizophrenic state" in *L'appel des appels* (2009) and also a very trenchant work on Google (*Google moi: La deuxième mission de l'Amérique*, 2007), and, to go on thinking about the different directions your work has taken since 1998, you've also developed a number of projects with Alain Badiou in recent years.

BC: In fact, this story dates back to when I had just published *La décision du sens* (2000). François Wahl and Paul Ricoeur were stepping down from editing the series *L'ordre philosophique* for the publisher Seuil. Badiou was to take over, but he was looking for a partner. He thought it ought to be a woman and that such a team could be more interesting and open minded. And *La décision du sens* intrigued Badiou the most.

PD: Since then, you also coauthored two works, published in 2010 and forthcoming in English with Columbia University Press: *Il n'y a pas de rapport sexuel: Deux leçons sur "L'étourdit" de Lacan* (*There's No Such Thing as a Sexual Relationship: Two Lessons on Lacan*) and *Heidegger: Les femmes, le nazisme, et la philosophie* (*Heidegger: His Life and His Philosophy*). Your collaborative work has prompted a considerable engagement from each of you with the question of sexual difference. And you often pit the position of "sophist" against Badiou's "Plato." How do you see this connection?

BC: I don't believe in truth. He does—and he wants to. We don't see language as playing the same role. So the point is to know whether this traverses our positions as man and woman. Is it a gendered position to be a sophist-philosopher? We are currently working on a new joint project that involves (very roughly) thinking about man, woman, philosophy. We began to deal with this when we were working together on Heidegger's correspondence with his wife—and in another way when we were working together on Lacan. What was so refreshing with our book on Heidegger was that we could play, as with a piano, with four hands. We found ourselves absolutely agreeing even though we don't at all think the same things. That's a good kind of consensus by the way—in that it's not at all a consensus but a continuous dissent traversing particular points.

We also became aware that we agreed on the following diagnosis: that we have absolutely opposed critiques of pure reason. But we share the same disgust for the critique of practical reason. And we have exactly the same critique of judgment. This is why we really can work together—and judge together—with generosity.

PD: Why do you consider it urgent—today—to develop a "consequential" relativism (*relativisme consequent*)?

BC: The "One" frightens me. I think that we need strategy and tactics to deal correctly with the "One." That's also why I am so happy to work with Badiou: because we have to be extremely aware of one another. The scenario between Plato and the Sophists is a microcosm of what can happen today as much in the context of philosophy as in the context of politics, love, science, and life. It's a question of how to take into account the one, the multiple, and diversity.

I call this "consequential relativism" because we have to choose at every moment what it is best to propose or to answer and for whom. I frame everything with the Protagorean affirmation: the point is not to make one change from falsity to truthhood but to produce change from a lesser good to a better state. Better for someone or for a city-state. Of course, many other dangers open immediately from that position. But they are less dangerous "for me." You see that I speak in a dedicated, comparative way. The comparative seems less dangerous, and less dangerous for me, than the "One" and the "One Truth" with a capital *T*.

This is also why John L. Austin is so important to me—and why relativism, performance (*epideixis*), and performativity are linked. Austin concluded *How To Do Things with Words*[10] with an expression of his inclination "to play Old Harry" with two fetishes: the true/false and the value/fact fetish. This is precisely the link between logology, performance, relativism, and politics.

PD: In recent projects you have used two phrases: "enough of the truth for" and a "better for" notion of relativism. Can I ask you more about these "fors"? How can we keep maximally open "for whom," "for which," and "for what" (individuals, peoples, events, moments, and futures) the truth and the relative are to be enough or better? You seemed to acknowledge that "This is better for us!" or "This is enough truth for us!" (or for the future or the circumstances) can also be adopted as intransigent stances and worse.

BC: Yes, there is a "for" in "enough truth" and "better relativism." But that "for" isn't absolute. Nor is it an ethical *metron*, a "just measure" regarding virtue. It's linked to time, to *kairos*, and to who is speaking to whom. Who is judging for whom. Who is proposing something to whom. This is certainly the link. Of course, you can always close yourself in whatever you want. No sentence can prevent that. But what I like in "Enough of the truth for . . ." is that it's not a complete sentence and that you have to go on . . .

Part I Unusual Presocratics

ONE

Who's Afraid of the Sophists?: Against Ethical Correctness

SOPHISTICS, substantive noun. A. The set of doctrines, or more precisely, the shared intellectual attitude of the main Greek sophists (Protagoras, Gorgias, Prodicus, Hippias, etc.). B. (Common noun) Used to refer to a philosophy of verbal reasoning, lacking solidity and seriousness.

—A. LALANDE, ed., *Vocabulaire technique et critique de la philosophie*

The Occasion

The set of doctrines or teachings associated with the individuals known as the sophists is termed *sophistikê*, in French, *sophistique*. The expression is lacking in English, which puts one in the position of either using the adjectives "sophistic," "sophistical," or of using the dismissive expression "sophistry." As I argue for a systematic role for these doctrines, I will ask your indulgence and introduce the neologism "sophistics" for now. The question is, why should one be interested in sophistics today?

As occasional causes are by far the most significant and the most efficient, I would like to explain first of all where my own interest in sophistics stems from. It arose from the encounter of two trajectories that were rivals in all senses of the word. The first phase of study, both triumphant and confused, took place under the sign of Heidegger. Because everything possessed a renewed intelligibility, everything also fit neatly into the palm of one's hand. The history of philosophy was philosophy itself, which the question of Being enabled one to scan and rework into epochs and turnings, with a hitherto unequaled skill that knew when to be self-effacing. It is very difficult to rid oneself of the idea that philosophers today do anything else besides rework Heidegger's gesture, even the anti-Heideggerians who sought their training in Kant, with a point of entry different from the *Kantbuch*. In order to move out from this circumscribed territory, no less is required, doubtless, than (a) a redefinition of philosophy throughout its history, in such a way that this widening of the scope does not produce a mere analytic restriction or moral rigidity that can immediately be traced back destinally to the technical and technological nature of our epoch, and (b) probably some new conceptual characters, to use Deleuze's expression. But the most frequent approach, which Deleuze himself initiated or at least made use of contemporaneously (using the Stoics, Spinoza, and Bergson), is to draw attention to the readings Heidegger failed to perform, or did not perform, inasmuch as they are held to be strategically impossible.

My own growing rigid, in this context, has to do with the determination of the origin and the dawn. The Greek morning which Heidegger arranged for us is monomaniacal and kleptomaniacal. It robs an entire array of texts and possibilities so that they may fit under the aegis of Parmenides's poem, such that the *Parmenides* of 1942–43 reads *polis* merely as *pelein*, the old Greek verb for *einai*: if the *polis* in itself is only the "pole of *pelein*," then "it is only because the Greeks are an absolutely nonpolitical people[1]" that they could found the *polis*, and did. The first reading that I found impossible to perform using Heidegger alone, in the truly grandiose perspective of Parmenides's unveiling, was Gorgias's *Treatise of Non-Being*, a treatise which, approximately a half century after the dawn, provides a full-fledged demonstration of the mechanisms or strategies thanks to which the poem conforms to Heidegger's dream; it is a text that critically exceeds ontology in its nascent state. Thus there was a different way of being pre-Socratic.

In order to confirm this diagnosis, it proved necessary for me to undertake the study of Greek, and ever more Greek, not so as to arrive at the bareness of meaning itself by digging through the thicket of semantics. It was a matter of acquiring the tools with which to respond in kind: amphibological appropriations of an emerging syntax and the extraordinarily imaginative rigidity of the various grammaticalizations. This was my counterapprenticeship, then: philology, with its ceaseless equivocations between the rights of the text and the rights of the interpreters, as taught tirelessly by Jean Bollack and Heinz Wismann, between Lille and Paris.

Now, certain texts are more corrupt than others, and these are the ones that are ultimately rejected or deemed unusable by the tradition, whether by chance or by choice, in a pattern that runs from the doxographer to the scribe and on to the great scholar, the German philologist. From Parmenides to Heidegger, there is a kind of textual Darwinism, a process of selection of the triumphant tradition which ends up defining our vantage point on philosophy and its history. As for the remainder, the tradition allows us to accede to it only through a paleontology of perversion. For example, we are left with Anaximander, Heraclitus, Democritus, and, paradigniatically, Gorgias's *Treatise*, which pushes ontology too far and hence cannot be treated indulgently as a token piece of rhetoric; in other words, we are left with all the figures who were pre-Socratic in a different way.

Of course, it turns out that the canonical texts, too, have to be treated in the same fashion, perhaps due to some contagion. This occurs in their heterodoxical moments, when they are obliged to confront the "others": witness the extreme difficulty of book *Gamma* of Aristotle's *Metaphysics* or Plato's *Sophist*. It also appears in the very singularity of the works that are created, torn between denials and inventions. Hence the philological passion, which considers that all of eternity may not be enough time to understand a sentence adequately. This passion attaches the same importance to all textual objects. This attachment proves to be particularly necessary in order to decipher what is left over, the remainder—here, sophistics.

This proved to be the moment when my object of inquiry was chosen: a fleeing *kairos* (right moment and occasion) typically represented as a bald beautiful young man with nothing but a single lock of hair on his forehead by which to catch him (always too late). After all, he could possibly be Nietzsche's Chiron, the limping philosophical-philological centaur.

For this choice to be deemed successful, the object had to enable me to bring to fruition a series of appealing projects that would be difficult or even impossible to carry out otherwise. The claim I will be making in what

follows may seem startling even if it is generally (or generically) character-
istic of those who are called, and call themselves, philosophers. However,
I can temper the overbearing arrogance of the claim with a caveat and de-
clare that it will be made "shamelessly" (*sans vergogne*), to use Francis Ponge's
term for the crafty *hubris* of the Sophists.[2] The arrogance of the claim lies
in the hypothesis that the chosen object, sophistics, is a good tool, maybe
even the best of the available tools to produce something like a new narra-
tive of the history of philosophy—the tale of a new morning, which makes
one want to count the fingers of the dawn. Sophistics produces a new de-
limitation of the entity called "philosophy" in relation to the other entities
it constructs (sophistics as rhetoric and then as literature).

The following remarks, then, will take the form of a philosophical and
literary stroll that responds to an aspect of things that does not belong to
our ordinary habits (but which, once one responds to it, is as good as they
are at monopolizing our attention). The stroll gives itself the right to stop
along the course of time and collect texts of a lineage different from that
which runs from Parmenides, Plato, and Aristotle to Hegel, Heidegger, or
Habermas. Once these texts have been gathered up, they begin to resonate
with one another. This should surely enable us to glimpse how artificial the
border between the rational and the irrational is and perhaps to reorganize
the cosmos of philosophy, starting from a richer, more complete, more con-
temporary, or otherwise effective point of view.

Sophistics as Historical Fact and Structural Effect

As the state of the corpus of translations and stubborn retranslations of the
same ancient texts reveals, we have until quite recently, in France in any
case, been prisoners of the image that antiquity sought to project of itself,
namely, a succession of moments of excellence. Yet my choice of sophistical
doctrine as an object of research does not, at least initially, solely stem from
an antiquarian zeal for ill-known texts that require a great deal of philo-
logical and historical work. Nor, thereby, does it originate in an interest in
the margin where these roughly crossed-out texts lie, an interest that would
make the margin into an area of research, legitimizing a militant pathos in

favor of accursed thinkers, against debarments and exclusion. Hence I will not be proposing a "rehabilitation," and especially not one of these rehabilitations that are grounded, by means of a circular argument, in the modifications and improvements they enable one to introduce into the persistent frame of the most traditional of all histories.

Indeed, the singularity of sophistical doctrine is to already be, inasmuch as it is a historical fact, a structural effect, that is, an effect of the structure: the "doctrine of the sophists" is a philosophical concept whose model is truly provided by the real practice of those who called themselves, and were called, sophists (individuals such as Protagoras, Gorgias, and Antiphon). This is definition A in Lalande's *Vocabulaire*. But it is also used in philosophy to refer to one of the possible modalities of nonphilosophy—this is definition B, which is as magisterial as it is mysterious: "a philosophy of *verbal reasoning*, lacking any solidity or seriousness." I frequently return to this definition.

This is Plato's starting point and the point where he welds together the two halves of the problem: sophistic doctrine, which is a historical reality, is at the same time artificially produced by philosophy. The essence of this artifact is simply to construct the sophist as the negative alter ego of the philosopher: his bad other. They have resembled each other ever since the Stranger's comment in the *Sophist* that the sophist resembles the philosopher "as the wolf does the dog, as the most savage resembles the most tame" (231b). They are so much alike that even when one reaches out with both hands to catch one, one catches the other (in the Platonic text itself, which plays with datives, one may ask with some justification who's who). Socrates's cathartic midwifery (maieutics), his practice of refutation end up belonging to the *genei gennaia sophistikê* (which one translates as "the genuine and truly noble art of sophistics," ignoring the emphasis that cements the bond). Conversely, at the end of the dialogue, when all dichotomies must be recapitulated, the final arborescence provides us with the same pair, when the issue is how to describe the demagogue or speechmaker: "wise man or sophist?" The decision is reached only when Theatetus states a thesis: "We posited him as not knowing" (268c). In any case, the sophist, who is an "imitator of the wise man," is his paronym to exactly the same extent as the philosopher himself is.

If we consider the Platonic dialogues as a whole, we can indeed discern the figure of sophistics, which will henceforth belong to the tradition. It is devalued on all grounds—ontologically, because the sophist is not concerned with being but seeks refuge in nonbeing and what is accidental; logically, because he is not in pursuit of truth or dialectical rigor but merely opinion, seeming coherence, persuasion, and victory in the oratorical joust; ethically, pedagogically, and politically: his goal is not wisdom and virtue for the individual or for the city but rather personal power and gain; the sophist is even devalued on literary grounds since the figures of speech he makes use of, his style, are merely the bulges of an encyclopedic vacuity. If one makes use of the standard of being and truth in order to judge the teaching of the sophist, it must be condemned as pseudophilosophy: a philosophy of appearances and a mere appearance of philosophy.

On this basis, however, another dimension of the *Sophist* comes to light which shakes up its strict organization: the artifact itself becomes a producer of philosophy. The sophist is the other of the philosopher, whom philosophy never ceases to expel from its domain and even from humanity itself, as we will see with Aristotle, because the philosopher in turn defines himself as (merely) the other of the sophist, an other whom he pushes further and further into a corner. Philosophy is the child of wonder, and, according to the first sentence of the *Metaphysics*, "all humans naturally wish to know." Yet "those who ask if one should honour the gods and love one's parents, or not, simply need a good lesson, and those who ask if snow is white or not only need to look."[3] The sophist exaggerates, as Protagoras does regarding the gods, Antiphon regarding the family, and Gorgias regarding that which is and that which one perceives. He always asks one question too many, he always derives one consequence too many. Due to this insolence, philosophy is beside itself. The love of wisdom is forced to transgress the limits that it assigned itself and to make gestures that surely do not belong to the rest of its procedure, such as pulling out the stick. In what follows, I analyze some of these gestures as a goal of my research. The doctrine of the sophists is indeed an operator that serves to circumscribe and define the scope of philosophy.

Thus the point of view I have chosen makes use of a philosophico-sophistical perception (Novalis, in his *Logological Fragments*, suggested the term *philosophistize* [*philosophistieren*][4]), the nature of which may be conveyed by the term *effect*. It is an effect, first of all, because sophistics is an artificial creation, a by-product of philosophy (*as the difficulty with terminology itself shows*). But it is an effect, second, because sophistics, a fiction of philosophy, reverses the direction of things and shocks philosophy, never ceasing to have an effect on it. This sums up the structural version of an infinitely complex history of ideas which, in my view, historians of philosophy are wrong to ignore.

The Sophistical Effect

My work has focused on showing how sophistical doctrine obliges philosophy to reflect on itself. It starts from three moments, three privileged bodies of text that enable one to express the sophistical effect and reconstitute a history of the limit.

A TREATISE AGAINST A POEM

The confrontation between Parmenides's *On Nature, or On What Is*, and Gorgias's *On What Is Not, or On Nature*[5] provides us with our primal scene. As Heidegger has shown, but not *only* as he has shown, everything hangs on the way in which being and saying are connected (recall Lalande's definition: "a philosophy of verbal reasoning").

"Nothing is; if it is, it is unknowable; if it is and it is knowable, it cannot be said to someone else [communicated]."[6] The three theses of the *Treatise* present themselves as a reversal of Parmenides's poem, which, from Plato to the present day, has been taken to say, first, that there is being since "Being is" and "non-Being is not"; second, that this Being is essentially knowable since "being and thinking are one and the same." Thereby philosophy was able to embark on the right path, to know being *qua* being and diversify itself commercially into doctrines, disciples, and schools. This series of reversals should not, however, be viewed as an idle little game, for it is a radical critique of ontology.

Gorgias's strategy, as displayed in his first thesis, is to have us realize that Being, which is the Parmenidean hero just as Ulysses is the Homeric hero, is never anything besides an effect of the poem. The sophist follows the way in which, at the starting point of the poem, the "word of the path: *Is*" (fragment 8), suffices to secrete the full subject, which is identified thereafter by means of the article (*to eon*, the Being, the entity), through a series of infinitives and participles; he thus dissects the way in which syntax creates semantics. If there is a "sophism," it resides in the "is" and its ontological treatment since the mere statement of the identity of being, which leads one to confuse the copula with existence, derives its entire worth from an amphiboly and a homonymy.[7]

The second postulate of the poem—which Heidegger translates paratactically as "being, thinking, the same" (fragment 3)[8]—marks the mooring point of truth as unconcealment and then as adequation. Here the catastrophe is perfect. It is enough for me to think something and, moreover, to speak it for that thing to be. By that token, if I say "war-chariots battle on the open sea,"[9] then war chariots are battling on the open sea. There is no room for nonbeing or for errors and lies. It is Parmenides's ontology alone, taken at face value and pushed to the limit, which guarantees the infallibility and efficaciousness of the discourse, which thereby is sophistical.

That being is a speech effect now takes on a twofold meaning: we are not simply faced with a critique of ontology—your purported being is nothing but an effect of the way you speak—but with a claim that is characteristic of "logology," to use a term coined by Novalis, also used by Dubuffet.[10] Novalis describes the redoubling: "It is amazing, the absurd error people make of imagining that they are speaking for the sake of things; no one *knows* the essential thing about language; that it is only concerned with itself."[11] What matters from now on is not a being that would supposedly be already there but the being produced by the discourse; one must assess the magnitude of the shift in landscape, from the primal scene onward. The safest identity principle is no longer formulated as "Being is" or "the entity is" but, to quote another sentence from the treatise, "he who speaks, speaks."[12] The presence of Being, the immediacy of Nature, and the evidence of a speech that aims to express them adequately all vanish at the same time; the physics discovered by speech makes way for the politics created by discourse.

Indeed, it is here, thanks to the sophists, that we reach the dimension of the political as *agora* for an *agôn*: the city as the continuous creation of language. The discourse of the sophists is to the soul what the *pharmakon* (poison and remedy) is to the body: it induces a change of state, for better or for worse. But the sophist, like the doctor, knows how to use the *pharmakon* and can transmit this knowledge; he knows and teaches how to move, not, according to the bivalency of the principle of noncontradiction, from error to truth or from ignorance to wisdom, but, according to the inherent plurality of comparison, from a lesser state to a better state. In the *Theatetus*, Protagoras, who professes virtue, states this through the mouthpiece of Socrates, who then defends him: "one has to effect a change from another condition to the better. But the physician effects a change by drugs, the sophist by speeches" (167a), and wise and good orators like him "make cities be of the opinion that the good things in place of the poor things are just" (167c). The entire rhetoric of the sophists is thus a vast performance which, time after time, by means of praise and counsel, produces the consensus required for the social bond. This consensus is minimal, even minimalist, because far from requiring a uniform unity, the sophistical consensus does not even require that everyone think the same thing (*homonoia*) but only that everyone speak (*homologia*) and lend their ear (*homophônia*). In this way, it is hinted that the final motor (*ressort*) of political discourse is homonymy ("that the sentence have a meaning for each of the meanings of each of its terms"), which alone can have an effect on "the metaphysician as much as on the cook," to speak like Ponge.[13]

At this point, the distance that has been achieved from the Heideggerian dawn begins to sink in. In the philosophizing Greece of *alêtheia*, the invention of the city is nonpolitical because the political *qua* political is in no way political; rather, it is always subordinate to Being, the True, and the Good. But in a philosophisticizing Greek, to which the ontological immediately reverts, backtracks toward the logological, *logos* enables us to grasp the very immanence of the political in its condition of possibility, in a perception that is more Aristotelian and Arendtian than it is Platonic and Heideggerian. "Humans live together according to the mode of speech":[14] the specificity of the political lies in the competition of the *logoi*, governed by the norm of taste (in the sense this term has had since Kant), which seeks to obtain the consent of the other in the midst of a plural condition. Arendt emphasizes that this is why doing political philosophy, that is, "to look upon politics from the perspective of truth . . . means to take one's stand outside the political realm."[15] Under the aegis of the first statement, namely, Antiphon's assertion in *On Truth* that "one citizenizes" [*politeuetai tis*, a Greek word not easy to translate] no longer refers to nature except as something that has escaped from a private crevice into the public realm, the autonomy of *logos*, which creates the legal sphere, and the autonomy of the political are henceforth intertwined.

THE *LOGOS* OF A PLANT

All of Aristotle's regulation of language, in which modernity is invented, may justifiably be seen as a rejoinder to sophistics: how can language be tamed, and how can it be rendered ethical both prior to and during its rhetorical-political life?

The response or comeback to the primal scene can easily be located: it is the demonstration of the principle of noncontradiction that is performed at the beginning of *Gamma* 4, a demonstration that is scientifically impossible since the issue is the first principle, yet can be carried out dialectically in the shape of a refutation of the opponents who claim to deny it.[16] Now, refutation is the paramount weapon of the sophists; Aristotle, following Socrates, borrows it here for the occasion. If Gorgias's treatise is read in the way we just proposed, it stands *in toto* as a refutation of Parmenides's poem. It starts with the speech of the other, as enunciative procedure and thematic statement, and brings to light its catastrophic consequence. Ontology taken literally means logology, or in other words, if Parmenides, then Gorgias. Quite symmetrically, the demonstration by refutation starts with the opponent's statement of the principle (if only to express his denial) and brings to light the unsettling consequence that the opponent obeys the principle at the very moment he denies it. Sophistics taken literally is Aristotelian; if Protagoras speaks (which sophists normally do), he can only speak the way Aristotle does.

The real dynamic of the refutation lies in a series of equivalent relations that, once they are stated, are as self-evident as ontology itself: to speak is to say something that has a meaning, and this meaning is the same for oneself and for another. Thereafter, indeed, I need only speak ("Hello") for the principle of noncontradiction to be proven and instantiated in the process:

it is impossible for the same (word) to have and not have the same (meaning) at the same time. All I need to do is speak ("so long as the opponent says something.")[17] Aristotle finalizes the procedure by ensuring that this necessary and sufficient condition is present in the very definition of man and excluding all those who do not fall under his demonstration from humanity, from the outset, "for such a man, as such, is like a plant, from the outset."[18] The requirement of meaning, once it is equated with the aim of univocity in this fashion, is first of all a formidable war machine against homonymy. Ever since Aristotle, all those who refuse to submit to this requirement have been reduced to so much silence or noise, something prior to language. They are free to inquire into "what is in the sounds of the voice and in words,"[19] into drivel or nonsense (*blah-blah*), or, in other words, into the signifier inasmuch as it does not signify. This freedom will not even extend to the conventional sphere of human language.

From Parmenides to Gorgias and from Gorgias to Aristotle, let us grant that the sophist has been checkmated. But much is to be learned from the game up to the present day.

It is up to us, in particular, to decipher the ambiguous status of psychoanalysis in light of this teaching—this speech which one pays for, this *pharmakon* which is bought and sold, just as the sophists were reproached for. For it is obvious that Freud, then Lacan, occupy the site that Aristotle assigned to the recalcitrant sophists, the site of the signifier. Yet there is a crucial difference that changes everything: they occupy this site as Aristotelians. Thanks to psychoanalysis, even drivel and homonymy fall into the embrace of meaning. Freud's definition of a "pun" (one of whose categories, let us not forget, is the "sophism") as "sense within non-sense"[20] stands as sufficient witness that speaking for one's pleasure or, as Lacan puts it, "speaking to no end" or, more literally, "speaking at a loss" (*parler en pure perte*) is today a sophistical activity that has been embraced or taken over by Aristotelianism.[21]

It is also up to us to grasp in what way Aristotle's gesture in the *Metaphysics* is repeated in front of our own eyes. Meaning, consensus, and exclusion are precisely the structure of what Karl-Otto Apel calls "the *a priori* of the communicative community."[22] The basic question for Apel, who views himself as following in the footsteps of Wittgenstein and Peirce but is really a follower of Aristotle, is "the condition of possibility of meaningful discourse or meaningful argumentation."[23] It is the same problematization of the notion of an ultimate ground; just like with the principle of all principles, one must both ground and cease to ground. The resolution of the aporia is also the same: one takes a step back, a regress toward the transcendental condition of human language. The proof strategy is the same: an opponent is required, be it Popper or Protagoras, whose argument is refuted by showing him that "the rules of the transcendental language-game" are such that he has "always already implicitly acknowledged their validity." In other words (those of Aristotle, precisely), "If one is to destroy *logos*, one must surely have a *logos* of one's own." Finally, and above all, one finds the same exclusion of the radical, evil other who persists in denying the "meta-institution of all possible human institutions," whether it is termed language game or decision of meaning, and must pay for this refusal by "losing his own identity as a meaningful agent," namely, suicide or dementia. In short, Aristotle's plants today would be headed for the morgue or the asylum. But, as you will have understood, the point of contention of this exclusion remains the same: by making an entire dimension of speech philosophically and ethically inaudible, one has confused otherness with nothingness.

FROM THE GOAT-STAG TO THE NOVEL

The consequence of the decision of meaning is twofold. First, and most radically, as we have seen, there is the exclusion from the community of all those who "speak for the pleasure of speaking," in the terms of *Gamma* 5.[24] The sophist, whom Aristotle and Apel find so disagreeable, is not human. But there is a second consequence that is more subtle and has to do with the topology of meaning sketched out by Aristotle's statement of equivalence. To speak is to say being; such was Parmenides's thesis, and such, again, *mutatis mutandis*, is the ordinary regime or daily lot of Aristotelian language. Ordinarily, indeed, when one speaks, the meaning of the word expresses the essence of the thing. This is the case when the thing exists; the essence of the entities is the meaning of the word that refers to it—if "man" means "animal with two feet," then, providing man exists, man is a two-footed animal—and it is precisely in this that the ontological necessity of excluding "idle talk" is rooted, all the way to Heidegger. Now, faced with the sophist, the Aristotelian response in kind opens up a radically new possibility. One is no longer forced to speak of something that exists in order to mean something; one can very well speak of the "goat-stag" (which is the great example in *De Interpretatione*[25]) without putting ontology at risk. One can speak *nonbeing* because one can *speak* nonbeing because with the language of possibility comes a meaning that is no longer bound to reference. This is in fact why truth values are nothing more than a question of *sun*, syntax, and synthesis, between a subject who is or is not, and a predicate that is or is not. Thus we may utter the truth when we speak about things that do not exist (the statement "A goat-stag is not a cow" is true), things which, when one speaks about them, continue not to exist. Aristotelian semantics, for its part, produces parallel worlds in which true sentences assign nonexistent predicates to nonbeings—stemming not from the false which is but from the true which is not. From the ontology that has thus been reassured by Aristotle, the possibility flows of an assumption of logology: by speaking of things that have no existence and therefore, in Aristotle's terminology, no essence or definition, by discarding the physical or phenomenal reference, one has opened up the possibility of promoting meaning alone, meaning itself. Just as Parmenidean ontology had always already become sophistical logology, here, on Aristotelian ground, sophistical logology is assigned to a new dwelling place: literature, as a case that is legitimized by the interpretation of the *legein ti* as *sêmainein ti*.

In the wake of rhetoric, which had already chosen the expression "to speak to" over the expression "to speak of," it is an entirely different corpus that becomes more intelligible, that of the second wave of the sophists, still Greek yet already Latin, and this marks the inception of the novel. If the novel is considered in this light, it shows itself to be an extremely original response to philosophical prohibition. For the novel is self-consciously a *pseudos* and presents itself as such; it is a discourse that forgoes any ontological adequation and follows its own demiurgical path, namely, speaking for the pleasure of speaking rather than speaking in order to mean something and thus producing a world effect, a novelistic "fiction." And the popularity of novels, which resumes the foundational tradition of the Homeric poems, ends up constituting the cultural avatar of a political consensus, extended to the limits of the inhabited world by means of the *pax Romana*. As Dion said, not everyone sees the same sky, but even the Indians know Homer.[26]

Thus the paradigm of truth has been transformed. From now on, sophistics no longer has to do battle with philosophical authenticity but rather with the exactness of historical fact. It is now the gaze of the historian which brings the accusation of the *pseudos* to bear against sophistics and its literary kin. Lucian's *How to Write History*, in particular, bears witness to the existence of this new conflict: the historian as mirror is completely opposed to the poet, who is entitled to "overthrow the fortress of the Epipoles with a stroke of the pen" and defines himself by not being a novelist. However, Lucian practices the art of the sophists on sophistics itself; in *The Genuine History*, his irony ends up jeopardizing his own practice: "I will tell the truth on one point, which is that I tell lies."[27] Here, "genuine" history takes up the liar's paradox again, and against the history of the chroniclers and the faithful account of events, it responds with the unmatchable power of invention.

When confronted with philosophy, the early sophists preferred a consensus-building discourse to that which sought to conform to the entity or to the being of the entity. This very shift from adequation to political and cultural consensus also influences the shift in the relevant opposition: the later sophists had to confront history rather than philosophy. We have thus moved from ontology to the human sciences and from the art of the sophists to literature.

Ethical Correctness

The epicenter of the history of philosophy, once it is rewritten under the influence of sophistics as the history of the delimitation of philosophy, becomes the problem of the regulation of language. Ordinary philosophy (of which I speak with the same respect as of ordinary language) musters up all its forces, at all levels and by all the means at its disposal—Platonic, Aristotelian, Kantian, Heideggerian, Levinasian, analytic, Habermasian, Foucauldian, and even Perelmanian—to reinforce this regulation ethically. As ideology is lacking, we are given moral lectures instead. As a result, from Allan Bloom to Václav Havel, the consensus that sophistics should be the prime target has reached remarkable dimensions, extending as far as politics.

Allow me to return once more to the mutual demarcation of the space between the philosopher and his bad other. Its most tangible effect is to relinquish the distinction between good and evil, the foundation of ethics, and hand it over to the most slippery genre, that of resemblance; as Nietzsche noted, "the boundary between good and evil is blurred—that is the Sophist."[28] As a result, the two major themes that philosophy develops in order to distinguish the good side from the bad side of resemblance are canceled out by sophistics in such a way that ethics is displaced.

The first theme is that of the mask of "hypo-crisy" which one slips on. We are familiar with the accusation of flattery and deceit that runs throughout the *Gorgias*: rhetoric and sophistry are *eidôla* which "slip beneath" justice and legislation. But generally one fails to notice that Protagoras, who proudly describes himself as showing his face, undoes this accusation when he shows, at the end of his myth, why the only mask one need wear is indeed that of justice:

> As for the other excellences . . . if someone wishes, for instance, to be good at playing the flute or some other art, while he is not, he is mocked and becomes angry, and those who are close to him come and reproach him for his folly. If, on the contrary, the issue is justice and the political virtue in general, when a man who is known to be unjust, when this man ends up saying the truth about himself in public, this frankness which previously was viewed as wisdom, is in the present case considered to be madness, and one states that all must declare themselves to be just, whether they are or not, and that he who does not put on the mask of justice is mad.[29]

The social bond is created by pretending it exists, and when philosophy reproaches the sophists for being hypocritical, this hypocrisy is none other than the essence of political virtue. Hence the sophistical alter ego is the one who drags ethics onto the political terrain.

The second elaboration in lieu of a distinction is, in Aristotelian terms, that pertaining to intention, *proairesis*. The sophists once again "slip" into "the same form as the philosopher,"[30] but this time, the difference between the two has to do with "their choice of a way of life."[31] The intimate character of intention makes it even harder to grasp the difference. This is seized upon by Latin rhetoric and the second wave of sophistics in order to lead the moral problematic to its other point of reversal. *"Philosophia enim simulari potest, eloquentia non potest"* ["For philosophy may be counterfeited, but eloquence never"].[32] In the second part of the sentence, Quintilian forces one to reevaluate the first part definitively. He leaves the question of intention to philosophy, both with regard to its contestable criterial status and its concretely or effectively ungraspable character. This is why philosophy "may be counterfeited," whereas eloquence, once again, as always, produces the effect that is unfailingly *index sui*. Philosophy never relinquishes its claim to unmask sophistics by banking on the concept of intention; sophistics never ceases to distinguish itself from philosophy by emphasizing the accounting of effects. The consideration of effects can match that of intention because the effect is no longer at the mercy of a dichotomy: faced with the polarized duplicity of intention, there is or there is not an effect, de facto, precisely. When one responds to the question of intention with the effect, one has shifted the grounds of the ethical problematic, the definitional shield of philosophy, onto another terrain, that of aesthetics.

This twofold destabilization or upsetting of ethics is obviously what leads one to cry wolf. The most common name for the wolf today is "relativism." This underscores in eminently philosophical, that is, Platonic fashion that the ethical upset is dependent on the refusal to subject discourse to the criterial verdict (*instance*) of truth. Unfortunately for whoever ends up repeating his views, Joseph Moreau is one of those who has maintained this most consistently. For example, with regard to the media in particular, he denounces "the great failing of a sophistical civilization," one defined (like ours) by "technological power and the power of the word." He regrets the absence of any function in this "sophistical" civilization that "could regulate the usage of technology and of *logos*, without which the one is in the service of boundless appetites, and the other consents to justify undisclosable interests."[33] This should be taken quite literally. Moreau considers that "sophistic reason" is responsible in particular for the demise of the gold standard in economics: "To be sure, gold is just an idol, but one which was indispensable for lack of universal good faith. We are merely beginning to see the damage that this sophistic challenge to common sense and honesty can cause."[34]

What is interesting in Moreau's argument is that he is intelligent enough to plead guilty at the right moment, thereby justifying the impression one might have from the outset. One feels annoyed but also stifled by his position, which I would venture to term "ethical correctness." As he writes, "one cannot avoid being accused of intolerance, when one invokes the right of truth, faced with those who proclaim the sovereignty of opinion. However, the accusation of intolerance is unjustified, for if I assert that truth must live up to absolute demands, of which one must take account, I do not thereby claim that I am in possession of it, or that I must impose my view at any cost."[35] This reflection enables one to distinguish two ways of being an antirelativist in the current debate. One is more "crude" or intolerable than the other because it is dogmatic and noncritical. A position is dogmatic when it operates as if truth were not merely a regulative idea, a site, but also a content that must be respected, that one must make people respect. François Furet's reaction against the "denunciation of European culture," which he finds characteristic of political correctness, most likely falls in this category. Furet regrets that this new political vulgate leads one, on the intellectual level, to "relativize all works of art and of the spirit, to wreck the idea of the universality of truth, without which the notion of education itself loses its meaning."[36]

Dogmatism and relativism become symmetrical for the second kind of antirelativist, who takes care to leave the site of truth empty. Allan Bloom, waging war against political correctness, thus specifies that "there are two threats to reason, the opinion that one knows the truth about the most important things, and the opinion that there is no truth in these matters; the first one asserts that the quest for truth is unnecessary, and the second one asserts that it is impossible."[37] Hence the right attitude, with due classicism, is the Socratic knowledge of ignorance.

Alain Badiou's modality of antirelativism makes for a radically different perspective insofar as he strives both to demarcate himself from the consensual discourse on ethics and to make room for a structural perception of sophistics. Notice in passing that it is hardly inconsequential for such different standpoints to come together on this issue. In *Conditions* (1992),[38] Alain Badiou reenacts a Platonic gesture, faced with "modern sophistry" (Nietzsche and Wittgenstein) and its "contemporary" form (Lyotard, Rorty, Vattimo, and Derrida). There is no philosophy without sophistics, and there are no philosophers who do not define themselves as opponents of the sophists ("every definition of philosophy must distinguish it from sophistics"[39]). However, it is not only the definition of philosophy in general that is dependent on sophistics but also the distinction between good and bad philosophy:

> Philosophy must never give way to anti-sophistical extremism. When it nourishes the dark desire to do away with the sophist *once and for all*, philosophy goes astray. This is precisely what defines *dogmatism*, in my view: claiming that the sophist should not exist, simply because he is a perverse twin of the philosopher. No, the sophist *must simply be assigned to his place*. (Badiou 1992, 73)

Faced with "disaster" (64, 72), with "dogmatic terror" (72), which lies in declaring that "the sophist must not be" and hence decreeing the "eradication of its other" (75), the "ethics of philosophy," on the contrary, maintains "the sophist as its opponent" and "preserves the *polemos*" (74): "At all times, the sophist is required for philosophy to keep hold of its ethics. For the sophist is the one who reminds us that the category of Truth is empty. To be sure, he only does so in order to deny truths, and in this regard he must be fought. But this fight takes place on the ground of ethical norms" (76).

For a dogmatic Platonism, the first type of antirelativism, the sophist as such is a danger to ethics. For a "Platonism of the manifold,"[40] which refuses to give up the category of truth as understood through sophistics (which then becomes ethically necessary, as "operation" and as "void"[41]), to keep a firm hold on philosophy can only mean to withdraw the manifold "from the authority of language"[42] and not to be obliged to "recognize the constitutive character of linguistic variation" (87).

In my opinion, it is exactly at this point that a more intelligent form of terror rears its head if we are to believe the philosophistical rewriting of the history of philosophy. Indeed, it teaches us that the margin, the degree of freedom separating the act of eradication from that of assigning a place, is perilously slim. How might one separate the initial gesture, which is good, from its chain of effects, which are bad? From Plato to Habermas, the issue is always Book X of the *Laws*, where the place that is assigned to those who speak as atheists is prison, followed by death without burial. In book *Gamma* of the *Metaphysics*, he who denies the principle of noncontradiction is a plant, whose place is outside of humanity. From this standpoint, the difference between morals and moralism, or ethics and morals, regardless of the chiasmas with added value, has yet to be fulfilled.

Anti-Platonism seems like such an outdated notion! Antisophistics, too, seems so outdated! Did we not move beyond these exchanges of threats long ago? Neither the Heideggerian problematic nor the return to Kant seems to me sufficient. They fail, in any case, to prevent the French scene, within philosophy and without, from reducing ethical discourse to something dangerously inane.

Translated by Charles T. Wolfe

Speak If You Are a Man, or the Transcendental Exclusion

> For people who are puzzled to know whether one ought to honour the
> gods and love one's parents or not need punishment, while those who
> are puzzled to know whether snow is white or not need perception.
>
> —ARISTOTLE, *Topics*, I, 105a5–72[1]

How does the ethical enter into language? The answer given from Aristo-
tle's time up to our own would seem to be: with the requirement of mean-
ing or sense.[2] Ever since the originary scene set up in the *Gamma* book
of Aristotle's *Metaphysics* as a war machine against the ancient Sophists,
those plantlike pseudomen who claim to speak for the sake of (the pleasure
of) speaking, the same structure—sense, consensus, exclusion—appears to
have been repeating itself over and over again; the repetition continues
right through the philosophies of consensus, ethics of communication, and
pragmatics of conversation developed by Karl-Otto Apel, Jürgen Haber-
mas, and Richard Rorty, whose diminishing demands for language never-
theless entail the same type of undesirable others to be excluded, to be
forced to exclude themselves from humanity. Thus, meaning, understood
as a transcendental necessity, that is, as a condition of possibility of human
language, is supported by, and only by, an exclusion no less transcendental

than the necessity itself. Or simply: common sense, being both sense and common, produces nonsense and senseless agents, noncommonality and inhumanity.

The Originary Scene

Aristotle has just articulated the first principle of the science of being as being, which posterity has tagged the principle of noncontradiction. Such a principle, the "firmest of all," is also the "most intelligible" and, like Plato's Good, is dependent on nothing else.[3] There are, however, those who deny it by asserting, and asserting their support for, the claim "that it is possible for the same thing to be and not to be" (*Gamma* 4, 1005b35–1006a1): these ill-bred boors oblige Aristotle to demonstrate a principle despite the fact that it is doubly impossible to demonstrate both because it is formally first and because it contains the very possibility of all demonstrations.

Nevertheless, Aristotle complies:

> But even this can be demonstrated to be impossible, in the manner of a refutation, if only the disputant says something [*an monon ti legêi*]. If he says nothing, it is ridiculous to look for what to say to one who does not say anything, insofar as he says nothing; such a person, insofar as he is such, is similar to a vegetable [*homoios phutôi*] . . . By "demonstrating in the manner of a refutation" I mean something different from demonstrating, because in demonstrating one might be thought to beg the original [question], but if someone else is cause of such a thing it must be refutation and not demonstration. In response to every case of that kind the original [step] is not to ask him to say that something either is or is not (for that might well be believed to beg what was originally at issue), but at least to signify something both to himself and to someone else [*sêmainei ge ti kai autôi kai allôi*]; for that is necessary if he is to say anything. For if he does not, there would be no speech for such a person, either in response to himself or to anyone else. But if he does offer this, there will be demonstration, for there will already be something definite. But the cause is not he who demonstrates but he who submits; for destroying speech he submits to speech. (*Gamma* 4, 1006a11–26)[4]

Aristotle's strategy consists of replacing the impossible demonstration with another type of demonstration that—unable to avoid begging the question—places all the responsibility upon the other. The demonstration becomes a refutation: showing that the opponent himself, by rejecting the principle, has always already presupposed it, the demonstration deduces the principle of its own negation through the claim "You said it."

Two insufficiently radical scenarios are to be rejected. Refutation is not, as is most often the case with Plato, the bringing to light of a logical self-contradiction by applying the thesis to itself; of course, if the same is and is not, is both true and false, by the admission of the one making the claim, this thesis is no less false than true. But then this scarcely matters since the opponent claims the right to contradiction. Nor does refutation function solely through pragmatic self-contradiction. Of course, as soon as the opponent agrees to take a thesis and defend it, he is pragmatically begging the principle he is trying to combat, but he can once again refuse to read his defeat as a contradiction even between theory and practice; or worse, he can simply refuse to enter into the dialectical game.

The weakness of both of these scenarios lies in the failure to give full consideration to the warning Aristotle pronounces at the start: "the original [step] is not to ask him to say something either is or is not . . . but at least to signify something both to himself and to someone else."[5] In other words, since dialectic, which nevertheless constitutes the very element of refutation, itself begs the principle, we must envisage a passage to the limit: something like a refutation at degree zero of dialectic that—because it entails conditions of possibility for dialogue and for language itself—we may call "transcendental refutation."

This entire refutation consists of a series of equivalences that take us from "saying something" (*Gamma* 1006a3, 22) to "signifying something both to himself and to someone else" (*Gamma* 1006a21). By this means, the injunction to speak ("Say 'Hi!'") can serve as the ultimate weapon: either the opponent shuts up, refusing to live up to the trait proper to man, who is endowed with the faculty of speech and thus counts neither as opponent nor as alter ego, or else he speaks, therefore he signifies, and thereby rejects the possibility of denying the principle, for the principle of noncontradiction is proven and instantiated only in the impossibility of the same (word) simultaneously having and not having the same (sense). Sense or meaning is thus the first experienced or experienceable entity that cannot tolerate contradiction. The refutation that serves to demonstrate the principle of noncontradiction implies if not that the world is structured like language, at least that Being, and beings, are constructed as sense, as meaning.

The Responsibility of Thought: Heidegger

At the other end of the temporal chain, Heidegger's appropriation of Aristotle's principle confirms this reading: Heidegger repeats, with modifications, this relegation of contradictory man. He discusses the question that Nietzsche asks concerning the principle of noncontradiction: if this is indeed the supreme principle, we must ask ourselves all the more "what sorts of assertions it already fundamentally *presupposes*"[6] Heidegger's emphasis). "The question that Nietzsche demands that we ask here," Heidegger continues, "has long since been answered—indeed by Aristotle—so decisively that what Nietzsche is asking about constitutes the sole content of this law for Aristotle." The exegesis of this singular answer combines two features. First, "something essential about beings as such: that every absence is foreign to presence," or in other words, "The essence of being consists in the constant absence of contradiction" But also, something essential about man, for the man who contradicts himself is not only failing to reach being but is also lacking in himself: "Through contradictory assertions, which man can freely make about the same thing, he displaces himself from his essence into nonessence: he dissolves his relation to beings as such."[7]

The passage immediately following shows clearly that, rather than maintaining an interpretive distance here, Heidegger takes sides: "This fall into the nonessence of himself is uncanny in that it always seems harmless, in that business and pleasure go on just as before, in that it doesn't seem so important at all what and how one thinks; until one day the catastrophe is there—a day that needs perhaps centuries to rise from the night of increasing thoughtlessness."[8]

Let us add that the very paradigm of "idle talk" as "a mode of being of Dasein" (which Heidegger discusses under the heading "Falling as a basic movement of Dasein") is the colloquium or congress, where "one is of the opinion that the cumulation of this lack of understanding will nevertheless eventually generate an understanding." The whole litany of notions bearing the prefix *Ver-* (*Verdeckung*, "covering up," *Verstellen*, "disguising," *Verkehrung*, "inversion," *Verfallen*, "falling") inevitably recalls the Sophistic pseudos: "Ancient sophistry was nothing but this in its essential structure, although it was perhaps shrewder in certain ways."[9]

The diagnosis remains the same, then, and so would the condemnation if Heidegger were not more Christian than Aristotle: failure, falling, and inauthenticity do not mean the person who claims to uphold the contradiction is a vegetable. Rather, he or she remains a person whose essence is, essentially, also nonessence. This intelligence of difference thus makes difference a self-difference proper to each person by virtue of being human rather than a difference among individuals. Philosophies of consensus appear to lack this at least theoretical cautiousness.

The Reiteration of Structure: Karl-Otto Apel

Apel, Habermas, and probably Rorty have in common a desire to rescue ethics from irrationalism when Kantian autonomy no longer seems sufficient to do so. Against the impasses of formalism, they seek universality in the regulation of language conceived as communication: a rational foundation for ethics includes the discovery of the fact that logic presupposes an ethics. Apel thus speaks of a "transformation of philosophy." I particularly wish to draw attention to identical points common to decision in the Aristotelian sense and to the a priori of the communication community.

What enjoins Apel from receiving and even from understanding the question is first of all his classical, neo-Hegelian-Heideggerian conception of the history of philosophy. As is well known, for Apel, philosophy obeys three paradigms in succession. First, the ontological paradigm, which addresses the question of being or of the Being of beings, *"l'être de l'étant,"* and defines truth using the classical theory of correspondence. This paradigm is shared by Plato and Aristotle, and its canonical definition is even found in the *Gamma*: "to say that that which is is not or that which is not is, is a falsehood; and to say that that which is is and that which is not is not, is true" (*Gamma* 7, 1011b 25–27). The second paradigm, that of Descartes, Kant, and Husserl, has to do with reflexivity of consciousness and with the transcendental subject, defining truth as what is evident. Finally, the third paradigm—that of Karl-Otto Apel himself, following Wittgenstein and Peirce—takes into account the linguistic turn: "The third paradigm is the paradigm in which the first question is not that of the conditions of knowledge, but that of the conditions of possibility of meaningful discourse (*sinnvollen Redens*) or of meaningful argumentation (*sinvollen Argumentierens*). This is for me the most radical question at this time."[10] The theory of truth that corresponds to this paradigm is a consensual one, which presupposes a shared interpretation of the world. As Apel writes in his essay "The *A Priori* of the Communication Community and the Foundations of Ethics," the ethics of logic "is sought in the reconstructive recourse to the transcendental-pragmatic preconditions for the possibility of logic and thus of science, namely in the a priori of the communication community."[11]

This third paradigm, rather than overtaking the other two, seems to me to hark back— precisely in what is most Apelian about it—to the Aristotelian gesture inscribed in *Gamma*. I propose to isolate four analogous points.

PROBLEMATIZATION OF THE NOTION OF AN ULTIMATE FOUNDATION

The double bind of an ultimate foundation is that there must be at once foundation and an end to foundation. Münchhausen's trilemma leaves us the choice of infinite regression, circular logic, or an unfounded interruption of the process of foundation. Apel freely acknowledges that Aristotle was conscious of the aporia: to the very extent that the principle of non-contradiction cannot be contested without self-contradiction or founded without begging the principle, "the foundation of the principle of non-contradiction by Aristotle can serve as an illustration of the classical problem of the ultimate foundation."[12]

RESOLUTION OF THE APORIA

This is where Apel, by his own account, diverges from Aristotle, but to my view he repeats Aristotle, and doubly so: both in the foundational gesture (of a transcendental nature) and in the contents of the foundation, that is, the requirement of meaning. Indeed, in Apel's eyes, Aristotle is "the artisan of the apodictic," that is to say, of an "organon of argumentation purged of any potentially disturbing elements of pragmatism." Because he differentiates philosophy, which is geared to the relation between discourse and things, from poetics and rhetoric, which are oriented toward the relation to the listener, Aristotle is even considered the initiator of the "sophism of abstraction"—abstraction from the pragmatic dimension upon which rests the contemporary logic of science, entirely oriented toward syntax and semantics. Instead, Apel himself proposes a "transcendental pragmatics," or "reflection upon the conditions of possibility of a verbally formulated knowledge, that is, a knowledge virtually valid from an intersubjective viewpoint."[13]

This strikes a less conventional reader of the *Gamma* as none other than the Aristotelian procedure. We have seen Aristotle replace the impossible demonstration with the refutation, whose unique, necessary, and sufficient condition is that the adversary speak / say something / signify something for himself and for the other. It is in the univocity that constitutes meaning—the "something"—that the principle is begged. It is now inevitable in the sense that no one can avoid it. Taking a step backward, which can quite adequately be designated as a transcendental search for the conditions of possibility of human *logos*, Aristotle's achievement is thus to convert the element of controversy itself into a ground that he has already conquered: *sinnvollen Reden* or *Argumentieren* is to "say something," to "signify something, both to himself and to someone else."

ADMINISTRATION OF THE PROOF

For Apel and for Aristotle alike, adversaries contradict each other not only with regard to the logical and formal and not solely with respect to the pragmatic and empirical. When Apel argues against Karl Popper's decisionism, according to which "irrationalism can be upheld without contradiction because one can refuse to accept arguments," he echoes the specific mechanism of Aristotelian refutation: the rules of the transcendental game are "rules whose validity has always already been implicitly recognized,"[14] or, as Aristotle says, "for destroying speech [*logos*] he submits to speech" (*Gamma* 4, 1006a26).[15]

THE RELATION TO UNIVERSALITY AND THE STATUS OF THE EXCEPTION

Along with me and all the other "me's" that are animals endowed with *logos*, two categories of bad others can be delineated: the assimilable bad other and the radical bad other. The assimilatable category consists of those who, saying what they want, nevertheless conform to the obligation to "subject themselves to argument" (*hupekhein logon, Gamma* 6, 1011a22), for they belong de facto to the community of those who signify and argue. This is the "Devil" of Apel's article "The *A Priori* of the Communication Community and the Foundations of Ethics": contrary to popular belief, the Devil does not constitute an exception to the universal; indeed, an objection to the universality of ethical foundation is that even the Devil, given an instrumentalist reservation—such as the improvement of his art of persuasion or the mastery of the "know-how" of scientific technology—could participate in Lorenzen's dialogue game for grounding logic and thus take part in the community of argumentation without abandoning his evil will. To state it in Kant's terms: he can behave "dutifully" without acting "out of a sense of duty." But one need only reply as follows: "It is not Kant's argument—that even devils who can use their intellect can, in principle, behave 'dutifully'— which is relevant, but rather the argument that even devils must behave dutifully if they wish to partake of the truth . . . This means that the Devil, inasmuch as he desired to be a member of the community of argumentation, would for ever more have to behave towards its members (i.e., all rational beings) as if he had overcome egoism and, consequently, himself."[16] In other words, the Devil's or the Sophist's evil intent to speak falsely and to deceive—their egoism—can function only if it is always already caught up in the universality of meaning.

But even more diabolical than the Devil is the man who refuses to sustain his discourse or even to act as if he wanted to say something. In this case, "persuasion" is of no avail; only "constraint" can be used: "the remedy is to refute what is said in the sounds of the voices and in the words" (*Gamma* 5, 1009a21–22). However, as Aristotle himself acknowledges, this constraint is "impossible," for those who speak in this manner "think that they *can* say contraries, as soon as they *do* say contraries" (*Gamma* 6, 10na15–16).[17] There remains only exclusion, which consigns a whole swath of speech to silence and deprives of speech those who speak without signifying. In Apel's terms, "the human being can be separated from the institution," which is the transcendental game of language—the "metainstitution of all possible human institutions"—"only by sacrificing the identity of the self as an agent of sense: through suicide, existential despair, or the loss of the self caused by the pathological process of autistic paranoia."[18] When it is not a death sentence, this is a life sentence: vegetables that speak are dispatched either to the morgue or to the asylum.

Reliance on meaning as the transcendental condition of *logos*, the elaboration of meaning through consensus ("both to himself and to someone else," *Gamma* 4, 1006a22), the passage to the universal by reducing the exception to the positive void that is inhumanity: the structure of philosophical consensus in the mode of Aristotle and Apel is entirely bound up with the problematics of meaning. "Sense and nonsense have a specific relation which cannot copy that of the true and false":[19] sense has no opposite; its nature is such that something either makes sense or else simply is not; someone either is an agent of sense or else is not human.

What Is at Stake in the Everyday: Habermas

Both Habermas and Rorty, each in his own way, retreat from the transcendental necessity at the root of consensus. The backward step that Habermas quite explicitly takes in his critique of Apel consists in refusing to see a foundation in the rules of the transcendental language game: if sense and consensus impose their necessity, it is simply because there is no replacement rule. They can be acknowledged or obtained only through and in discussion. In Aristotelian terms and hewing squarely to Aristotelian doctrine, Habermas does not admit that a refutation may ever constitute a demonstration. Thus, with every Sophist, every time someone refuses to admit the ethical a prioris, an effort must be made to demonstrate that by the same token he contradicts himself and betrays the intention of his discourse, which is to convince and to reach an intersubjective agreement. Instead of a foundation, we come finally to definitions: a discussion aims at consensus or it is not a discussion; every instance of communication is ethical, or else it is not communication.

But such an approach only renders more formidable the problem of the exception to the universal. At this point, the topos of exclusion is strictly unaltered. This time, the most diabolical of all is the *"consistent skeptic,"* who "will deprive the transcendental pragmatist of a basis for his argument. He may, for example, take the attitude of an ethnologist vis-à-vis his own culture, shaking his head over philosophical argumentation as though he were witnessing the unintelligible rites of a strange tribe. Nietzsche perfected this way of looking at philosophical matters, and Foucault has now rehabilitated it." The height of strangeness is, of course, that he chooses to remain silent and that "through his behavior the skeptic voluntarily terminates his membership in the community of beings who argue." Habermas, it seems, does not see how Apel's theory could accommodate this silence. However, in his own treatment of the recalcitrant one, he merely repeats—using Apel's very terms—the exclusion invented by Aristotle: one who refuses argumentation "may reject morality, but he cannot reject the ethical substance (*Sittlichkeit*) of the life circumstances in which he spends his waking hours, not unless he is willing to take refuge in suicide or serious mental illness."[20]

Here, the characteristic schism of the senseless is no longer found in the domain of language but rather in the dimension of behavior, of everyday authenticity, echoing Aristotle's assertion that the "something" of "to signify something"—the identity required by language and noncontradiction—does not differ from the "something" necessary to the "rather than"—from the identity required by practical choice and by the principle of reason. For Aristotle as well, it is clear that the adversary cannot do what he says (or does not say), nor can he behave as his discourse or silence requires him to: "Why does he not proceed one morning straight into a well or over a precipice, if there is one about: instead of evidently taking care to avoid doing so, as one who does not consider that falling in is equally a good thing and not a good thing?" (*Gamma* 4, 1008b15–17; cf. 5, 1010b9–11, and 6, 1011a10–11). Here Habermas simply ups the ante: "As long as he is still alive *at all*, a

Robinson Crusoe existence through which the skeptic demonstrates mutely and impressively that he has dropped out of communicative action is inconceivable, even as a thought experiment."[21]

In order to be truly consistent with himself, Cratylus—a true Heraclitean, who, unable to make his discourse conform to the flux of phenomena, was content merely to wiggle his finger (either in silence or whistling furiously)—would have had to let himself die. As Habermas correctly emphasizes, not only the argumentation of reason but also all of everyday life are pervaded with the ethical, and one is subject to sense not just as soon as one opens one's mouth but as soon as one is alive. This is true to such an extent that the reverse of this necessity must finally be more than a relegation. It is a liquidation.

Socrates, or Conversation According to Rorty

The backward step taken by Rorty is apparently so big that he might as well take it all the way back to a Sophistic position—and indeed, his work is sometimes refuted with the scorn usually reserved for Sophists.

Rorty's watchword is "conversation," as prized in his American usage as idle talk is denigrated in Heidegger's German. Rorty's definition of pragmatism hinges on the notion of conversation: "pragmatism . . . is the doctrine that there are no constraints on inquiry save conversational ones."[22] Such a definition has the merit of introducing "a renewed sense of community" to compensate for the loss of "metaphysical comfort" associated with essentialism. Such pragmatists are at once "relativists" in the sense that they believe that "our culture, or purpose, or intuitions cannot be supported except conversationally."[23]

For Rorty, conversation—unlike Apel's argumentation or Habermas's discussion—has neither foundation nor finality beyond itself. Thus, Habermas is by definition an antipragmatist insofar as he believes "that conversation necessarily aims at agreement and at rational consensus, that we converse in order to make further conversation unnecessary."[24] In contrast, the only aim of pragmatic conversation is itself rather than any goal of sense or consensus: this conversation for conversation's sake ought to be placed alongside the "speaking for the sake of speaking" that Aristotle ascribes to Sophistic vegetables.

And yet such is by no means the case. It is as if, unable to produce the *topos* of exclusion from within the system, Rorty de facto reproduced the same exclusive impulses, which now have the force of mere commonplaces. Indeed, all he comes up with is "the prolepsis of the moral subject," to borrow Jacques Poulain's terms.[25] He quite explicitly takes Socrates as his model—not the complex, shades-of-gray Socrates of Plato's dialogues but a postcard Socrates, at odds with the Sophists, who are too caricatural ever to have existed. "This is the issue between Socrates on the one hand and the tyrants on the other—the issue between lovers of conversation and lovers of self-deceptive rhetoric. For my purposes, it is the issue about whether we can be pragmatists without betraying Socrates, without falling into irrationalism."[26]

The clinical profile of the bad other has hardly altered: tyranny and irrationalism are the effects of "self-deceptive rhetoric," the *apatê*, or deception, about which Gorgias said, conversely, that "someone who proffers it is more just than one who does not, and someone who suffers it is wiser than one who does not."[27] Rorty's response is to unabashedly assimilate the Socratic virtues (goodwill applied to speaking and listening to the other, to weighing the consequences of one's acts for others) to the virtues of conversation, and the virtues of conversation, quite simply, to the ethical virtues.[28]

Socrates and conversation: a rather unexpected pairing for the reader of Plato's dialogues in their concrete unfolding since the interlocutor is regularly, and often summarily, reduced to acquiescent monosyllables. What authorizes Plato's Socrates, in contrast to Rorty's, to eschew true dialogue is that his constantly proclaimed goal is not the love of conversation or of words themselves but rather the search for the true and the good—the things themselves. The conversation lovers Rorty describes as if he were dizzy even at this remove from the ancient parapets are still and always the lovers of wisdom. Thus, speaking for the sake of speaking becomes, like saying what occurs to one, the final metamorphosis of the moral constraint of sense.

Examining Apel, Habermas, and Rorty in sequence makes it obvious that less and less is required in order to escape the condition of a vegetable:

to enter into the transcendental game of language, to survive, to speak for the sake of speaking. The world of sense constantly swallows up what is outside it. But the exclusion retains its litigious dimension: this is the obligation to confront alterity and nothingness. In Jean-François Lyotard's terms, this contentiousness is even a paradigm of the differend, for undoubtedly it can be said that the semantic regime does harm to all other discursive regimes by depriving them of the means to prove this harm: every other regime is inaudible, unnamable, foreclosed.

Translated by Jennifer Curtiss Gage

THREE

Seeing Helen in Every Woman: Woman and Word

"Seeing Helen in every woman" is a phrase from Goethe, from *Faust*. "With this drink in him / He'll see a Helen in every woman," Mephistopheles says to Faust in the witch's kitchen, making him drink the love potion.[1] Indeed, Marguerite walks by in the street, and Faust, who sees her reflection in a mirror, says to himself, "Helen." He sees Helen in Marguerite and falls hopelessly in love.

This phrase spread throughout Germany like wildfire after Goethe. Two occurrences in particular struck me. The first is in Nietzsche in 1872, in *The Birth of Tragedy*, which says of Greek art: "It sees Helen in every woman: the avid desire for existence hides what isn't beautiful."[2] Thus, to see Helen in every woman is to see beauty even in ugliness.

The second is in Freud, in a letter to Jung dated 1909, a fairly extravagant letter in which he explains why he is sure he will die between the ages of 61 and 62. I will skip all the reasons for his belief; in any case, he even reads the number 61 in the number of the hotel room he is given in Athens, room 31, which "with fatalistic licence could be regarded as half of 61 or 62."[3] To explain this adventure with the number 61, he speaks of "the unconsciously motivated attention of the sort that sees Helen in every woman." Just like chance compliance for a delusory interpretation or somatic compliance for a hysterical symptom, like linguistic compliance for a play on words, according to the same mechanism, the unconscious sees Helen in every woman—thus meaning even in the insignificant and trivial.

But what is there then in Helen, what is there in the essence or nonessence of Helen such that she can be "every woman"? Such that, depending on the idiom chosen, she can be the *eidos* woman, woman as woman, exemplary femininity in each—in short, W/woman.[4]

In truth, to explore the question it would be necessary to consider Helen as a multimedia cultural object. Music is evidently of considerable importance, the operas and operettas that have been written about her in particular.[5] But whatever the medium, there is a powerful characteristic—let's call it methodological—of the world of Helen, which is that it is decompartmentalized. Against the fixed mastery of strict orders, all of the genres communicate, including literary genres: painting, music, philosophy, but also the epic, tragedy, comedy, lyric poetry, even the novel. A second trait of its configuration, which unfixes time, must be added to this first: the texts, music, or words which make phrases about Helen, are palimpsests, and palimpsests of palimpsests, ironically structured by their reuse. There is no text that isn't woven from other texts, no music that isn't woven from other music, no figure on a vase that isn't woven from all the others, and that is both profoundly Greek and profoundly cultural: Helen is an entirely fabricated object. In this world in circulation and layered expansion, which I would willingly range on the side of the feminine, one cannot have the deep and serious on one side and the surface and superficial on the other. "Oh those Greeks, they knew how to *live*. What is required for that is to stop at the surface, the fold, the skin, to adore appearance, to believe in forms, in tones, words, the whole Olympus of appearance. These Greeks were superficial—out of *profundity*."[6] In a single phrase, Nietzsche replays all of the separations since the Platonic distinction of the sensible and the intelligible; one will no longer say this is philosophy, male / this is literature, female. Helen's *kosmos*, an expanding world, goes from cosmetics (her mirror, her makeup) to cosmology (Castor and Pollux, her brother constellations). I propose to call such a relation between cosmetic and cosmology, beauty.

To define Helen's beauty, there is a syntagm that returns constantly since the *Iliad* and the *Odyssey*: "she resembles terribly" [*ainôs eoiken*]. She resembles terribly, her beauty is a beauty that resembles terribly. This is how we must read one of the most beautiful poems about her, one of the most beautiful poems ever, taken from Aeschylus's *Agamemnon* (verses 739–44, which I translate as best I can):

> What first entered the city of Ilion
> I would say it was the thought
> Of a windless calm
> The peaceful statue of splendour
> The tender arrow of the eyes
> The flower of love that bites the heart

The poem as an exchanger of resemblances, between the pensive organization of the world (the thought [*phronêma*] of a windless calm) and all its concrete finery, splendor, the arrow of the eyes, the flower of love: cosmology and cosmetics. So much so that, seeing the vases, the first work that the painter Matieu and I did together was to let ourselves be surprised by the number, the variety, the invention, and the design of Helen's dresses: Helen's wardrobe is Helen already, perhaps what is most real in Helen. "Hold tight . . . let not the garment go," says Phorcyas to Faust, and Hector to Paris in Giraudoux's play: "In other words: she was undressed, so neither her clothes nor her belongings have been insulted. Nothing except her body, which is negligible."[7]

Let's go back to my question: how has Helen been constructed since Homer, such that she is seen in every woman? In gathering together her textual world, one notices a red thread: in a rather striking manner, her reality, her consistency are entirely linked to language in all of its forms. If she is seen in every woman, it is because she has a discursive or linguistic consistency and existence. Hence my subtitle, "Woman and Word," a subtitle to be grasped under four headings. First heading: her proper name—and here I will read a little Aeschylus; second heading: her voice—and here I will read a little Homer; third heading: the relationship between word and thing—and here I will read a little Euripides; fourth and final heading: the relation to *logos*, to discourse in general, in its difference from being—and here I will read a little Gorgias. Finally, to tie up all of these threads, I will try to implicate them in Lacan's *Encore* and see how that holds together.

Helen's Name: Aeschylus

First of all, Helen's name. What I am doing is not orthodox: for example, if you consult Chantraine's excellent *Dictionnaire étymologique de la langue grecque*, you will be told that "whatever the interpretation attempted by the historians of religion . . . it is pointless to look for an etymology." That being said, there is a plethora of them and in which the whole of Greece believed. For example, "Helen" comes from *helein*, past infinitive of the verb *haireô* [I take, I remove, I capture]: here, say all the Greeks, is a good eponym, in accordance with the *etumon*, in the true sense, the etymological sense of the word. Especially because an uncertainty resides in the final syllable of "Helen," one cannot know whether it is active and she is a ravishingly beautiful abductor or whether it is passive and she is ravished, kidnapped, and enraptured. This ravished, ravishing beauty is so in all of the poems: Helen the culpable victim, active insofar as she is passive. As Giraudoux says without any care for correctness in *The Trojan War Will Not Take Place*, "you know women as well as I do. They are only willing when you compel them, but after that they're as enthusiastic as you are."[8]

I will quote only one poem with regard to Helen's name—all the others could follow. Again, it is Aeschylus's *Agamemnon*, verses 681–701:

> Who could have given this name
> authentic through and through [I translate *etêtumos* as "authentic"]
> if not someone we cannot see,
> who knowing in advance the marks of fate
> steers language to its target,
> —the wife of spears, the disputed:
> Helen? Is it not as Helen that,

Taker of ships, taker of men, taker
Of cities [*helenas, helandros, heleptolis*—every possible declension of the
    way in she takes and is taken] leaving the secrecy
Of magnificent veils, she leaves across the sea
By the gentle breath of a giant zephyr?
Many men, hunters with shields, set off on her trail . . .

This Greek *etumon* is the palimpsestic matrix of the very French Ronsard, who is sometimes violent ("Nor lamentable tear nor gentle pity / lent thee thy name. 'Tis Greek, and means to slay, / to ravage, storm, despoil and sack the city / of my poor heart, thy miserable prey"[9]), sometimes languid ("My golden Helen, nay my gold inhaling / that tempers my hot heart with its cool air"[10]). But it is also like a Marlow playing with English, sometimes writing Helen with two *l*'s—*Hellen*—as in *Hell*: "that heavenly Hellen."[11]

Especially as Helen with a single *l*, her name, or rather the signifier of her name, also assonates as "Hellenes" with two *l*'s. The cause of the Trojan War, Helen ceaselessly appears as the cause of the fact that the Hellenes are Hellenes: the "war for Helen" is constitutive of Greek identity. Isocrates testifies to this in *Encomium to Helen*: "It is with justice that we think that Helen is the cause of our not being the slaves of barbarians, thanks to her we will in effect find the Hellenes consensual, making a common army against the barbarians, and Europe then erecting for the first time a trophy of victory against Asia."[12] This is impossible to perceive in the translation published by Budé, which runs "We see the *Greeks* united"—the Greeks and not the Hellens. No one is able to understand that it refers to the signifier Helen/Hellene, of this little pair of syllables LN.[13] Helen as a relationship to language (the Hellenes faced with the barbarians' blah-blah-blah), Helen as a relationship to a territory (at the end of Euripides's *Helen*, she becomes Helen, the true name of Pharos, the island that guards the Attican coast), Helen, then, as a way to make Europe consensual through a sacred union against Asia. Helen's name constitutes her as a language, a people, a continent, a civilization. Helen or Greece itself: a ravishing ravished who, conquered, will always conquer her conqueror. To say it more strongly and more generally, Helen's name makes it manifest that love, like war, is most essentially, very explicitly, across a whole chain of texts, a question of words, a relationship between words, a signifying performance.

Helen's Voice

Helen's voice has an entirely singular consistency and existence. Here, too, there is a no less magnificent matrix text. If I am a philosopher *and* a philologist, it is because, when I read these texts in the translations that are commonly found in bookstores, it makes me furious to see just how unreadable they are even when they are well translated.

In the scene in question from the *Odyssey* (IV, 121–90), the verses that interest me, truly extraordinary verses, are verses that are usually, at least in the French tradition, cut, athetesisized, if you will, placed between square brackets, which are the philological guillotine. From the first Greek scholars to Victor Bérard (who nevertheless really does translate, to the point that to our ears his language sounds Homeric), everyone says, "Homer can't have meant that; it doesn't make sense," and the verses are cut. One has to be free like Lucian to be able to laugh when affirming that all of the verses that have been cut from Homer are indeed his—I have met him in hell, "and he claimed responsibility for them all without exception."[14] Here is the scene. Helen has returned; she has been captured and recaptured by Menelaus. He hasn't killed her, he hasn't avenged himself, she is at home as the mistress of the house, she spins, just as her servants spin around when she arrives, she makes some food when unexpected guests turn up, including Telemachus, who is seeking his father, Ulysses, the only one not to have returned. In any case, it is the very day of the wedding of one of the children, one of Menelaus and Helen's children, and, unfortunately, Telemachus is whining, and his tears are going to spoil the dinner. So, Helen—I'm paraphrasing, but the following phrases really are Homer's—Helen has an idea, she brings a *pharmakon*, a "poison-remedy" that she has brought back from Egypt to put in the wine so that all those who drink it will be cured of their sadness and can see their father and brothers assassinated before their very eyes without crying. This *pharmakon nepenthes takholon*, "which diminishes pain and anger," serves, it is said, to allow one to give in to the pleasure of discourse (*muthois terpesthe*, "enjoy each others' stories"). So she pours this drug into the wine, everyone drinks it, talks, and everyone is happy.

Who speaks and who recounts what? Helen starts and delivers a very complex eulogy to Ulysses—there would be much to say about this scene, mixing ruse and duplicity, in which Helen recognizes Ulysses, who has broken into Troy, but doesn't give him away and delights deep down to hear him massacring some Trojans. Then Menelaus says, "Ah, my dear, you speak rightly in all that you say," and lays it on a bit to recount the exploits of Ulysses: "What Ulysses did, what he achieved with his energy! We all sat in the wooden horse, the pick of the army, waiting to bring death and slaughter to Troy." The wooden horse, in which the Greek warriors hid themselves, has entered the city; it is inside Troy, where Helen has lived for ten years; she has married Paris and, after Paris is killed, his brother Deiphobus.

"But you came up," says Menelaus, speaking to Helen, "some god brought you to this place to give some chance for glory to the Trojans [Deiphobus followed you, fine like some god]—*athetesis, because why would Menelaus recall how many arms Helen passed through before being returned to him, notes Bérard, who has a sense of proprieties*—and three times you circled around our hollow lair, touching it. You called out to each of the pick of the Danaeans one name at a time [mimicking the wives of each Argive with your voice]—*unanimous athetesis, says Bérard*—[15] . . . Me, the son of Tydeus, and the divine Ulysses were sat in the middle, we heard you calling, we couldn't help being tempted, we jumped up to come out, but Ulysses held us back and checked our impetuosity."

See the complexity of the situation: Helen is in the process of betraying the Greek warriors, including Ulysses and her husband; she wants them to give themselves away. And, so that they might do so, she drives them crazy with desire by imitating the voice of each one's wife, whom they haven't seen for ten years, and she calls out to each one by name. So, she says "Menelaus" with her own voice, "Ajax" with the voice of Ajax's wife, and "Ulysses" with Penelope's voice. Evidently, "the imitation of voices is impossible, entirely ridiculous," says the scholiast, "as for verse 279, it is completely incomprehensible: how could Helen imitate the voices of each of the Achaean queens, and why?" Bérard asks himself *ad loc* in his translation. Just the same, Jaccottet, who has nevertheless read Freud and Lacan, clarifies the passage: "this verse, which has seemed suspect to more than one critic, can simply be understood to mean that Helen speaks Greek and not Trojan.[16]"

From this I retain the lesson that voice is the *pharmakon*, the remedy-poison par excellence, that the essence of desire is the voice that calls each man by his name. But above all, I deduce that Helen is a general equivalent for all women, that is, W/woman. And this is so by virtue of her voice, which serves to create desire because it is the voice of each one of the women for each one of the men, one by one.

The Word/the Thing: Euripides

The third level: the word is more real than the thing, and this is the case with Helen. Euripides dramatizes this in his *Helen*, which created quite a stir at the time, a "new Helen," it was said. In Euripides, what is new is that there are two Helens. Let's say that there is a Helen who is Helen and whom Hera, the wife par excellence, has taken to Egypt to Proteus, an old king who can no longer do her any harm, so that she can escape all of this unhealthy aspect of abduction, breaking of the contract, infidelity, There, she waits for it to pass. She is the embodiment of the perfect, faithful wife of a husband who has gone off to war.

And then there is a second Helen, who is nothing other than "flatus vocis," a fog of sounds, an *agalma* of cloud, an *eidolôn*, a phantom: the name Helen. It is this Helen who navigated to Troy, this Helen that Paris abducted, who climbed up onto the battlements, for which the Greeks were fighting and dying. This is the Helen that Menelaus rescues, with whom he arrives at the coast of Egypt to find himself confronted with the other, the "true" Helen. So, there is the name or the shadow, the shadow named "Helen" and Helen herself, Helen of Troy, Helen of Egypt.

This play is the most anti-Platonic of all because, in it, the word is more real than the thing. The name is more real than the body because it has more effects. Menelaus tells us so, and it is recounted ceaselessly—by Bloch in *The Principle of Hope*: "I trust the weight of sufferings endured more than I trust you"[17]—I believe in these "ten utopian years, the bitterness and the love-hatred of the cuckold, the many nights spent far from home" and not in you that I see, not in you that I touch and who is speaking to me, even if it is a mirage, I believe in what has had so much of an effect on me and on us.

That isn't easy to read in the translations, either, even if it is so present that it can't be eliminated completely. For example, when Helen says, "I was named Helen," it is translated in the current French edition as "I am Helen" [*je suis Hélène*], which really isn't the same thing in the scenario![18]

Here is the way that Helen puts everything into place in her first monologue:

> Hera, who reproaches Paris for not having made her triumph over the
>   goddesses,
> has made my bed nothing but wind for him,
> she does not give him me, but, similar to me,
> an idol that breathes, made from pieces of sky
> for the son of King Priam. And
> by having not me but an empty appearance, he believes I was his
> . . . Under the protection of the vigor of the Phrygians was placed, not me,
> but my name, the battle prize for the Greeks.[19]

There is no possible equivocation; it really is the name that is in Troy, the name in its form of breath-wind-cloud. In any case, the play finishes when the *eidolon* name, idol-phantom-image, flies off, back into the sky, because as is said at the end, "Helen has only to lend her name to the gods" (v.1653). So, the two Helens are joined together to make just one, a single Helen who is both her body and her name. Finally, it is she who leaves with Menelaus for a *happy end*.

But prior to this, a marvelous scene of mis/recognition takes place, which I can't resist recounting [v. 557–596]. When Menelaus disembarks on the shores of Egypt, he sees a woman who resembles Helen—in the end, it is Helen, even "Helen" whom Helen terribly resembles—and he says to her something like, "Ah . . . What is your name?" She replies, "Helen." "Come on, you can't be Helen because I have her here, I left her over there in a cave." In turn, she says, "How you resemble Menelaus." As she understands everything, she tries to explain to him that "the name can be found in many places, not the body." And it is then that Menelaus resists, with all the strength of this magnificent phrase: "It is the magnitude of my sufferings over there that persuades me, not you."

However, they soon leave together, but it will have been understood, once and for all, that the word is more real than the thing and that what is real in the word is the effect it has.

Logos, *or the* Encomium of Helen: *Gorgias*

In a general manner, Helen is a product of discourse. She is even *logos* incarnate.

That can be read via Gorgias's *Encomium of Helen*, the first great text on Helen after Homer. As an ambassador, Gorgias arrived in Athens with a delegation to deal with the affairs of Sicily. Gorgias then relates how he offers to give an *epideixis*, a monstration, a performance, a lecture in front of the Athenians in the agora: a relatively ordinary *one-man show* about Helen, in which he shows how she is guilty—no one is surprised, everyone knew it: she left her husband, her country, her children, and so on; she is the guiltiest of women, thousands of Greeks died for her. But, he adds, "come back tomorrow at the same time." The next day, same time, same place, Gorgias delivers the only speech that has been preserved for us: the magnificent speech, the *Encomium of Helen*.[20] And the *Encomium of Helen* is there to explain—I was going to say from A to Z—to what extent Helen isn't guilty and how she is precisely the most innocent of women.

She is not guilty for a series of interconnected reasons, an interlocking structure that one still finds in *Encore*. Helen is not guilty because fortune, "the intentions of fate, the will of the gods, and the decrees of necessity," have willed it thus. That is the aspect of *fatum*, Offenbach, fate, "fatalité!" So, if it was her fate to be guilty, she is not guilty. Or—second hypothesis— she was taken by force, she was abducted, the barbarian abductor is to blame, and, once again, she is not guilty. Or—the third possibility—she was "persuaded by speech," and so, if she believed what was said to her, she was not guilty, more so than ever. The *Encomium of Helen*, the model for and the paradigm of praise, is a praise to *logos*; it is a eulogy to the powers of *logos*:

> But if it was speech that persuaded her and deluded her mind, it is also not .
> difficult to defend her from that accusation and to dispel the accusation thus:
> Speech is a powerful master, which by means of the smallest and most invisible
> body accomplishes most divine deeds. For it can put an end to fear, remove
> grief, instill joy, and increase pity . . . [21]

She is exonerated because she believed *logos*, and it is *logos* that exonerates her as well and performs her innocence to the Athenians, who this time are so flabbergasted that they forge the verb "to gorgianize." Now, *logos*—you know which untranslatable entity it is a matter of—is nothing other than a *pharmakon*, as Gorgias says very precisely:

> There is the same relation [*logos*] between the power of discourse [*hê tou logou
> dunamis*] and the disposition of the soul [*tên tês psukhês taxin*], the administra-
> tion of drugs [*hê tôn pharmakôn taxis*] and the nature of bodies [*tên tôn somatôn
> phusin*]: just as one drug expels a humor from the body, and some stop illness,
> and others life, so among discourses, some distress, some charm, cause fear,
> make the hearers bold, and some, by some wicked persuasion, drug the soul
> and bewitch it. [22]

This performance finishes as it should: "I have made the bad reputation of a woman disappear by this speech . . . a eulogy for Helen, a plaything for me." [23] We see in its full range the consistency of Helen, from the least bit of signifier that enters into her name (so easy in French: Queneau made it L/N, *elle/haine*, she/hate), to the major conception. It is what I would characterize as counterontological, according to which it is speech that produces being. Starting from there, or from her, one sketches out the orbit of sophistic in the following manner. On the one hand, from Parmenides to Heidegger: ontology, there is being, *es gibt*, and man, as a good shepherd, is committed to say what there is. On the other hand, to borrow a term from Novalis: logology, where it is in the first place a matter of discourse and where being is nothing but the effect of speech, a discursive performance. *Logos* gives objects being, consistency, and existence; such is the case in politics (the Greek *polis*, the most talkative of all, is a continuous creation of discourse), such is the case in love, and more generally for every object of culture. Such is the case, at the intersection of these reasons, for Helen. That is how she is constituted, and not otherwise.

Helen Once More: Lacan

I would now like to gather together these threads and explain how Helen gave me the desire to reread *Encore*. I asked myself the following (even if it is too risky, too badly formulated a question): is it Helen's relationship to language that makes of her W/woman? In other words: does sexual difference have an impact on language? How are woman's desire, pleasure, and jouissance linked to language?

I propose some tracks through Lacan via my very partial reading of *Encore*. In the first place, it is clear that there is at least one negative track in relation to the "real" of the thing or the object. Helen's desire, Helen's pleasure, Helen's jouissance, in both senses of the genitive—objective and subjective, what one has from her and what she has—is nothing, is not "*rem*," not something. Let's have a little Giraudoux, that subtle boulevardier, for support:

Paris: Hasn't she the ways of a young, gentle gazelle?
Cassandra: No.
Paris: But you were the one who first said she was like a gazelle.
Cassandra: I made a mistake. Since then I have seen a gazelle again.
Hector: To hell with gazelles! Doesn't she look any more like a woman than that?
Paris: She isn't the type of woman we know here, obviously.
Cassandra: What is the type of woman we know here?
Paris: Your type, my dear sister. The fearfully unremote sort of woman.
Cassandra: When your Greek makes love she is a long way off, I suppose?
Paris: You know perfectly well what I am trying to say. I have had enough of
    Asiatic women. They hold you in their arms as though they were glued there,
    their kisses are like battering-rams, their words chew right into you. The
    more they undress the more elaborate they seem, until when they're naked
    they are more overdressed than ever. And they paint their faces to look as

though they mean to imprint themselves on you. And they do imprint themselves on you. In short, you are definitely *with* them. But Helen is far away from me, even held in my arms.

Hector: Very interesting! But, one wonders, is it really worth a war, to allow Paris to make love at a distance?

Cassandra: With distance. He likes distant women, but from close up.

Paris: Helen's absence in her presence is worth everything.[24]

As for the desire that Helen may have . . . Helen's desire is always either the desire of Aphrodite or of Paris, but since the *Iliad* and the *Odyssey*, it is never hers. Look at the first domestic scene in the *Iliad*, a piece of bravura. To understand it, it must be situated (III, 335–449). Helen is watching the singular combat between Paris and Menelaus, the lover and the husband, from the height of the ramparts. It could bring the war to an end because, if one of them were to win, he would carry Helen off, and everything would stop. Well, no! One of them doesn't win because Aphrodite is there: when Menelaus is going to win, she seizes Paris just like that, she hides him in a thick mist, she carries him off on a cloud (all the goddesses take off on clouds), and puts him in bed. No sooner has she done this than she takes on the figure of an old woman, she tugs at Helen's sleeve on the ramparts and says to her "come this way, Paris is demanding you go back home. He is in the bedroom, on the carved bed, resplendent in his beauty," hurry up. Helen recognizes the goddess by her desirable breasts, her sparkling eyes, yet she dares to reply: "Well, go and sit by him yourself, abandon the paths of the gods, don't let your feet go back to Olympus, but feel sympathy for him, look after him until the day that makes you either his wife or his slave! I will not go to him, to serve his bed; that would be unworthy of me."

Helen thus places Aphrodite in the face of her own desire. But however divine she may be, Helen is right to fear the goddess's anger ("do not provoke me, willful girl, beware of me growing angry and abandoning you") and allows herself to be taken to the bedroom. The domestic scene follows. Lowering her eyes, Helen rebukes her husband: "you have come back from fighting, what a favor it would have been if you were dead, broken by the powerful man who was my first husband. Before, yes, you boasted . . . Well, go now . . . ," and so on. Now, the scene finishes thus: "Woman, don't hound me with your painful taunts, come, let us lie together, the two of us, never has love so enveloped my lungs, not even on that first time . . . He spoke and led the way to their bed, his wife followed." After Aphrodite's desire, Paris's desire instead of Helen's.

It seems to me one finds a consistent and outrageous thematization of that in Lacan, in *Encore*:[25] it stems from dumbly dotting the *i*'s in what I would call a *Treatise on the Nonbeing of Female Jouissance* so as to make the repetition of the structure that inhabits and constitutes Gorgias's *Treatise on Non-Being*, which has already been seen at work in the exonerations of Helen. Gorgias's *Treatise on Non-Being* is composed of three theses assembled according to a rather remarkable recoiling structure: 1. "Nothing is." 2. "If it is, it is unknowable." 3. "If it is, and if it is knowable, it is incommunicable." You will find this recoiling structure in Freud's story about the borrowed kettle, for example: "I never borrowed a kettle; the kettle had a hole when I borrowed it; I returned the kettle in one piece." These are truly joke-stories, the inverse of the blooming of physics, this *phusis* that burgeons and grows.

I find the three theses of the *Treatise of Non-Being* in Lacan applied to female jouissance. It's no mystery. In the first place, she doesn't come: " 'Were there another one,' but there is no other than phallic jouissance . . . It is false that there is another one, but that doesn't stop what follows from being true, namely, that it shouldn't be/could never fail to be that one."[26] So, she doesn't come.

Then, if she comes, she doesn't know it: "There is a jouissance that is hers, that belongs to that 'she' that doesn't exist and doesn't signify anything. There is a jouissance that is hers about which she herself perhaps knows nothing if not that she experiences it—that much she knows. She knows it, of course, when it comes. It doesn't happen to all of them."[27] So, if she comes, she doesn't know it.

Finally, if she comes and she knows it, she cannot say it: "The plausibility of what I am claiming—namely, that woman knows nothing of this jouissance—is underscored by the fact that in all the time people have been begging them, begging them on their hands and knees—I spoke last time of women psychoanalysts—to try to tell us, not a word! We've never been able to get anything out of them."[28] So, then, in any case, she cannot say it.

Now, can we try to speak positively of this non-thing that doesn't stop retreating? We will start again from the major thesis, that it fails, that failure is the only form for the realization of the sexual relation. The major thesis of *Encore*. So, on the man's side, it fails because of the body, anatomy, because of phallic jouissance. "Phallic jouissance is the obstacle owing to which man does not come, I would say, to enjoy woman's body, precisely because what he is enjoying is the jouissance of the organ."[29] That is why he enjoys himself but not her. In sum, it is of him that one ought to say that anatomy is destiny.

But on the woman's side, it fails differently. Lacan's provocation is to assert the following: "A woman can but be excluded by the nature of things, which is the nature of words, and it must be said that if there is something that women themselves complain about enough for the time being, that's it. It's just that they don't know what they are saying—that's the whole difference between them and me."[30] One hears it here, but once one has heard it, can it be taught? It fails in a "crazy," an "enigmatic" way, says Lacan, because of language. What does that mean: "because of language"? "The sexed being of these not-whole women does not involve the body but what results from a logical exigency in speech."[31] A relation to speech then, and not to the body. That is what I propose to hear as a "fail better," to the extent that jouissance is linked to language and language, as we know, is the apparatus of jouissance: "There's no other apparatus than language"— certainly not the body. "That is how jouissance is fitted out in speaking beings."[32] These are just quotations placed next to each other. But they make me say that, for woman, it fails better. Very precisely: it fails better insofar as she is Helen, that is to say, of the order of the word and of language rather than of the thing, of the order, and in the order of discourse rather than of being.

Hence this joke, this whimsy, to finish: man fails and enjoys as a philosopher; woman fails and enjoys as a sophist.

Translated by Andrew Goffey

Part II   Sophistics, Rhetorics, Politics

FOUR

Rhetorical Turns in Ancient Greece

"Rhetorical *turns* in Ancient Greece." Why the plural? What happened in Greece could certainly be read in terms of a "rhetorical turn," but the point is that there was more than one. Each turn has its own meaning and implications, which I now try to describe.

The First Rhetorical Turn, or: How Philosophy Tamed Logos

When we, as patient scholars, read about the beginnings of rhetoric, we always learn that it begins, like any *tekhnê*, by a practice improving upon chance. We can trust Roland Barthes's "The Old Rhetoric: An Aide-Mémoire," as well as George Kennedy's basic *The Art of Persuasion in Greece* and even John Poulakos's more recent *Sophistical Rhetoric in Classical Greece*[1] when they say that rhetoric began, more or less, with the sophists. Its origins may lie with Corax and Tisias's attempts to help their Sicilian coc-itizens to win their lawsuits against the two tyrants Hiero and Gelo and to recover their properties (the beginnings of forensic speech); or with the embassy of Gorgias, who attempted to convince the Athenians not to make war on Sicily (deliberative speech), or when the same Gorgias in a public speech depicted Helen as an innocent woman (epideictic speech), or with the many foreign teachers and lawmakers who traveled from city to city, and so on. These are all very good stories, regardless of whether they are credible. What clearly merges from all of these accounts, however, is that rhetoric comes into existence very early and that practice and training of the Sophists are two of the earliest manifestations of its existence.

In this widely held view, the Sophists are orators and rhetoricians, both described by one single Greek word: *rhêtores*. Since, however, they are only beginners, they are not very good ones. They are "not yet," just as "phlo-gistic" is not yet oxygene. Aristotle says this in a very Maoist way at the end of the *Sophistical Refutations*:

> The teaching which they gave to their pupils was rapid but unsystematic; for they conceived they could train their pupils by imparting to them not an art but the results of an art, just as if one should claim to be about to communicate knowledge for the prevention of pain in the feet and then were not to teach the cobbler's art and the means of providing suitable foot-gear, but were to offer a selection of various kinds of shoes; for he has helped to supply his need but has not imparted an art to him.[2]

To give someone a few fish, Mao said, is not the same thing as teaching him how to fish. But, of course, one has to know how to fish before one can teach it, and these early rhetoricians were "not yet" good enough to under-stand that.

But this description is a very biased one. In fact, it is a pure Platonic-Aristotelian description, that is to say, it is a strictly philosophical one even if Barthes or Kennedy or Poulakos are not aware of it. And it matters be-cause it makes a difference. My claim is that rhetoric is a philosophical in-vention, an attempt to tame *logos*, in particular the Sophist's *logos* and its effects. The creation of rhetoric by philosophy is itself the very first "rhe-torical turn": in other words, the first rhetorical turn is in fact a philosophi-cal turn. Let me explain how.

The word "rhetoric" itself is a pure Platonic invention. In this I am entirely in agreement with Edward Schiappa. "Did Plato Coin *Rhêtorikê*?" is the title of one of Schiappa's best articles.[3] And the answer is clearly "yes." To put it simply, there is no known occurrence of the term *rhêtorikê* before Plato's *Gorgias*, written about 385 B.C., the subtitle of which is "On Rhetoric" (*ê peri rhêtorikês*). Of course, one cannot infer anything from a mere absence, but it is clear that all of the sophistical texts to have survived use *logos* but never *rhêtorikê* to describe what they are doing (except in a very controversial and possibly late text by Alkidamas). It is very likely that Plato coined the term *rhêtorikê*, just as he did *eristikê*, *antilogikê*, *dialectikê*, and probably *sophistikê*. This much has been known for years (Werner Pilz first commented on it in 1934),[4] but no one has yet attempted to explore the possible implications. Why? Because Plato himself did not want us to and was clever enough to prevent us from doing so. He is so skillful that that the word, and the thing, seem to have been there long before Gorgias.

Just listen. We are at the beginning of the dialogue.

Socrates reproaches Polos, who never gives a straight answer to any of his questions, for being "better trained in what is called rhetoric [*tên kaloumênên rhêtorikên*] than in dialogue [*ê dialegesthai*]" (448D). So Socrates turns directly to Gorgias and says, "Gorgias, do tell us yourself in what art it is you are skilled, and hence, what we ought to call you." And Gorgias replies, "Rhetoric, Socrates." So, says Socrates, "are we to call you a rhetorician?" "Yes," answers Gorgias, "and a good one" (449A).

So there we are. It is as if the word "rhetoric" had always been available and that it was, in fact, the true name for sophistry. Gorgias himself has, after all, just said as much. But why should it matter? It matters because the strength of *logos* has been made to vanish, caught and subsumed under rhetoric. And rhetoric itself has also been made to vanish as soon as it is born. That is why it is such a clever and quasi-diabolic rhetorical turn—a philosophical trick.

The paradigmatic expression of the strength of *logos* is to be found in Gorgias's *Encomium of Helen*. The best way to demonstrate this is by way of quotation. Gorgias's praise of Helen is in fact a praise of *logos*: "Discourse is a great sovereign [*logos dunastês megas estin*], who by means of the smallest and least apparent of bodies accomplishes the most divine of acts [*theiotata erga apotelei*]."[5]

The point is that *logos* acts. It makes things happen, new things, which take place both inside people and outside. What occurs inside is obvious and falls under what Plato has persuaded us to call rhetoric, influence, persuasion. The sentence I've just quoted continues as follows: "Discourse is a great sovereign, which by means of the smallest and least apparent of bodies accomplishes the most divine of acts, for it has the power to put an end to fear, push aside sadness, produce joy, increase pity."[6] But—and this is more important and far less Platonic—*logos* also does things *outside* the subject, in the world.

I can show this more effectively by reading the very beginning of the *Praise of Helen*. It is in itself a demonstration of how to produce new *koina*, new common objects and values. In it we can see, from the first set of sentences to the second, this passage from a consensus about commonplaces to invention, from liturgy to *happening*.

The first vector is orthodoxy. Gorgias says the following:

> Order, for a city, is the excellence of its men, for a body, beauty, for a soul, wisdom, for an action, value, for a speech, truth. Their opposite is disorder. Man, woman, speech, deed, city, thing, should be honored with praise if praiseworthy and incur blame if blameworthy; for to blame the praisable or to praise the blamable is of equal error and ignorance.[7]

All of those immense Greek words are here, divided into positive and negative according to a system of values that requires no explanation: *kosmos* (order, the structured world and beauty—from "cosmology" to "cosmetics") and *akosmia* (disorder, chaos).[8] There is here not a single term, not a single sentence that does not both derive from and at the same time sum up the entirety of Greek poetry and philosophy. We are at the point where words first acquire their meaning, when they exist together as a conventional semantic system. The communion around values roots itself in the sharing of common language.

The second vector—heterodoxy—follows immediately:

> It is to the same man that it befalls to say with rectitude what must be said, and to contradict those who blame Helen . . . I want . . . [to] put an end to the accusation against her of whom we hear so much abuse, demonstrate that those who blame her are wrong, show the truth and stop ignorance.[9]

Gorgias—the "I," speaking by himself—is the challenger of the consensus, which gathers "into only one voice and one soul [*homophônos kai homopsukhos*]" all the poets, all the auditors, even the evidence that is deposited in the language itself, in the eponymy of Helen's name, forever underlined by poets from Aeschylus ("loser of ships," "loser of men," "loser of towns," *helenas, helandros,* heleptolis[10]) to Ronsard ("son nom grec vient de ravir, de tuer, de piller, d'emporter"[11]). Gorgias, however, is going to prove that Helen belongs among those things to be praised, not reviled. Praise thus supports itself by the consensus implied in the first set of sentences in order to recreate a new consensus, a new *koina*. The Sophist has cast into the world a new Helen, who, from Isocrates and Euripides, all the way up to Hofmannsthal, Offenbach, Paul Claudel, and Jean Giraudoux, is all innocence and worthy only of praise.[12]

And the key to this change is found in the performative power of speech, in a regime of generalized speech acts before Austin—performance or performativity before any thematization of illocutionary acts. What matters is not a being who was supposedly already there, but the being produced by the discourse—what I call, with the word stolen from Novalis and Dubuffet, "logology." It is here, thanks to the Sophists, that we can arrive at the dimension of the political as *agora* for an *agôn*, at *polis* as a continuous creation of language.

"Calling on common opinion," starting with banalities and widely accepted objects, Gorgias plays, or displays, *logos* to make these objects seem a little different, so as to recast them as other. There is a moment in any act of praising when language takes the upper hand with respect to the object, when language crafts the objects, when description and the commonplace (*topos*) are exposed. From ontology to logology, from *phusis* to *polis*, from description to performance, it is the moment of creation and of the creation of values: new *koina* which allow us to start again, new common places, new common thoughts. We are now in politics, manipulating evidence in order not to deal with preexistent proofs but to contrive new types of obviousness.

Such is the power of *logos* that Plato had to tame and to challenge with philosophy.

How did he manage this? He tames *logos* by means of a double stratagem. First he discards, devalues, annihilates, phantomatizes what may now be called, after his own invention-intervention, "sophistical rhetoric." This happens in the *Gorgias*. Then he makes a "savagely hostile takeover bid" so that philosophy may take possession of rhetoric. This happens in the *Phaedrus*. So Plato gives "rhetoric" its name and then immediately makes it disappear. He does this twice. Either rhetoric is sophistical, a "persuasion maker" (*peithous dêmiourgos*), which is to say it is nothing, or less than nothing, and has no place in the *politeia*, for it is this that gives rise to the fickle mob rule which is democracy. Or it is true dialectic, that is to say, it is the pure philosophy, dialectic indeed, which provides us with the philosopher-king. In this rhetorical turn, rhetoric vanishes as rhetoric. Two rhetorics, one good and one bad, make zero rhetoric. It is a severe equation. Creation and *aphanisis*.

Let us now take a closer look at the *Gorgias*.

Rhetoric is defined as *peithous dêmiourgos*, a "persuasion maker." The irony *stricto sensu* is that it is precisely the "other" which defines it. Poor others, always playing the part of Socrates:

> *Socrates:* The art of rhetoric as you conceive it, and if I at all take your meaning, you say that rhetoric is a producer of persuasion and has therein its whole business and main consummation. Or can you tell us of any other function it can have beyond that of effecting persuasion in the minds of an audience?
>
> *Gorgias:* None at all, Socrates, your definition seems to me satisfactory; that is the main substance of the art. (453A)

He has said it again! This well-known definition has an immediate consequence. It leads inexorably to the devaluation and the fall of rhetoric. Rhetoric becomes a phantom. I will not quote the text at length but only emphasize a series of slippery equivalences. From the epistemic point of view, rhetoric is not a science (*epistêmê*), not an art (*tekhnê*), but an *empeireia* (an empirical practice), a *tribê* (a routine—the word means "rubbing," as when making love, wearing, wasting, spending . . .). From the ontological point of view, rhetoric is an *eidôlon*, an imitation, a phantom of *eidos*. From the ethical point of view, it is a *kolakeia*, a form of flattery, as bad for the health of the soul as cookery is for the body. It leads us to the well-known analogy shown in figure 1 (465 C):

1		2		1'		2'	
legislation		justice		gymnastics		medicine	(*eidos, tekhnê/epistêmê*)
-----------	=	--------	=	------------	=	---------	
sophistic		rhetoric		cosmetics		cookery	(*eidôlon, kolakeia*)
(soul)				(body)			

Figure 1. Proportions 1 and 1' express norm and structuration: way of life, regime. Proportions 2 and 2' express corrective items and, depending on circumstances, remedies.

As a corrective, and one that depends on circumstances, rhetoric is even less valuable than sophistic, just as justice is less valuable than legislation. It acts in case after case (you can hear the French *au cas par cas*), so that it means nothing.

Just consider how Socrates silences Callicles (520 AB). The rhetoric you praise, Callicles, he says, is even less beautiful than the sophistic you despise, and I, Socrates, as an authentic expert in politics and in political discourse, will be treated in Athens—in fact, I have already been treated and condemned as we all know—as "a physician prosecuted by a cook in front of a children's court" (521D).

Now the *Phaedrus.*

Phaedrus's point of departure is precisely *Gorgias*'s definition of rhetoric as *atekhnos tribê* (*Phaedrus*, 260 E, and *Gorgias*, 463 B), a routine without art, dealing with mere opinions (*doxas*), appearances, images, and falsehoods (*eikê*). But in the *Phaedrus*, Socrates exhorts himself to be cool and kinder with Tisias, Gorgias, Prodicus, Hippias, and Protagoras, all these sophists-orators because, as he points out, they are "not-yet"; they are merely "preliminaries" to genuine rhetoric. "Socrates, be lenient," says Phaedrus (269 B), those people do not know *ti esti rhêtorikê*, what rhetoric *is*.

Two remarks may help to understand just what it is. First, rhetoric deals not only with public but also with private speech (*idioi* and not only *dêmosioi sullogoi*, 261 B)—and we should keep in mind that thought itself is defined as a private dialogue with oneself or with one's own soul. Second, those who deal best with *eikê* and *pseudê* are the very ones who know the truth (237 D). It is a tradition that leads from Aristotle's characterization of metaphor (those who know the truth are always the best in discovering likenesses), to Quintilian, for whom, thanks to *ethos*, the *vir bonus* is, and always will be, the best liar. So, *Phaedrus*'s definition of rhetoric is nothing but dialectic. It is only when you know dialectic (*epistamênoi dialegesthai*, 269 B) that you are able to define and to practice rhetoric and to produce it as a whole or a system [*to holon sunistasthai*, 269 C]. You can then adapt different types of speech to the different types of souls: this is *psychagogia*, or how to "drive souls" (261 B, 270 E-272 B). But the whole undertaking is so difficult and so lengthy that it has two puzzling consequences. Although we cannot but forgive the Sophists for trying to speed up the process, the *sophoi*, the philosophers or wise ones will never take time to do such a thing for their compatriots but only for gods (273 DE). So rhetoric is dialectic—philosophy for an audience of gods!

This is the *aphanisis* of rhetoric. Rhetoric disappears, and the first rhetorical turn is therefore a philosophical turn. By means of a Platonic trick, rhetoric becomes either illusory (*Gorgias*) or divine (*Phaedrus*). But it never counts as political speech.

Contemporary theoreticians of rhetoric are mostly, consciously or not, implicated in this framework. Perelman's objective is characteristic. How can one fulfill the program of the *Phaedrus* with the help of Aristotelian rhetoric? His answer is to substitute a Kantian universal audience for the audience of gods. But the universal audience, the "*auditoire universel*," is not a real audience but merely a regulatory principle. It implies a confusion between rhetoric and ethics, but whereas rhetoric is at least linked to ethics, rhetoric and politics receive their norm from outside, from the world. We live in the heteronomy of rhetoric and politics, and the norm outside being is an ethico-philosophical one. Remember Arendt speaking about Plato/Heidegger in her interview with Günter Gaus.[13] I would not call myself a "political philosopher," she said, for ever since Plato/Heidegger such a thing is no longer possible. But what was no longer possible for Arendt is desirable for Alain Badiou, whose claim is to have inherited Plato. Good rhetoric will be truth in politics, ontological truth, rhetoric for and by truth, the rhetoric of a philosopher-king. "Plato, our dear Plato, with him, and by all means possible, let us affirm the true Idea, the Principle, against the phantom of this freedom which is overwhelming us, this freedom which depends on insignificant objects and tiny desires."[14]

The Second Type of Rhetorical Turn, or Rhetoric as a Social Bind

I propose to remain with Plato in order to provide an account of the second type of rhetorical turn, which this time is a genuinely rhetorical one, made by and for rhetoric. Of course, I could have used material from much later, from any time in the second moment of the war, from Cicero and Quintilian, for example, or later still, from the second Sophistic, with Philostratus for example. But Plato, "our dear Plato," if you read him in a sophistical way, is by himself able to give voice to the Sophists exceeding Plato. For some Platonic Sophists do indeed employ a truly rhetorical rhetoric rather than a philosophical one.

Our starting point will be the dialogue *Protagoras*, subtitled *or the Sophists*. This time we are thrown into politics. Here Protagoras's question is: "Is there, or is there not, some one thing whereof all the citizens must needs partake, if there is to be a city?" (324 E).[15] It is answered twice, first by a myth, and then by a *logos*.

We all know the myth as *the* myth of the origins of politics. The gods charge the brothers Epimetheus and Prometheus with the task of ensuring that all the creatures on earth are "dealt to each the equipment of its proper faculty [*kosmêsai kai neimai dunameis hekastois hôs prepei*]" (320 D). First, Epimetheus hands out to all those qualities which respect proportion and balance: either fur or feathers, and if weakness, then speed (this, by the way, is the source of our two concepts of justice, distributive and retributive). But in the end nothing is left for people, "naked, unshed, unbedded, unarmed" (321 C).

Then Prometheus "philanthropos" steals from Hephaestus and Athena *tên entekhnon sophian kai puri*, "artful wisdom with fire" (321 D). With *sophia*, man acquires religion (he worships gods, makes altars . . .) and *logos* (the skill to articulate speech and words), and because this wisdom is art or technique, the power to create, man would seem to have all he required, from a dwelling place to clothes, to bed and food. Except for one thing. Men still lack *politikê tekhnê*. Either they are destroyed by wild beasts because they do not know how to defend themselves, or they protect themselves by gathering together into "cities," but there they fight among themselves because they do not know how to live in peace. One way or the other, they all perish.

To preserve the race of men, a supplementary gift from Zeus is needed: the art of politics, that is to say, *aidôs* and *dikê*, "respect," or "shame," to use Bernard Williams's terminology,[16] and "justice" or "right." But things do not end there. A question now arises which is often forgotten. Hermes asks Zeus how to distribute this supplementary gift: to a few like the other arts and crafts (for most ordinary men, one can be either a medicine man *or* a shoemaker but not both) or to all? "To all," replies Zeus, "let all have their share; for cities cannot be formed if only a few have a share of these as of other arts. And make thereto a law of my ordaining, that he who cannot partake [*ton mê dunamenon metekhein*] of *aidôs* and *dikê* shall die the death as an illness of the city" (322 E).

In this familiar scenario, *aidôs* and *dikê* are the social boundaries. Speech does not help, nor does religion. We are once again in the heteronomy of politics. The supplementary norm comes from outside, and this norm is a kind of ethical value, a "shame civilization."

This, at least, is the standard interpretation.

But I now propose to make my own rhetorical turn to this interpretation. This shift can already be read in Plato's *Protagoras*, and it is dramatized, or reshaped, in a remake of the myth, which we owe to Ælius Aristides, who wrote his well-known but now largely forgotten *Platonic Discourses* in the middle of the second century A.D.

Let me begin with Plato's *Protagoras*, in which Protagoras says a few things that go against the standard ethical interpretation. I pick up on two of them.

First, there is a strange contradiction at the end of the myth. Zeus orders everybody to partake of *aidôs* and *dikê* (*pantes metekhontôn*, 322 D), but he also orders that "he who cannot partake be put to death [*ton mê dunamenon . . . metekhein*]" (322 D). So is it all or not all? Protagoras explains this contradiction with regard to Athens by pointing out that there every citizen has an equal right to speak in the *polis* and in all political deliberations. Athenian *isêgoria* means that "it is held that everyone should partake of this excellence [*metekhein tês aretês*[17]], or else that state cannot be" (323 A). There can be no specialist in politics. He offers a "further proof" of this that deserves our attention. In all the other "excellences," when you claim to be good but in fact are not (in flute playing, for example), you will make a fool of yourself, people will laugh at you, and you will be compelled to recognize you are not good, but with *aidôs* and *dikê*, it is only when you claim *not* to have them that you are thought to be mad:[18]

> To tell the truth [*talêthê legein*], which in the former arts they would regard as good sense [*sôphrosunên*], they here call it madness [*manian*]. And they **say** [*phasin*] that everyone must **say** [*dein phanai*] he is just, whether he is or not, and that the one who does not **pretend** to be just [*ton mê prospoioumenon dikaiosunên*: the one who does not slip under the mask of justice] is mad. (323 B, my emphasis)

This is certainly not a matter of ethics. We have here a political claim that also turns out to be a logical (*logos*) or rather a rhetorical one. You must "say" it, be it or not. And you begin to be it as soon as you say it; that is, you partake in it by saying it. It is a species of illocutionary act. Even if you are not, when saying you are, you are making yourself a part of the community. (Sade might have called it an "homage which vice pays to virtue.")

A second piece of the same evidence is provided by *logos*, which explains and helps to interpret the myth. There we learn what it is that provides the genuine model for political excellence: not flute playing but *hellenizein* (327 E). This verb conflates four distinct meanings: to speak Greek, to speak well, to think well, and to participate in Greek culture. All of which are contrasted with *barbarizein* (a word that derives from the onomatopoeia *blah-blah-blah*, which was believed to characterize all non-Greek speech). Everybody teaches their child to *hellenizein*, beginning with the nurse, just as everybody teaches political virtue; that is precisely why you can so easily come to believe, mistakenly, that in politics there can be no teacher.[19] Nevertheless some teachers—Protagoras, for example, and that is why he deserves his fees—are better than the others. What this rhetorical turn means, therefore, is that politics is nothing but a matter of *logos*.

Of *logos* and, namely, of rhetoric.

Let us now read Ælius Aristides's reflection on the myth in his *Against Plato, in Defense of Rhetoric*.[20] Here Protagoras's explanations became straight "mythemes." In this reshaped scenario, men perished in silence. Prometheus, who did not steal anything, goes to see Zeus to tell him what is happening, and "Zeus, much impressed by Prometheus' just remarks, when he had considered the matter by himself, ordered Hermes . . . to go to mankind with rhetoric" (396–97). With rhetoric, not with *aidôs* and *dikê*! This is the first obvious change that we need to underline.

Then Zeus ordered Hermes not to divide up rhetoric so that everybody might share it equally but "to select the best, the noblest and those with the strongest natures, and to hand the gift to them so that at the same time they would save themselves and the others" (397). This, then, is the second main change. Rhetoric is only for the happy few, an expertise, not a shared blessing.

But it is able to create a community. "When rhetoric had come in this way . . . , men were able to escape from the beasts, and all men stopped being enemies to one another, and they found the principle of community" (*koinônias arkhên*: "principle" and "beginning" of community) (398). Here is the paradox or at least one of the paradoxes of democratic subjectivity. Some are more equal than others, and it is from this inequality that the community eventually derives.

Aristides's discourse now becomes a eulogy of rhetoric. "Man uses things on earth as he wants, taking *logos* for his shield instead of any other means of protection" (399).[21] Rhetoric becomes our "sleepless guard" (401). So rhetoric is politics, and politics is nothing but *logos*, just as a rose is a rose is a rose . . . *Logos* has not yet been tamed.

FIVE

Topos/Kairos: Two Modes Of Invention

My simple—perhaps even simplistic—thesis is in fact heavy with conse-
quence. On the basis of a close reading of Plato's *Gorgias*, I hold that on-
tology invented rhetoric in order to domesticate—to spatialize—time in
discourse. Through rhetoric time is modeled as and reduced to space: a
discourse is primarily an organism that unfolds (it has a "plan"), and it is
articulated (for Plato one has to know how to "divide it up"). From a "nar-
row" perspective, it is woven out of "tropes" and "metaphors" (here again
one can hear space being spoken of). In short, it is a question of shifting
from the thread to-be-followed and the capture of the *kairos*, the point of
time, to the *topos* and the *topoi*, the places of crafted speech. And so if there
is a sophistic particularity of rhetoric, a strictly sophistical *inventio* of
rhetoric and within rhetoric, it would entail identifying something like
a "rhetoric of time," which would be to the rhetorics of space as sophistic dis-
cursivity is to Platonico-Aristotelian ontology. It will come as no surprise

that this distinction between space and time coincides with the distinction often made between "rhetorics of the statement" and "rhetorics of enunciation."

Improvisation and Rhetorics of Time

My point of departure is the eponymous text of the second sophistic, the very beginning of Philostratus's *Lives of the Sophists*. Whatever differences there might be between the old sophistic, the "philosophizing rhetoric" founded by Gorgias, and the second sophistic—which is actually just as ancient since its patron is Æschine, but it practices hypotyposis and history—the founding fathers have at least one feature in common upon which Philostratus discourses at length (482–84): they improvise. While reviewing all possible inventors of improvised eloquence, Philostratus concludes that Æschine "must have engaged in the greatest number of improvisations" but that it is Gorgias who "began" (482). Improvisation has such an important place in the *Lives* that one could ask whether it alone is not *a* or *the* defining characteristic of sophistics. It is Polemo, a veritable Sarah Bernhardt, who staged the most mediatized dramatizations of this feature in imperial sophistics (537ss). Improvisation, which is well named *ex tempore*, is a key element which sums up an entire series of features of sophistic *logos*.

The generic trait of rhetorics of time is that discourse, in its to-be-followed, is not projected as a closed totality, an organic *holon* to be dissected according to a "plan" and its "articulations"; it is not even a *pan* (piece) but rather a *panta*, a plurality of singular emissions that are necessarily in succession: hence the evident link stigmatized in Plato's *Theatetus* as in book *Gamma* of Aristotle's *Metaphysics* between the *panta rhei* and Heracliteanism if not atomism. What I propose after Novalis to call "logology" (being is an effect of saying) is in fact a chronology: time is the acting or efficient principle of discourse—hence a series of differential characteristics to be classified.

1. The present, and in particular the present of enunciation as produced by the latter, is included in the chain and cannot form an exception to it.

There is no residual presence of the present, nor any place for a metalanguage. This is the source of the contradictions and inversions, in short, the entire paradoxology. The anecdotal paradigm is the well-known dispute between Protagoras and Euathle: "It is said that once, when he asked his student Euathle for his fees, the latter responded: 'But I haven't won any victories yet [*oudepô . . . nenikêsa*, perfect]!' 'Well,' said Protagoras, 'if I win [*all' egô men an nikêsô*, future], because it's I who will have won [*ego enikêsa*, aorist], you will have to pay me [*labein me dein*, present]; and if it's you, because it is you [*ean de su, hoti su*, verbs omitted].'"[1] This is the very model of judicial eloquence; it can be found at work in a paradigmatic manner in Antiphon's *Tetralogies*. What fictionalizes the fact or the case is the immersion of *logos* in time, in particular in the time of enunciation of the defense speech (first accusation, then first defense, second accusation then second defense), such that every argument is apt to turn into its contrary the following moment. What is important to understand here is that it is not a matter of proving that, given any argument, a counterargument can be produced, as in the *Dissai Logoi*, but that every argument turns into its own contrary as soon as it is enunciated because it has been enunciated (the more suspect he is, the more guilty he is; no: innocent. The fewer witnesses there are, the more innocent he is; no: guilty). This follows the model of the *kata-ballontes*, the "reversing arguments," the "catastrophe arguments," which Protagoras is said to have invented.

This movement is brought to a halt by spacialization, by the *hama* of the principle of noncontradiction: the "at the same time as," which produces the spread-out vision of the *tota simul* and stops the to-be-followed by means of the copresence of residual presents. This is the correct reading of the work of *Gamma*; it opens up the space of writing, of formalization, of truth "tables" via the simple efficacy of the *sun*: *sul-logismos*, or, transposed into the Stoician world, *sun-êmmenon*.

2. In turn, sense is created as the enunciation goes along, not only, as we have seen, at the level of argumentation, of the arrangement of phrases, but at the level of syntax, of the arrangement of words. This is what Gorgias's *Treatise of Non-Being* alerts us to with his exploitation of the slippery nature of any proposition of identity: "non-being is . . ." (therefore it exists) ". . . non-being" (here again it does not exist). This is precisely what is blocked by the

spatialization of syntax as established after *The Sophist* in *The Categories* and *On Interpretation*, a spatialization in which subject and predicate are constructed as nonnegotiable places.

At this point one could reflect upon the difference between languages: are there both temporal languages and spatial languages? Perhaps Greek is a temporal language in that it presents a series of flexible unities, while German could be a spatial language through the verb being posed at the end, thus delimiting a *holon*. One could also reflect on the difference in styles: Aristotle forever Germanizing Plato's language; the Attic orators fabricating "periods" in which the phrase is given in its entirety (its greatness, like that of the city, is *eusunopton*, it "can be embraced in a single regard"),[2] and in which the meaning is completed and delimited— until Dionysus of Halicarnassus deperiodizes the phrase by working on it via ascent and descent, substituting a kind of circumflex at the level of style.

3. At the level of the words themselves, the focus is on the sounds and the signifiers: hence the privilege of the voice and the rhetorical on the one hand, as Philostratus endlessly insists, and, on the other hand, the privilege of homonymy, carried by sounds, silences, inflections, accents, and tonalities, as can be seen in any *Sophistical Refutations* from Aristotle's to Galen's. Joined to the quickness of the instant this gives the joke, also heavily emphasized by Philostratus (in the same text, at 483). The spatial strategy— distinguishing and fixing meanings—is a response to this, as is the return to sender, which at least marks the place of the respondent when a definition is lacking and when dialectic must replace any critique.

This kind of focus generates certain kinds of figures. This was my starting point. "Gorgianize," the word Philostratus invented,[3] says a lot, both by its phonic power alone and by its construction around a proper name.[4] With his sonorous figures Gorgias gives prose both meter and music. This is why Aristotle accused him of having a "poetical style" (*poietikê . . . lexis*) and of not having understood that "the style of *logos* is different from that of poetry."[5] The *Souda* says that Gorgias gave rhetoric its "phrastic" and attributes to him the use of more or less all figures (tropes, metaphors, allegories, hypallages, catachreses, hyperbates). The properly Gorgianesque figures, however, are—or at least would have to be according to my overly systematic perspective—first of all those audible or sonorous figures in which an enumeration is completed: "and doubling [*anadiplôsesi*], and repetitions [*epanalêpses*] and returns [*apostrophais*] and correspondences [*parisôsesin*]." In any case it is these figures that Diodorus retains when he describes the surprise of the Athenian philologists on hearing Gorgias and his "extraordinary" figures for the first time: "and antitheses [*antithetois*] and isocolons [*isokolois*] and parisons [*parisôsin*] and homeoteleutons [*homoioteleutois*]."[6] This is why the *Encomium of Helen* can really be heard and properly understood only in Greek: the repetition of alliterations, which, as Ronsard says of the source, "en sussurant de suit" ["wanders in whispering"]— *ho smikrotatôi sômati kai aphanestatôi theiotata erga apotelei*: a succession of sounds to describe the nature of *logos* and testify to her dynasty.[7]

Our spatial tropes are opposed to the Gorgianesque tropes. Metaphor and metonymy are two ways of doing panoptical geometry by establishing an analogy of proportion ("the evening is the old age of the day") or by counting the part for the whole (the sail for the boat): it is always a question of "seeing the same," integrating the scene of the world and producing its well-ordered graph.

4. In the end it is *ex tempore* eloquence that is the primal manifestation of the rhetoric of the time. Philostratus searched, literally, for the person in whom "the waves of improvised speeches found their source [*skhediôn . . . pêgas logôn . . . ek . . . rhuênai*]" (482): the metaphorics of time is evidently a metaphorics of flux, of waves. The time of discourse and the time of becoming: this is the perspective—it has been remarked—from which the alignment of sophistics with Heracliteanism appears correct; "everything flows" in the world of those who speak. But what has not yet been understood is how *ex tempore* is said in Greek: *skhedioi logoi*, "improvised speeches," *skhediazein*, "improvise." The adverb and the adjective indicate proximity, whether it be spatial (that of two warriors in close combat) or temporal (the approach of death, as well as the unexpectedness of an event); such that *skhedia*, for example, is the word used by Zeus in book V of the *Odyssey* to designate the "stout binding" [*epi skhediês poludesmou*, V, 33] of the ties as numerous as those that bind Ulysses himself to the mast when he sails past the Sirens. This conjunction of spatial adjustment and precarity, of temporal immediacy, makes up the approximative essence of the "raft" Ulysses

fabricates to escape his love for Calypso. Improvised discourses are the rafts upon which man embarks along the course of time.

"It's Gorgias," Philostratus thus continues, as I gloss him, "who was at the origin of improvisation: advancing into the theater at Athens he had the audacity [*etharrêsen*, from *tharsos*, the "bravery" and "boldness" of the Homeric hero, also designates "recklessness" and "impudence," all the more so since everything is happening in full view of the public, in the theater] to say: "Propose!" [*proballete*, "throw first"—just as we say: "Dear Englishmen, shoot first"—is juridical terminology referring to the leveling of accusations: with *pro-* one secures the beginning, never the outcome], and he was the first to take such a risk without flinching [*to kinduneuma touto . . . ane-phthegxato*: "he articulated"—since the *phtoggoi* characterize voice as a set of sounds, accents, and articulations that are specific to man for Aristotle—what he articulated is the "danger" linked to the uncertainty of chance and precisely, as Chantraine notices, to the "cast of the dice"], showing by this, on the one hand, that he knew everything [*endeiknumenos dêpou panta men eidenai*: Gorgias incarnates the Philostratean definition of the old sophistic, which lays out, in contrast to philosophy, its omniscience; which is exactly why philosophy has always held sophistics to be the mere appearance of wisdom] and, on the other hand, that he would speak about everything by allowing himself to be led by opportunity [*ephieis tôi kairôi*]." Here we find ourselves in the crux of the matter: led by Philostratus to the emergence of the *kairos*.

Kairos *and* Topos

The *kairos* of *kairos* is already instructive. Gorgias, Philostratus supposes, had had enough of Prodicus's hoary chestnut: the fable of the young Hercules caught between vice and virtue at the crossroads, a fable that he took with him from town to town with success and money, a "stale turn" (*heôla* from *heôs*, the "dawn," the "morning," characterizes yesterday's food, stale bread, for example) an oft-repeated turn (and God knows it was repeated by others after Prodicos until nobody could take it any more). "Allow oneself to be taken up by the *kairos*" frames the tale of Prodicus's grand tour: this is the reaction of sophistics to hackneyed moralism.[8]

On the basis of the Hippocratic corpus on the one hand and Pindaric poetry on the other, *kairos*, one of the most untranslatable of Greek words, is certainly specific to sophistic temporality.[9] I will underline, without further ado, several of its pertinent features for the rhetoric of time. First of all, why is *kairos* dangerous? Like the Zen instant of archery, it is the moment of the opening of possibilities: that of the "crisis" for the doctor, the decision between cure and death; that of the unleashed arrow for the Pindaric or tragic archer, between hit and miss. *Kairos*, as different from *skopos* (the "goal," the bulls-eye at the center), names, for Onians, the point at which "a weapon could penetrate in a fatal manner": what is at stake is the arrow as destiny, striking the heart.[10] It is the name of the goal inasmuch as the goal depends entirely upon the instant, the name of place inasmuch as place is entirely temporalized: one can understand how the Latin *tempus* means not only "time" but also "temple"; in considering the *kairos* we glimpse how "temple," "time," and "religious temple" belong to the same family of words, from the Greek *temnô*, "to cut."[11] With *kairos*, it is a question of both opening and cutting: precisely at the "weak point of the armor," as in *The Iliad*,[12] at the joints of bones, and at the "opportune moment" (in the French "*opportunité*," both *port*, "harbor," and *porte*, "door," are to be heard).

Onians's superb hypothesis, which Gallet retains, fleshing it out and rendering it far more precise through the study of texts and drawings, is that *kair'os* ("the correct point which hits the goal," as Chantraine says) and *kaîros* ("the 'rope' which fixes the end of the warp to the loom"—Chantraine again, who is not hostile to this assimilation) "were originally the same."[13] For Onians, *kairos* is the name of the spacing, of the void, of the opening created by the warps of fabric. Gallet shows that it is not in fact the opening itself but more exactly that of the "regulating braid" which, like a comb, "separates the threads of the chain by keeping them parallel such that they do not become tangled," tying them together at the same time. This braid thus regulates both the vertical and the horizontal order of the insertion of the weft by marking out the work zone;[14] it is sometimes paired with an apparatus installed at the top of the loom "which maintains the summit of the entire work."[15] Pindar uses the term in this manner, by syllepsis, both in the literal and the figural sense, to refer to the "procedure of weaving themes together."[16] Within the articulation of the *kairos*—and articulation should be understood in all of its senses in English: *kairon ei phthegxaio*, "if it is articulated," "if it is stated"[17]—words are both shot off and woven.

This brief inquiry allows us to understand the relationship between *kairos*, the time of the moment, and *telos*, purpose: *kairos* is *autotelic*; it contains its own purpose within itself. It is the moment in which *poiêsis* and *tekhnê* (characterized by the exteriority between the *ergon*, the work, and its end, and also caricaturized by the worst of architects—unlike the bees—possessing an idea of the house that he constructs), at the height of their inventiveness, approach *praxis*, approach a divine interiorization of purpose. But perhaps this is not yet radical enough; perhaps one should go so far as to say that *kairos* is *poros*, the "passage." One could economize on *telos* and the idea of purpose (hence the monotonous secondhand ends ascribed to those who let themselves be led by the *kairos* or by the sophists in general: money, success, victory). It would also underline the relation between *kairos* and singularity: with *kairos*, one is engulfed in a particular case, and there is nothing apart from the case; all invention is singular because it is perfectly adapted. It is Aristotle, picking up the Platonic critiques at the beginning of the *Meno* (from the "swarm of virtues" to a "beautiful cooking pot, a beautiful woman, a beautiful lyre"), who demands generality precisely against such a conception; he demands that, instead of presenting pairs of shoes, one should teach the art of shoemaking.

It is exactly on these two points that the two rhetorics—of *kairos* and of *topos*—are most clearly distinguished. As Jacques Brunschwig points out in the preface of his translation of the *Topics*, "the place is a machine for making premises *on the basis of a given conclusion*": with *topos* we have the *telos* and all we have to do is follow the predetermined route, whereas with *ex tempore*, we have the autotelic opening of the beginning.[18] As for the singular, Brunschwig cites the sole Aristotelian definition of place—and it is, by the way, the operative definition: "commonplace is that embracing a large number of particular kinds of enthymemes,"[19] thus showing that "the same commonplace should be able to deal with many different propositions, and one should be able to deal with the same proposition via many different commonplaces."[20] In short, there are no cases save those taken on a general, or a topical, level. Accordingly, as both Barthes and Brunschwig observe in the same terms, commonplace is no longer definable save through an extravagant series of spatial metaphors: mold, seam, matrix, circle, sphere, region, well, arsenal, reservoir, headquarters, storehouse, treasure (not to forget the most surprising metaphor, which hints at the *Theaetetus*'s dovecroft but superimposes some *kairos*: Ross's "pigeonhole").[21] This is where the kinship between a *logos*, which harvests the real, and a *topos*, which harvests arguments, falls apart.

These two conceptions of rhetoric, which are based on two conceptions of *logos* and two different comprehensions of time, can also be laid out in figure 2:

Rhetorics of Space   **Rhetorics of Time**

Logos

space	time
saving	spending
plan	improvisation
organism, articulations	course
hierarchy of *sun* (syllogism, syntax)	reversal
hama of noncontradiction	paradoxology
statement	enunciation
meaning	signifier, homonymy
periodization	joke, witticism
visual figures (metaphors)	sonorous figures (alliterations)
stock of *topoi*	opening of the *kairos*

Time

spatial time (movement, size)	temporal time
physical, cosmical (totalized)	logical (involves the raft)
past-present-future	now
presence of the present	performance

Figure 2. The space of saving and the time of spending.

Figure 2 depicts the difference between ontology and logology. To conclude, I shall sketch a hypotyposis of this contrast, portraying its ideal type with the help of a few citations.

The ontological paradigm can be easily identified in a number of Heidegger's texts. It should not be forgotten that it is presented, in one of its clearest and most developed expressions, as an interpretation of the Heraclitean *logos*, which is also at work in the exegesis of Protagoras's famous phrase on man as a measure. "Phenomena" are *onta*, time is spatialized into presence and the power of speech into a space of savings:

Who would want to deny that in the language of the Greeks from early on *legein* means to talk, say or tell? However, just as early and even more originally—and therefore already in the previously cited meaning—it means what our similarly sounding *legen* means: to lay down and lay before. In *legen* a "bringing together" prevails, the Latin *legere* . . . *How does the proper sense of* legein, *to lay, come to mean saying and talking?* In order to find the foothold for an answer, we need to reflect on what actually lies in *legein* as laying. To lay [*legen*] means to bring to lie. Thus, to lay is at the same time to place one thing beside another, to lay them together. To lay is to gather [*lesen*]. The *lesen* better known to us, namely the *reading* of something written, remains but one sort of gathering, in the sense of bringing-together-into-lying-before, although it is the predominant sort. The gleaning [*Aehren-lese*] at harvest time gathers fruit from the soil. The gathering of the vintage [*Trauben-lese*] involves picking grapes from the vine . . . But gathering is more than mere amassing. To gathering belongs a collecting that brings under shelter. Accommodation governs the sheltering; accommodation is governed in turn by safekeeping. That "something extra" which makes gathering more than a jumbling together that snatches things up is not something only added afterwards. Even less is it the conclusion of the gathering, coming last. *The safekeeping that brings something in has already determined the first steps of the gathering and arranged everything that follows.* If we are blind to everything but the sequence of steps, then the collecting follows the picking and gleaning, the bringing under shelter follows the collecting, until finally everything is accommodated in bins and storage rooms. This gives rise to the illusion that preservation and safekeeping have nothing to do with gathering. Yet what would become of a vintage [*eine Lese*] which has not been gathered [*gezogen*] with an eye to the fundamental matter [*Zug*] of its being sheltered? *The sheltering [Bergen] comes first in the essential formation of the vintage.*[22]

To speak, for ontology, is to gather together and save.

Faced with this position, logology should take as its motto Ælius Aristides's phrase "speeches march with the same pace as time."[23] Being contemporary with time is being from one moment to the next immediately there: what characterizes the present is not its persevering presence but its transition; discourse, explicitly tied to the *kairos*, to the "opportunity," to the propitious "occasion" seized by the orator, "immediately hits a bullseye." "Immediately" is *parakhrêma* in Greek: the adverb, which hypostatizes the locution *para to khrêma*, "available for use," says a little more. It's a question of what is there, ready to hand, with the utility of a utensil available for any occasion, like those "riches" (*khrêmata*) that are so precious and yet surpassed by *logos*. This is the most surprising characteristic of *logos*: its sempiternal immediacy makes it inexhaustible. Ordinary riches, those that are cumulative and accumulable, are doubly tied to use: they use up the earth, which produces them (410), and they diminish when they are spent (409). On the contrary, "the possession and power of discourse is not spent when one uses it" (*para tên khrêsin*, 409). In other words, real wealth lies in always having *logos* ready to hand, in being an orator. Not only is discourse not used up when it is spent, but it increases (410). A more banal transposition is possible: in the terms of a capitalist economy, spending is profitable; in terms of linguistics, competence increases with performance—and it is certainly not by chance that these two models happen to be superimposable.[24] We should insist on this point because in Ælius Aristides's oeuvre there is a thematization—and for the first and perhaps the only time related explicitly to its proper object, *logos*—of one of the most original problematics of sophistics: that of being, not as gathering and collection but as expenditure and "consumation" (Bataille's word). Sophistry plays time against space: this engages, in a formidably precise analogy, one interpretation of being (and in saying an interpretation "of being" I recognize he won) against another, expenditure against accumulation; one interpretation of *logos* against another, *logos* discourses, *logos* extends; the choice of a prevalence, that of *logos* over being (being is thought in terms of *logos*) or that of being over *logos* (*logos* is thought in terms of being). Finally, it implies a choice between two models of time: the coursing of discourse versus the presence of the present, which ends by turning the exsistant into the shepherd of being.

A contemporary echo of the sophistic model appears in an "Essay in General Economy," for which "the expense (the consumption) of riches [is], in relation to production, the primary object."[25] This echo—admittedly shot through with a no doubt one-sided reading of the valorizations that can be developed on the basis of Nietzsche or Freud—may well have its dated and unpleasant aspects. However, Bataille does allow one to clearly situate the terms of the opposition. On the side of restricted economy one has the thing, accumulation, useful or commercial exchange, ordinary life, whereas on the side of general economy one has energy and its squandering (the sun, luxury, sex, potlatch, the gift, sacrifice). With the systematization of both economies—which always comes down to the triumph of the first— one cannot, Bataille says, avoid "giving the principles of 'general economy' a fairly ambiguous foundation: this is because squandering energy is always the contrary of a *thing*, but it only enters into consideration inasmuch as it is registered in *the order of things*, as transformed into a *thing*."[26]

Literature and Philosophy: A Mimêsis of the Second Order

One last remark to conclude on Philostratus's *Lives*, with which we began. It is as though the difference between the old philosophizing sophistics (Gorgias) and the second, historicizing sophistics (that of Æschine) was subsumed under the generic unity of improvised discourse. Thus one finds excellence defined as fluency of expression (*tous xun euroiai hermêneuontas*, 484): this confers upon the best philosophers the status of sophist. From this standpoint what Philostratus essentially does is blur boundaries: the boundaries between what—at the end of the entire process—appear to be "genres," "characters," "tendencies": philosophy, history, rhetoric, and literature are unified in sophistics, which is to say, in discursive practices. Philostratus also blurs the boundaries between epochs: the very essence of *paideia* and cultural *mimêsis*, joined to the passion he has for his own great men and his own modernity, undoes chronology in an aesthetic and "kairic" manner.[27] As such one genuinely enters another world in which philosophy is no longer (or no longer only or no longer primarily) the generator of signposts, criteria, names, meanings, epochs, temporality: taking sophistics into consideration gives one the means to examine the difference between philosophy and literature.

I believe that with the triumph of sophistical rhetoric one can even say that one has entered into literature. How does one write outside these two great patented genres when one is neither a poet nor a philosopher? An abundant and unstable inventiveness unfolded over more than two centuries, throughout that late and genial antiquity, in a kind of melting pot born from rhetorical exercises—jazz and its variations, the Anglo-Saxons would say—such that progressively and for a retrospective point of view, new genres emerged, genres so profoundly transformed that the very genre of genre came into question: biography, autobiography, hagiography, doxography, historiography, literary criticism, and finally the novel.[28]

What does it mean to say that one enters into "literature"? No doubt it is anachronistic and imprudent, even if unavoidable, to use a term forged across the Latin world but whose concept was stabilized only in the second half of the eighteenth century.[29] However, Lacoue-Labarthe and Nancy are quite right in noting that "when it is determined and established, the concept of literature—whatever it covers in its most general sense—tends to designate by predilection 'literature itself' as what imposes itself as the beyond (the truth, the critique, or the dissolution) of what ancient poetics and rhetoric had constituted as the genres of the written or spoken thing." They then specify that "consequently literature tends to fundamentally designate the novel, especially as the latter is understood by romanticism." It is quite striking to see how this definition and this diagnostic, based on German romanticism, agree with what Roland Barthes proposed but on the basis of antiquity. In his article on ancient rhetoric, Barthes insists on the fact that Aristotle's rhetoric is defined in opposition to poetics and that all the authors who recognize such an opposition could be ranked on the side of Aristotelian rhetoric. Barthes writes, "That rhetoric will cease when the opposition is neutralized, when Rhetoric and Poetics unite, when rhetoric becomes a poetic *technè* ('of creation')." He then adds: "This fusion is crucial, for it is at the very source of the notion of literature."[30]

Inventio is thus no longer simply one of the five parts of rhetoric (before or besides *dispositio, elocutio, memoria, actio*) but rather forms the characteristic, the very essence of rhetoric as open rhetoric. This fusion in literature, characterized by a "poetic" rhetoric in the sense of "productive," is certainly what is at stake in the second sophistic. The second sophistic is constantly characterized by its *mimêsis rhêtorikê*—what Bompaire or Reardon propose to translate as "literary culture." *Mimêsis rhêtorikê* is the appropriation by imitation—which is developed throughout the entire cursus in those schools in which the director was a sophist—of all the works of classical antiquity: poetry, philosophy, history, rhetoric strictly speaking, and with it political deliberation. All of this is thus absorbed as species of a quasi-universal genre constituted by general rhetoric as placed under the sophistic aegis via the same movement with which Philostratus baptized the second sophistic, as we have seen. The striking feature of this mimetic rhetoric is clearly its innovative nature: it is inventive and creative. The most violently new of all the new "genres" is of course the one that will become literature par excellence: the novel.

But one should not mistake the meaning of this inventiveness. Although I grant, as Bompaire does, great importance to *mimêsis rhêtorikê*, the position I adopt is nevertheless completely opposed to his. In *Lucien écrivain*, the subtitle of which is "Imitation and Creation," he insists in every possible way on the historical continuity and the logical compatibility of what he calls, with Stemplinger's categories, "philosophical imitation" and "rhetorical imitation." For example, he writes: "The imitation of books is only a particular case of the imitation of the world."[31] In my opinion this kind of evaluation leads to a rehabilitation of literary *mimêsis* as philosophically and literarily insufficient as those "rehabilitations" of sophistics that turn the latter into a complement of philosophy. This kind of evaluation is determined by a quite recognizable ethics, one that is foreign, or rather contrary, to the phenomenon in question: "Many excesses have been committed in its name [*Mimêsis* in literary history] . . . But if it is well managed in its technical detail and great and lofty in spirit, imitation does not dishonour ancient literature."[32] These evaluations concern style as well as content, and the least little detail: "Let's simply recall that Aristotle mocks Gorgias' reflex as the victim of a passing swallow, the reflex of an amateur pedant in mythology."[33] To take the occasion, upon being hit by swallow shit, to exclaim "Shame on you, Philomela!" is solely pompous or "tragic" in the name of the separation of poetics and rhetoric.[34] From the standpoint of general rhetoric, of sophistics, of literature, the difference between "the evening is the old age of the day" and Gorgias's exaggerated figure (no less exaggerated than Ponge's prawn) is absolutely pertinent. It could even symbolize the difference between a first-order *mimêsis* of nature and a second-order *mimêsis* of culture. On the one hand art imitates nature and perfects it: with Aristotle's *Poetics* it becomes possible to describe carrion.[35] On the other hand it is "only" a matter of *logos*, of mimesis transmitted by reference, according to the most ironic mode of the palimpsest. Again: ontology and phenomenology against logology.

That one enters, with this, into "literature" is also the sign, once and for all, that Platonico-Aristotelian philosophy has won—hence the natural, appropriate, and thus unavoidable character of Bompaire's judgment. One cannot escape the imperious conclusion: even if rhetoric and sophistics triumph upon the scene of the world, become the mistress of the ears of youth, of the ears of princes and crowds, it is philosophy that will have chosen the ground: their terrain as literature, not as philosophy, and quite precisely as nonphilosophy. Aristotle's metaphysical gesture excluding "he who speaks for the pleasure of speaking" from the community of rational beings has repercussions: literature as such is projected into an elsewhere. Philosophy can quite easily treat it as an object and draw up its aesthetic rules; no doubt it is also obliged to occasionally recall, at least from time to time beyond the wealth, risks, and inversions of the discursive regimes that Plato tries out, that it is itself a discourse and to reflect upon the styles that suit it. But "writers," orators, or novelists, for their part, do not have, as such and philosophically, the right to believe themselves to be philosophers. And this, regularly but not without contestation, commotion, and exceptions (obviously Nietzsche) until today—Derrida will not have been doctor *honoris causa* at Cambridge.

Translated by Oliver Feltham

SIX

Time of Deliberation and Space of Power: Athens and Rome, the First Conflict

The conflict between Greece and Rome was, in a manner of speaking, the first international conflict in history. The way in which this conflict took place has often been described as a relationship between military might, *imperium romanum*, and the power of civilization, Greek *paideia*. It is known that, although vanquished, Greece conquered its conqueror: Greek culture, with its poets and philosophers, was "imitated," or, to be more specific, reinvented and adapted by every *vir bonus dicendi peritus*—for instance, Horace, but also Cicero, Lucretius, Virgil, Seneca, or Quintilian, who all contributed to the glory and domination of Rome.

The *pax romana*, in fact, reduced all to silence, and silence itself is an integral part of the conflict I am about to describe. One of the most interesting approaches to and interpretations of this conflict, as a conflict about the uses of language, the uses of deliberation, and the game played by the genius of the Greek and Latin mother tongues, underscores the fact that this conflict is utterly about language and rhetoric. The best way to approach it is to look into how the great Sophist Ælius Aristides conceives it.

Ælius Aristides, a Greek from Asia Minor who lived under Roman rule at the time of Antoninus and Marcus Aurelius, delivered a great number of orations on a variety of occasions. Most of them have been preserved. Although it is common practice among philologists to divide this sizeable and largely unanalyzed body of work into three parts, of interest to philosophers and historians alike, these parts must be treated as a whole.

First of all, the *Sacred Tales*, a sort of personal diary, exceptional in its kind, relate how hypochondriac Ælius talks about his minor and more serious ailments and convalescence. They are called *Sacred Tales* because Ælius wrote them while sitting under the gates of Asklepios in Pergamon, sleeping, dreaming, taking baths, and also deliberating in order to support the healing process through language.[1]

The second part deals with his orations on rhetoric and in particular his highly remarkable *Against Plato: In Defence of Rhetoric*, in which he pitches Plato against Plato, the *Gorgias* against the *Phaedrus*, all of this in order to highlight Plato's role as "the father and teacher of orators" (465):[2] wildly but still respectfully ironic, Ælius brings Plato back into the realm of rhetoric "like a slave on the run" (463).

The third aspect of his work, which is of specific interest to us, is how Ælius, as a political orator, intervenes in conflicts between different cities. In particular, he is known as the author of two famed panegyrics, the *Panathenaic Oration* and the *Roman Oration*.[3] The two orations are a contrapunctic analysis of a language of power and a language of culture, Latin and Greek, a way to keep silent and to act, and a way to speak in order to talk further.

Politics, as it was practiced in every Greek city at the time of Ælius, is effectively described by the three oratorical modes explained by Aristotle—deliberative, forensic and epidectic. As Pierre Vidal-Naquet put it, politics gave way to "political fiction" linked to an inflation of rhetoric in schools, compensating for the real political impotence of the empire's subjects.[4] The directors of these schools called themselves "sophists," and their students excelled at *meletai*, declamation exercises on anachronical topics. André Boulanger, whose greatest achievement was to expel preconceived

wisdom, nevertheless emphasizes the extraordinary development under-
gone by "epideictic [praise and blame] genres, which, under the Empire,
assumed the first place and gave Sophists an official position."[5] With re-
gard to the Greeks' ceremonial genre, *ad ostentatione* in Latin, literally, "for
show," Quintilian notes that "Roman custom had made use of it even in
public life":[6] hence, under the empire, rhetoric of praise replaces delibera-
tive rhetoric, for all (serious) intents and (noninnocent) purposes.

Ælius the orator is the only one to my knowledge who delivered one
speech praising Rome and another praising Athens. Here is how Boulanger
introduces the praise declamations: "Attention must be paid to those two
famed panegyrics which, in Ælius's works, undoubtedly have the most so-
phisticated thinking."[7] Yet, in the conclusion of his analysis of the *Panathe-
naic Oration*, he writes: "[It is] a vast collection of all the common places
which, for centuries, had encumbered ceremonial rhetoric and school
speeches. . . . The *Panathenaic Oration*, devoid of any originality, is other-
wise of no great interest. . . . In sum, if the *Panathenaic* admired by rhetori-
cians of later centuries is the triumph of the art of sophistry, it is also its
downfall."[8] One would have noticed the quaint ambiguity of the middle
sentence.

From a rhetorical point of view and that of a rhetoric taught by Sophists,
it is apparent how Ælius's work offers, with some risk, the possibility of a
signal reassessment: I believe that, in this instance, sophistry produces
an effect of enhanced lucidity both at a philosophical (a reflective anti-
Platonism) and a political level. These two orations—at least when viewed
in combination—fulfill the paradoxical criteria of a praise speech: at once
the perpetuation, protection of value judgments regarding "future objec-
tions," and modification or creation of values that will determine—in this
instance up to this very day—our perception of something we call Rome
and something we call Athens.[9]

"The whole exordium is a mere rattle of words," says Boulanger:[10] my
own interest lies in the modalities of the "rattle" in an exordium aimed at
capturing the attention (*captatio benevolentiæ*) of both worlds.

One world, "the Ruling Power": Rome's invention, Rome's "brainwave"
(*eurêma*) lies in "the science of government" (*to arkhein eidenai*), with which
the Greeks are not familiar (*R.* 51). Another world, "the Civilizing Power":

Athens is the "source [*arkhê*] of nourishment, which is sciences and speeches" (*A.* 2). To be prince (*arkhein*) is opposed to being the principle (*arkhê*); put differently, Rome governs space, whereas Athens frames time.

Let us, first of all, briefly paraphrase in order to bring together the paramount elements the space called Rome contains, Rome, that is, the world. Rome is, so he begins, "like snow": wherever one stands, it is all around you (*R.* 7). One cannot speak of Rome as one can of other cities; "she is here [*entautha estêken*]" (*R.* 9) as she has no assigned boundaries, no more than the ocean has any (*R.* 10). This is why one can visit the entire world *or* this single city, inasmuch as Rome is like the workshop and market of the whole world (*R.* 11). In short, "whatever one does not see here neither did nor does exist" (*R.* 13): Rome is Being. With Rome, the Parmedian sphere equates physically the terrestrial globe, and there are no longer any limits. Ramparts from now on no longer circumvent cities, but power itself and those ramparts are no longer actual walls but men, the legions that become coterminous with the limits of the globe itself (*R.* 84). This is how Rome's praise is conveyed to the Romans themselves by means of promulgating Roman values.

Ælius, however, by using other metaphors contends that this world is akin to a "well-tended enclosure [*aulos ekkekatharmenos*]" (*R.* 30) and the earth to a "pleasure garden [*paradeisos sugkekosmethai*]" (*R.* 99). If Zeus, in terms of physics, transformed chaos into cosmos, Rome, in terms of politics, turned chaos into cosmos by expelling *stasis*, that is, civil war. Rome has "established order in the *oikoumenê* [*anakekosmisthai tên oikoumenên*]" (*R.* 98). The "*oikoumenê*," the civilized world, has shrunk down to the size of an *oikos*, a homestead (*R.* 102), or even a courtyard or a garden. Rome is the world, but the world is minuscule.

The same inversion appears in the context of Rome's relationship with *logos* and by way of consequence in the panegyric itself. Indeed, the shift from global level and power vested in the public to the confines of a private household cripples *logos* and reduces it to "idiocy."

Initially, Ælius proclaims that Rome loathes deliberation and exposes the flaws of her omnipotence: "For it is she," he says, "who first proved that rhetoric cannot fulfill all functions" (*R.* 6). In her case, both the panegyric and even the (its) simple designation are bound to fail: there can be no *horos* (spatial "limit" and logical "definition") of Rome, the—"unnameable" (that which one is not allowed to name and is an object of disgust), given that no lookout point allows one "to put together the seven hills under the name of one city" (*R*. 6).

Hence, Rome remains mute even when she is noisy. Like a "well-tended enclosure," already quoted, "the whole inhabited world utters a single sound, far more accurate than a choir's [*khôrou akribesteron hen phteggetai*]" (*R*. 30). The monody for which Aristotle, in the *Politics*, accuses Plato spreads across the globe in a totalitarian manner, accompanied by a new kind of terror—Ælius, considered a flatterer, nonetheless does not hesitate to spell it out. As he tells us, the chorus produces the same pitch and holds it, and everyone follows the cues in a world where a mere "plucking of a chord" suffices. The choir-master-emperor governs by fear (*phobos*), and "country and race all in one, obey in silence [*hupakouei siôpêi*]" (*R*. 31). The model is, of course, the army itself, a "permanent chorus" (*R*. 87).

It becomes evident at this point how, with Ælius, we have already shifted from shared Roman values to the Greek invention of Rome.

Faced with the fact that Rome has no limitation, Athens geographically defines itself as an infinitely reduced space, the virtual space of a single point. Athens, placed at the core of the center, which Greece represents, is indeed symbolized by the Acropolis (*A*. 15). It is comparable to the way in which climate, for example, refers to the point of neither too much nor too little: the right measure of current weather. This infinitesimal space is never more than the representation of time as originating power. First and foremost, Athens is the "first country of man" (*A*. 25). Whereas Rome takes up all space, Athens takes up all the time: it is expressed in the myth of her autochthonous origins ("she finds her origin in herself," *A*. 26), a myth now raised to a superior level and applied to the very relationship between Athens and Rome. Romans, as the *Roman Oration* states, are the Greeks' "foster fathers" (*R*. 96), but Greeks, argues the *Panathenaic*, are the foster fathers of the foster fathers, "fathers' fathers" (*A*. 1).

Athens's relationship to *logos* is symmetrically inverse to Rome's. In the case of Athens, which provides us with all of our discursive nourishment, there is at once a perfect "rational" adequacy, if you will, between the panegyric and the object of the panegyric: "For the expression of thanks for oratory delivered by means of oratory not only is fair in itself but also first of all confirms the name given to this kind of speech. For it alone is, to be precise, 'the use of fair speech'—*eulogos*" (*A.* 2). Put differently, if the panegyric of Athens comprises the very essence of panegyric, this is due to its essentially being a panegyric of *logos* itself. The birthplace of humankind is nothing other than the birthplace of *logos*, as *logos* stands for Greek language and Greek is Attic: "Athens has created a nonmixed and pure *phonê*, which does not hurt and sets the example for all conversation among Greeks [*pasês tês hellenikês homilias*]" (*A.* 14). Within Athens then, discursiveness and interdiscursiveness, language, speech, and idiom are all one. Beyond doubt, this is the sole veritable universality we encounter, and although not spatial, it is ever logical: "All without exception speak the unique *phonê* common to that race, and, thanks to you, the *oikoumenê* has become homophonic" (*A.* 226). Set against the imperialist monody with its silencing effect, the homophony of a highly contagious consensus effectively broadens public life, given that all other languages—in comparison with Greek, which has become the definition of and criterion for education and culture (*horos tina paideias*)—are merely "childish babble" (*A.* 227). As the only language which is always adapted to public life, Greek is the one that causes a lack of interest in other languages: "In tune with all the solemn festivals, all assemblies and all councils, the Greek language presides over time and place and to everyone is always equally fitting" (*A.* 227). *Ho logos kai hê polis*: the last words of the panegyric seal the equivalence between the Greek language and the political, *logos* and *polis*.

Hence, when the world is mute, it is spatial and Roman. When the world talks, however, it is temporal and Athenian. Rome guarantees unicity of uniformity, which establishes an undifferentiated space: "Now indeed it is possible for Hellene or non-Hellene, . . . to travel wherever he will, easily, just as if passing from fatherland to fatherland. . . . for security it suffices to be a Roman citizen, or rather to be one of those united under your hegemony" (*A.* 100).

Everybody, however, has two native countries. Rome is the physical home country, but Athens is the logical home country, watching out that, from one generation to the next, over time, the like-mindedness that will allow people to converse with each other is preserved. Ælius is not to be accused any longer—in a rather Platonician manner—of being a mere flatterer, a "collaborator." For, although his *Roman Oration* exposes Roman values, he abolishes them at the same time with the use of ever-missing Athenian values. Athens's values are undeniably extolled: Athens talks, and, once defeated, Athens takes action solely by means of talking. This is the culmination of a sophistic approach to politics. The mute space opposed to the time of discourse is, according to Ælius Aristides, the proper way, highly rhetorical, to evaluate the conflict between Greece and Rome and, ultimately, to give speech the last word.

Translated by Nathalie Rosa Bucher

Part III   Sophistical Trends in Political Philosophy

SEVEN

From Organism to Picnic: Which Consensus for Which City?

> Among all those magnificent horned beasts at the head of which
> Monsieur le Préfet does us the honour of being seated, him standing at
> the prow of the splendid herd of the local bovine race, and taking the
> helm with a clear and watchful eye, while the sails, propelled by the
> magnificent native draught horse, carry along the straight course of
> prosperity the man of Champagne, who does not fear its twists and turns.
>
> —*The Prisoner of the Buddha*, by FRANQUIN, GREG, AND JIDÉHEM[1]

Here I investigate, from the standpoint of ancient Greece, a notion that strikes me as increasingly central to the space of our current political and philosophical imagination, to the point where it may seem constitutive of maturity or modernity in politics: the notion of consensus.

Consensus is in fact a pivotal concept that allows three different domains to be linked together:

The logical, in the broader sense (*logos*), since language is the
instrument of consensus par excellence, whether it is obtained
by the dialogical route, putting into action what is today known
as "communicative reason," or by the rhetorical route of
persuasion;

The ethical, since consensus is signatory to the choice of the good or
the best or, failing that, attests to the calculation of an optimum

capable of safeguarding, if not each and all together, then at least, in
Rawlsian mode, the worst off;

Finally, the political, since consensus is perhaps the condition of the
political or in any event a condition of civil, social, and national
peace, indeed of international concord between states.

I ground my analysis in three distinct philosophical corpora that are
nonetheless, either implicitly or explicitly, in a relationship of dialogue,
contradiction, or polemical engagement with each other: the corpus of so-
phistics, that of Plato and that of Aristotle. I might have chosen nonphilo-
sophical corpora (that of the tragedians, for example, or of the historians)
and different philosophical corpora (that of the Stoics in particular). But
my intention is not to undertake, as a historian of philosophy, an exhaustive
survey of these corpora, which have their own internal significance; rather,
it is to try to see whether and how certain models continue to function to-
day. Now, it seems to me that in the sophists and Plato we already have the
basic components in place and in Aristotle something like their combina-
tory pattern. It also seems to me that by accentuating certain features and
so moving, at worst, into caricature, at best, toward a template, it is possible
to sketch out a taxonomy that would allow a number of contemporary posi-
tions to be allocated: for example, Heidegger alongside Plato and Arendt
alongside a sophisticated Aristotle.

In any case, what is different each time is the modality of this linkage
between the logical, the ethical, and the political. By way of a guiding
principle, this is how it seems possible to me to characterize each of the
positions:

1. Rhetorical consensus: continually creating the city
through *logos*

A consensus of the sophistic type is the always precarious result of a
rhetorical operation of persuasion, which produces, opportunity after op-
portunity (this is the *kairos*), an instantaneous unity entirely made up of
differences. The *phusis* of the Ionians and the Being of the Eleatics, to
whom it was the task of the nascent ontology to give adequate expression, is

replaced by the politics that speech creates: nature does not therefore serve as a model for the city, quite the reverse, even; it is the city that serves as a model for the individual. With the sophistic *homonoia* and *homologia*, *logos* becomes the political virtue par excellence.

2. Ethico-political consensus: agreeing to the fixist hierarchy of differences

In Plato's *Republic*, the city is an enlargement of the soul, and *homonoia* determines one of the four virtues characteristic of the city as of the individual: "temperance" [*sôphrosunê*]. It is defined as the sense of hierarchy. With justice, the virtue of the structure ("let each take care of his own affairs"), it arranges the fixism of functional differences within an organic unity. Politics and ethics are but one, submitted to the same idea of the Good (the philosopher-king).

3. Specificity of the political mixture: optimizing deficiencies

The relations between politics and ethics in Aristotle are so complex that they may seem contradictory. But the city is defined from the outset as *plêthos politôn*, the "mass" or "quantity" of citizens. It is thereby understood that the democratic constitution may at times be called straight on the "constitution" since it alone takes account of the *plêthos* as such. In the *Politics*, we witness the implementation of a decreasingly Platonic set of paradigms for the city: as a soul, but really more as a crew, as a chorus, and finally as a picnic, where the organization of functions gives way to the mixture that alone is capable of optimizing differences and of enhancing the quality of the whole through the simple accumulation of individual deficiencies. The virtue of the good man and that of the citizen, ethics and politics, become carefully distinguished at this point, and consensus within the *plêthos* ends up being a point of equilibrium in the conflict of egoisms.

The Sophistic Homologia, *or the City as Performance*

Homologia, "identity of speech," and *homonoia*, "identity of thought," which are normally translated as "agreement," "consensus," sometimes "concord," are terms that belong first of all to the vocabulary of the atomists (Heraclitus and Democritus) and the sophists (Gorgias, Antiphon, Critias, Thrasymachus). Both Gorgias and Antiphon wrote a *Peri homonoias*, for example. For the purposes of characterizing *homonoia*, I restrict myself to a few fragments by Gorgias and Antiphon, or revolving around them, and to an analysis of the role of *logos* in politics, grounded in the myth of Protagoras.

GORGIAS: PRODUCING *HOMONOIA* THROUGH *LOGOS* BY INTEGRATING STASIS

Homonoia is obtained by means of *logos*. This is already manifest in Gorgias. The *Encomium of Helen*, for example, which thematizes the almightiness of speech by explicitly connecting it to time ("If everyone on every subject possessed memory of the past and present and knew the future in advance, speech would not be such as it is"[2]), is the very model of a *logos* that brings about a change of *homonoia*. Helen is in fact presented from the outset as "a woman who brought together, *in one voice and in one soul*, the *credence* of the poets' auditors, as well as the *sound* of a name which bears the memory of misfortunes" (I am hereby translating, very badly, *homophônos kai homopsukhos . . . hê te . . . pistis . . . hê te . . . phêmê*).[3] This is precisely what occurs with Gorgias—"but I myself wish, by giving a certain discursivity to the discourse [*logismon tina tôi logôi dous*], to put an end to the accusation"— whose encomium has the effect of producing a different Helen, a different consensus on Helen, stretching from Euripides and Isocrates to Claudel, Offenbach, and Giraudoux.[4]

As Socrates says, speaking for Protagoras in the Apology of the *Theaetetus*, the sophist does with his speeches what the doctor does with his drugs and brings about the change, the inversion of states, by effecting a movement not from false to true but from worse to better (166e–167b). What is at issue in *logos*, understood in this way, is not knowledge but political practice and virtue. This may well be the very meaning of Gorgias's audacious utterance, which Plutarch relates to tragedy (B23): "the one who charms," indeed, "the one who deceives" (*apatêsas*), "is more just than the one who does not deceive, and the one who is deceived is wiser that the one who is not deceived."

In a speech on *homonoia*, or one that aims to produce it, what must be charmed and won over is, in fact, *stasis* itself. Plutarch records the judgment of Melanthius concerning the speech *On Concord*, which Gorgias is supposed to have pronounced at Olympia: "He exhorts us to concord, he who is not even able to get himself, his wife, and his servant, three private individuals, to agree."[5] From this it would be possible to deduce that identity of feeling— they both love him; he loves them both—is not the way to *homonoia*. The remark is more serious than it seems if one considers the judgments that Philostratus, in the *Lives of the Sophists*, brings to bear on the *Olympian Oration* and on the *Funeral Oration*.[6] The first intervention was of great political importance: "Seeing Greece in *stasis*, [Gorgias] became its councilor in *homonoia*, turning the Greeks against the Barbarians and persuading them to take by force not each other's cities but the land of the Barbarians." But in this attempt to produce *homonoia*, the sophist expels *stasis* only from inside to outside.

The second speech is thus more potent still, composed "with a wisdom beyond compare," "for, although [Gorgias] set the Athenians against the Medes and the Persians and battled for that same spirit as in the *Olympian Oration* [*ton auton noun agônizomenos*], he breathed not a word about *homonoia* among the Greeks, for he was addressing himself to the Athenians, who were in love with power . . ." It seems to me that the *Funeral Oration* is the prodigious speech that it is only because it produces *homonoia* in the surest way possible: not by preaching it directly but by integrating the fact of *stasis*, Athenian imperialism, as something necessary for concord itself, by charming and winning over *stasis* in the guise of *homonoia*. Consensus is thus the effect of a logical operation, in the broader sense, that is able to turn to its advantage the contradictory opinions or practices that would otherwise prohibit it.

ANTIPHON: *HOMOLOGIA* DEFINES THE CITY

In the papyrus script *On Truth*,[7] the first thing in evidence is not that "being is" but that "one citizenizes [*politeuetai tis*]":[8] the first reality is not *phusis*, "nature," but the *polis*, the "city." Nature thereby becomes the escapee from the laws of the city; it constitutes the secret of the privacy as that from which there can thenceforth be no escape [*ei an lathêi, mê lathôn, di' alêtheian*].[9] In the end, the difference between the city and nature comes down to the difference in the laws that govern them: there is a lawful and prescriptive element in the city just as there is in nature [(*ta nomima*) *ta men . . . tôn nomôn . . . ta de tês phuseôs*],[10] but the lawfulness of the laws is "instituted," the "result of an agreement" (*homologêtenta, homologêsantas*),[11] whereas the lawfulness of nature is "necessary" and "grows" with it (*phunta*).[12] Thus for Antiphon, *homonoia* characterizes the very essence of the law that constitutes the city.

This is confirmed in the *Peri homonoias*[13] (which is also usually translated more with an eye to the Latin than the Greek as *On Concord*) even if this second treaty is, like the figure of Antiphon himself, a doxographical artifact. Thus in Diels and Kranz, at the head of the fragments preserved from the *Peri homonoias*, the most "sophistic" of the sophist's speeches according to Philostratus (356, 4), we are presented with two fragments geared to clarifying the title word, *homonoia*. But these two fragments, which are not in any way attributable to Antiphon, are the only ones in which the term appears. Let us admit that we are dealing with an effect of *homonoia* on *homonoia*.

The first of these fragments is an extract of a conversation between Socrates and Hippias, taken from the *Memorabilia* by Xenophon (IV, 4, 16), where Socrates—for it is he who is speaking here and not, as one might well expect, the sophist—having chosen to die in obedience to the laws, upholds the thesis that "it is what is lawful that is just."[14] He then goes on to give a eulogy to *homonoia*, the greatest asset a city can have. Greece is distinguished from the rest of the world by the law that requires all citizens to take the oath of *homonoia*: "Throughout Greece there is a law decreeing that citizens must swear to agree to—*omnunai homonoêsein*—and throughout [the land] they swear this oath."[15] *Homonoia* is thus the political equivalent of the great oath of the gods.[16] The content of *homonoia* is described in a remarkable fashion: it is not about sharing the same opinions, judgments, or values; the aim of the oath is not that "citizens vote for the same choruses, praise the same flute players, choose the same poets, take pleasure in the same things."[17] It is not a question of "fellow feeling" (*sumpatheia*); all that matters is that "they are persuaded by the laws," that they "obey" them (*ina tois nomois peithôntai*). The law of the Greeks is thus the law for an oath to be taken to obey the laws. *Homonoia*, the condition that allows a city to be a city and a household to be a household (*polis eu politeutheie, oikos kalôs oikêtheie*), which is thus the essence of the political, is in this way not a unity of identity but a unity that is truly formal, free, and empty, the form of a unity open to all contents.

A passage in Iamblichus, quoted by Stobaeus (II, 33, 15), confirms that "sameness"— the *homo* of *homonoia*—must be understood more fully in terms of *sun*, or "gathering": "*homonoia*, as the word itself tends to suggest, conjoins [*suneilêphen*] community and unity in a gathering [*sunagôgên*]."[18] Once this notion is advanced and begins to be put into effect, we leave the city, and passing by the household on the way, by all public and private "gatherings [*sullogous*]," we arrive at what falls within the realm of "natures and kinships [*phuseis te kai suggeneias pasas*]"; *homonoia* even "circumscribes" the relationship of consistency and constancy that the individual in the unity of his "I" entertains with himself (*homognômosunê, homophrosunê*). It is thus politics, *homonoia/stasis*, that is used in the analysis of nature and the individual, of whom it is required that he not be "unstable [*astatos*]," "maladjusted [*astathmêtos*]," or "at war with himself" [*polemios pros heauton*]. Here, the Parmenidean model is quite clearly turned on its head: the unity of "with," the collective and plural unity of the city, becomes the matrix of unicity.

The fragments attributed to Antiphon himself are certainly more difficult to interpret. Often brief and highly disparate, these mainly propose notations of vocabulary and a large number of commonplaces. But they do perhaps display a revival of interest in the perspective we are working from here: far from being congealed in the unicity of an eternal now, *homonoia* must take account of the diversity of opinions, the mediocrity of peoples' actual behavior, and finitude in its lived reality. This concerns life as it occurs in time (49–53a, cf. 77); the time of hesitation and of fear, of cowardice and desire (55–59), the time of education (60–65), the wear and tear (*l'usure*) of time, but also its usage according to the *kairos* and to the difference of past, present, and future. In actuality, like money or any other possession, time acquires presence not by being preserved but only by being spent, put into play. In the tale of the miser (54), as in the maxim of Protagoras, we encounter the importance of the etymological meaning of the *khrêmata*, what the hand makes use of and is meant to be used: "whatever someone has not used, nor will use in the future, whether or not it is his makes no odds"; this is what has to be said to console the miser, who, instead of "releasing as much as possible," like Callicles and his leaking barrels, has had stolen from him the treasure that he had buried in his garden.[19]

Analogously, in his work *On the Interpretation of Dreams*—if we are to go by the examples taken by Cicero[20]—Antiphon brings into focus the ambivalent specificity of relation. To the runner bound for Olympia who dreams that he is driving a quadriga, he does not say, like a certain other interpreter, that he will be victorious, given the speed and strength of the horses, but that he will be beaten, as he has four ahead of him. And when he dreams that he is an eagle, it is not that he is the mightiest but that in pursuing others he always lags behind.

In a more general fashion, *gnômê*, or common sense, which in this way often gets preached by the sophists along with orthodoxy in behavior, is, it seems to me, always capable of going one way or the other: "like father like son," or "to the thrifty father the wasteful son"—a fitting *gnômê* can always be found. Nothing could be less rigid than common sense, for in its lability and contradictoriness it is always ready for a new *kairos*.

The "concord" put forward in sophistics appears, therefore, as the implementation of an identity—which can be reduced to a *flatus vocis*—and results from a plurality that is at once conflictual and temporalized.

THE *LOGOS* OF PROTAGORAS

The myth of Protagoras related by Plato is the longest and most explicit text we possess on the politics of the sophists. Now, contrary to what we are deducing from Gorgias and Antiphon, *logos* appears in the myth as radically unsuited to constituting the dimension of the political: "the art of articulating sounds and words" comes from Promethean know-how, and yet Promethean men get devoured or kill each other for lack of the "political art" (321c–22b). What is needed—and herein lies the whole myth—is a supplementary gift from Zeus, *aidôs* and *dikê*, to enable the constitution of "the orders that constitute the city and the ties that gather in bringing friendship [*poleôn kosmoi te kai desmoi philias sunagôgoi*]" (322c).

But on closer inspection, it very much seems that the constitutive importance of *logos* in politics has to be maintained for several reasons. First, because *aidôs* and *dikê* have to exist in relation not simply to the articulation of sounds and words but also to speech in a public space. *Aidôs* is the "respect for public opinion," the "sense of human respect,"[21] and so is by no means a sense of moral obligation whose transgression would make for an uneasy conscience but rather the advance sense of what the other expects. Likewise, *dikê*, from *deiknumi*, "I show," before being the natural disposition of the just man, refers to the rule, the use, and the public norm of behavior. *Aidôs* is thus no more than the motivation to respect *dikê*, and *dikê* has any force only insofar as each person experiences *aidôs*: "respect" and "justice," then "justice and temperance [*dikaiosunê, sôphrosunê*]" (323a), acquire meaning in the sophistic conception only when mediated by the gaze of the other. This is why Protagoras, in concluding the myth, proclaims that "in matters of justice and political virtue in general, even when it is known that a man is unjust, if he publicly tells the truth about himself [*talêthê lege*], what was earlier believed to be wisdom (telling the truth) here becomes madness. By the same token, it is said that everyone must say they are just [*kai phasin pantas dein phanai*], whether they are or not, and that whoever does not make some pretence of justice [*prospoioumenon*] is a madman" (323b–c). The principle of publicness is necessarily a principle of hypocrisy, as with Antiphon, who defines the right use of justice by the observance of the prescriptions of the laws when in the presence of witnesses and by the observance of the prescriptions of nature when in the solitude of the private realm.[22]

This is indeed what is developed by the *logos* of Protagoras, following from the myth: virtue is like *logos*, an apprenticeship in convention. The city as a whole teaches "value," *aretê*, at the same time that it teaches citizens how to speak. The apprenticeship begins as soon as the child "pays attention" or "understands what is being said to him [*suniei ta legomena*]" (325c7) or as soon as he carries out the convention that is words. This convention pursues its course through the study of the increasingly refined forms of *logos* up to that most eminent of proceedings that consists in the settling of accounts at the end of the magistrate's term of office (326e). This is why there are no more masters in virtue than there are masters in Greek (328a): the power of justice, the political virtue, merges with the power of *logos*. But this is also why Protagoras considers himself to be one of the best teachers.

To conclude, what emerges from *logos* subsequent to the myth (namely, that *logos* itself constitutes the political virtue par excellence) becomes the essential element of the myth in the amended version that Ælius Aristides proposes in the second century of the common era, when the Second Sophistic reflects upon the powers of rhetoric at the height of the Pax Romana. In his speech "Against Plato in Defense of Oratory," men "die in silence" (II, 396) for so long as Zeus refrains from granting them, no longer *aidôs* and *dikê*, but the rhetoric that Hermes brings them (397).[23] It is the "victory of *logos*" that allows the city to be constituted (398); rhetoric "connects and orders [*sunekhei kai kosmei*]" (401, cf. 424): like "a guard that never sleeps," it always manages to "give coherence to what never ceases to occur [*aei to paron suntithêmenê*]" (401).

In short, *logos* is the actuality, the topicality of the political, its continuous creation, contradiction after contradiction, volte-face after volte-face. *Homonoia-homologia* bespeaks this perpetual construction of the artifact that is the city and bears witness to the fact that the city is first of all a performance.

The Social Body, or the Meaning of the Hierarchy

Plato presents us a completely different model of consensus. In bringing this out, I restrict myself to the metaphors for the city used in the fourth book of the *Republic* and to the characteristics of *homonoia* that ensue.

THE CITY IS LIKE THE SOUL

In truth, it is not so much a question of metaphor in Plato as of enlargement and miniature. Faced with the difficulty of defining justice, Socrates in effect puts forward an expedient:

> It were as if a sequence of small letters were given to short-sighted people to read from afar; if one of them noticed that the same letters were written elsewhere on a larger scale and a larger surface, it would, I think, seem like a stroke of good fortune to be able to read these first and then to examine the smaller letters to see if they are the same. (368d)

Justice, and then injustice, in the city are thus a transposition for the benefit of the myopic of justice and injustice in the individual. The passage foretold, the "epanaphora (434e)," from city to individual begins to take effect in chapter 11 of book IV, culminating in the statement that the city has well and truly made legible the "principle and model" of justice [*arkhên te kai tupon*] (443b).

But things are clearly a little more complicated. For having set his sights on defining, in broad brushstrokes, justice in the great theater of the city, he constantly has recourse to what goes on in man, in the individual. I will take just one example, which is crucial for my purposes here: that of *sôphrosunê*, apparently one of the four virtues "clearly" contained by the "perfectly good" city (427e). It is a term that tends to be translated as "temperance" precisely because of the priority given to the "psychological" model. Temperance, then, says Socrates, is "a kind of order and dominion over pleasures and desires" (430e); to explain it better, he uses the expression "being master of oneself [*to kreittô hautou*]": "it seems to me that this expression means that within the soul of man himself there is a better part and a worse part, and that when, as is natural, the better part governs the worse, then one is said to be 'master of oneself'" (431a). It is now and only now that Socrates suggests that "eyes be turned" [*apoblepe*] (431b) toward the "temperate" city in order to note how there, as in the temperate man, the better part governs the worse. In the light of this, there is no longer any cause for surprise in the reading put forward by Diès concerning "social justice and individual justice, order in the city and order in the soul": "We do not have to enquire, then, which is the primary subject and which the secondary; the subject is one . . . ,"[24] with the proviso that, when all is said and done, this unity is that of the soul. Indeed, the soul never ceases to function as a model of intelligibility for the city, making it possible to understand the difference between the "social bodies," "classes," or "castes" [*ethnê*], between their functions, their virtues: it is inherent to the city as a metaphor, before being the metaphor for the city.

THE VIRTUES OF THE STRUCTURE

There are therefore, in the state as in the soul, then in the soul as in the state, three parts, "the same and same in number" (441c): "the part that decides [*to bouleutikon*]," represented in the city by the "rulers" or "accomplished guardians," and in the soul by the "logical principle [*ho logos, to logistikon*]," whose virtue is to be "wise [*sophos*]"; "the part that brings assistance [*to epikourêtikon*]," in the city, the "warriors," in the soul, high spirit [*to thumoeides*], whose virtue is "virility" or "bravura" [*andreia*]; and finally, "the part that is concerned with objects," "that is attached to possessions [*to khrêmatistikon*]," in the city, the producers and tradesmen, in the soul, "desire [*to epitumêtikon*]," whose virtue is precisely "temperance."[25]

However, when compared with the other two virtues, temperance has one characteristic that brings it into relation with that mysterious fourth virtue, the object of the dialogue: justice. Instead of belonging solely to one of the parts of the city or the soul, it is in fact a kind of "consonance" or "harmony" [*xumphônia tis kai harmonia*] (430e; cf. 431e): "it literally stretches out across the whole city, taking in all citizens, and giving them the ability to make as one the same chant [*xunadontas . . . tauton*], be they weak, strong or average, in intelligence, or if you will, in physical strength, in number, wealth, and so on . . ." (432a). It is at this point that Socrates brings in the term *homonoia*: "such that we could in all accuracy say that temperance is this consensus [*homonoian*], the natural consonance [*xumphônian*] of the worst and the best as to determine which of the two is to rule both in the city and in each individual."[26] As we know, Socrates goes on to define justice by the fact that each person, each class, each citizen, each part of the soul "does what it has to do without getting mixed up in what the others are doing"[27] and so stays in its place in every sense of the term. If justice is the virtue of the structure, safeguarding the taxonomy, then *sôphrosunê*, which we might translate as "control" (*self-control*, even, as we read in Liddell, Scott, and Jones),[28] is the virtue of the hierarchy and safeguards the cohesion of the individual soul as of the social soul (a better term here than "body"), a virtue that might well be thought of initially as harder to obtain from, and thus more characteristic of, subjects than masters.

THE PART AS A FUNCTION OF THE WHOLE

It is clear, in any case, that in the *Republic* there can be no question of some part or other, the guardian class, for example, being "differentially happy [*diapherontôs eudaimon*]," only of ensuring "the greatest possible happiness for the city as a whole" (420b),[29] just as the God of Leibniz has no need to be concerned with the lone fate of Lucretia in order to create the best of possible worlds. By way of example, then, Socrates imagines that he is painting a statue; if reproached with not using the most beautiful color, purple, for the most beautiful part, the eyes, he would be able to reply:

> Do not think I have to make the eyes so beautiful that they cease to be like eyes, any more than with the other parts, but rather look to see whether, in giving each part its due, we make the whole beautiful. Likewise, in the present matter, do not compel us to bestow upon the guardians the kind of happiness that will make them much more than guardians. For we might just as reasonably clothe the farmers in long, flowing robes, shower them with gold, and ask of them only that they work the soil for their own pleasure. (420d–e)

There are two opposing conceptions of apportionment: that which functions in terms of the individual and that which is a function of the whole. And Socrates concludes that in order for there to be a city, the guardian must indeed be a guardian, just as "the farmer is a farmer and the potter a potter" (421a).

In the end, as we can see, it is the organic model that wins out even if it is neither the most explicit nor the most detailed in its overall form: the city/soul functions like the body. The difference between the parts is necessary on the same grounds as the difference between the hands and the eyes. Moreover, the city has a pain in its citizen just as a man has a pain in his finger (IV, 462c–d), and, more generally, justice is the health of the soul as of the city (IV, 444c–e) in the same way that the deviant forms of constitutions are illnesses, according to the metaphor that runs through book VIII.

In Plato, *homonoia* describes the manner in which the parts conspire to become whole. Of course, as soon as one part lays claim to autonomy, this can only mean a perversion, in the strictest sense, that is at once dangerous and culpable. Unlike the sophistic whole, the Platonic whole is either unable or unwilling to entertain open competition among the singularities that constitute it.

The Picnic, or the Ruse of Democracy

"THE CITY IS A PLURALITY OF CITIZENS"

This is precisely the object of Aristotle's retort in the *Politics* (*Politikôn*, not *Politeia*), with his proposal for alternative images of the city and, at the same time, for an alternative model of consensus. "For happiness is not like evenness: the even number may well be the attribute of the whole without being that of any of the parts, but with happiness, this is impossible."[30] Whether dealing with happiness or with the virtue of the city, Aristotle constantly opts for the synthetic order: if each, then all—"for even if it is possible for all to be politically dedicated without each of the citizens being so, it is nonetheless the second modality that is preferable: for all is also a consequence of each."[31] The difference between Plato and Aristotle lies in their intuitive starting positions: for Plato, the city is first of all one; for Aristotle, it is first of all plurality, *plêthos*. The whole Aristotelian critique of Plato follows from this: Plato conflates economics and politics because he climbs the unity of the household and the unity of the city down to the unity of the individual (and even to that of the soul, even to that of the body):

> The household, like the city, must to a certain degree be one, but not completely. For in the progressive movement toward unity, there comes a point where the city no longer exists, or, if it still exists, where it is very close to being a noncity, and is an inferior city; as if a symphony were made into a homophony, and a rhythm into a single foot.[32]

In order to distinguish himself from Plato, Aristotle uses, as he always does, right up to the *Metaphysics*, the concepts and demands of sophistics even if it means dodging the ultimate consequences of sophistics and coming back at the last minute, as if for want of something better, to Plato. Be that as it may, the Aristotelian critique of Plato returns us at once to the sophistic interpretation of *homonoia*: it is a case of interpreting the "same" not as a "one" but as a "with." Or, to put it another way: the Aristotelian definition of the city and of the constitution takes as its model not the unicity of an organism but the composition of a mixture, as the early definitions of book III demonstrate:

The constitution is a certain organization [*taxis*] of those who inhabit the city. And since the city is a mixture [*tôn sugkeimenôn*], like any other totality that is first composed of several parts [*sunestôtôn d'ek pollôn moriôn*], clearly what is first at issue is the citizen. For the city is a plurality of citizens [*he gar polis politôn tis plêthos estin*].[33]

FROM CREW TO PICNIC

Contrary to the monoideism of *Republic* IV, the *Politics* is awash with metaphors. It is only to be expected that the paradigm of the parts of the body, the parts of the soul, indeed the relation between the soul and the body should be in operation in book I, where the matter in question is the organization of the family and the household, the relation between master and slave, husband and wife, father and child. But as soon as it becomes a question of the actual city itself, the paradigm is used in a way that is the exact opposite of the way it is used in Plato. Its primary function is thus to provide proof of the difference between virtue in the individual and virtue in the city: ethical virtue, that of the *agathos anêr*, the "virtuous man," is not to be confused with that of the *spoudaios politês*, the "dedicated citizen,"[34] for while there is only one ethical virtue, there is a differentiated plurality of political virtues (something that does not fail to recall the beginning of the *Meno*):

> Since the city is composed of dissimilar elements [*ex anomoiôn*] (as a living being is from the outset made up of a soul and a body, and the soul of reason and impulse, the household of a man and a woman, and property of a master and a slave, so too is the city made up of all this, and other kinds of dissimilar elements besides), then necessarily, the virtue of all the citizens is not one and the same, any more than in a chorus is that of the coryphaeus and that of his assistant.[35]

Hence, if there is to be political *homonoia*, its first characteristic must be that of being *ex anomoiôn*, made up of a plurality of political virtues.

But as the paradigm requires, these differences are still susceptible to being interpreted in a Platonic vein as a functional hierarchy. In chapter 4, the model of the chorus, frequently taken up and allowing virtues to be declined according to constitutions (the Dorian mode, the Phrygian mode; cf. 1276b4–9), and the long-lived model of the ship's crew (1276b20–31), which brings to light the difference between public and private, individual competence (oarsman, navigator, helmsman) and common goal (the saving of the ship, 1276b20–31), always fall within a taxonomy of an organicist kind, even allowing for changes in mode or employment; finally, the difference in virtues or capacities still corresponds to something like the division of labor.

Thus, in chapter 11, when asked whether it is fitting to entrust power [*to kurion*] to the plurality (*to plêthos*, "the mass," if you will, but in the sense where this mass of citizens is, by virtue of the definition given at the beginning of the same book, as you will recall, constitutive of the city),[36] there appear a number of original metaphors, which, while less and less compatible with those used initially, are more and more in keeping with the despecialized and stochastic mixture, so to speak, that is the city. At one and the same time, the image of the body and that of the soul work themselves into a frenzy. Here is the key passage:

> A plurality of people, who as individual men are without political value, is nevertheless capable when gathered together [*sunelthontas*] of being better than an elite [*ekeinôn* takes up *tous aristous men, oligous de*, 1281a40f.], not when taken one by one but collectively [*oukh' hôs hekaston, all'hôs sumpantas*], in the same way that those meals where everyone contributes their share are better than the ones where a single person treats all. Indeed, when there is a plurality [*pollôn gar ontôn*], each part has a share of virtue and practical wisdom, and when the plurality is gathered together [*sunelthontôn*], then just as the crowd [*to plêthos*] becomes a single man with many feet, many hands and many senses, so it is with moral and intellectual dispositions [*ta êthê kai tên dianoian*]. This is why the plurality is better at judging musical and poetic works: each judges a part and all judge the whole [*alloi gar allo ti morion, panta de pantes*].[37]

Unlike in a body or for Plato, the quality of the part is not that of being adapted to the whole and staying in its place. It is simply that of having some quality or other for the whole to latch on to. In Plato, the whole optimizes the parts by making their inadequacies as individuals into the condition of their quality, of their role as organs. In Aristotle, the whole optimizes the parts by retaining only their qualities and forming a compound thereof.

With the image of the picnic (this is how Liddell, Scott, and Jones translate *ta sumphoreta*), which is again taken up in 1286a29, it is diversity on its own that makes up the quality, for what would it be like if instead of "with" there was a "same," and everyone brought tomatoes?

Finally, diversity may even give way, quite simply, to number. In this event, quantity becomes in and of itself a quality, as witnessed, above and beyond the crazy image of the tentacular body,[38] by the end comparison, which serves to justify the fact that "the mass of citizens," that is, "all those who have neither wealth nor any claim to virtue whatsoever [*to plêthos tôn politôn . . . hosoi mête plousioi mête axiôma ekhousin aretês mêde hen*]" (1281b24f.) take part in the deliberative and judicial assemblies:

> For when everyone is gathered together [*sunelthontes*], they possess an
> adequate sensibility, and, mixing with the best, they aid the city, just as
> nonpurified food combined with a small quantity of pure food makes the
> whole more nourishing; whereas each person taken separately lacks maturity
> of judgment. (1281b 34–38)

This dietetics is far removed from the organic model.

It may be that this is how certain physical mixtures come to settle and decant, going through the processes of purification by themselves: the sediment disappears of its own accord by sinking to the bottom. But it is doubtless more accurate to surmise that we here come by the singularity of that object that is the city, as whatever its constitution or regime, it defines itself by being "a plurality of citizens"—indeed, we come by the very specificity of the political: of all mixtures being the one that by itself constitutes such a procedure of decantation.[39]

POLITICAL FRIENDSHIP

If plurality is indeed the condition of the political, what then becomes of *homonoia*? The first thing to say here is that the term does not belong to the vocabulary of the *Politics*[40] but to that of the *Nicomachean Ethics*. This is in fact the work that, in IX, 6, undertakes to define *homonoia* as *politikê philia*, a friendship whose framework is the city. It is not about having the same opinions or conceptions (in astronomy for example); put briefly, it is about being in agreement on the ends and means of practical importance. The definition gives pause for thought, for how can friendship, which in its perfect form unites similar elements in a *sunaisthanestai*, a mutual perception or shared sense of their excellence (VIII, 4), be reconciled with the city, that is, the mixture made of up a plurality of dissimilar elements?

The answer would seem on this occasion to have to allow diversity of regimes, as is suggested by the differential analysis of forms of friendship corresponding to forms of constitution (VIII, 12–13). In fact, Aristotle at once stipulates that political friendship "occurs between good people [*en tois epieikesin*],"[41] as they are already "in concord with themselves and with others."[42] Among such people, the political problem of dissimilarity does not arise; in other words, in them, ethical friendship and political friendship are united or merge. This is indeed also what characterizes aristocracy: "it is in effect the only form of government where the goodness of the man and that of the citizen are but one [*en monê gar haplôs ho autos anêr kai politês agathos estin*]."[43]

But what happens in the perfect city when one takes into consideration not the good people alone but the *plêthos* itself, including "ordinary people," "common folk" [*phauloi*]—what happens, then, in a "constitution," pure and simple, and in that constitution which makes the *plêthos* as such govern, in a democracy? First of all, there exists a democratic substitute for "sameness": equality. "While in tyrannies, friendships and justice count for little, in democracies they count for much more, for those who are equal have a lot in common":[44] here we come across the importance of alternation and isonomy for the *Politics*. But from the point of view of ethics, this answer is quite inadequate, for the *phauloi* "are not capable of concord, or only to a very small degree, any more than they are of friendship."[45] If the city is not then plunged into disaster, it is because, among the *phauloi*, what safeguards the "common interest" is not *homonoia* but, on the contrary, *stasis*. Each person, looking only after himself and having no other aim than to receive from the city the greatest assistance and the smallest burden of responsibility, "spies on his neighbor to prevent him from gaining similar advantage: for if he fails to keep a lookout, the common interest is lost. They therefore come into conflict [*stasiazein*], keeping one another in check without wishing to do what is right themselves" (b13–16). Being careful to stick to one's position, to remain in *stasis*, is thus the only means for the *plêthos*, and so for the complete city, of safeguarding the common good.

Homonoia is hence the state of equilibrium produced when the exercising of singularity and self-interest is taken to an extreme: once more the democratic mixture puts the deficiencies themselves to good use. There is an objective ruse at work here, not on the part of reason but of democracy. On the condition, that is, as may need emphasizing once more, that the movement not end, democracy is the opposite of an "idea"; it consists only in its becoming. In this, on the hither side of Aristotle, we meet up with sophistic practice, going right back to the exemplary gesture of Heraclitus, as recorded by Plutarch:[46] in response to his fellow citizens asking him what he thought of *homonoia*, Heraclitus is supposed to have concocted a *kukeôn* (a mixture, probably, of water, barley meal, and mint) and stirred it "without saying a word . . . before the dumbfounded Ephesians" before drinking it and taking his leave. For it is mixture, and the creative movement of mixture, that brings about consensus in democracy.

ARISTOTLE THE SOPHIST

In the wake of these analyses, it is not difficult to give an account of everything that the political, anti-Platonic Aristotle owes to sophistics.

The first feature, which may seem the weightiest (and we will come back to this in relation to Hannah Arendt) but which requires the utmost care in interpreting, is the importance of *logos* in politics. For a sophist, *logos* is the political virtue par excellence. Now, right from the start of the *Politics*, Aristotle places in series two definitions of man: man as a "city animal," or "political animal," and man as an "animal with the gift of *logos*."[47] It is because man is capable not only of expressive vocal sounds but also of *logos*, that is, capable simultaneously of conventional effects, or words, and of syntactical articulation, or judgments, that he is "more political" than the other political animals. Nonetheless, the way in which *logos* is implemented in the *Politics* makes it less of a *tekhnê*, a rhetorical competence, than a *telos*, the very end and purpose of our nature.[48] In Aristotle, in other words, a rhetoric of the sophistic kind, the very kind that is able to sway the decision of the judges and the choices made by the assembly or, through eulogy, to create common values has the political aim of making us logical *in actu*; above all, it must work in such a way that each of us can, with nouthetics and education, become what we are, oriented toward *logos* and *nous* by *logos* and *nous*—something which, in truth, comes close to a Platonic ruler: insofar as we live in a city, we are all, potentially at least, philosophers.

The second common feature is the immediate, "physical" perception of man as citizen and of the city, whatever its constitution, as plurality, that is to say, a plurality of dissimilar elements.

The third, related feature is, in this kind of *plêthos* at least, the apprehension of *homonoia* as the pure effect of a continual *stasis*.

Whatever the complexity of the linkage between politics and ethics in Aristotle, it seems to me possible in any case to recognize in these last two features a certain specificity of the political. Corresponding to this, as the beginning of the *Nicomachean Ethics* attests, there is an autonomy, indeed even a hegemony to politics, "the mistress and architectonic *par excellence*,"[49] while for its part, the inquiry that takes place into the good is still "of a political nature [*politikê tis ousa*]."[50] No doubt the relevant paradigm is that there exist two distinct books, the *Politics* and the *Nicomachean Ethics*, compared with the unicity of Plato's *Republic*.

I therefore propose two criteria that would make it possible to differentiate between two models of consensus. The first comes down to the relative autonomy of the political: is this a domain that has its foundation, its *raison d'être*, somewhere other than in itself, in the ethical, for example, as it does in Plato, or is it rather a potentiality unto itself, an architectonic, if you will, as in sophistics and Aristotle? The second comes down to the relative autonomy of the individual in relation to the whole: is it a question of hierarchical subordination, where singularity is never considered as such, never referred to itself, or it is a free play of differences, a linkage formed by competition?

Contemporary Perspectives

To close, I would like to outline how it might be possible, using as a yardstick the difference hereby forged, by means of sophistics, between Plato

and Aristotle (a certain kind of Plato and a certain kind of Aristotle), to in-
terpret a few differences between contemporaries capable of provoking
passionate reaction. Martin Heidegger and Hannah Arendt do not have the
same perception of the Greek city, nor did they have the same relation, ei-
ther in a theoretical or a concrete way, to the political. Heidegger's city is
tragic and Platonic, that of Arendt sophistic and Aristotelian: for him, the
political has nothing political about it; for her—and this is what she herself
endeavors to think—there is a specificity to the political, or it has transcen-
dental conditions.[51]

THE SYRACUSE SYNDROME

It is possible to maintain, without too much exaggeration, that the matrix
of the Heideggerian corpus of material concerning the city is verse 370 of
the chorus from Sophocles's *Antigone* and, at the center of centers, the pas-
sage to which he devotes many a commentary, *hupsipolis-apolis*, "high in
the city—out of the city."[52] It is from the standpoint of this expression that
Heidegger, in *An Introduction to Metaphysics*, for example, chooses to inter-
pret the meaning of the word *polis*:

> *Polis* is usually translated as city or city-state. This does not capture the full
> meaning. *Polis* means, rather, the place, the there, wherein and as which
> historical being-there is. The *polis* is the historical place, the there *in* which,
> *out* of which, and *for* which history happens. To this place and scene of history
> belong the gods, the temples, the priests, the festivals, the games, the poets,
> the thinkers, the ruler, the council of elders, the assembly of the people, the
> army and the fleet. All this does not first belong to the *polis*, does not become
> political by entering into a relation with a statesman and a general and the
> business of the state. No, it is political, i.e., at the site of history, provided there
> be (for example) poets *alone*, but then really poets, priests *alone*, but then really
> priests, rulers *alone*, but then really rulers.[53]

To be sure, the explanation of "alone," repeated with Heidegger's own
emphasis, is at once given in terms of creative violence: the singular au-
thenticity possessed by each makes of him the placeless founder of the
place or, in the manner of a work of art, the one who opens up the world.

Clearly the horizon is of an entirely different sort from what we have in Plato. But I would like to suggest that the treatment of singularity is not fundamentally different. Indeed, it is the exclusive, definitive character of what might somewhat hastily be called a specialization of the individual that alone is fit to constitute the "there is" of the whole. In this I hear, *mutatis mutandis*, an echo of Socrates's words in response to the objection that "the guardians will not be happy":

> If you manage to persuade us, then the farmer will not be a farmer, nor the potter a potter, nor will any other have the character which when combined with those of all the rest means that there is a city.[54]

Each, in other words, reproducing the complementarity of organs in the division of labor—even were it the most inventive or creative—is always like an eye, a heart, or a foot, but, in contrast to what Aristotle or Marx intended, never like a hand, the organ that takes the place of organs, the "capable" organ, and capable in its singularity of outstripping this singularity.

But *hupsipolis-apolis* still and above all implies, along with a delocalization of man in relation to the city, a delocalization of the political as such. In Plato, the Good alone is *anupothêton*, "unconditioned," and by dint of this a condition of the political. Likewise, the issue for Heidegger is to understand the political from the standpoint of something other than it or, if you wish, from the standpoint of what it truly is: not the ethical but the history of being. This is why he is able, in reinterpreting the passage in the *Parmenides*, to assert that "the difference between the modern state, the Roman *res-publica* and the Greek *polis* is essentially the same as that between the modern essence of truth, the Roman *rectitudo* and the Greek *alêtheia*." If by *polis* is understood "the pole of *pelein*," the old verb for *einai*, "to be," then "it is only because the Greeks are an essentially non-political people" that they were able and obliged, in the end, to found it.[55] The invention of the city is nonpolitical because the political *as* political has nothing political about it.

The consequences of this subordination of the political to the ontological or the *historial* are immediately evident in the interview given by Heidegger in 1966 to the magazine *Der Spiegel*: "A decisive question for me today is: how can a political system accommodate itself to the technological age, and which political system would this be? I have no answer to this question. I am not convinced that it is democracy."[56] If democracy can seem like a "half truth," then this is effectively because it does not correspond to the modern essence of truth because it misapprehends technology in continuing to assume that "technology is in its essence something over which man has control": for the philosopher that Heidegger always remained, it is, beyond question, on the aptness of the philosophical assessment that the soundness of the political position depends.

Hannah Arendt's diagnosis is arresting in its intelligence: "we . . . can hardly help finding it striking and perhaps exasperating that Plato and Heidegger, when they entered into human affairs, turned to tyrants and Führers. This should be imputed not just to the circumstances of the times and even less to preformed character, but rather to what the French call a *déformation professionnelle*."[57] The Syracuse syndrome would in this way traverse "our philosophical tradition of political thought, beginning with Parmenides and Plato, from the moment that "the way of life chosen by the philosopher was understood in opposition to the *bios politikos*, the political way of life,"[58] and equally, then, from the moment that the political becomes thinkable only under philosophical tutelage.

THE SPECIFICITY OF THE POLITICAL

So it is that Arendt constantly rejects the name "philosopher" in favor of "professor of political theory"—Protagoras had previously signaled his preference for "master in virtue" or "teacher of excellence." Arendtian political theory might in truth serve as a template for our second model of consensus: indeed, it defines the specificity of the political by the "with," which is characteristic of an irreducibly plural condition.

It is easy to demonstrate everything that Arendt owes to Aristotle, as it is something she herself never ceases to insist upon. As is the case for Heidegger, it is the Greek *polis* that is present in politics, but the city emerges not tragically, ecstatic of itself, but in the extraordinary and entirely everyday circumstance of "living together" (*suzên*), through the "sharing of words and deeds."[59] As Jacques Taminiaux has emphasized,[60] it is against a Heideggerian interpretation of Aristotle, with the Platonic premium it puts on the *bios theorêtikos*, that Arendt is reacting in marking out the irreducible specificity of *praxis* in its double connection to human plurality on the one hand and to *doxa*, or opinion, on the other.

But these philosophemes of a non-Platonico-Heideggerian Aristotle are to my mind precisely those of Aristotle the sophist. Throughout her work, the dominant features of the Greek city for Arendt are Aristotelico-sophistic. It is first of all the political itself that emerges, and can only emerge, out of the sophistic distinction, which goes on to structure book I of Aristotle's *Politics*, between public and private, law and nature, convention and biological necessity, city and family, economy and indeed society.

The specificity of the political would thus consist in its disqualification, pure and simple, of the oppositions that are canonical for theory and the *bios theorêtikos*. In politics, there is no opposition between the multiple and changing *doxa*, the supposed mother of errors, and the eternal, solitary constraint of *alêtheia* any more than there could be any conflict or even any significant difference between appearing and being in that space of "appearances" that is the city: "*Doxa* was neither subjective illusion nor arbitrary distortion, but . . . that to which truth invariably adhered"—this was the teaching of a less than Platonic Socrates, then, a Socrates, rather, brought up in the agora on the school of the sophistic *dokei moi* ("it seems to me," says the truth that in what appears there is) and formerly on that of the Homeric poem, which hymns at once Achilles and Hector, and so brought up since he was capable as a result of "seeing the world . . . from the other's fellow's point of view" and of "exchanging" points of view on "the political kind of insight *par excellence*."[61] This indeed is attested to in Aristotle by the characterization, to which Arendt also gives emphasis, of *phronêsis*, or "prudence," that properly political virtue, as a "doxastic virtue."

But more radically still, Arendt makes language the political faculty par excellence and makes the kind of speech adapted to the moment and occasion the political action par excellence: "Wherever the relevance of speech is at stake, matters become political by definition, for speech is what makes man a political being."[62] In this manner, she continually refers to the inaugural definition of man as an "animal with the gift of language," protesting against the misconception that turns this into an *animal rationale*, but within the compass of Aristotle's *Politics*, her intention is to work back toward the "the current opinion of the *polis* about man and the political way of life," an opinion that is *de facto* sophistic, and the only one suited to creating and maintaining that marvelous system, "the most talkative of all bodies politic," which is the Greek city.[63]

"Men live together in the manner of speech":[64] the specificity of the political is the competition of *logoi*, normed by what after Kant might be known as taste, which courts the agreement of the other in the midst of a plural condition. This is why for Arendt, unlike for Plato/Heidegger, "to look upon politics from the perspective of truth . . . means to take one's stand outside the political realm."[65]

To conclude, I wish to ward off a misunderstanding. Recognizing the specificity of the political does not, for all that, imply that one knows how in politics to avoid errors, avoid horrors: Carl Schmitt and Max Weber or Raymond Aron think the political as such. It still has to be known which specification is retained and how and why it is put into effect. But whatever this specification may be, it can never, by definition, be confused with either the ethical distinction between good and evil or with the theoretical distinction between true and false, which would doubtless offer us immediate assurance, only to terrorize us later. And even if it were to take special account of *logos*, this would not mean that we would thereby be done with tyranny or demagogy. My intention, then, has simply been to bring forward out of the Greek imaginary or metaphorical space these two major ways of thinking the political, that of the (philosopher as) ontologist or the (philosopher as) political scientist and, with the problematic of consensus, to indicate the necessity of connecting these with the manner in which the individual relates to the whole.

Translated by Jake Wadham

EIGHT

Aristotle with and Against Kant on the Idea of Human Nature

Aristotle: "Reason and thought is the ultimate end of our nature" (*ho de logos hêmin kai ho nous tês phuseôs telos*);[1] Kant: "rational nature exists as an end in itself."[2] Nature, end, reason, rational nature—it seems that Aristotle and Kant are making use of the same ingredients and, what is more, the same kind of argumentative move, whereby what is given is also what we must strive to attain. I would like, with the assistance of Kant and in the light of certain of the uses to which Aristotle is put today, to return to this idea of "human nature" (uncertain, as I am, whether it is anachronistic or timeless), an idea that lies at the very heart of Aristotelian thinking about politics and education ("lead to the *logos* by way of the *logos*") in the hope of gaining a clearer understanding of its meaning.

Never before has greater use been made of Aristotle's practical philosophy. Aristotelians are abundant, at least in this particular domain. Neo-Aristotelianism has become a political issue, at times even a burning issue in its contemporary relevance, whether one is for or against, whether one finds in it the necessary conditions of real democracy or sees it as the symptom of an arid conservatism.[3] The debate began in Germany and has since spread to the Anglo-American world. The Italians, more so than the French, currently occupy the impartial observer's position and are able to assess, wisely and in full knowledge of the facts, the lineage and authenticity of Aristotelianism in the various positions.[4]

What I find striking about this "neo-Aristotelianism" is the philosophically contradictory use that it makes of the term *practical philosophy*. This contradiction does not correspond—as is broadly the case with other tensions in this movement—to the difference between the analytic and the hermeneutic traditions. Rather, this contradiction, which crosses the boundaries between traditions, is more as follows: on some occasions, Aristotle is presented as a way out, a happy alternative to the unlivable rigidity of Kantian formalism and one that deserves to be championed once again. Yet on other occasions, Aristotelian prudence and free choice have been considered evidence of an intuition approaching Kant's, of the will and its freedom, but one that is capable of tempering and perfecting the life of practical reason. Thus two quite different ends and means are bound up in today's insistence on the importance of Aristotelian ethics. This either forms part of a reappraisal of the past, a reaction against Kantian modernity in its various incarnations, an attempt to rediscover ourselves as differently (or other than) Modern—and attempt in which Aristotle is definitively pre- (that is, non-) Kantian: Aristotle against Kant. Or, on the other hand, it is a syncretic blueprint for the future, whereby Aristotle can help us become what we, in any event, are striving to be: Kantians, only a little more comfortable; here, Aristotle is a post-Kantian, Aristotle is with Kant.

It is worth adding that what these two alternatives clearly have in common (irrespective of their particular decisions and methods) is a concern with what we might call, along the lines of the rediscovery of "everyday language," the recapture of everyday practical experience: an ethics in and of the quotidian. We could, accordingly, ask whether this is not in fact something approaching a sign of the times, a sign that is perhaps alone sufficient to allow these times to be characterized if not as Aristotelian, then at least as "Aristotelizing."

Aristotle and Kant: Two Incommensurables?

Whether Aristotle can be used to perfect or undo Kant entails anyway that one think Aristotle-and-Kant. However, this very conjunction cannot be taken for granted. "Any discussion of the notion of *proairesis* which proceeds in terms of the problem of the 'freedom of the will' is doomed to look for things in Aristotle's work that are not there and to miss what is there."[5] Implicit in this remark by Pierre Aubenque is an entire thesis on (or of) the history of philosophy, one that is attuned to the incommensurability of what, after Heidegger, may be called different "epochs." There is a danger of our completely misunderstanding both thinkers if we attempt to measure Aristotle and Kant by the same yardstick, to place them side by side, even to recompose or perfect one with the aid of the other, as though they were contemporaries, or colleagues, both speaking to us of the same things. Or such is the tenor of the complaints, *mutatis mutandis*, addressed by philosophers from what is known as the hermeneutic tradition to those from the so-called analytic tradition, when the latter, convinced of both the unity of reason and the inevitability of its advancement, endeavor to correct, for example, the formulations and proofs of the principle of noncontradiction with the help of advances in propositional logic made by Frege, Peano, and Russell.[6] Yet on this occasion, it is Arendt and Gadamer,[7] no less than MacIntyre and Nussbaum,[8] who emphasize, each in their own way, by turns the conflict between and the complementarity of "Aristotle-and-Kant." Before we get swept along on this particular tide, let us attempt to specify those considerations that can (or should) hold it in check.

"Excellence," "merit," and "authenticity": these are the characteristics that define the sequence of the "three ages of ethical thought."[9] Luc Ferry has done well to state simply something that we all knew but which, nonetheless, there is a tendency, or a desire, to forget in discussions of "practical philosophy" entangled between Aristotle and Kant. According to Ferry, to speak of excellence (*arête*) is to say that classical morality makes sense only in the context of a certain worldview, a "nature which establishes the ends of man and thus provides a direction to his ethics."[10] But we no longer all live in the same, shared world. When the Moderns made the transition "from the closed world to the infinite universe," they were forced to "seek within the subject itself" for reasons to justify a "limitation that must from now on be thought of as *autolimitation*, as *autonomy*." "[W]here the ethics of the ancients began from a reflection on man's natural *finality*, that of the moderns begins with a theory of the 'good will,' of the free and autonomous will."[11] Virtue could no longer consist in excelling in our nature but lay rather in the fight against that which is natural within us: this, then, is the meaning of "merit." Kant spoke of "Two things: the starry sky above and the moral law within;" "two things," caught in a disjunctive use of "and," in a radical rupture of continuity. Aristotle or Kant: the choice is yours—or, rather, since we are all prisoners of our time, the choice has already been made.

Unless, that is, we are living in a third epoch, one no longer characterized by the Modern subject but rather by the contemporary individual. In that case, the appropriate ethical characteristic would be that of "authenticity," which Luc Ferry defines (in what is, admittedly, a rather unconventional manner) as the conjunction of two demands, both of which seek to deny the legitimacy of the very notion of limitation: self-fulfillment and the right to difference.[12] In fact, we cannot be characterized by authenticity alone, for authenticity is never alone: "What is unprecedented in the contemporary period is the fact that the three ages of ethics, though they would seem to be antithetical, do not in fact cancel each other out—the requirement of authenticity does not imply a total and definitive withdrawal of the principles of excellence and merit."[13] Authenticity, if it is to be valorized, must bear witness to something other than itself: "the courage of virtue," "the power of seduction." Today's world is, according to Ferry, in essence syncretistic and eclectic.

So perhaps today we have finally gained the right to negotiate (albeit in aesthetic terms) the incommensurable and may accordingly speak legitimately of Aristotle-and-Kant. Luc Ferry places a cautionary emphasis on the importance of the idea of human nature in understanding the ethics of the ancient world and, in particular, on the amalgam of skill and practice, which is as necessary a part of becoming a good flautist as it is in learning to become morally "excellent." Yet this warning of Ferry's nevertheless echoes the following comment by Pierre Aubenque: "Even though it does not necessarily exclude a certain exercise of the will, only a *natural gift* can point out the path to follow and clear it of the obstacles with which it is strewn" (and this, Aubenque argues, is the way to read Aristotle's remarks on "deliberation"—not as prefiguring a Modern theory of the "freedom of the will").[14] If we are to affirm the validity of both a distinction between epochs and the essentially syncretistic character of our own, the conclusion to be drawn is simply that contemporary philosophy—which is in the process of becoming—has rights that the history of philosophy would do better to desist from claiming.

The Idea of Nature in Aristotle: The Slave by Nature and the Nature of Man

Yet before concluding that the present discussion will be concerned more with philosophy than the history of philosophy, I would like first, as a historian of philosophy, to revisit what appears to be the key notion of "nature" or "human nature" in Aristotle. My aim in so doing is to make rather clearer why the practical use of this concept is so difficult and perhaps also to cast a few doubts on this notion of clear-cut divisions between epochs.

Aristotle is, in essence, not Kant, and only a fool would claim otherwise. Aristotle makes no distinction between the phenomenal and the noumenal and has no sense of a subject involved in the construction of reality nor of the freedom of the will. Accordingly, in Aristotle, there is a continuity between the starry sky and that which could not at the time have been the moral law and so on. Yet even in the light of these considerations, is it true to say that, in the ancient world represented by Aristotle, "[o]ne can never raise oneself above one's nature, and each person's definition constitutes, so to speak, the prison from which one cannot escape"?[15] This claim of Luc Ferry's concludes his discussion of what is, to a Modern, or contemporary, audience one of the least acceptable aspects of Aristotle's practical philosophy: the idea of the "slave by nature," expounded in book I of the *Politics*. We must concur, initially, with Ferry that this aspect of Aristotelian doctrine is in no sense either marginal or accidental: the house, with its structure of different levels (free men on the one hand, slaves and beasts on the other) even functions as a metaphor for the universe.[16] Jacques Brunschwig has shown how Aristotle, far from trying to justify the institution of slavery as it was in the society in which he lived, chose to skirt around the realities of the day—the "slave-producer" and the "slave-commodity"[17]—and instead to propose a new definition of slavery "as it should be." (By contrast, there may be cause to criticize today's neo-Aristotelians for attempting to legitimize the established order in their own societies.) There are slaves by nature, but nature has failed to give us the ability to recognize them. ("There are some slaves who have the bodies of freemen, as there are others who have a freeman's soul . . . though it is not as easy to see the beauty of the soul as it is to see that of the body."[18]) Brunschwig continues as follows: "What good is it to know that nature has ordained some to be slaves and others to be free, if we are unable to tell one class from the other and if we have no right to assume that the actual status of a person corresponds to the one allotted him by nature?"[19] Yet Brunschwig's is a particularly shrewd variant on a classic line of defense against Aristotelian "slavism": he insists on the difference between theory and practice, between law and fact. For Jacques Brunschwig, Aristotle intends to cast the shadow of a doubt on the institution of property owning. For Martha Nussbaum, the definition of the slave by nature (he who cannot "exercise forethought," which she renders as being unable to "plan a life for oneself"[20]) establishes a condition so restrictive that this class of person proves to be almost entirely empty. Most radical of all readings, finally, is that of W. W. Fortenbaugh: "clearly, there is no such thing as slaves by nature in the world. Aristotle's, accordingly, remains a theoretical proposition."[21]

Yet we cannot let Aristotle off the hook quite this easily. These various lines of defense suggest merely that Aristotle's thought has failed to move with the times, that he is simply stuck in the "ancient world." For the key point, as Luc Ferry has shown, is precisely that there are slaves and free men by *nature* and that the ideal situation (even if it remains unrealized) is one in which the former obey and the latter govern. The "abyss" separating the hierarchies of the Ancients from those of the Moderns consists in the fact that those of the former are "in principle full" (even if they happen to have been "badly filled"), whereas those of the latter are "a priori empty." "Fact and law thus take up inverse positions in the two universes."[22] So we are confronted over and over again by this ubiquitous concept of "nature" in the philosophy of the ancient world, whether in the context of "excellence" (as a natural goal prescribed in the order of things) or in terms of social hierarchy (where inequalities may be *"ascribed to the nature of individuals* and were, as such, *insuperable."*[23]

This concept of an "aristocracy" based on "individual natures" also demands further investigation (Ferry opposes "aristocratic excellence" to "democratic inspiration"). In Aristotle's work, the word "nature" applies at once to the physical world, to man (the human species), to every man in his particularity (insofar as he belongs to a "class" such as that of slaves by nature) and even to what sets him apart as an individual (his variety of *êthos,* rhetoric, ethics, even psychology). Man, and every man (every "individual," then), is "by nature" such and such and, therefore, if you will, has such and such a nature to the extent that he is in the world, that is, in nature. There is, however, a nature that all men share by virtue of their being men, in accordance with the familiar, differential, definition of man as being "alone among the animals" in possessing *logos.*[24] Such is the nature that nature has prescribed for man.

So the question I ask myself is as follows: in what sense is "a person's definition" purely a "prison from which one cannot escape"?[25] Phrased differently, are we entitled to affirm, without further ado, *by treating as equivalent all the meanings of "nature"* (cosmic nature, human nature, and individual nature), that the slave by nature stands beneath the free man in the same way that a stone falls to the ground and in the same sense that the human being stands forever above the plants and the animals and beneath the gods? Or does Aristotle's work suggest a certain conception of the nature of the human being as specifically different, a conception which, for example, would allow the human being to escape, to some extent (and, to be precise, to the extent of its difference from other kinds of animal), from the fixed hierarchy of differences, which is the order of things? (I think, however, that it would be wrong to speak of Aristotle as having "anticipated" such a conception without also adding that such a conception preceded and "influenced" his work, namely, by way of tragedy, the Sophists, and indeed followed with Stoicism). Is not human nature that property of every individual which is *exceptional as a matter of course,* and does it not constitute, whatever the definition of each individual, the path of the transformation, or evolution, of this definition? We return here to the passing remark of a moment ago, which may be banal but on this occasion is by no means anachronistic: it is laid down in the order of things that human nature will be culture.

Before we can develop this particular line of argument, there is one critical objection that must first be addressed. Can we be sure that a slave by nature is a human being and thus that the definition of a human being applies in his case? We know that, in one sense, the slave constitutes a part of the "house" (*oikos*), the "economic" domain, and that he never rises to the rank of citizen. This objection is all the more serious in view of the fact that the opening of the *Politics* makes the ability to live in the city dependent upon possession of *logos*. Moreover, slaves are merely cattle by analogy;[26] indeed, a slave is even described as an "animate article of property" (*ktêma ti empsukhon*).[27] Here, then, are two reasons for doubting that the slave is truly a human being. "The element which is able, by virtue of its intelligence [*têi dianoiai*], to exercise forethought is naturally a ruling and master element; the element which is able, by virtue of its bodily power, to do the physical work is a ruled element, which is naturally in a state of slavery."[28] According to this view, the slave by nature is not a human being but simply a body, the body of the master.[29]

I suggest that, in spite of this division into two separate classes and against the grain of the definition of the slave by nature—shocking, as it is, to our ears—we are nonetheless able to find the resources that will allow us, so to speak, to climb back up the ladder of humanity and to question again all such fixed hierarchies. The slave by nature is a body, granted. Yet a body, a *sôma*, is certainly not just the handle of a rudder—it is not made of "ebony"—for the simple reason that such a handle is never "animate," whereas a body (that is, an animal or a human body) is always animate. Moreover, Aristotle states explicitly that the slave exists, for the master, as "a living but separate part of his body."[30] In the same way that there is always, whatever happens, some amount of soul in a body, there is also, always, in one way or another, something of the *logos* in every soul, even the soul of a slave.

This emerges clearly when Aristotle, at the end of book I, comes to divide up ethical virtues among members of the household:

Here a preliminary question may be raised in regard to the slave. Has he any "excellence" beyond that of discharging his function as an instrument and performing his menial service—any "excellence" of a higher value, such as temperance, fortitude, justice, and the rest of such moral qualities? Or has he no "excellence" outside the area of the bodily services he renders? Either alternative presents difficulties. If slaves have an "excellence" of the higher sort, in what respect will they differ from freemen? If they have not it would be surprising since they are human beings, with a share in the *logos*.[31]

The resolution of this aporia is straightforward enough: there must be different kinds of excellence which correspond to differences between natures. The virtues of one who governs are not the same as those of one who obeys, no more than those of the male or the father can be confused with those of the woman or the child. However, there is more at stake in the resolution of this difficulty: it is striking, first, that the most fitting model to illustrate the relationship between the master by nature and the slave by nature is less that of the relation of the soul to the body which it animates and more that relation which exists between different parts of the soul. It is not enough to assert merely that the master may be likened to the ruling part, "that which has the *logos*" and the slave to the ruled part, "that which does not have it [*tou alogou*],"[32] for Aristotle adds immediately thereafter that "all these people (i.e., slaves, women, and children) possess in common [*enuparkhei*] the different parts of the soul; but they possess them in different ways."[33] The way to loosen the conceptual snare of the slave by nature is not to object that there is no way of knowing whether so-and-so is really a slave of this sort but rather to acknowledge that, by rights, every slave by nature has, to however limited a degree, some share in the *logos*[34] or to recognize, as Aristotle puts it, that the slave is, nevertheless, a man.

If one concedes this point, it seems to me that the slave by nature cannot, in fact, any longer be considered a "prisoner" of his nature. *Logos* alone allows him to transcend (or, more precisely, to transform) this slavish nature. The slave has just enough *logos* to be susceptible to *logos*, that is, to be open to *paideia*, or education. This, moreover, is the last word on slaves in the first book of the *Politics*. As Aristotle puts it: "those who withhold reason from slaves, and argue that only command should be employed, are making a mistake: admonition ought to be applied to slaves even more than it is to children."[35] This relationship between the slave and the child, and particularly the status of the child, is a point of fundamental importance (and, perhaps, as we shall see, a touchstone) with respect to the radical character of the divide between epochs. If the slave may be compared to the child (as indeed the *Meno*, a dialogue which puts *paideia* into practice, already invites us to do by a turn of phrase that is surely far from incidental: "tell me, little one . . ."), this is because both, in their different ways, are imperfect human beings: their *telos* lies beyond them, in a father or master,[36] who represents for them *logos* and the *nous* in complete possession of themselves, in action. The slave has just enough *logos*, as does the child, to be susceptible to cultivation, to reproach, to exhortation. This treatment, despotic though it is, bears a resemblance to the more kingly, paternal task of bringing the child to *logos* by way of *logos*.[37] The effect is to make the slave, as Fortenbaugh notes, "the judge of his own actions" (*Rh.*, 1391 b 10 s). Accordingly, regardless of whether this was the intention, the slave becomes more and more human. Yet none possess *logos* from the beginning, nor indeed is it sufficient to have grasped it once to hold it forever. The definition of man reiterated in book VII of the *Politics*, which addresses this very question of education, may be better understood by recalling that "Reason and thought is the ultimate end of our nature" (VII, 13, 1334 b 15). This suggests the following line of argument: the slave by nature is a man, a man is an animal in possession of *logos*, *logos* is what allows man to come closer to *logos*; so how could the slave by nature, insofar as he is a man, be denied this possibility of self-betterment?

Finally, a clear indication of the importance of this "insofar as he is a man" is to be found in the discussion of *philia*, in book VIII of the *Nicomachean Ethics*, where Aristotle specifies that "I cannot feel *philia* for a horse, an ox, or indeed for a slave *qua* slave. For there is nothing common to the two parties." However, he goes on to add that "*Qua* slave, then [*hêi men oun doulos*], one cannot be friends with him. But *qua* man [*hêi d'anthrôpos*] one can; for there seems to be some justice between any man and any other who can share in a system of law or be a party to an agreement; therefore there can also be friendship with him insofar as he is a man."[38] "One can never raise oneself above one's nature"[39]—except, that is, by way of *paideia*, which is an aspiration by way of the *telos*. It may be objected that this argument is contradicted by the reality of life in ancient Greece, for slaves, when freed, were not usually then educated and, even if they were, they never became citizens. Yet it would then be our turn to reply that we are talking here about principles rather than facts and that the theoretical question of the slaves' humanity remains in spite of this objection.

We must at least acknowledge that there are two opposing forces in play here. The first insists on the difference between the natures of slave and master, whereas the second stresses that all human beings have a nature that is identical. The former appears to be entirely committed to positional fixity, whereas the latter allows room for development. Yet even the former is not quite so positionally fixed as it first appears: its function is to describe the structure of the household (master by nature/slave by nature, but also male/female and father/child). While the structure as such is set in stone, he who is by nature a child, who is born a child, will become, by nature, a man. It will already be clear where the crux of our discussion lies: is the slave by nature more like a woman or more like a child? Indeed, the idea that a slavish nature is inscribed in the body has only been evoked (*banausoi*) in order to finally be rejected. There is no such thing as a biology of the *Untermensch* in Aristotle. Furthermore, the emphasis on exhortation, the insistence on *logos*, the fact that the treatment of slaves and children often goes hand in hand suggests that slaves are closer to children than to women. For no amount of education will ever free women from the world of silence.[40] If the slave is closer to a human being than to an animal and closer to a child than to a woman, then the expression "slave by nature" must primarily denote a place within a structure—that is, within a hierarchy which, in the final analysis, is empty *a priori*, just like that of Modernity.

I trust it will be clear that the point of honor at stake in this last stand is not Aristotle's "slavism," for Aristotle is, *in addition*, "slavist." Rather, this discussion focuses on the concept of nature in all its cosmo-anthro-logical ambiguity. This ambiguity, inherited and handed down by Aristotle, combines a fixed order with the transformative potential, which is a specifically human characteristic. This is why his understanding of the child's place is of such importance. During the era of excellence, the child (*l'enfant*) was required to be nothing more than a small animal whose sole right was the etymological one to remain silent (*infans*). In the age of merit, the child was supposed to be a man in miniature and was expected to already be a morally responsible subject. There really ought to be an unbreachable divide between these two conceptions. And there is, but only if you ignore *paideia* on one side and *Bildung* on the other, both of which would be entirely (if inversely) deprived of their respective *raisons d'être*. This, to my mind, is the thought underlying Martha Nussbaum's objection to Terence Irwin's description (which Nussbaum calls "Kantian") of Aristotelian education. Irwin makes out that education for Aristotle is a sort of behaviorist manipulation, necessary in order to provoke the metamorphosis of the child into an adult capable of making moral choices. Yet Irwin's account fails to lend due weight to the way in which *aisthesis* and *logos* are conjoined and fails to do justice to the complexity of the concept of *logos* itself, a concept that grounds the continuity between the child's animal nature and the pursuit of the *telos* of adulthood.[41]

A different way of phrasing the same reservations would be to suggest that the concept of nature as a teleological prison, which Luc Ferry ascribes to Aristotle, is the direct consequence of a Kantian reading of Aristotle. This is a reading which privileges the formal identity of concepts (nature, end) over and above differences of content (it is only for man that the end of nature is *logos*). Thus what we have rediscovered here—in what is, essentially, simply a rather more "Aristotelizing" reading of Aristotle—are the appropriate methodological principles of *neo*-Aristotelianism.

From Aristotle to Kant: The Slave by Nature and Radical Evil

The concept of nature probably represents, in all honesty, one of the most considerable of the difficulties which each and every practical philosophy is called upon to face. It is a problem which is prone to cross the boundaries between epochs and which, I suggest, contorts the thought of two figures as different as Aristotle and Kant in analogous ways.

I would like to prepare the ground with some cursory, even programmatic, comments that highlight the extent of the difficulty facing any comparative endeavor of this kind and to summarize the entire field of discussion by setting forth the issues which will demand further scrutiny. I then indicate how, latent in the concept of nature, is what I propose to call an *analogy of contortion* between the Aristotelian aporia, of the slave by nature and the difficult Kantian doctrine of radical evil.

I. ARISTOTLE COMES SO VERY CLOSE TO "INVENTING THE WILL"

In favor: Hannah Arendt,[42] among others: "No other Greek philosopher came so close to recognizing the strange lacuna . . . in Greek language and thought";[43] Aristotle introduces "a new faculty into the old dichotomy and thus settle[s] the old quarrel between reason and desire."[44] The choice in favor of reason or desire is a matter for the faculty of choice (*proairesis*): "It opens up a first, small restricted space for the human mind."[45] Let it be noted here that in order to justify what has in fact become a rather common feeling about Aristotle (shared, indeed, by both Irwin and Nussbaum), what is required is a thorough reexamination of the three concepts of *boulêsis*, *proairesis*, and *phronêsis*.

Against: the general line of argument pursued, in particular, by Pierre Aubenque, according to which Aristotle was bringing two different debates into contact with one another. The first was the traditional view that *proairesis* was the basis of imputability, and the second, Aristotle's own, that *proairesis* has no bearing on the end but only on the choice of means. Thus what had formerly been known as *proairesis* (the determination of the end) became *boulêsis*, a process entirely rooted in nature and therefore never "responsible," whether it strives for good (as a result of its definition and therefore without merit) or evil (against nature and therefore implying a pathology or teratology, yet still not implying responsibility). Thus, according to Aubenque, "Aristotle's ethics is the only coherent ethics in Ancient Greece because it locates good and evil not in the absolute of the will (as was later to be the case with the Stoics, who nonetheless also managed without a concept of sin), but in the choice of the means."[46]

The problem with such an interpretation, which Pierre Aubenque makes no attempt to disguise, is that it splits the concept of *proairesis* into two different and incompatible meanings such that, in the final analysis, *proairesis* proves to be inarticulable. On one hand, in book VI, for example, virtue is defined as "a state of character concerned with choice" (*hexis proairetikê*) and is linked to *proairesis* understood as a "deliberative desire [*horexis bouleutikê*] of things in our own power."[47] Yet on the other hand, in book III, *proairesis* is thought of simply as the free choice of means, subject to a prior act of will (in other words, it is the "predeliberated."[48] In contrast to the first interpretation, which retained throughout a place for a practical will analyzable in terms of its end or means, what we appear to have here is the mere juxtaposition of two concepts that are alien to one another, only the second of which is truly Aristotelian.[49]

The strength of the "Kantianizing" reading of Aristotle is also derived from a second observation.

2. ARISTOTLE COMES SO VERY CLOSE TO INVENTING THE DIFFERENCE BETWEEN HETERONOMY AND AUTONOMY

Here we deal with the distinction between acting in conformity with duty but not from duty. Tricot, in his commentary on the *Nicomachean Ethics*, gives voice to a common view when he notes that "we are getting close, here, to the rigorism of Kantian ethics."[50] Here are the two most salient passages:

Aristotle levels the accusation of vicious circularity against his own argument that we become virtuous by doing virtuous things: for if we do virtuous things, he objects, does that not mean we are already virtuous? His answer: no more so than in the case of the *tekhnai*. For it is indeed by doing grammatical things that one becomes a grammarian, provided that one does them grammatically, which is to say neither by chance nor at another's behest. There is, nonetheless, one remaining difference: the property of being grammatical resides in the result, the product, whereas the property of being ethical resides in the subject. Thus "if the acts that are in accordance with the virtues have themselves a certain character it does not follow that they are done justly or temperately. The agent must also be in a certain condition when he does them: in the first place he must have knowledge, second he must choose the acts, and choose them for their own sakes [*proairoumenos di'hauta*] and third his action must proceed from a firm and unchangeable character."[51] Equally, "it is not the man who does these that is just and temperate, but the man who also does them as just and temperate men do them."[52] The weak reading of these passages would have it that their aim is simply to rule out chance and obedience and to specify the importance of an understanding of the means adopted in the practical syllogism (and thus a declension of the act in accordance with the *kairos* of the categories). The strong reading—which is the more plausible—rules out, in addition, action which is merely in conformity with virtue.

The second passage is as follows: "As we say that some people who do just acts are not necessarily just, i.e., those who do the acts ordained by the laws either unwillingly or owing to ignorance or for some other reason and not for the sake of the acts themselves (though, to be sure, they do what they should and all the things that the good man ought), so it is, it seems, that in order to be good one must be in a certain state when one does the several acts, i.e., one must do them as a result of choice and for the sake of the acts themselves [*dia proairesin kai autôn heneka tôn prattomenôn*]."[53] Then comes the distinction between skill (which is independent of the end) and prudence (which cannot exist without skill but which should not be confused with it) and Aristotle's analogy with what is sometimes called "practical mutation," which is to say the difference between "natural virtue" (*arêtê phusikê*) and "ethical virtue" (*arêtê êthikê*). Whence Tricot's note and his translation of *ariston* as "Highest Good," one which is all the more suspect for having been presented as self-evident from the very beginning!

3. YET KANT HAD HIMSELF BLOCKED IN ADVANCE THE POSSIBILITY OF SUCH A CONFLATION OF THESE TWO POSITIONS

The reason for his opposition is as follows: any other practical philosophy aside from his own, and in particular that of Aristotle, is in reality a philosophy of nature and will characteristically be dominated by the notion of the end. For a practical philosophy to be qualified as Kantian, it is not enough for there to be causation by the free will, or choice (which is very probably implied in *boulêsis-proairesis-phronêsis*); rather, in contrast to causality as it operates in the natural world, the will must be subject only to the concept of freedom, to a principle of law entirely divorced from reference to either ends or intentions.

Yet this is quite simply unthinkable from Aristotle's perspective. The notion of an act which proceeds from virtue rather than merely being in conformity with virtue cannot be expressed, nor can such an act be performed, in the Aristotelian universe, without also willing the good or willing happiness; nor can it be performed without also taking into consideration the calculus of ends and means. There are Kantianizing and Aristotelianizing readings, and both Luc Ferry and Pierre Aubenque are right to emphasize the difference. In Aristotle, there is always—at least to some extent—a natural dimension to the end (the will for good) and a natural dimension to the organ best able to discern this end (the "eye" for the good). Accordingly, the alternative which Aristotle himself brings to the fore—is man given his end by nature, or does he provide himself with an end of his own?—is always balanced in favor of the first option. This is particularly apparent in chapter 7 of book III of the *Nicomachean Ethics*: "Whether, then, it is not by nature that the end appears to each man such as it does appear [*mê phusei . . . phainetai*], but something also depends on him [*ti par' auton estin*], or the end is natural but because the good man adopts the means voluntarily [*hekousiôs*] virtue is voluntary, vice also will be none the less voluntary: for in the case of the bad man there is equally present that which depends on himself [*to di' hauton*] in his actions even if not in his end" (1114 b 16–21). The cautious way in which this is phrased ("something also depends on him") indicates that we are never more than "joint causes" (*sunaitioi*) of the dispositions which lead us to posit any particular end. This suffices for responsibility but not for freedom.

In Kantian terms, the will to an end (which refers either wholly or partially to the concept of nature) is not a will to act in accordance with the law (which refers exclusively to the concept of freedom and no other). This is especially clear in the First Introduction to the *Critique of the Power of Judgment*:

> The critique of pure *theoretical* reason, which was dedicated to the sources of all cognition *a priori* (hence also to that in it which belongs to intuition), yielded the laws of nature, the critique of practical reason the law of freedom, and so the *a priori* principles for the whole of philosophy already seem to have

been completely treated. But now if the understanding yields *a priori* laws of nature, reason, on the contrary, laws of freedom, then by analogy one would still expect that the power of judgment, which mediates the connection between the two faculties, would, just like those, add its own special principles *a priori* and perhaps ground a special part of philosophy.[54]

Hence the recurrent distinction (which is also apparent in the *Groundwork to the Metaphysic of Morals*) not just between a "skill" (a "technical imperative" indifferent to its end, whether good or evil) and "prudence" (a "pragmatic imperative" which establishes a nonarbitrary end for itself, namely, happiness), but also between a skill and this new arrival, the categorical imperative. Thus the concept of the "pragmatic" (a free act but one not determined solely by the concept of freedom) allows for the rejection of all "moral" doctrines of prudence and accordingly fends off the baleful misunderstanding that would end up making prudence and thus ethics into a technical branch of the human sciences.

All of the foregoing is made quite explicit in the work of Pierre Aubenque and Luc Ferry alike.

4. CAN THIS REALLY BE THE LAST WORD ON THE MATTER?

It seems to me that the Aristotelian reader's counteroffensive can really be targeted only at the internal difficulties generated by Kant's own use of the concept of "human nature," with all the limitations it imposes.

"Nature," in the Kantian sense of *kuriôs*, is quite clearly the other face of freedom. This is manifestly the case when, for example, Kant asks: "is man by nature morally good or bad? He is neither, for he is not by nature a moral being. He only becomes a moral being when his reason has developed ideas of duty and law."[55] So what does it mean to say, as Kant himself does in *Religion Within the Boundaries of Mere Reason*, that "*The human being is (by nature) either morally good or morally evil*"?[56] Answer: "This only means that he holds within himself a first ground (to us inscrutable) for the adoption of good or evil (unlawful) maxims, *and that he holds this ground qua human, universally*—in such a way, therefore, that by his maxims he expresses at the same time *the character of his species*."[57] This is an "*innate* characteristic," yet one for which Nature is nonetheless not "responsible." For to avoid witnessing the collapse of his entire ethical system, Kant is obliged to hold to the principle that "this subjective ground must, in turn, itself always be a deed of freedom";[58] it is "thus represented as present in the human being at the moment of birth—not that birth itself is its cause."[59] In other words, human "morality" has nothing to do with nature but is nonetheless a characteristic expression of the species.

From this point of view, there are three "original dispositions" which together constitute "human nature":[60] the disposition to animality (the human being as living entity—*The Critique of Pure Reason*), the disposition to humanity (the human being as both living and rational—*The Critique of the Power of Judgment*), and the disposition to personality (the rational human being capable of responsibility—*The Critique of Practical Reason*). The position of the concept of "radical evil" is pinpointed with utmost precision and should be perfectly clear: radical evil is the remainder once all "systematically" impossible meanings have been eliminated. Yet it is hardly surprising if this concept has, as Alexis Philonenko remarks, been "constantly misunderstood."[61] Here, for example, is one of the definitions which typifies Kant's use of this residual compatibility approach: "The statement, 'The human being is *evil*,' cannot mean anything else than that he is conscious of the moral law and yet has incorporated into his maxim the (occasional) deviation from it. 'He is evil *by nature*' simply means that being evil applies to him *considered in his species*; not that this quality may be *inferred from the concept of his species* (i.e., from the concept of a human being in general), for then the quality would be necessary."[62] This paragraph deserves to be quoted in its entirety. For in order to safeguard both freedom (and thus "contingency") and universality (and thus the connection to the species), Kant ends up positing the existence of this "*radical* innate evil in human nature (not any the less brought upon us by ourselves)." The term *nature* refers to a characteristic of the species, universal but not necessary.

It might be thought that, for our purposes, it would be possible to overlook the contortions to which original sin gives rise in Kant's practical philosophy. However, the definition of radical evil, in all its subtlety, determines not only the concept of nature but also that of education, to which it is clearly connected. Radical evil—fragility, impurity, malice—is "perverse" only because it "inverts" the ethical order by prioritizing the motive of self-love over that of obedience to the law. It is this reversal which education is charged with correcting in the child; furthermore, we know that because the child is a moral subject, he or she is aware from the outset of the presence of the moral law within. Thus the "Methodology of Pure Practical Reason"[63] should allow the child to become better aware of the fact that the motive of obedience to the moral law ("virtue only has so high a value here because it comes with such a heavy price") is of greater worth than that of self-love in however altruistic a guise ("not because it brings any profit"). Moreover, there is perhaps the prospect of the human race putting right this same inversion in its own species. Moral education is both a progressive "reform" of the way we feel (virtue, for Kant as for Aristotle, is acquired little by little, through the performance of virtuous acts from the still inappropriate motive of self-love) and a "revolution" in our way of thinking, whereby the maxim of self-love is cast aside for that of saintliness. Moreover, Kant accepts the paradoxical notion that this revolution—just like the child's awareness of the law—must be always already present in order for reform to take place. "With education is involved the great secret of the perfection of human nature. It is only now that something may be done in this direction . . ."[64] The human being will become "disciplined" (tamed), "cultivated" (skillful), "civilized" (prudent), and "moral" (capable of choosing good ends, namely ones which may be universalized). To this list of stages Aristotle would probably have added that the human being will, finally, become "political." Either way, for both thinkers, "All the natural endowments of humankind must be developed little by little out of man himself, through his own effort";[65] in other words, that these potentialities be transformed into realities.

For "Aristotle-and-Kant," then, "a man can only become a man through education."

There is no doubt that the tone changes markedly when Kant assigns determinism and freedom, respectively, to the phenomenal and noumenal realms, as indeed it does with the conception of progress as generic. Yet the method remains the same: it is education that perfects nature's work. Between "rational nature exists as an end in itself"[66] and "Reason and thought is the ultimate end of our nature,"[67] there is certainly more than just a passing resemblance.

The slave by nature is also by nature a man. Man is evil by nature but is naturally neither evil nor good. Are not both these paradoxes—which are formally analogous—symptoms arising from the use of this concept of human nature? Practically impossible though the use of this concept proves, it still seems to be required from time to time in order to convey with a minimum of confusion, if, too, with a strong dose of ideology, that a "reality" (slavery, sin) is being worked on by philosophy.

On the Uses of a Practical Philosophy

Radical though the differences may be between practical reason in Aristotle, a composite concept, and Kant's view of the moral subject as constituted by the freedom of the will, what we have been calling, for the sake of convenience, neo-Aristotelianism, puts forward a series of reconciliatory solutions, the accuracy of which as history of philosophy is quite openly inflected by the strategic needs of a philosophy in the process of becoming. In order to scrutinize the contradictions between these various responses, I suggest that it is worth taking into account the "third man" in each case—not he who benefits from the interpretation but he in whose shadow it takes place. Thus on the chessboard which the history of philosophy quickly becomes (for better and for worse), the respective positions of Aristotle and Kant are determined by that of an other, of the other—by the choice of a third term. Once again in other words, I am suggesting that the typology of the Aristotle-Kant relationship comprises the two pure cases we have briefly discussed[68]—Aristotle/Kant, through a Kantian lens (Ferry), and Aristotle/Kant through an Aristotelian one (Aubenque)— and a virtually indeterminate variety of somewhat finer blends, of which I wish to question neither the interest nor the legitimacy. To make matters clearer, I choose two of these, drawn from the recent work of Anglo-American philosophers, both of which have had a decisive influence in terms of the large body of critical discussion they have generated, discussion which helps make them susceptible to comparison.

One of the interests of Martha Nussbaum's work lies in the way she attempts—with the assistance of Aristotle—to "deplatonize" Kantianism. This is certainly not her main objective—this being, rather, the "fragility of happiness"—but it is nonetheless a necessary phase in order to "justify and give point to the ethical practices in which we actually engage"[69] and to address "the daily conduct of our lives."[70]

In order to demonstrate more fully the complexity of the bond between Aristotle and Kant, united against Plato, I begin by drawing on an article of Nussbaum's, which I have already quoted, one that is devoted to an Aristotelian critique of Plato: "Shame, Separateness, and Political Unity: Aristotle's Criticism of Plato." The Greece of the *aidôs*, which is that of Plato no less than that of Aristotle, is a civilization of "shame" or, if you prefer, of "self-respect"; the question is whether, as Aristotle suggests but as Plato denies, "separateness and autonomy of choice are . . . necessary for self-respect."[71]

The question that preoccupies Martha Nussbaum's Aristotle is accordingly: "What is the relationship between self-respect and autonomy of choice?"[72] Aristotle privileges, as he constantly states in the *Politics*, the distributive over the collective,[73] the properly political interrelation of separate free beings over and above organic unity (which is simply "economic," in the sense of familial) and prefers to look for an ethical foundation in "the considered consensus of the greatest number and of the wise" rather than in "the vision of a single expert." By contrast, to return to the topic of slavery, almost all of Plato's human beings are no more than slaves by nature in relation to the philosopher-king; what is more, they are probably ineducable in the Aristotelian sense. In short, Aristotle tolerates "a certain amount of disorder for the sake of autonomy."[74] Martha Nussbaum is careful to emphasize the fact that this is a "deliberative autonomy,"[75] the very form of freedom which the slave qua slave lacks and without which no life could really be a "good life." For a life to be "good" in the Aristotelian sense, it must be chosen "from within" by the power of practical reason, which is common to all. This limited form of freedom, which is compatible with—and may even demand—the distinction between slaves and masters, is by no means identical to the kind of absolute freedom which resides in the realm of the Kantian noumenon, upon which any restriction whatsoever would be a contradiction in terms. This notwithstanding, it is clear that Aristotle and Kant are on the same side: against Plato.

Yet the relationship between these philosophers changes in *The Fragility of Goodness*. For here, Nussbaum is first concerned with guarding against any Kantian, or indeed Kantianized, reading of the Greek texts on the grounds that the immediate effect of such a reading would be to make an irrelevant distinction between moral and nonmoral values, for example, "luck" (the "hap" in "happiness"). Nussbaum equips the reader with a handy table of reference in the form of a purposely sketchy list in two columns, intended to allow the reader to identify two (and perhaps the only two) of the "normative conceptions of human practical rationality."[76] On one side there is the entirely active agent who cuts himself off from all external influence and leads a good life in isolation. On the other, the combination of positive elements with elements rejected from the first column produces an agent who is both active and receptive, who strikes a balance between control and risk, between internal and external influences, and who aims to lead a good life alongside friends and loved ones—in a community. The first is a Platonic vision; the second, an Aristotelian one, which reaches back, past Plato, in a return to the origins of tragedy. Yet at this point in Nussbaum's account it is already assumed—as it will be throughout the work— that the Platonizing tendency is also a Kantian tendency, as the following remark, typical of many, suggests: "The middle-period Platonist (and the modern Kantian) might reply. . . ."[77] On this occasion, Kant is on Plato's side: against Aristotle.

Yet I do not believe for one moment that these two approaches are incompatible. When Aristotle and Kant are aligned against Plato, Aristotle is with Kant in seeking to recognize the existence of something like freedom—the capacity and the duty to choose freely in practice, shared by all men insofar as they are men. But Aristotle is also opposed to Kant, who here is on Plato's side, when Aristotle argues against the right of the moral agent to live in exclusion, one which would exclude any relation between his inner being and outer reality. As I have already suggested, it is this continuity of the inside with the outside and similarly of the animal and child with the adult man that provides the most compelling reason to reject Irwin's indissolubly Platonic-Kantian perspective on the appearance of *proairesis* and the supposed mutation into a moral subject. After all, we do not bring up our children as either Plato or Kant would have.

According to the interpretation outlined by Nussbaum, which becomes more intelligible once the presence of Plato is acknowledged, if Kant may at times have gotten in the way of our reading Aristotle, it is now Aristotle's turn to let us live Kant.[78]

KANT, NIETZSCHE, ARISTOTLE

Alasdair MacIntyre, at least in *After Virtue*,[79] orchestrates the confrontation between Aristotle and Kant to the accompaniment not of Plato but Nietzsche, a philosopher who, in that he hardly risks being confused with either of the other two, perhaps makes one of the fiercest of third parties.

The key to MacIntyre's argument—which is dramatized at the beginning of his book in the "disquieting suggestion" of a catastrophe affecting the discourse of the natural sciences—lies in becoming aware of the fact that "modern moral utterance and practice can only be understood as a series of fragmented survivals from an older past."[80] This is why the project of the Enlightenment must itself fail, for as Kant acknowledged magnanimously, it remains within a theological frame, a frame presupposed explicitly in the concept of pure practical reason, the disappearance of which renders the entire project quite simply incomprehensible. It is at this point that Nietzsche steps in, "as the Kamahameha II of the European tradition," one competent to inform us Polynesians that "good," "right," and "obligatory" are linguistic vestiges that have become severed from their historical roots and today have no more meaning than "taboo." Thus in *The Gay Science*, ethics takes a kind of *linguistic turn*.

It is in this context that MacIntyre seeks to promote Aristotle. For if the defeat of Kant goes without saying, Nietzsche's triumph still depends upon a hypothesis: "the only alternatives to Nietzsche's moral philosophy turn out to be those formulated by the philosophers of the Enlightenment and their successors"[81] or, in other words, those of "liberal individualism in some version or other."[82] But this is not the case; indeed quite the opposite is true. The failure of the Enlightenment and subsequently the failure of Nietzsche's demonstration of its failure are in fact "nothing other than an historical sequel to the rejection of the Aristotelian tradition."[83] Thus MacIntyre calls upon Aristotle on two occasions: first, because his theology and his teleology provide the interpretative matrix without which any form of Kantianism is little more than a tattered garment; second, because Aristotle's is the only other available conception of morality and even the only form of moral reasoning that is truly consistent,[84] which means that the underlying question is and always has been: "was it right in the first place to reject Aristotle?"[85]

MacIntyre's Aristotle stands, of course, in the great tradition of Greek anthropologico-philosophical thinking (*aidôs, agôn, polis*), in which virtue denotes the excellence required on each occasion by the role or function of a mortal being. Furthermore, from the Sophists to Cicero, it is a question not of virtue in the singular but of *virtues*.[86] By anchoring the domain of the practical in the nature and specific end of man, Aristotle forges the moral thinking that undergirds the "classical conception of man" and lends such weight to the allegation of naturalistic fallacy, effectively overloading it such that it ceases to hold. This is the happy chance of an ethics of happiness: the individual is, by nature, in continuity with both the world and his fellow beings.

Education adds the finishing touches to this harmonization of feeling and action: "To act virtuously is not, as Kant was later to think, to act against inclination; it is to act from inclination formed by the cultivation of the virtues. Moral education is an *éducation sentimentale*."[87] Education also adds the finishing touches to the perfect harmony of goods distributed in accordance with *philia* within a human community. It is only when "men came to be thought of as in some dangerous measure egoistic by nature; it is only once we think of mankind as by nature dangerously egoistic that altruism becomes at once socially necessary and yet apparently impossible and, if and when it occurs, inexplicable. On the traditional Aristotelian view such problems do not arise."[88]

Nietzsche's critique loses all foothold once it ceases to be the case that rules determine virtues (or, worse still, that the formalism of the moral law determines virtues), and instead it is virtues that govern rules. However, the requirement for intelligibility is entirely satisfied: Aristotle's insistence on the practical syllogism amounts to an attempt to elaborate the necessary conditions for accounting for any human action, such that a life may indeed have the appearance of a "narrative unity." It will come as no surprise, then, to find that the Aristotelian tradition can be "restated in a way that restores intelligibility and rationality to our moral and social attitudes and commitments."[89]

None of these analyses are surprising. However, the conclusion is unexpected and strives to surprise by its brutal naïveté: Nietzsche *or* Aristotle, Trotsky *and* St. Benedict. Exactly what kind of worlds or communities does that particular partnership promise? It is quite likely that liberal discourse is made up entirely of bits and pieces. But could one imagine a fragment more kitschy than this Aristotle who allows us to read only Aristotle yet who is immersed in a form of society that is so very opposed to the Aristotelian vision? Unless perhaps MacIntyre is asking us to imagine the virtues of Aristotle's practical philosophy in a non-Aristotelian world—in the world of merit and authenticity, of Kant and Heidegger. In which case, the first of these virtues will surely be to restore the intelligibility of the everyday, along with a degree of good conscience, to "us," to every "I," in daily life. For we do not think of ourselves as phenomena at one moment and noumena the next, as physically determined, then morally free, bridging the gap with an ever-resourceful philosophy of judgment. Rather, we perceive ourselves, and accordingly conceive of ourselves, as individuals who—body and soul—have but one single history. "Thus, the history of nature begins with goodness, for it is the work of God; but the history of freedom begins with evil, for it is the work of man."[90] If instead of this dichotomy and this noumenal anguish we were now to begin to look instead to something along the lines of Aristotle's dictum that "Every art and every inquiry, and similarly every action and pursuit, is thought to aim at some good,"[91] we would show ourselves to be more Aristotelian than we are Kantian in our elaboration of an inalienable right to well-being.

I would now like to draw together the various strands of the preceding discussion, one prompted by the constant juxtaposition of Aristotle and Kant in contemporary thinking: the distinction between epochs, the difficulties of the concept of nature and the presence of philosophical third parties who serve to suggest that Aristotle and Kant are, by turns, staunch allies and bitter enemies.

Nature—as we have seen both in the case of the slave by nature and in that of radical evil—is the cross which every form of practical philosophy is obliged to bear. The use of this concept of nature as a means of distinguishing one epoch from another can lead only to further difficulties. We might use the concept more profitably to mark out a transhistorical difference between, let us say, one style of philosophizing and another.

Were I, from this perspective, to propose a new grouping, it would be the following: the Sophists, Aristotle, and Kant. It would then be immediately clear that the idea of nature is by no means a characteristic of antiquity in its entirety even after we had distinguished between the various different meanings of the concept. This is a commonplace in the work of the Sophists, at any rate, which gets repeated on every possible occasion and in every possible domain: there is no such thing as nature, and, in particular, there is nothing natural about so-called human nature. Gorgias wrote a treatise titled *On What is Not or On Nature,* in which it is convention par excellence, *logos,* which finally provides the antiphysical model of this nature which is not, or is not one. Protagoras maintained that all is relative to a standard which differs on every occasion, to a convention which it may prove expedient to extend and make stable or preferable to attempt to improve. Nor indeed are ethics and politics ever matters of nature, even in the case of the famous myth of the *Protagoras* (of *aidôs* and *dikê,* this additional gift from Zeus, which is the source of all "political virtue"), which is reinterpreted by Protagoras himself in the course of the very narration which gives meaning to the myth in terms of a sharing of *logos* by way of pedagogy throughout the entire city, from the wet nurse to the magistrate. Antiphon is renowned for being (unlike Aristotle) on the right side with respect to the question of slavery in that "by nature we are all just as much barbarians as we are Greeks" and because we all breathe the air "through our nose and mouth"; yet even he makes of nature a mere horizon which is always secondary and forever being pushed into second place, beyond the initial sphere of the *nomos*, which governs the arrangement of the public sphere in which we are immediately immersed. (And this complicates quite considerably the task of those of his interpreters who seek to present him as a precursor of "natural law.")

I would assert with confidence that some of the tensions which permeate Aristotle's work, in particular in the area of politics and rhetoric, of which the problem of the slave by nature is a clear example, can be explained only in terms of a hesitation on the philosopher's part between the Sophists and Plato. Aristotle's final decision to stand with the Sophists represented an attempt to guard against a danger inherent in Platonism that was felt to pose the more serious threat. That aside, the idea that antiquity could be distinguished by the undisputed preeminence of the concept of nature can probably be rejected: in Aristotle's time there existed, moreover, a critical awareness with respect to this concept that was often lacking in Kant's era, indeed even in Kant's work itself.

All this has repercussions when it comes to deciding on the nature of democracy. "If excellence is in essence aristocratic, merit on the other hand is of democratic inspiration. Since it is ascribed to a domain other than that of innate talent, no one can be said to be a priori wanting of it."[92] A claim of this sort can, it seems to me, be dismantled in the following manner. On the one hand, we reencounter here the same ambiguities with respect to the concept of nature and the idea of ascribing constitutive sense to the concept of human nature. For nor is anyone (any man) deprived of humanity *a priori*. There is no formal difference between having *logos* and having a good will. The concept of nature can only ever fix in place the *a priori*.

On the other, let us for a moment examine the matter not from an ethical standpoint but rather from the sociopolitical perspective called for by these very terms, aristocracy and democracy. When we say that a democratic society functions, or should function, "on the basis of merit," we mean that instead of valuing so-called natural inequalities (race, strength, beauty), it should endeavor instead to encourage work and effort—but also, most probably, skills and results. It is accordingly no coincidence that, in republican schemes of value, excellence and merit are closely intertwined (excellence awards for kids and merit awards for for farmers). The Sophists, in this sense, were true republicans. They held that one skill alone—*logos*—was the equal of every other and perhaps also their one source. This skill is both shared by all (hence Zeus's demand that everyone be given their portion of political virtue) and is capable of achieving excellence (hence the idea that Protagoras both speaks and teaches others to speak better than anyone else).

Once again, merit and excellence are not to be found in the ethical domain but, from the very beginning, in the political. This distinction, at least in theory, is perhaps among the most important of those elements of democracy handed down by the Sophists—through the intermediary of Aristotle, who chose to write both an *Ethics* and a *Politics* rather than a single *Republic*, and through Kant—to the world of today.

Translated by Oliver Davis

NINE

Greeks and Romans: Paradigms of the Past
in Arendt and Heidegger

Philosophy and Political Thought

If we are to compare Arendt with Heidegger—or indeed with any philosopher—it is best, I think, to take as our clue or guideline a fact which she herself continually stresses. "I am not a philosopher," she insists, not even "a professor of political philosophy" but rather "a professor of political theory" or of "political thought." Or again, using the terminology of Kant (who represents in her eyes the grand exception to the normal relationship between philosophy and politics), she writes: "I am not a thinker by profession." Thus in a television interview made in 1964, Günter Gaus introduced her as a philosopher. She retorted: "I'm afraid I have to protest: I do not belong to the philosophers' circle. My profession, if one can even speak of it at all, is political theory. I neither feel like a philosopher, not do I believe that I have been accepted into the circle of the philosophers, as you kindly suppose."[1] Gaus was unconvinced and asked her to explain the difference between political philosophy and her work as professor of political theory. She replied with complete assurance: "The difference, you see, depends on the thing itself. . . . [Philosophers] do not behave neutrally toward politics—since Plato's time it's no longer possible. . . . It is in the very essence of the thing—I mean, in the question of politics as such—that the hostility lies."[2]

This sharp distinction between political philosophy and political thought determines the structure of her essay "Martin Heidegger at Eighty": "We who wish to honour the thinkers, even if our own residence lies in the midst of the world, can hardly help finding it striking and perhaps exasperating that Plato and Heidegger, when they entered into human affairs, turned to tyrants and Führers. This should be imputed not just to the circumstances of the times and even less to preformed character, but rather to what the French call a *déformation professionnelle*."[3]

This repulsion—in the proper sense of the word—is set out more analytically (if not more philosophically) in *Thinking*, the first volume of *The Life of the Mind*. In chapter 3, Arendt raises the question: "What makes us think?" Sections on "The pre-philosophic assumptions of Greek philosophy" (§14) and "The answer of Socrates" (§17)—which is itself less philosophical than it seems—enclose the two "professional" answers of Plato (§15) and of the Romans (§17). Plato's answer is contained in a single word: *thaumazein*, "to wonder." Philosophy, according to the *Theætetus* (155D), is "the daughter of Thaumas." Arendt adds: "The Platonic wonder, the initial shock that sends the philosopher on his way, was revived in our own time when Heidegger, in 1929, concluded a lecture entitled 'What is metaphysics?' with the words . . . 'why is there anything at all and not, rather, nothing?' and called this 'the basic question of metaphysics.'"[4] Heidegger's conceit of connecting *denken* (to think) with *danken* (to thank), which leads to the untranslatable notion of *Gelassenheit*, is evidently not Platonic. Nonetheless, for Heidegger, to philosophize or to wonder is quite certainly a matter of looking for the invisible in the visible.

The answer given by the Roman philosophers, of whom the Stoics are the paradigms, turns for its part on the "divorce" between man and the world: "The trick discovered by Stoic philosophy is to use the mind in such a way that reality cannot touch its owner."[5] That is why Hegel, who relocates the whole world inside consciousness, is in the end their legatee. As Arendt subtly observes, whenever philosophy is construed as science, we find ourselves back in the old Stoic position.

These two factors—Platonic wonder and the Stoic divorce between man and the world—are "different to the point of being opposites."⁶ Yet at the same time they are closely related to one another, for in both cases, "thinking leaves the world of appearances." Thus from Parmenides to Plato and from the Stoics to Hegel, "this bracketing of reality . . . has remained one of the great temptations of the professional thinkers."⁷ Hence the *déformation professionnelle*.

It should be noted that Heidegger does not merely echo Plato. At bottom, he represents the intersection of the two answers. From Parmenides to Plato—and to Heidegger, philosophy is a matter of looking for the invisible in the visible, of seeking the Being of being. And yet from the Stoics to Hegel—and to Heidegger, philosophy is also found in "the merging of acting and thinking."⁸ In her "Conclusions," Arendt analyzes "Heidegger's will-not-to-will" and his "reversal," which she places between the two volumes of his *Nietzsche*. She writes of Heidegger's "History of Being"—in which the main event is the change in the concept of truth, which must be accepted, and not the invention of the telescope—that it simply looks like "another, perhaps a bit more sophisticated, version of Hegel's ruse of reason . . . , or divine Providence."⁹ The difference is, if anything, to Heidegger's disadvantage: "With Heidegger, this Nobody, allegedly acting behind the back of acting men, has now found a flesh-and-blood incarnation in the existence of the thinker, who acts while he does nothing, a person, to be sure, and even identifiable as 'Thinker'—which, however, does not signify his return into the world of appearances. He remains the '*solus ipse*' in the 'existential solipsism,' except that now the fate of the world, the History of Being, has come to depend on him."¹⁰

Despite her revulsion to professional thinkers, Arendt is herself a thinker. She conducts, as she puts it, "exercises in political thought" (the subtitle of *Between Past and Future*). And it is here that the past—that antiquity—comes in.

In the preface to *Between Past and Future*, Arendt describes the activity of thinking as a matter of "settling down in the gap between past and future."¹¹ Moreover, she defines the modern era as the age in which the condition of the thinker becomes the condition of everyman: "When the thread of tradition finally broke, the gap between past and future ceased to be a condition peculiar only to the activity of thought and restricted as an experience to those few who made thinking their primary business. It became a tangible reality and perplexity for all; that is, it became a fact of political relevance."[12] It follows simply enough that Arendt, inasmuch as she is a modern, is herself, like the rest of us, in the condition of the thinker. That is how we must understand her favorite appeal to Char's epigram: "Our inheritance was left to us by no testament."

Nevertheless, when, at the end of the first volume of *The Life of the Mind*, Arendt wishes to draw attention not to her method or her criteria or her values but rather to what she calls her "basic assumption,"[13] this is how she gives substance to the activity of thinking: "I have clearly joined the ranks of those who for some time now have been attempting to dismantle metaphysics, and philosophy with all its categories, as we have known them from their beginning in Greece until today. Such dismantling is possible only on the assumption that the thread of tradition is broken and that we shall not be able to renew it."[14] In referring to the attempt to dismantle metaphysics, she is in effect calling herself a Heideggerian, for it is Heidegger, and Heidegger alone, to whom she pays tribute for the fact that the dismantling or "collapse took place in a manner worthy of what had preceded it"[15]—and here she is a thinker and nothing but a thinker. However, she continues, "historically speaking, what actually has broken down is the Roman trinity that for thousands of years united religion, authority and tradition. The loss of this trinity does not destroy the past, and the dismantling process itself is not destructive; it only draws conclusions from a loss which is a fact and as such no longer a part of the 'history of ideas' but of our political history, the history of our world."[16] Arendt expresses her fundamental difference from Heidegger immediately after her tribute to him: she does not think, she thinks politics—she thinks our political history.

Out of Antiquity

Only on this basis, I think, can we compare Arendt and Heidegger with regard to their relationship to antiquity.

First, both Arendt and Heidegger, the relationship can only be a "free" one: no philistinism, they say, no scholarship, no philology. Arendt pays tribute to Heidegger in the following terms: "There was someone . . . who, precisely because he knew that the thread of tradition was broken, was discovering the past anew . . . Thinking has come to life again; the cultural treasures of the past, believed to be dead, are being made to speak, in the course of which it turns out that they propose things altogether different from the familiar, worn-out trivialities they had been presumed to say."[17] And she speaks of her own work in the same way: "With the loss of tradition we have lost the thread which safely guided us through the vast realms of the past, but this thread was also the chain fettering each successive generation to a predetermined aspect of the past. It could be that only now will the past open up to us with unexpected freshness and tell us things no-one has yet had ears to hear."[18] Culture is "a field of ruins": that is "the great chance" which allows us "to discover the past for ourselves," to "read its authors as though nobody had ever read them before."[19]

Moreover, for both Arendt and Heidegger, the free relationship with the past is allied to the fact that interpretation and criticism are forms of experiment. Thus, in the preface to *Between Past and Future*, we hear an echo of what Heidegger, in §7 of *Sein und Zeit*, calls "the phenomenological method of inquiry": we must, Arendt says, "discover the real origins of traditional concepts in order to distill from them anew their original spirit which has so sadly evaporated from the very key words of political language . . . leaving behind empty shells with which to settle almost all accounts regardless of their underlying phenomenal reality."[20] The "original spirit" is necessarily tied to phenomenal experience and to a phenomenological attention.

This, moreover, is why the constant focus of attention is language—key words and their etymologies. We shall find examples aplenty in both authors. Yet there is still the same difference between them, and it must be stressed. In *Men in Dark Times*, referring to Walter Benjamin, Arendt observes that "any period to which its own past has become as questionable as it has for us must eventually come up against the phenomenon of language, for in it the past is contained ineradicably, thwarting all attempts to get rid of it once and for all." Thus far, Arendt is Heideggerian. Then she speaks in her own voice: "The Greek polis will continue to exist at the bottom of our political existence—that is, at the bottom of the sea—for as long as we use the word 'politics.' "[21] The Aristotle whom we hear at this point in Arendt's text is not the descriptive phenomenologist: "Wherever the relevance of speech is at stake, matters become political by definition, for speech is what makes man a political being."[22] Thus the term *logos* is not taken, either uniquely or primarily, with the same tone and sense.

This attention to language implies that, for Arendt as for Heidegger, we may finish up with fragments. At the end of the first volume of *The Life of the Mind*, the "empty shells" which constitute our key concepts are found to be echoed in some lines from Shakespeare's *Tempest*:

Full fathom five thy father lies,
Of his bones are coral made,
Those are pearls that were his eyes. Nothing of him that doth fade
But doth suffer a sea-change
Into something rich and strange.

"It is with such fragments from the past," Arendt comments, "after their sea-change, that I have dealt there . . . If some of my listeners or readers should be tempted to try their luck at the technique of dismantling, let them be careful not to destroy the 'rich and strange, the 'coral' and the 'pearls,' which can probably be saved only as fragments."[23]

Here, however, the difference between Arendt and Heidegger can once again be seen. For Arendt, the crucial point about fragmentation is that it involves a story: what we need is not eyes for the phenomena but ears for the past. With this, we touch upon Arendt's conception of history, which is made explicit in, for example, "Understanding and Politics": "Whenever an event occurs that is great enough to illuminate its own past, history comes into being. Only then does the chaotic maze of past happenings emerge as a story which can be told, because it has a beginning and an end."[24] The crises of the modern age allow us to transmute the sublime chaos of empty shells and pearls into a story. The past becomes a story: Arendt does not offer us a history—whether historial or historical—of concepts or of thought; she tells us the stories or histories of concepts and of thought. *Out of Antiquity*—as one says *Out of Africa*.

Greeks and Romans

The thread I shall follow is the contrast between political thought and pro-
fessional thought or thought about thought. And with its help I shall ana-
lyze more closely the different dealings that Arendt and Heidegger have
with the past.

We must, I think, begin with the most impressive piece of evidence:
Arendt and Heidegger refer to different pasts. Arendt makes a double refer-
ence—to the Greeks and to the Romans. For Heidegger there is only one
reference point: the Greeks—and again the Greeks.

One may say, with only a little exaggeration, that for Heidegger the rela-
tion between Rome and Greece is one of translation and betrayal. When
Heidegger invokes Latin it is usually to show how the translation of Greek
terms betrays the Greek experience of *alêtheia*. *Veritas* bolts the door on
alêtheia, and Heidegger's intellectual journey takes him "upstream" (by
what René Char calls a *retour amont*) from the Latins to the Greeks—and
then from the Greeks to what is more Greek than the Greeks.

To indicate the tone and substance of this relation, one quotation may
suffice. It comes from Heidegger's essay "The Origin of the Work of Art":

> By these [Greek] determinations . . . the Western interpretation of the Being
> of beings [is] stabilized. The process begins with the appropriation of Greek
> words by Roman-Latin thought. *Hupokeimenon* becomes *subjectum*, *hupostasis*
> becomes *substantia*, *sumbebêkos* becomes *accidens*. However, this translation of
> Greek names into Latin is in no way the innocent process it is considered to
> this day. Beneath the seemingly literal and thus faithful translation there is
> concealed, rather, a translation of Greek experience into a different way of
> thinking. *Roman thought takes over the Greek words without a corresponding,
> equally original experience of what they say, without the Greek word*. The
> rootlessness of Western thought begins with this translation.[25]

Heidegger's *Parmenides*, written in 1942–43, treats expressly of the reper-
cussions which this rootlessness has had on political thought: "We think
politics in a Roman way, that is to say in an imperial way."[26] "Since the im-
perial age, the Greek word 'political' has meant something Roman. Noth-
ing of the Greek remains but the bare sound."[27] *Imperium* (*im-parare*, "to

provide oneself with"), "Thou shalt," *ius*, which no longer derives from *"dikê"* the goddess who shows, but from *iustitia*: all these terms point to the transformation of *alêtheia* into *veritas*. And the difference emerges even more markedly with the transposition of *pseudos* (what dissembles) into *falsum* (what fells or lays low). Eliane Escoubas rightly suggests an analogy between *imperium romanum* or *pax romana* (from *pango*, "to fix") and *falsum/verum*. In fact, "if we consider more closely the process by which the Romans took over the language, thought, and culture of the Greeks, we can see how *falsum* (what lays one low) has changed the sense of *pseudos* (what dissembles), assimilating and thereby supplanting it. Such an assimilation is always the most dangerous—and also the most enduring—form of domination. From then on, the West has known *pseudos* only in the form of *falsum*."[28] Thus in every area at once the Latin translation of Greece constitutes a first and decisive check on disclosedness.

The reaction against Latinity and the concern for the Greek original hidden beneath the translation is certainly one of the elements in Arendt's attitude to the past. Here are two particularly fine examples. First, her analysis of the notion of a "spectator" in *The Life of the Mind*. The passion for seeing, a fundamental Greek attitude which at one and the same time determines the *polis* as the space of appearances and philosophy as a theoretical concern, loses all its sense in Lucretius's celebrated line: "To see from what troubles you yourself are free is joy indeed." Seeing is here simply a matter of being present in safety at the unleashing of a storm. "Here of course the philosophic relevance of spectatorship is entirely lost—a loss that befell so many Greek notions when they fell into Roman hands."[29]

A second example, more strictly Heideggerian, bears on the Latin translation of Aristotle. To render *zôion politikon* by *animal sociale*, as Seneca and Aquinas do, completely suppresses the Greek experience: instead of the distinction between public and private, *polis* and *oikia*, to which Aristotle alluded, it invokes the fellowship of the human species, of a biological rather than a political entity. "More than any elaborate theory, this unconscious substitution of the social for the political betrays the extent to which the original Greek understanding of politics had been lost."[30] The translation of *zôion logon ekhon* by *animal rationale* "rests on no less fundamental a misunderstanding."[31] For once again—for Aristotle and for all the Greeks—the definition was exclusively political. This is plainly indicated by the fact that barbarians and slaves can be called *aneu logou*, "deprived, of course, not of the faculty of speech, but of a way of life in which speech and only speech made sense."[32] So, too, Heidegger, for example, in his *Parmenides*, observes that *zôion*, "living thing," should be thought of in its relation to *phusis*, or "nature," and not in its relation to biology, as has been the case since the Roman era.[33]

Thus the Romans had no ear, whether philosophical or political, for Greece. But their deafness, according to Arendt, can be explained. In her view, the Roman experience cannot be analyzed as a modification of a single and fundamental original experience, namely, the experience of the Greeks. Rather, it constitutes in its own right an experience no less fundamental. The experience, however, is not an experience in thinking—it is not theoretical or philosophical. It is an exclusively political experience—and indeed it is precisely here that its originality lies.

"Common opinion on philosophy was formed by the Romans, who became the heirs of Greece, and it bears the stamp, not of the original Roman experience, which was exclusively political, . . . but of the last century of the Roman republic."[34] In fact, in the conservation of "the Greek heritage, which the Romans, but never the Greeks, knew how to take care of and how to preserve,"[35] we may trace with precision the nature and form of the betrayal which the Roman translation signified, for it may be said that Rome preserved Greek political philosophy as if it were the whole of philosophy. And this is the basis on which we now live. "Even today we believe that Aristotle defined man primarily as a political being endowed with speech or reason, which he did only in a political context, or that Plato exposed the original meaning of his doctrine of ideas in *The Republic*, where, on the contrary, he changed it for political reasons."[36] "In spite of the grandeur of Greek political philosophy, it may be doubted that it would have lost its inherent utopian character if the Romans, in their indefatigable search for tradition and authority, had not decided to take it over and acknowledge it as their highest authority in all matters of theory and thought."[37]

Now, the slide from Greek political philosophy to philosophy *simpliciter* and the subordination of Rome to Greece are merely consequences of the original Roman experience of politics: the experience of foundation. The "tradition," which is defined by the Roman trinity of authority, culture, and religion and which the modern age sees in crisis, derives precisely from the decision to subordinate Roman culture to Greek thought, or, in other words, to "found" it. In "What Is Authority?" and also in *The Human Condition*, Arendt contrasts *polis* and *patria* term by term in an incomparable piece of analysis. "There is no more elemental difference between Greece and Rome than their respective attitudes toward territory and law."[38] "Wherever you go, you will be a *polis*"—that is the motto of the Greek colonists."[39] On the other hand, *ab urbe condita* roots in the soil; it is the motto of an empire that would make the Western world Rome's hinterland. There are several *poleis*, several cities: there is one *urbs*, one town. The founder and the legislator in a Greek city are foreigners, sometimes barbarians, for the laws are never more than a rampart behind which a *polis* may shelter itself. It is only after the foundation and after the legislation that political life begins. For Rome, on the other hand, the founder and the legislator are *patres patriae*. In the same way, Roman religion "ties back," *re-ligat*, to the foundation; *auctoritas*, from *augere*, "increases" the foundation. Political authority at Rome lies with the Senate, which is characterized by its *gravitas*, that is to say, by its ability to carry the weight of the past and to provide ballast for the ship of state. To grow old is to lean toward the past, to lean toward the source of authority, and when you are a Roman, you aim to imitate. But if you are a Greek, then—to borrow Goethe's epigram, which Arendt herself cites in this context—to grow old is "to withdraw from the world of appearances." A Greek does not imitate: he competes.

This fundamental opposition between the two political experiences—the space of appearances in the *polis*, the foundation of the *patria*—leads us to the "historically all-important fact" that "the Romans felt they needed founding fathers and authoritative examples in matters of thought and ideas as well, and accepted the great 'ancestors' in Greece as their authorities for theory, philosophy, and poetry."[40] This is the way to explain the paradox inherent in the Roman idea of foundation. Unlike the Jewish foundation, whose chronology begins with the creation of the world, it was necessary—to avoid breaking the thread of tradition—that the Roman foundation be at one and the same time primary and nonprimary. This is how

Virgil's *Fourth Eclogue* must be interpreted: the foundation of Rome is also a rebirth of Troy.[41]

The subordination of Rome to Greece was a consequence of this search for authority, which was itself a consequence of the fundamental political experience of the Romans.

This is why Greece silenced Rome no less than Rome silenced Greece. "The Greek concepts, once they have been sanctified by the Romans through tradition and authority, simply eliminated from historical consciousness all political experiences which could not be fitted into their framework."[42] All political experiences—and certainly the experience of foundation. The great chance given us by the ruin of culture—to return to *Between Past and Future*—is that we can at last "look upon the past with eyes undistracted by any tradition, with a directness which has disappeared from Occidental reading and hearing since Roman civilisation submitted to the authority of Greek thought."[43] We can at last listen to the Romans: we can hear them, with Arendt, alongside the Greeks—two fundamental experiences which do not form a sequence, two irreducible events. We need no longer think of the Romans, with Heidegger, as, following the Greeks, a mere running out.

Greeks and Greeks

Here, too, we should no doubt first stress the similarity. For Arendt and for Heidegger alike, there is an opposition internal to the Greek corpus itself—a divide within the Greek world, a sort of relationship between Greeks and Greeks.

I deal briskly with Heidegger inasmuch as I am concerned here only with the comparison between him and Arendt. For Heidegger, the relationship between the Presocratics on the one hand and the other Greeks, like Plato and Aristotle, on the other, is analogous, *mutatis mutandis*, to the relationship between the Greeks and the Romans. Marlène Zarader's paper, "Le miroir aux trois reflets, histoire d'une évolution?"[44] helpfully distinguishes three phases in Heidegger's thought. First, there is a period in which the Greeks are opposed to Rome and to the tradition which Rome represents: "the Greeks thought what the later tradition would forget." No divide yet between the Presocratics and Plato, and when, during his Marburg period, Heidegger speaks of a "step back," it is a question of returning to Greek ontology (i.e., essentially to Aristotle). In a second phase, the distinction comes, on the contrary, to be made between the early Greeks and Plato or Aristotle: preference is given to "the Greek dawn," when "the first Greeks experimented in ways which no-one had thought before"; Being was expressed in its original terms—φύσις, ἀλήθεια, λόγος, μοιρα—and thus displayed its true form as presence. "Platons Lehre von der Wahrheit," which shows how already in Plato *mimêsis* functions as *adæquatio*, thus furnishes a parallel for the way in which *veritas* was to bolt the door on *alêtheia*. I leave aside the third phase, marked by "The end of philosophy and the task of thinking," when *alêtheia* would at once be *homoiôsis* and when nothing but a sidestep could show how everything original is derived without mediation. It must suffice here to underline Aristotle's fascinating ambiguity: he is at the same time Presocratic and Platonic, concerned both with "unveiling" and with "adequation," as Heidegger showed in his repeated and contrasting analyses in *Metaphysics* and of Aristotle's *De Interpretatione*. The divide within Aristotle—just like the divide between Greeks and Greeks and between Greeks and Romans—always represents a running out—or a running down—in this History of Being, which is also the History of Truth.

For Arendt, there is indeed a divide and an analogous appeal to the Presocratics. But here, too, we find—and easily—the thread which we are following. For Arendt does not talk about the same Presocratics . Her Presocratics are the paradigms of an experience that is not original but rather "prephilosophic."[45]

Insofar as it is "philosophical" or "theoretical," the Greek *corpus* stretches—for Arendt—from Parmenides to Plato and Aristotle and then to Heidegger. It is characterized by the primacy of truth, *theôria*, and the *vita contemplativa*. Heidegger's Presocratics including Anaximander,[46] are modern in Arendt's eyes. The only genuine Presocratic experience is political experience (an echo of which can still be heard in Aristotle), where the focus is not truth but freedom. For freedom, by definition, is not a philosophical concept: it is "an exclusively political concept, indeed the quintessence of the city-state and of citizenship. Our philosophical tradition of political thought, beginning with Parmenides and Plato, was founded explicitly in opposition to this *polis* and its citizenship. The way of life chosen by the philosopher was understood in opposition to the *bios politikos*, the political way of life."[47] The entry of freedom into philosophy was not made until very much later, with St. Paul and the Christian identification of freedom and free will. It culminates magisterially in Heidegger's *Vom Wesen der Wahrheit* with the affirmation that the essence of truth is freedom.

Arendt's Socrates

The point of contact between what is prephilosophic and political and what is philosophical in the strict sense is represented by Socrates. Or, to put it more pointedly, Socrates, for Arendt, is a Presocratic. Françoise Collin[48] observes that "the history of western philosophy is a 'sequence of footnotes' not to Plato's works but rather to those of Socrates—or, rather, since he wrote none (and in this he is eminently political), to his trial and his condemnation." The trial of Socrates is the event that marks the division between the prephilosophic (the *bios politikos*) and the philosophical (the *bios theorêtikos*).

Arendt, it must be confessed, offers us a very odd Socrates—a split personality who is already philosophical and yet still Presocratic. Insofar as he is Presocratic (in Arendt's sense, not in Heidegger's), Socrates seems to me to have all the characteristics of a sophist. This emerges, I think, from "the answer of Socrates" to the question "What makes us think?"[49] and also from the short essay "Philosophy and Politics."[50]

Indeed, if in Plato we get a little Heidegger, in Socrates we see a great deal of Arendt. Socrates is the nonprofessional thinker whose position Arendt claims for her own. He is a thinker "who always remained a man among men, who did not shun the marketplace, who was a citizen among citizens, doing nothing, claiming nothing except what in his opinion every citizen should be and have a right to,"[51] and he "decided to lay down his life . . . simply for the right to go about examining the opinions of other people, thinking about them and asking his interlocutors to do the same."[52]

To say of Socrates that he is a nonprofessional thinker is to make two assertions at once: it is to say that he is a thinker and to say that he is a citizen. In the thinker, we have Plato's Socrates or the platonizing Socrates. In the citizen, Socrates the sophist.

Socrates is certainly a thinker, given what Arendt, in her analysis of Plato's *Gorgias*, takes to be his two key assertions: two replies to Callicles and hence two professions of antisophistic faith. The first assertion is that "to commit an injustice is worse than to suffer one." It cannot be the citizen who here speaks through Socrates's mouth but only the thinker; for as far as the citizen is concerned, crime is a transgression of the law and therefore demands punishment. The second assertion is *homologein auton heautôi*. According to this maxim, it is better to be in disagreement with everyone else than to be in disagreement with yourself. And this constitutes the essential structure of thought, that relation of a thinker to himself which Arendt calls "the two-in-one." The philosopher stands alone against his judges, alone against his friends—but in agreement with himself. In this way, it was Socrates who discovered the principle of noncontradiction, upon which Aristotle grounded Western logic and which still finds echoes in Kant's categorical imperative. "Because I exist, I shall not contradict myself. And I can contradict myself because in thinking I am two-in-one."[53]

But in itself the "two-in-one" is more complicated than this, for when we are thinking, we are not thereby philosophizing. The criterion of the two-in-one is not truth but agreement, and the duality inherent in agreement points toward a plurality and hence to the essential condition of politics. "As the metaphor bridges the gap between the world of appearances and the mental activities going on within it, so the Socratic two-in-one heals the solitariness of thought; its inherent duality points to the infinite plurality which is the law of the earth."[54] It is perhaps worth remarking here—although Arendt does not mention the fact and no doubt did not know it—that *homologia* (literally "identity of discourse"), along with *homonoia* ("identity of thought"), is a key word in the political thought of the sophists. There it means at the same time "concord" between states, "*consensus*" among citizens (something which must be continually renewed and which constitutes the very life of the city), and also the "agreement" between me and myself, which was to become characteristic of Socratic thought.[55] Thus despite appearances—Socrates sitting in a corner preoccupied by his daimonion—in the very act of thinking Socrates is a citizen. Thus I think it is illuminating to suggest here a series of analogies which are not made explicit by Arendt but can be read between the lines of her text: the analogies hold between Socrates the citizen, Socrates the sophist, and Socrates the Aristotelian (or at least Socrates the political animal in Aristotle's sense).

A Sophistic Polis

As Arendt insists, Aristotle's celebrated definitions of man as a "political animal" or an "animal endowed with *logos*" do no more than articulate the common view in the *polis* of man and political life. Thus our whole comparison of Arendt and Heidegger could be organized in terms of their different perceptions of Aristotle. Heidegger has two Aristotles, one of them Presocratic and the other already modern. Arendt has two Aristotles, one of them prephilosophic and political and the other Platonic and theoretical. But as Jacques Taminiaux has shown well,[56] Arendt gives an Aristotelian and not a Platonico-Heideggerian interpretation of the *bios theorêtikos* that therefore does not absorb all the characteristics of *praxis*. *Praxis* in Aristotle is tied to human plurality and to *doxa*: Arendt, as Taminiaux stresses, revives the Aristotelian concepts of the *polis*, of politics, and of citizenship.

For the sophistic movement, I think, shares certain features of great significance with what Arendt thinks of as Greek political thought and ascribes in particular to Socrates and to Aristotle. This is true even though, as I have already said, it is sometimes difficult to discern it in Arendt's writings, for she—like Heidegger, and indeed like us all—writes under the spell of Plato's philosophical fiction which made the word "sophist" so repellent that it still seems perverse or scandalous to give it an honorable sense.

The first feature is constitutive and structural. It is so prominent that one is liable to overlook it. It was precisely against the sophists and against the *bios politikos* that Platonic *theôria* was developed.

Again, in order to define the *polis*, Arendt adopts Aristotle's phrase "the interchange of words and deeds,"[57] and this is how she characterizes "the Greek solution" to the fragility of human affairs. The distinctive elements in this solution are so many sophistic *topoi*. First, there is the distinction between the public and the private, between the domain of nature and the domain of necessity. Long before Aristotle wrote the first book of the Politics, and before Callicles and Thrasymachus had spoken in their Platonic personae, Antiphon, in his *On Truth*[58] had already expressly discussed this contrast and its consequences: in the city, we play the citizen, and the private is defined as that which escapes the public grasp.

Second, there is the difference between *doxa* and *alêtheia*, between the plurality of *doxai* and the single and solitary constraint of truth. In the Greek *polis*, *alêtheia* exists only as the product of *doxai*, with which it is identified. It is this idea which Plato attacks—but it is the very essence of the political thought of the sophists and also, to some extent, of Socrates. Compare what Arendt says of Socrates when she contrasts him with the sophists in "Philosophy and Politics," with what she says of the sophists themselves in "The Concept of History." "In contrast with the sophists, [Socrates] had discovered that *doxa* is never a subjective illusion or an arbitrary distortion, but that truth is invariably tied to it."[59] "In other words, when Socrates brings to birth a *dokei moi* or an irreducibly singular "It seems to me" from one of his interlocutors, he nevertheless indicates that it is the same world which shows itself differently to different men and that therein lies the truth of *doxa*. And "this sort of understanding—seeing the world . . . from someone else's point of view—is political perception par excellence."[60] In *Between Past and Future*, it is thanks to the sophists and by "an inexhaustible flood of arguments which the sophists offered to the citizens of Athens" that the Greeks learned "to exchange their own point of view and their own 'opinions' . . . with those of their fellow-citizens . . . and to envisage the same world from the perspective of another Greek."[61] In this sense, Homer is the first sophist as well as the first historian, for he sings both of Achilles and of Hector, and Hesiod and Thucydides follow in his footsteps. In other words, like anyone who can reveal the truth in each point of view and thus create a common world, Socrates is a thoroughgoing Protagorean.

The third element is inseparable from the second. It is the distinction between appearing and being, a distinction of the last importance to the philosophers and of absolutely no concern to the politicians. In the *polis*, being is produced from the plurality of appearances. Here Arendt observes that Gorgias was a very early critic of the schism between being and appearing, for he pointed out that each is impotent without the other. She cites a text that Proclus ascribes to Gorgias: "Being is invisible [*aphanes*] when it does not hit upon appearing, and appearing is weak [*asthenes*] when it does not hit upon being."[62]

All these elements converge on a fourth, the status of *logos* as the condition of politics. Arendt follows Burckhardt and maintains that the *polis* is "the most talkative of all bodies politic."[63] There is a ceaseless competition among logoi and an effort to secure conviction by adapting your logos to the *kairos* or occasion. For a *logos* uttered at its *kairos* is a *praxis*, an action—it is political action par excellence. The trial of Socrates thus marks a turning point, introducing a distrust of *peithô* or persuasion—that is to say, of *logos* in its political form. But Socrates, for his part—"gadfly," "midwife," "electric ray"[64]—"was the greatest [of all the sophists] because he thought that there are or could be as many different *logoi* as there are men, and that all these *logoi* unite to form the human world, insofar as men live together through the medium of speech."[65]

Socratic discourse, then, insofar as it is sophistic, is for Arendt a paradigm of unity: not the unity of uniqueness but a unity constituted from divergent singularities in such a way that plurality can appear as the condition of politics. Here, in contrast to the organic and hierarchical structure of Plato's republic, we find Aristotelian metaphors, which give both equality and individuality their due. Individual faults may even work to the advantage of the whole, as in a choir or on a ship—or with meals to which, as to modern picnics, "many bring their contributions" and which are "better than those supplied at one man's cost."[66] We know—from Plato himself—that the practice of persuasion, which can confer power and even riches, is not philosophical: on the contrary, it is the practice which made the sophists, in Hegel's phrase, "the masters of Greece" and, according to Grote, the inventors of democracy and the precursors of the Enlightenment.

More radically, Socrates the sophist and the Socratic sophists who practice "the sophistry of noble lineage"[67] apply a powerful purgative and introduce us to "the most political of human faculties"—the faculty of judgment. It was Socrates who took the step from thinking to judging: the liberating force came from his critical activity, and it was linked to the two-in-one and to the demand for agreement with oneself. Arendt cites the one passage—in *Was heißt Denken?*—in which Heidegger speaks explicitly about Socrates: "Throughout his life and up to his very death, Socrates did nothing other than place himself in this draft, this current [of thinking], and maintain himself in it. This is why he is the purest of the West. This is why he wrote nothing. For anyone who begins, out of thinking, to write must inevitably be like those people who run for shelter from a wind too strong for them."[68] But she cites Heidegger the better to confute him: "The manifestation of the wind of thought is not knowledge; it is the ability to tell right from wrong, beautiful from ugly. And this, at the rare moments when the stakes are on the table, may indeed prevent catastrophes, at least for the self."[69] In other words, Socrates poses the question of meaning in contrast to the question of truth. At the very beginning of her book, Arendt stresses that "the need of reason is not inspired by the quest for truth but by the quest for meaning. And truth and meaning are not the same."[70] Heidegger thus provides "the latest and in some respects most striking instance" of "the basic fallacy": it occurs in *Being and Time*, "which starts out by raising anew the question of the meaning of Being. Heidegger himself, in a later interpretation of his own initial question, says explicitly: 'Meaning of Being' and 'Truth of Being' say the same."[71] The same holds when, in the role of professional thinker, he identifies the faculty of knowing with the faculty of judging under the name of "the wind of thought."

And yet it is Protagoras rather than Socrates who ought here to serve as the model.

In *The Human Condition*, Arendt suggests a complicated and ultimately critical interpretation of "man the measure." Protagoras appears there initially as "the earliest forerunner of Kant, for if man is the measure of all things, then man is the only thing outside the means-end relationship, the only end in himself who can use everything else as means."[72] And yet Plato's paradoxical retort in the *Laws*, according to which not man but "the god is the measure [even] of mere use objects,"[73] suggests that Protagoras is in the last analysis the forerunner of Marx, for whether he means to or not, he extends the concept of *homo faber* to the world as a whole, thereby running the risk of transforming the world and public space into a simple marketplace.[74]

Protagoras could be defended in more ways than one. According to Heidegger, we may interpret the proposition as a limitation on—or a proper measure of—disclosedness or Parmenidean truth.[75] But it may be feared that in Arendt's eyes this amounts to a further accusation against Protagoras— the accusation of professionalism in thought. It would be better, then, to observe that the proposition deals exclusively with *khrêmata*[76] (taken very literally the word means "use objects": goods or property which you use); it does not deal with *pragmata* (the word means "things" in general and refers both to works and to actions). Yet there is a more radical and a better defense of Protagoras. It was given by Socrates himself in Plato's *Theaetetus*. Neither Arendt nor Heidegger, so far as I know, has ever taken note of it even though Socrates-Protagoras there takes the political stand that Kant, on Arendt's reading, takes in the *Critique of Judgment*. Protagoras, who expresses himself through the mouth of Socrates, claims to care for others by the therapeutic force of his discourse and to help them undergo a "change of condition": he does not of course convert them from false beliefs to true beliefs (that, he says, is neither possible nor desirable) but rather from less good beliefs to better beliefs.[77] Protagoras is mindful of the distinction between meaning and truth as he teaches us how to make better judgments, and in doing so he exhibits two features characteristic of Kant's thought. For "he woos the consent of everyone else" (*peitheien* and not *dialegeisthai*, as Arendt notes, and he thinks of judgment in terms of taste. And in this way, since "for judgments of taste the world is the primary thing, not man, neither man's life nor his self," the supposed arbitrariness of taste is a feature of public life and the common world—in short, of the mutual dependency of culture and politics, which is the city itself.[78]

In the end, we might maintain, following the analysis of Etienne Tassin, that Protagoras pushes the Socratic view to its extreme—or, rather, that he goes beyond Socrates and as far as Machiavelli. In the celebrated myth of the Protagoras, *aidôs* and *dikê* constitute political virtue in the strict sense, and this virtue was bestowed by Zeus as a supplementary gift to be shared equally among all men: Protagoras concludes the myth by asserting that we learn this virtue as we learn our mother tongue—we suck it in with our nurse's milk. As for those who do not possess it, if they do not even pretend to possess it, then they are madmen who thus exclude themselves from the human community.[79] Hence politics is necessarily a politics of appearance, and Greek politics speaks the language of the sophists and deploys all its possibilities: plurality, the space of appearances, persuasion, judgment.

To end this discussion of Arendt and the sophists, I shall note the fluctuation of her thought on politics, which is sometimes bold and sometimes not. This can be explained in terms of the influence of the philosophical. It is noteworthy that once she sets foot outside politics, the judgment she passes on persuasion changes. The best evidence for this is her assessment of lying in "Truth and Politics." On the one hand, the liar is "an actor by nature," for "he takes advantage of the undeniable affinity of our capacity of action, for changing reality, with this mysterious faculty of ours that enables us to say 'The sun is shining' when it is raining cats and dogs."[80] Thus our capacity to lie is a confirmation of human freedom. On the other hand, persuasion is a form of violence, used by those who have power. "Persuasion and violence can destroy truth but they cannot replace it" (259) since truth "is the ground on which we stand and the sky that stretches above us" (264). One might almost say, Arendt remarks, that "to consider politics from the perspective of truth . . . means to set foot outside the political domain" (259). It is in philosophical Latin that one says: *Fiat veritas et pereat mundus.*

Of the Transcendental in Politics: Sophocles or Pericles?

If in politics judgment must be thought of in terms of taste, then there arises in an acute form the problem of the relationship between aesthetics and politics, between works and actions in the city. Here the difference between Heidegger and Arendt reaches its peak. We shall best see this if we compare their interpretations of the first chorus of Sophocles's *Antigone* and of Pericles's funeral speech in book II of Thucydides's *History.*

(And note at the outset, as a pointer of some significance, the different na-
tures of the works they choose: tragic poetry, historical prose.)

Man, who is "the most strangest thing of all" and who is "everywhere
journeying, inexperienced and without issue," is at the same time *upsipolis
apolis*:[81]

> *Polis* is usually translated as city or city-state. This does not capture the full
> meaning. *Polis* means, rather, the place, the There, wherein and as which
> historical Being-There is. The *polis* is the historical place, the There in which,
> *out of* which, and *for* which history happens. To this place and scene of history
> belong the gods, the temples, the priests, the festivals, the games, the poets,
> the thinkers, the ruler, the council of elders, the assembly of the people, the
> army, and the fleet. All this does not first belong to the *polis*, does not become
> political by entering into a relation with a statesman and a general and the
> business of the state. No, it is political (i.e., at the site of history) inasmuch
> as the poets (for example) are *only* poets (and truly poets), the thinkers *only*
> thinkers (and truly thinkers), and inasmuch as the priests are *only* priests (and
> truly priests), the kings *only* kings (and truly kings). Now, "are" here means
> "use force"—inasmuch as they are actively involved in force and become
> eminent in historical being as creators and men of action. Pre-eminent in the
> historical place, they become at the same time *apolis*, without city and place,
> lonely, strange, and alien, without issue amid Being as a whole, at the same
> time without statute and limit, without structure and order, because they
> themselves as creators must first create all this.[82]

By way of this long quotation we may see how essential it is for Hei-
degger that the city be thought of as what is behind and beyond it—of its
negation. This is Heidegger's "apoliticism." Agents, creators, founders: all
are one. It is their violence which is explained in "The Origin of the Work
of Art," which dates from the same period: "The temple-work, standing
there, opens up a world and at the same time sets this world back again on
earth, which itself only thus emerges as native ground."[83] Here we also see
that the Greek experience of the *polis*, insofar as it is thought of as the expe-
rience of a "location" or a "There," is always bound to be identified with the
Roman experience of a *patria*, giving it its tone or lending it its metaphors,
as you will. In any event, politics is, as far as possible, thought of as, or in
terms of, a work of art.

The nonpolitical essence of politics is confirmed when Heidegger rein-
terprets the same verse in his *Parmenides*, written eight years later. Here he
proposes to understand *polis* in terms of *pelein*, the archaic verb for *einai*.
The city is in itself the place for the total unveiling of Being, and "the dif-
ference between the modern State, the Roman *res publica*, and the Greek
polis is essentially the same as the difference between the modern essence
of truth, the Roman *rectitudo*, and the Greek *alêtheia*."[84] Unveiling, unlike
disguising or forgetting, essentially involves conflict: it is manifested in
terror, in horror, in unhappiness, which, as Jacob Burckhardt saw, were
features of the Greek city. "It is not by chance that these thoughts about
man occur in a Greek tragedy. For it is from the unique source of the con-
flictual essence of *alêtheia* that the possibility and necessity of 'tragedy'
itself arise."[85] If the *polis* is in itself only the *polos tou pelein*, the "pole" of
being, then "it is because the Greeks are an absolutely non-political people"
that they both could and had to found it.[86]

In order to give us an understanding of what a *polis* is, Arendt for her
part likes to adduce the Periclean epigram: *philokaloumen te gar met'euteleias
kai philosophoumen aneu malakias*. She suggests something like the following
translation: "We love beauty within the limits of political judgment, and
we philosophize without the barbarian vice of effeminacy."[87] To the Hel-
lenist, Arendt's interpretation will seem no less forced than Heidegger's.
The central point is this: she boldly understands "limit" and "effeminacy"
as two "strictly political" terms.[88] *Malakia*, which means in the first instance
softness (of a bed, of a fabric, of a meadow, of skin, of a face or a look), often
does connote weakness (of shell-less mollusks), physical or mental feeble-
ness, effeminacy. "We philosophise like men and not like pansies"—that is
Pericles's thought. But it is much harder to understand *euteleia* as a positive
term. The word is grand enough in itself: *eu*, "well" or "in a good fashion,"
and *teleios*, "complete" or "finished" or "perfect" (from *telos*, "end" or "aim").
It is this etymology that leads Arendt to see behind *euteleia* "the faculty to
take aim in judgment, discernment, discrimination, in brief . . . that curi-
ous and ill-defined capacity we commonly call taste."[89] But if the privative
term *ateleia* regularly denotes a state of imperfection, nevertheless *euteleia*,
too, seems most often to have strongly negative connotations: "medioc-
rity," "parsimoniousness," "cheapness." This in Aristotle's "nature does not

imitate those craftsmen who, *for economy's sake*, make a spit and lamp-holder in one."[90] According to the *Metaphysics*, no one would dream of counting Hippo among the natural scientists, like Thales, "because of the *mediocrity* of his thought."[91] In the *Poetics*, *euteles* is predicated, in contrast to *semnos* ("grave," "dignified"), of poets who represent low people and actions that lack grandeur.[92] (The low, *phauloi*, contrast with the *spoudaioi*, noble people whose actions are fine: the contrast governs the whole of Aristotle's ethics and politics.) The *Poetics* also applies the word to a style or mode of expression (*lexis*) which is "flat" and not elevated.[93] Liddell and Scott's *Greek English Lexicon* suggests "without extravagance" for the Periclean passage. And no doubt the sense should be looked for in the financial domain, for just as *ateleia* can mean exemption from a charge or tax, so *euteleia* may also indicate that something is cheap or a "good buy." (In modern Greek *telos* means "tax.") Pericles, I think, means to assert that the Athenians "love beauty without ruining themselves" (i.e., without making it a cause of excessive taxes or even—more simply—a financial matter at all). After all, that is the very best way to have taste: in a democracy one does not act in the way one does in the extravagant and hybristic empire of the Great King. "Taste debarbarizes the world of the beautiful by not being overwhelmed by it."[94] In the end, then, Arendt is right to understand Pericles's epigram as a subordination of work to action, of love of beauty and love of truth—items which occupy the first place in the hierarchy of souls described in the myth of the *Phaedrus* (248d)—to the sphere of politics.

That is why Arendt also likes to cite, again selectively, another passage from the "Funeral Oration": "We shall not need the praises of Homer or of any other panegyrist whose poetry may please for the moment, although his representation of the facts will not bear the light of day. For we have compelled every land and every sea to open a path for our valour, and have everywhere planted eternal memorials of our friendship and our enmity" (*Life of the Mind*, vol. 2, 4).[95] Athens has no more need of poets. The cities which she has founded take over Homer's baton. She can produce geographers and historians.

But Thucydides and Pausanias do not produce an engaged art any more than Homer did. "Athens . . . never settled the conflict between politics and art unequivocally in favour of one or the other," and "the Greeks, so to speak, could say in one and the same breath: 'He who has not seen the Zeus of Phidias at Olympia has lived in vain' and 'People like Phidias, namely sculptors, are unfit for citizenship.'"[96] Arendt repeats the paradox, and it fascinates her: "This conflict [between art and politics] cannot and must not be solved."[97] Or, again: "We need not choose here between Plato and Protagoras."[98] Politics needs art: if the world is to be what it is always deemed to be, the fatherland of men during their life on earth, then human ingenuity must avail itself of actions and also of words. Without Pindar, no Olympic Games. Nonetheless, the *polis* dethrones art, for it elevates action, without of course reifying it, to the first place in the hierarchy of the *vita activa*, and it characterizes speech as the decisive difference between men and animals—"both of which bestowed upon politics a dignity which even today has not altogether disappeared."[99] This paradox is a corollary of the paradox inherent in the status of works of art themselves. For a work of art is a work in the fullest sense—that is to say, it is the most intensely tangible object in the world, an object that belongs to the same public space as politics. And at the same time it is also a nonwork, which frees itself from the goals and designs of *homo faber* no less than from the biological necessity of toil.

Hence—and with all these qualifications made—it seems to me that the difference between Plato and Protagoras remains. It is, if you prefer, the difference between a powerful tendency on Heidegger's part and a powerful tendency on Arendt's part.

A final example—the example of tragedy—may serve to sum this up. Tragedy, which is essentially Greek, is for Heidegger, as the Parmenides explicitly avows, the tragedy of *alêtheia*. For Arendt, it is "the political art par excellence"[100]—not because it necessarily represents the conflict between private and public but because it is the imitation, with a minimal reification, of action, of drama, and of those nongeneralizable individuals who are the "acting people"—the "agents" or "actors" of history. (And the chorus, which extracts the meaning of the piece, is thus less tragic than the drama itself.) That is why, *pace* Aristotle, tragedy and history are equally philosophical—or equally unphilosophical. They are equally resistant to universalization, equally averse to any ruse of reason.

Thus in Heidegger's case, the dignity of politics consists in not being itself—while the philosopher runs the risk of Syracuse. And in Arendt's case, the dignity of politics consists in being nothing but itself—and the "philosopher" (if Arendt is one) must think only of the conditions under which politics, in its specific form, is possible.

Translated by Jonathan Barnes

Part IV Performance and Performative

How to Really Do Things with Words: Performance
Before the Performative

> [W]hat may fairly be called a modern Rhetoric, another systematic
> study of ways of effecting or affecting action by or in speech,
> J. L. Austin's How to Do Things with Words, a set of lecture notes
> (as Aristotle's texts are), edited and published posthumously.
>
> —STANLEY CAVELL, "Performative and Passionate Utterances"[1]

> It does not seem to prevent the drawing of a line for our present
> purposes where we want one.
>
> —J. L. AUSTIN, How to Do Things with Words[2]

How Exactly Does Logos "Act"?

I would like to begin by tracing a horizon of problems and an angle from
which to attack them.

My starting point is the too famous phrase by which Gorgias character-
izes *logos* in the *Encomium of Helen*: "*Logos dunastês megas estin, hos smikro-
tatôi somatôi kai aphanestatôi theiôtata erga apotelei*," which I propose to
translate as follows: "Discourse is a great master, which with the smallest
and least perceptible of bodies performs the most divine of acts."[3]

Three terms are to be underlined, which refer, if not to the speech act, at
least to language as act. The difference between the two—speech act and
language as act—is precisely what I am seeking to interrogate.

Dunastês: this is the first determinant of *logos*. Let us note, so we can be
rid of it, that I render *logos* as "discourse" (of course, one might propose

"language" or "speech" here), wishing to cover under the mantle of this term all the previous distinctions incubated in French. So as to understand how "this discourse" given by Gorgias (*hode ho logos*, §3) can legitimately serve as a starting point for a reflection on the act of language, it is actually a matter of remarking that the semantic amplitude of the Greek *logos* is very broadly mobilized here, if only via the constant play between singular and plural. One could, for example, translate (or overtranslate) the occurrences from paragraphs 9 to 13, depending on the case, not only in the singular as "language," "speech," "discourse," but in the plural as "literary genres," "doctrines and treatises," "discussions," "phrases and words." It is simultaneously a question of the relation to *ratio* as rational formalization (*egô de boulomai logismon tina tôi logôi dous* [§2]: "Me, I want, giving logic to *logos*," "discursivity to discourse") and as proportion (*ton hauton de logon ekhei hê te tou logou dunamis pros tên tês psukhês taxin* . . . [§14]: "there is the same relation [*logos*] between power of discourse [*logou*] and disposition of the soul as between the disposition of drugs and nature of bodies"). In short, *logos* which Gorgias produces, like the one able to persuade Helen, that of poets and oracles, that of meteorologists, of orators, of philosophers, *logos* is a "dynast." Following Chantraine,[4] *dunastês* is one who has "the power of acting" in general, and notably "political power," like Zeus (Sophocles), the chiefs of a city (Herodotus, Plato), a prince or a king (Thucydides). Speech is immediately (a) power of acting.

Apotelei: such is the first verb that defines this power of acting. It is composed of *teleô*, "to complete, bring to term, accomplish" an oeuvre, an enterprise, an action, in conformity with the ambiguity of *telos*, the "end" as term and goal, and of *apo*, which insists on the completion of a right to the end, exactly like the *per* of "perform." One might render it as "complete"—I choose "perform" to make its actuality audible, and I will come back to this choice.

Erga: this is what is performed. The term, with the same root as *work*, enters into two major systems of opposition: action/inaction (in Hesiod, for example), and act/word, vain word (in the singular as in the plural, from Homer to Thucydides, passing via the Tragics). This traditional opposition of speech and act, of the verbal and the real, is evidently what the phrase we started with short-circuits. It does so not without profiting from the amplitude of the sense of *ergon* and of its plural "oeuvre, work, occupation, labor, affair, operation," which joins together the real of the act and that of the oeuvre: *logos* performs the most divine acts/oeuvres. It seems to me that this ambiguity, which we will not interrogate further, ought to accompany the question of performance such as it is posed in Antiquity, even for always.

Let us pursue the phrase to make the angle of attack explicit: *"Dunatai gar kai pausai kat lupên aphelein kai kharan anergasasthai kai eleon epauxêsai"* [In fact, it has the power to put an end to fear, to remove pain, to produce joy, to increase pity].

Two new verbs are to be put into the file, confirming the power of *logos* to act. *Dunatai*: the *dynast* "has the power of/to," the most powerful "can." Do what? Increase or diminish primary passions (*pathêma, epathen,* §9). One of the verbs that name action over a passion is more remarkable than the others and is apparently rather infrequent. It is *anergasasthai*, badly translated by "to produce" joy (which, in turn, is far from saying *kharis*, the "grace" that Athena pours on the head of Ulysses so that he appears in his strength and beauty, "favor" and "recognition," "pleasure" and "jouissance"). The term picks up *ergon*, the act/oeuvre that language performs as an act; in truth, *ergazomai* (here in composition with *ana-*, maybe in the sense of producing "again" or "to increase" joy) is, for its part, already rendered as *to perform* in Liddell, Scott, and Jones.[5] Joy is one of the most divine performances that *logos* accomplishes.

Here is the question that I would like to pose, then: how does everything that is described here exceed rhetoric? Can one not simply reduce the first phrase to the second, the second to a subjective therapy of the soul, and the whole thing to a persuasive function of a rhetorical type? In short, isn't the action of language confused with rhetoric? In any case, isn't this the way that one usually thinks, each time that a philosopher reads a sophist?

I would like precisely to try a different perspective, with the help of the notion of performance. Hence my translations. The stake, which appeared to me in all its clarity when I reread *How to Do Things with Words*, is that of the status of rhetoric.

To put it tersely: in matters of discourse, must one count two or must one count three? The questions follow at once. What is the identity of the third term? For philosophy, the third term, the intruder, is sophist logology,[6] and philosophy makes this third term inexist as far as it is able so to do, to its own benefit and to the benefit of rhetoric, which it subjects or subjugates. For Austin, the third term is rhetoric, which arises unexpectedly but whose place he tries to ensure, between the illocutionary, which he "invents," and the locutionary, which he circumscribes. Greek philosophy and Austin do not start with the same evidence, but they are both confronted with a third dimension of language—or "dit-mension," to dot the i's and cross the t's orthographically with Lacan.[7]

Counting two is what philosophy has habituated us to. When one speaks, one can either "speak of" or "speak to," according to an "or" that is evidently not exclusive. "To speak of," to unveil, to describe, to demonstrate, is of the major register of philosophy, considered as ontology and phenomenology. "To speak to," to persuade, to have an effect on the other, is of the register of rhetoric. From the point of view of *philosophia perennis*, there is no third dimension of language.

At once the second dimension of language is sucked up by the first.

One effectively witnesses a double reduction. On the one hand, what might exceed rhetoric, that is, something like sophistic performance, grafted onto language as act, is reduced to rhetoric. On the other hand, for its part rhetoric becomes more or less quietly the concern of philosophy. The third dimension, the one that could serve to sketch out something like sophistic is appropriated, at the same time as rhetoric, by normal, normed, normative philosophy, and the potentially powerful, active, and autonomous flux of the language act thus finds itself domesticated by ontology.

We have already described very precisely these two points of reduction.[8]

First point: sophistic is rhetoric. Plato's *Gorgias* institutes this equivalence as a self-evident starting point, only then to rework it in the remainder of the text. "Gorgias—Socrates asks—tell us yourself what you should be called as learned in what art (*autos hêmin eipe tina se khrê kalein hôs tinos epistemona tekhnês*). Gorgias's reply: *tês rhetorikês, ô Sôkrates*, "in rhetoric, Socrates." "You should be called an orator then?" "And a good orator, Socrates" (449a). Sophistic is rhetoric, and it is the sophist in person who will have said so. Even if, in all probability and against the machination by Plato of the appearance of a rhetoric that is always already there, one witnesses the moment of the invention of the word *rhêtorikê* (*sc. tekhnê*), like that of the word *sophistikê* by Plato himself in this exchange.[9]

Second point: now, rhetoric is the affair of philosophy. This is true for Plato since *Gorgias* and its rhetoric-sophistic, the "worker of persuasion" (*peithous dêmiourgos*, 453a) are comprehended only when subsumed under or transcended by the *Phaedrus* and the advent of a philosophical rhetoric, which this time is confounded with the dialectic and is directed at an auditorium of gods. Good rhetoric is thus philosophy itself. One can also maintain that with Plato, rhetoric disappears since it is confounded either with sophistry—when it is bad—or with philosophy—when it is good.

This philosophical extremism, which is equivalent to the annihilation of rhetoric as such, is consequently less convincing than the Aristotelian perspective, according to which rhetoric is a *tekhnê*, indeed a complete *epistêmê*: its "proper function is not to persuade," as it is for Plato, but rather "to see the means for persuading that each subject includes,"[10] and it must "make the theory of the persuasive that is appropriate in each case."[11] Rhetoric, antistrophe of the dialectic,[12] thus incontestably exists by itself and belongs by rights to the *Organon*. In this perspective, sophistic would be a semblance of philosophy, linked to rhetoric distorted by bad intention and poorly conceptualized, proposing a series of recipes in place of a theory and a method. Sophistic doesn't want to understand that rhetoric arises from the general discursive regime of apophantics, that "speaking to" is and must be submitted to "speaking of."

Now this submission is, I believe, the crucial point that determines the philosophical anchoring of rhetoric, *grosso modo* right up to Perelman (included, even if he did not agree!). The violence of the gesture may be read in the following paradox, which Aristotle plants right at the start of his *Rhetoric*: "rhetoric is useful because the true and the just are naturally stronger than their contraries."[13] But why the devil would something like rhetoric then be necessary if the true and the just are "naturally" stronger than the false and the unjust? The only response—which is not explicit—is in my opinion that rhetoric must help the truth, which has a greater natural strength, exactly like art helps or "perfects" nature: "in certain cases art completes what nature is incapable of accomplishing right to the end, and in other cases, [it] imitates" (*Physics* II 8 199a 15s).[14] Philosophy counts two, speaking of and speaking to, but regardless of what happens in the bosom of the one, they always come back under the regulation of the truth that governs speaking of.

No third dimension: speaking as act is not taken into consideration as such. What might resemble it the most here, that is, *legein logou kharin*, "speaking for speaking's sake" or "for the pleasure of speaking," is even radically excluded by book *Gamma* of the *Metaphysics*.[15] There are certainly statements that, for Aristotle, escape the regime of the truth: thus prayer is neither true nor false. But no statement escapes the regime of sense that founds the principle of noncontradiction, in conformity with the "evident" equation according to which to speak is to say something, to say something is to signify something, one thing only, for both oneself and for the other. Now, precisely, those who refuse the decision of sense and the principle of noncontradiction are the very same that Aristotle describes as "speaking for speaking's sake": sophists, upholders of what a language is capable of as act. This doubling of *legein lou kharin* is in effect able to exceed not only the truth but also *a fortiori* persuasion since "speaking to" (persuasion) is philosophically ruled by "speaking of " (truth). Or again—to anticipate Austin's distinctions—the autonomous power of language thus put to work could arise from force rather than effect. But this "logology" is dismissed by Aristotle as being outside of sense, assimilated to the *logos* of a plant, that is to say, a *nonlogos*, at the same time as are excluded from humanity those who—like Protagoras—maintain their refusal of the principle of noncontradiction.

I am evoking the normal regime of sense, that is to say, the regime given as a norm by Aristotle, which still determines us today whether we know or want it or not, because it is only against this background that Austin's invention and its ambiguities stand out.

Locutionary, Illocutionary, Perlocutionary

"A THIRD KIND OF ACT": WHICH THIRD?

"Let us contrast both the locutionary act *and* the illocutionary act with yet a third kind of act."[16] Austin's invention consists in counting three. My aim is comparative: what are the points of resemblance between the sophistic three repressed by philosophy and the three "invented" by Austin and misunderstood, he says, by philosophy until him? What is the relation between logology and the illocutionary? The question that I am posing is retrograde, like the force of the true according to Nietzsche: in what way can Austin contribute to clarifying that which, in antiquity, exceeds philosophy and rhetoric, at least rhetoric thought philosophically, that is to say, reduced to philosophy? In other words: how to think performance before the performative? The following reflections merely start this project.

Yet, in order to pose the question of the relation between logology and illocution properly, an essential difference must first be noted: that of the order of appearance of the protagonists. The order in antiquity: philosophy (1), rhetoric (2), and then sophistic (3) which philosophy denies (assimilates or expels). The modern order: the locutionary (1), the illocutionary (2), and the perlocutionary (3). Because the perlocutionary—and evidently not the illocutionary, even if the illocutionary is the focus of attention—is the "third type of act." It is striking to note that the perlocutionary, which as we will see functions as the Austinian name for rhetoric, is presented only after the evidence of the locutionary and the finding of the illocutionary. What comes second for philosophy, as well understood and controlled (rhetoric),[17] is what occurs third in the economy of Austin's argument, as a third to reexplore: I take that as an invitation to shake up the status of rhetoric.

The relevant relation to interrogate is thus, on the Greek side, that between "speaking of," "speaking to," "speaking for the sake of speaking," that is to say—in adopting current philosophical terminology—philosophy, rhetoric, sophistic. On Austin's side it is locutionary, illocutionary, perlocutionary. My interrogation bears on the limits of the analogy between these tripartite divisions. I propose to fix the ideas by means of the following table, which the rest of this chapter in its entirety will have to interrogate and explain. It will already have been understood that the column order retains the mark of a point of view: the order here (1. Philosophy; 2. Rhetoric; 3. Sophistic) is effectively a philosophical and not an Austinian order. It indicates that "for us" philosophers and historians of philosophy, it is the logological/illocutionary that poses the question.

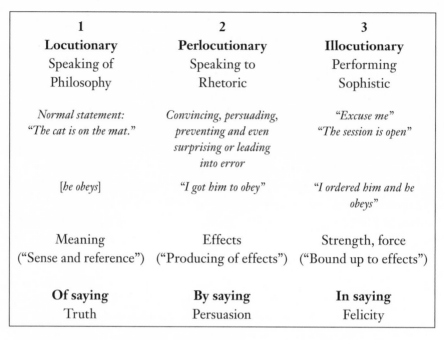

1 **Locutionary** Speaking of Philosophy	2 **Perlocutionary** Speaking to Rhetoric	3 **Illocutionary** Performing Sophistic
Normal statement: *"The cat is on the mat."*	*Convincing, persuading,* *preventing and even* *surprising or leading* *into error*	*"Excuse me"* *"The session is open"*
[he obeys]	*"I got him to obey"*	*"I ordered him and he* *obeys"*
Meaning ("Sense and reference")	Effects ("Producing of effects")	Strength, force ("Bound up to effects")
Of saying Truth	**By saying** Persuasion	**In saying** Felicity

Figure 3. The three dimensions of language.

THE ILLOCUTIONARY REVOLUTION?

Austin wakes philosophy up from its apophantic sleep. Let us begin from this awakening, which—if Austin is to be believed—is in the process of "producing a revolution in philosophy": "if anyone wishes to call it the greatest and most salutary in its history, this is not, if you come to think of it, a large claim" (*How to Do Things with Words*, 4). The revolution consists in isolating utterances that grammatically are statements,[18] are not nonsense, do not report, do not describe, do not constate anything, are not true or false, and are such that "the uttering of the sentence is, or is part of, the doing of an action, which again would not *normally* be described as, or as 'just,' saying something" (ibid., 5). There is indeed something exceptional here in relation to the Aristotelian ontological norm: an assertion (not a question or a prayer) that, without being outside of sense, is outside of truth. It is, however, true, true in an Aristotelian way, that the whole question of fiction, via no matter what statement about the goat-stag, sense without reference, is likely to be engulfed in this characterization if one stops the description there. For his part, Austin scarcely dwells on this awkward question.[19]

The examples, Austin warns, are "disappointing": so acute, small, exceptional, the "yes" of the wedding couple, "I leave my watch to my brother," "I name this ship *Queen Elizabeth*," "I bet you sixpence it will rain tomorrow." However, it is evident that they have one characteristic and highly resistant property in common: to utter the phrase is neither to describe what I am doing nor to affirm that I am doing it; *it is to do it* (ibid., 6). The speech act, one will have understood, is not the act of speaking but the act of which one speaks, the act that one utters. That is what is acted, executed, when one utters it. Or, as Benveniste (commenting on Austin's lecture at Royaumont) puts it perfectly: "the act is thus identical with the utterance of the act. The signified is identical to the referent" and—even more clearly— "the utterance *is* the act."[20]

Some remarks are necessary in order to clear the comparative terrain.

In the first place it is manifest, at least for a medievalist or a jurist, that the Austinian invention is not as new or as little theorized as he seems to say. His examples of bequeathal or of baptism testify to this, like all formulae for the taking of sacraments, for oaths and laws. The speech act has always intervened in the history of thought in a manner that is both crucial and marginal. One of the stakes of this collection is to mark out, in relation to the apophantic norm, the domains of exception that are the sacred and the magical—from the divinity of creation to the sacramentary formula, the juridico-political (with Roman law), the literary (with the status of the poet and the *auctor*).

It is equally manifest that the "third dimension" of language, affirmed by Austin's little examples, does not have a great deal to do with the amplitude of the "dynasty" of *logos*, from which I began and which it cannot, in any case, be confused with.

To try to better understand the relation between the "performative" tip and the much vaster, vaguer, and more generic notion of "performance," I would like to begin with some remarks about their terminological family.

I would then like to make the comparison between these "third" dimensions—not directly but indirectly by their difference from what they are not (the other two dimensions). And to show how, for Austin himself, it is finally the difficulty of tracing a clear frontier between the perlocutionary and the locutionary on the one hand and the perlocutionary and the illocutionary on the other hand that leads him to propose a notion that is itself much vaster and much more generic: that of the *speech act*, a notion that is much closer to "performance."

I will then find sophist logology at two very precise points: with Gorgias, a reader of Parmenides, in the manner it carries out a reading of philosophy in terms of the *speech act*, and with *epideixis*, in the manner it exceeds both philosophy (or the normal locutionary regime) and rhetoric (or the perlocutionary). *Epideixis* doesn't describe in terms of truth her simply produces an effect of persuasion: it accomplishes with felicity what I call a world effect.

"TO PERFORM"—"PERFORMANCE" AND "PERFORMATIVE," PER-FORMATIVE AND PER-LOCUTIONARY

Performative is Austin's own invention, acclimated to French by Austin himself at a colloquium held at Royaumont;[21] thereafter it was immediately justified and appropriated by Émile Benveniste: "Since *performance* is already in use, there will be no difficulty in introducing *performatif* in the special sense it has here. All that has been done is to bring back into French a lexical family which English took from Old French."[22]

Klein's Comprehensive Etymological Dictionary of the English Language maintains that in English "performance" was coined from Old French "parfournir" (from Medieval Latin *perfurnire*) and/or "parformer"; in addition, French borrowed the term at least three times, if the *Dictionnaire historique de la langue française* is to be believed: in 1869, by analogy with the vocabulary of horse races, to mean the "manner of developing a subject, of executing a work in public"; in 1953, to denote "individual result in the accomplishment of a task"; and in 1963, in the wake of Chomsky, it enters into opposition with "competence." The word is a mobile, bilingual term that bridges sport (performance/record), technique (performance/the output of a machine), psychology (performance of a test), linguistics (performance/competence), and modern art (performance—happening, not forgetting, in English, performance as theatrical representation). It is difficult to not add that in France today, performance is center stage, with evaluation and the culture of results—which risks destroying the very core of our crafts.[23] From the most objective to the most subjective it is equally the act, its actuality, and its actualization that are at stake.

As for *performative*, Benveniste simply adds, it is regularly formed, like *resultative, predicative*, or its Austinian other, the *constative*.

However, what interests me is the difference between the name and the substantivized adjective. It is the adjective *performative* (*sentence* or *utterance*, elided elliptically, as with *rhetorikê* or *sophistikê* <*tekhnê*>) that is invented and marked by Austin; as for the verb *to perform* and the substantive *performance*, it is not easy to distinguish the current meaning and the marked meaning. Although my inventory is not systematic, I tend to think that it is the habitual English meaning that regularly functions even if it cannot *not* be contaminated by the terminological invention of the adjective. Thus, in chapter VIII of *How to Do Things with Words*, the one in which the third kind of act appears, Austin says: "We shall call the performance of an act of this kind the performance of a 'perlocutionary' act and the act performed . . . a perlocution" (101).[24] Performance is clearly indifferent to the type of act performed (Austin concludes the preceding phrase with the expression "the performance of the locutionary or the illocutionary act").

"The performance of a perlocutionary act." In passing, I would like to signal a terminological trouble that I am apparently alone in experiencing—Austin himself not seeming to be bothered by it: one shouldn't let oneself drift into confusing the *per-* of *perlocution* with the *per-* of *performative*. The two have nothing to do with each other. The *per-* of *performative*, like that of *performance*, denotes the accomplishment of a "right to the end" (*apo-telei* in Gorgias's phrase), whereas the *per-* of *perlocution* denotes the means, that is, the "*by*" of "*by saying*": it is "*by means*" of saying and not "in" the saying itself ("*in saying*," characteristic of the illocutionary or performative) that the perlocutionary acts. In the performative, the utterance is the means of acting and of producing an effect. However, when, with *L'effet sophistique*, I chose the word "performance" for rendering *epideixis* (Plato's terminology for the discursiveness of the sophists; I will come back to this at length), it is because this term seemed appropriate to graft something of the order of the *Wirklichkeit* onto rhetoric in operating, if one may say so, a confusion of *per.*

Let's now see how the old and the new can be coupled term by term.

LOCUTIONARY/APOPHANTIC

I believe that one can accept without too much difficulty the equivalence between Austin's "locutionary" or "constative" and Aristotle's "speaking of" or "apophantic." In both cases, what it is at stake is the normal regime of discourse, that which philosophy thinks and practices, linked—in antiquity at least—to ontology and phenomenology and which one can designate reductively as "descriptive fallacy" and which Austin considers at once as the only regime to which philosophers have paid attention.[25] A *normal statement* is a *logos apophantikos*: "the cat is on the mat" is equal to "Socrates is white." Both say something, *legein ti* for Aristotle and *say something* for Austin, and even "say something about something." In both cases they have a relation to *meaning*, to *sêmainein*, to signification, that is to say, generally, to sense and to reference, and they are susceptible to truth and falsity, *true/ false, alêthes/pseudos.* In short, one can, without difficulty, superpose the description that Aristotle gives at the start of *De interpretatione* (chapters 1 and 4) of the propositional utterance and the description that Austin gives of the *statement* right at the beginning of *How to Do Things with Words*—a rapid description but one which is taken up again, explained, or completed more than once in what follows.

PERLOCUTIONARY/RHETORIC OR THE AVOIDANCE OF "RHETORIC"

But for a certain number of oddities, it isn't very difficult either to accept the equivalence between perlocutionary and rhetoric. A first difference as to the emergence of the notion, as a third term after the constative-apophantic and performative, has already been underlined. In fact, it is only in the eighth lecture—the eighth of twelve, thus in the final third—titled "Locutionary, Illocutionary, and Perlocutionary Acts" that our "third type of acts" intervenes.

Rhetoric as third, then, except that the word "rhetoric" doesn't appear in this chapter or—short of an error on my part—anywhere at all in the book.

All the characteristics are there, but not the name. Now, Austin, who gave great lectures to the Aristotelian Society undoubtedly knew Aristotle—Aristotle, who, along with Kant, served to allow him to sketch out the contours of philosophy transmitted by a tradition that he did not call continental. There is here an omission that is never explained. Allow me to make an observation. If reading Austin gives me so much pleasure, it is because, like Aristotle, he is too honest and never hides the points that are able to thwart the machine that he puts into place: regularly explaining them even makes the machine advance. That is also why what it never occurs to him to say, although one would expect it—his blind spot, if you like—is of the greatest interest for an interpretation and a follow-up.

The avoidance of the word "rhetoric," I believe, arises from a difficulty of definition or, more exactly, from an awareness of an incommensurability. Besides, rhetoric—like philosophy or sophistic—is not a "statement." But one must go one step further: if there is a statement that is normal or proper to philosophy, that is to say, to the constative in its difference from the performative, there is no statement proper to rhetoric. Austin never gives an example of the *perlocutionary* statement, one that would be analogous to "the cat is on the mat" for the traditional locutionary or to "the session is open" for the revolutionary illocutionary (the latter kind giving rise for its part to a series of inventories, distinctions, and taxonomies, all as voluntaristic as they are problematic, always resumed with energy and all based on a host of examples). For the perlocutionary, instead of a statement susceptible to appearing in quotation marks, we constantly find something like a description of *statements*, or more exactly, a description of perlocutionary *acts*. "Thirdly, we may also perform *perlocutionary acts*: what we bring about or achieve *by* saying something, such as convincing, persuading, deterring, and even, say, surprising or misleading" (109). Under the heading of the key distinction *of saying, in saying, by saying*, one rediscovers, at the heart of *by saying*, the traditional traits characteristic of rhetoric, the "worker of persuasion" (*peithous dêmiourgos* in Plato's *Gorgias*)—capable of misleading, but no proper utterance. The impossibility of defining the intrinsic traits of a perlocutionary utterance or enunciation is corroborated by the fact that "clearly, *any*, or almost any, perlocutionary act is liable to be brought off, in sufficiently special circumstances, by the issuing, with or without calculation, of any utterance whatsoever, and in particular by a straightforward constative utterance (if there is such an animal)" (110). Thus, in remarking that this is your wife's handkerchief, I produce a major perlocutionary effect: I persuade you that she is cheating on you.

This extensive lability is linked to the complex definition of perlocutionary acts, which may not be reduced to a *single* statement or to the statement *only*. They engage not just an argument and a discursiveness that is extended in time but reception by an audience: "what we bring about or achieve *by* saying something" (109). For better or for worse, this *or*, which links an act (an act that we accomplish) and a consequence for another (an act that we bring about), organizes the difference between the speaker and the listener that is characteristic of rhetoric as "speaking to," polarized between an orator and an audience. The *statement* cannot, then, be the unity of measure appropriate to rhetoric.

THE "SEA-CHANGE"

In a certain manner, Austin treats rhetoric/the perlocutionary as does philosophy: he confers on it the vocation of vanishing. One will note, besides, that the perlocutionary appears (at the end of lecture VII, then VIII, IX, X) only the better to disappear (it is no longer a question of it in the last two lectures). However, the intervention of the perlocutionary plays an essential role: that of a catalyzer for the celebrated *sea-change* that allows the general theory of discursive acts to be attained (150).[26] Hannah Arendt uses the same syntagm in the preface to *The Crisis in Culture*, next to René Char's phrase "our inheritance was left to us by no testament."[27] Like Arendt, Austin wishes to signify that the "thread of tradition is broken." This naturally nondialectical "sea-change" lets nothing subsist but also makes nothing disappear, as Ariel says in *The Tempest* (act 1, scene 2): "Full fathom five thy father lies / Of his bones are coral made / Those pearls that were his eyes / Nothing of him that doth fade / But doth suffer a sea-change / Into something rich and strange."

The *sea-change* is designated as such only in the twelfth and final lecture and is soberly defined in terms of the transition "from the performative/ constative distinction to the theory of speech acts" (150). But it refers to the "tangle" evoked at the end of the seventh lecture, which obliges a "fresh start to the problem" to be taken:

It is time then to make a fresh start on the problem. We want to reconsider more generally the senses in which to say something may be to do something, or in saying something we do something (and also perhaps to consider the different case in which *by* saying something we do something). Perhaps some clarification and definition here may help us out of our tangle. For after all, "doing something" is a very vague expression. When we issue any utterance whatsoever, are we not "doing something"? (91–92)

So, it is the eighth lecture, titled "Locutionary, Illocutionary, and Perlocutionary Acts," that really brings about the *sea-change*. The nomothetic aspect is underlined: Austin "dubs" the locutionary act (94), "calls" the illocutionary act (98),[28] and introduces the "third kind of act," which he "calls" perlocutionary (101). Thus he then distinguishes three, and no longer two, types of entity, which he subsumes under the common genre of "speech-acts." Finally he defines them in a harmonious or commensurable manner: "to say something" (94) becomes an "act *of* saying something" (100), symmetrical to the *by saying*, characteristic of the perlocutionary, and the *in saying* of the illocutionary.

Here, so as to fix the ideas, is an elementary schematization of the *sea-change*:

First Taxonomy	Sea-change	Second Taxonomy
Constative/		Locutionary/illocutionary/
Performative		perlocutionary
(chaps. 1–8)		(chaps. 8–12)
statements, sentences		speech acts

Figure 4. The Sea-change.

However, on closer inspection, nothing is resolved. The intervention of the perlocutionary makes the illocutionary—the proper object of Austin's inquiry—pass from one difficulty to another. The first difficulty was that of making the strict distinction at the heart of the first taxonomy between performative and constative. Hence the intervention of the "third type of acts," the perlocutionary as a resource for resolving the difficulty and the *sea-change*. Now, this transformation, which produces a new taxonomy with three and not two elements—locutionary, illocutionary, and perlocutionary—leads to a second difficulty: that of bringing about the strict distinction between illocutionary and perlocutionary without counting the fact that the locutionary is itself no longer strictly distinct, either.

We will come back to these difficulties.

But it must be emphasized forcefully that if nothing is resolved, everything is transformed. Because the *sea-change* has brought about the passage from a conception in terms of *statements* (which is not appropriate for the perlocutionary, and that is perhaps its principal catalytic effect) to a conception in terms of *speech acts*, with a new focalization of interest. "The total speech-act in the total speech-situation is the *only actual* phenomenon which, in the last resort, we are engaged in elucidating."[29]

SPEECH ACT AND PERFORMANCE

With the passage to *speech acts* we get another point of view on the relation between performance and performative and a different appreciation of the relation between act of language and language as act. I would like to underline what changes.

Locutionary and Illocutionary: Truth and Felicity

Let's start again from the constative/performative distinction. It intersects with the truth/happiness distinction:

> The truth of the constative utterance "he is running" depends on his being running. Whereas . . . it is the happiness of the performative "I apologize" which makes it the fact that I am apologizing: and my success in apologizing depends on the happiness of the performative utterance "I apologize." This is one way in which we might justify the "performative/constative" distinction—as a distinction between doing and saying. (47)

Aristotle says it in the same way for the constative: it is because the snow is white that "the snow is white" is a true proposition. However, the difference between the tip (it is because I say "excuse me" that I excuse myself) and sophistic logology, with the "rhetorical" amplitude of its world effect, appeared considerable to us; that is why the analogy *stricto sensu* between philosophical apophantic/sophistic performance, on the one hand, and constative/performative, on the other, seemed so difficult to us.

Now, it is this difference, which is filled in when the separation between the constative and the performative becomes fuzzy. As Cavell quite rightly signals,[30] what produces the crisis in the dual distinction at the start, between constative and performative, is the fact that the distinction between truth and felicity cannot be maintained as such. In my understanding there are two ways to describe this interference. Cavell's way, which rests on what comes before the *sea-change* and brings happiness back under the condition of truth, "commits us to saying that for a certain performative utterance to be happy, certain statements have *to be true*."[31] As Cavell reminds us, Austin then observes that "at least in some ways there is danger of our initial and tentative distinction between performative and constative utterances breaking down."[32] And Cavell turns this crisis into a victory:

> I do not wish so much to deny these descriptions as to insist that this critical juncture also represents a signal victory for Austin, for what it shows is that performatives bear the same ineluctable connection with, assessment by, fact, with and by what is the case, that statements do.[33]

I would much rather see the victory elsewhere, basing my arguments on what comes after the *sea-change*. In fact, "to perform a locutionary act is, we may say, also and *eo ipso* to perform an illocutionary act, as I propose to call it" (98).[34] That is why the "doctrine of the performative/constative stands to the doctrine of locutionary and illocutionary acts in the total speech-act as the *special* theory to the *general* theory" (148; italics in original). *Eo ipso* the locutionary is also an illocutionary because first of all it is an act. With the integral speech act it is performance that collects the winnings. The relation of force is inverted. Truth is found after happiness, as a particular case. What counts, what is surprising in the truth-happiness relation is not so much that the truth is required for a performative to be happy (yes, there is a state of the world, with conditions and intention, which determines felicity) but that the session finds itself open when the performative is given under conditions of felicity. In other words, when the performative is happy, the constative that it becomes is true. It seems to me that that is where we pass beyond the performative, *stricto sensu* undefinable, to touch on a performativity broadened out to performance. I would like to make this comprehensible on the basis of a recent and remarkable example. "Yes, we can" is an utterance that in all appearances is formally constative, apophantic. But when one considers it as a speech act in a situation, one understands that this constative was first and foremost a performative until "Chicago night," when it gained its status as a constative, according to conventional use. As Gorgias says, "It isn't discourse that represents the outside, it is the outside that becomes revelatory of discourse."[35] Under certain circumstances, which the example of sophistic will perhaps allow us better to determine, every constative is a happy performative that has become true. Far from "the desert of comparative precision" (55), we recognize that "the same phrase can be employed in two different ways depending on the circumstances" and that, considered from the speech act point of view, the constative/performative difference is *eo ipso* broadened out to the ontology/logology difference via the difference between truth and happiness. Thus the difference between utterances is not a difference of nature but a difference of use, with everything that is vague and dangerous for ontology in that notion, in the profoundly sophistical mode of Greek *khrêsthai* and *khrêmata*.[36]

The Apophantic as Act of Saying Something

I would add that, instead, it is happiness that wins, sharing as a sophist the satisfaction that Austin experiences in *playing old Harry* with the true/false fetish (151). Truth is a particular case of felicity, and it is in this sense that the true/false difference is a fetish put in jeopardy—and it is precisely what we find in the analysis that Gorgias offers of Parmenides's poem *On Nature*. To come back to philosophy, it seems to me that what is really new in relationship to Aristotle in Austin's description arises when the normal, that is to say, philosophical, point of view on the *normal statement* gives way to the properly Austinian point of view of the generalized *speech act*. It is then, effectively, that in the second taxonomy, the constative becomes the *act* of *saying something*.

For this at least I see no possible Aristotelian equivalent. To speak is, without doubt, for Aristotle, as also for Homer and all Greeks, a certain type of action, this action implying besides a whole series of physical acts (phonation, articulation, etc.) and mental acts (intention to signify, to designate, to communicate) that Aristotle's treatises on physics, logic, and metaphysics allow us to detail.[37] But no taxonomy before Austin is inscribed under the notion of three types of acts distinct in their relation to *logos*, with this radical prepositional economy, and none puts the apophantic on a common level, not in a dominant position, in this way. One will note—honor to whom honor is due—that in the first place it is this act of saying something, in the Aristotelian fullness of its normal sense, that is baptized *performance*: "The act of 'saying something' in this full normal sense I call, i.e., dub, the performance of a locutionary act" (95).[38]

It is in this way that philosophy is integrated as a modality, a tonality of performance. Performance is confused with speech as act and is distinguished from the performative, which is something like its tip. Consequently it can no longer be a matter of trying to establish a list of "explicit performative verbs" but only "*a list of* illocutionary forces *of an utterance*" (150). So, here we are back with rhetoric: is differentiating illocutionary and perlocutionary value so simple?

Illocutionary and Perlocutionary: Force or Effect?

Let's start again from the perlocutionary and the "third kind of act":

Let us contrast both the locutionary *and* the illocutionary act with yet a third kind of act. There is a yet a further sense (C) in which to perform a locutionary act, and therein an illocutionary act, may also be to perform an act of another kind. Saying something will often, or even normally, produce certain consequential effects upon the feelings, thoughts, or actions of the audience, or of the speaker, or of other persons: and it may be done with the design, intention, or purpose of producing them. . . . We shall call the performance of an act of this kind the performance of a "perlocutionary" act, and the act performed . . . a "perlocution." (101)

Several connected remarks follow.

First, the passage from one type of act to the other (*therein*, a first way of saying *eo ipso*) is normal, and the limits are fuzzy. Even if criteria for differentiation or marks of recognition are possible, the *sea-change* obliges us to abandon all the dichotomies (and not just the constative/performative dichotomy that Austin mentions) and all the "pure" races ("what will *not* survive the transition, unless perhaps as a marginal limiting case . . . is the notion of the purity of performatives") to the favor of "more general *families* of related and overlapping speech-acts" (150). In fact, the examples of performative acts are immediately impure. Sometimes they are hybridized with locution—thus "he persuaded me to shoot her," baptized *Ca, C* for perlocutionary and *a* so as to refer to the *A* of locution (which for its part is uttered *"He said to me 'shoot her!' meaning by 'shoot' shoot and referring by her to her"*) (101). Sometimes they are hybridized with illocution: *"He got me to shoot her,"* baptized *Cb, B* designating the illocutionary (which for its part is uttered *"He urged (or advised, ordered, etc. . . .) me to shoot her"* (102).[39] In any case, that is why "it does not seem to prevent the drawing of a line for our present purposes where we want one" (114).

The criterion for the differentiation of the perlocutionary, strongly stressed, is the production of effects, which must be intentional, willed, not accidental, which is precisely why they arise from something that resembles the art of rhetoric. However, in rhetoric, it is not very frequent to take into account the effects produced on the orator himself, nor on people other than the audience (who? viewers? readers? Or perhaps the people one is speaking about—Helen, for example, as praised by Gorgias—those who constitute the rest of the world and even the world itself—via them?). In this way, the perlocutionary in turn joins up with logological performance of the sophistic kind, as described in Lyotard's emblematic phrase: "it is not the addressee who is seduced by the addressor. The addressor, the referent, the sense are no less subject than the addressee to the seduction exerted."[40]

Effects, precisely. That is where the difference between the perlocutionary and the illocutionary is constantly stressed and where it constantly gets away. We were warned: "it is the distinction between illocutions and perlocutions which seems likeliest to give trouble" (110). Let us recall the criteria one last time. The illocutionary does something *in saying* ("excuse me"); it has a "force" and is susceptible to success or failure (*felicity/infelicity*). The perlocutionary does something *by saying*; it has an "effect" and produces consequences—in which regard, it is worth noting, it is immediately on the side of happiness rather than truth. But the difference between the illocutionary and the perlocutionary, between force and effect is all the more labile given that in order to be happy or achieved, the illocutionary is itself "bound up with effects." The speech act may well be "bound up" with effects, but unlike the perlocutionary, it does not pertain to the illocutionary to "produce" effects.[41] On the one hand, there is an extrinsic link; on the other, there is consequential production—one should be able to distinguish them.

But it is decidedly not so simple because, when describing this illocutionary link, Austin writes that *"an effect must be achieved on the audience if the illocutionary act is to be carried out."*[42] That is the first of the ambiguous (to say the least) three ways in which illocutionary acts are "bound up" with effects. Let's examine all three of them more closely.

Securing Uptake

> Unless a certain effect is achieved, the illocutionary act will not have been happily, successfully performed. This is not to say that the illocutionary act is the achieving of a certain effect. I cannot be said to have warned an audience unless it hears what I say and takes what I say in a certain sense. An effect must be achieved if the illocutionary act is to be carried out. (116)

If no one heard that the session was open or that I excused myself, then it is as if I hadn't said anything. The role of the audience is crucial, much as it is with rhetoric, and casuistry has a wonderful time with it (can one do a baptism if one is mute or speaking a foreign language?).

TAKING EFFECTS

"Taking effect," not to be confused with "having consequences"; the example is perfectly clear: "'I name this ship the *Queen Elizabeth*' has the effect of naming or christening the ship; then certain subsequent acts such as referring to it as the *Generalissimo Stalin* will be out of order." (117)

The arbitrariness here is clearly acknowledged: "it does not seem to prevent the drawing of *a* line for our present purposes where we want one, that is, between the completion of the illocutionary act and all consequences thereafter" (114). Because, where, exactly, does the effect on the world stop?

The difference with the response to a perlocutionary is even more delicate, as it is the other's action that constitutes the response. The examples also exemplify the difficulties in making the distinctions. The truly bookish difference, a paper difference that seems not to refer to any linguistic sentiment, is that between "I ordered him and he obeyed" and "I got him to obey".[43] If I have understood properly, the second formulation implies a perlocutionary act of persuasion, linked to diverse means, of a rhetorical type such as "incitations," a "personal presence," but also, possibly, an "influence that can go as far as constraint." This ensemble can contain an illocutionary act different from an order ("as when I say 'I got him to do it by stating *x*'" [118]). I admit that these subtleties trouble me, to the point that I no longer seek to trace a line between force and effect.

The examples indicate to us already that we would find it difficult to stick to a grammatical criterion, however loose it may be.[44] Even the "in/by" difference, which is definitional and seems particularly apt for recognizing illocutionaries and perlocutionaries, cannot provide us with a reliable test.[45] In fact, the real singularity of the illocutionary, which I haven't yet granted, is convention: "illocutionary acts are conventional acts, perlocutionary acts are *not* conventional" (121). "The [illocutionary] act is constituted not by intention or by fact, essentially, but by *convention* (which is, of course, a fact)" (128). It is convention that can clarify the difference between effects and consequences: "there is clearly a difference between what we feel to be the real production of effects and what we regard as mere conventional consequences" (103). However, once again things do not seem so simple. It comes down to the arbitrariness of the line: when I said "yes" on my wedding day, was the simple conventional consequence (i.e., I'm married now) separable from real effects? And can rhetoric, for its part, be conceived without conventions, *topoi* and *endoxa*, to manipulate? Doubtless it is not about effects/consequences/conventions in the same sense but about where the lines of sense pass.

It is certain that the distinctions are rendered arbitrary by the *sea-change*. I simply wanted to show here how the passage to the general theory of speech acts not only troubled the difference between constative and performative and the difference between locutionary, illocutionary, and perlocutionary but also the difference between performance and performative.

Points of Sophistic Application: Critique of Ontology and Politics

Right at the end of his conferences, Austin delights in "play[ing] Old Harry with two fetishes which I admit to an inclination to play Old Harry with, viz. (1) the true/false fetish, (2) the value/fact fetish" (151). This point of arrival doubtless constitutes the best starting point for a comparison with sophistic. I will take two examples, which I will treat here all the more schematically for having developed each one of them for itself elsewhere.[46] To consider, along with Gorgias, *On Nature* as a speech act is to play Old Harry with the true/false fetish and to make felicity take primacy over truth. To consider, along with Gorgias, the *Encomium of Helen* as a performance able to produce an innocent Helen is to play with the fact/value fetish.

HOW GORGIAS READS PARMENIDES'S *ON NATURE* AS A SPEECH ACT

In the reading that Gorgias's treatise *On Non-Being, or on Nature* proposes of Parmenides's poem *On Nature, or on Being*, everything manifestly revolves around the way in which being and saying are knotted together. It is one of two things, brutally distinct: either there is being, *esti, es gibt sein*, and the task of man, the shepherd of Being, is to speak it faithfully: apophantic and constative ontology, unveiling and truth, from Parmenides to Heidegger and from Aristotle to Austin as a reader of philosophy. Or: Being is and is there only in and by the poem, the constative is apparent solely because it is only ever the product of an illocutionary performance: being is an effect of saying, a successful speech act, from Gorgias to Austin, a discursive production, what I propose to call a performance: "logology," to use Novalis's term.[47]

Gorgias's procedure, treatise against poem, consists simply in drawing attention—an insolent attention—to all the maneuvers, whether of the Greek language or discursivity itself, which allow the unveiling between being and saying to be put in place. In particular, the manner in which *On Nature* passes from *esti* to *to on*, from the verb to the subject-substantive participle (by a sort of linguistic "secretion"), by playing on the ensemble of meanings of *esti*: it is possible, it is true that (as one says "it is the case that") "is," in the sense of the copula and of identity, "is" in the sense of existence, to put it in post-Aristotelian terms, by playing on homonymy or *pollakhôs* at least and on amphiboly. Being, the famous *to eon* of fragment VIII, has been woven together by the poem; it is a result and not an observation. It seems to me that here there is a radical way of understanding The Poem as a *total speech act in a total speech situation* rather than as a series of *statements* and of making the illocutionary force of each constative phrase felt. The Poem, then, as a speech act (*acte de langage*), with the additional precision that the speech act is, or at least is also, what I would like to call a "language act" (*acte de langue*)—but why wouldn't that be suitable for a "*total* speech act"? The difference of languages doubtless remains foreign, nontopical, to Austin, but it is certainly not the same for the idiosyncratic intimacy and singularity of the language that he speaks and of which he speaks.

The limit effect or catastrophe thus produced consists in showing that, if the text of ontology is rigorous, that is to say, if it does not constitute an exception in relation to the legislation that it sets up, then it is a sophistic masterpiece. What matters for the moment is not a being that would be already there, so to speak, but the being that discourse produces. Gorgias makes the full extent of the change of landscape measurable: the surest principle of identity no longer has as formula "Being is" or "Being is being" but—also a phrase in the treatise—"whoever speaks speaks" and even "whoever speaks speaks . . . a speech."[48] Parmenides's Poem, like Gorgias's *Treatise*, is a language act, the difference being that it tries to hide—or hide from itself—its "third dimension."

The presence of Being, the immediacy of Nature, and the evidence of a speech bound to say them adequately all disappear together: the physics that speech uncovers gives way to the politics that discourse creates. Wherein thanks to the Sophists—the "masters of Greece," as Hegel put it—one effectively attains the dimension of politics, as *agora* for an *agôn*: the city is a continuous creation of language pertaining to success and not truth.

The status of *epideixis* is central from this point of view, and the term, which can quite rightly be translated as "performance"—in the broad sense, whose Austinian legitimacy we have seen—makes lingering on it worthwhile.

Epideixis is the very name that tradition attributes, par excellence, to sophistic discursivity. The term is consecrated by Plato (in, for example, *Hippias Major* 282c and 286a, *Hippias Minor* 363c, and *Gorgias* 447c) and designates the speech delivered by Prodicos, Hippias and Gorgias. In opposition to the dialogue through questions and answers, which Socrates is fond of, it can only be repeated, reproduced *expressis verbis*, so much does it count formulation and enunciation.

Referring to *deixis*, monstration, with one's index finger extended, *epideixis* can be understood only in contrast to *apodeixis*. *Apodeixis*, which refers to all the *apo* (*apophainesthai*, *apophansis*) characteristic of phenomenology,[49] is the art of showing, "starting from" what is shown, using it as a basis to "de-monstrate." It signals the domain of the apophantic/constative and of unveiling/truth. *Epideixis* is the art of showing "before" and of showing "as well," according to the two main senses of the prefix. To show, publicly, "before," in everyone's eyes: an *epideixis* may thus be a demonstration of force (the deployment of an army, in Thucydides, for example, or the demonstration of a crowd), an exhibition.[50] But also showing "more" on the occasion of this publicity: by putting an object on display, one makes use of it as an example or a paradigm, one "overdoes" it—"making of a fly an elephant," Lucian says. This is consonant with the practice of paradoxical eulogies—to baldness, as, too, contemporaneously, to the pitcher of water, by Francis Ponge, a shameless vindication of *hubris*.[51] And one thus shows oneself "as well," as a talented orator, capable of contraries, or as a real "poet," a fabricator. It is a matter, then, in the broad sense, of a "performance," whether improvised or not, written or spoken, but always related to the show, the public. In the restricted sense, precisely codified by Aristotle's rhetoric, it means epidictic eloquence, praise, or blame, which speaks the good or the shameful and aims at pleasure.

With sophistic, the two senses of performance and of eulogy are conjugated and amplify one another: the most memorable *epideixis* (the *one-man show*, which made him a celebrity in Athens, that is to say, for always throughout the world) is an *epideixis*, the *Encomium of Helen*, where, "praising the praiseworthy and blaming the blameworthy," he nonetheless succeeded in clearing the infidel that everyone since Homer has accused. The supplement of *deixis*, which is *epideixis*, succeeds in turning the phenomenon into its contrary: the phenomenon becomes the effect of the all-powerful *logos*. In any case, that is why every eulogy is also or above all a eulogy to *logos*, and that is where we started from: "Discourse is a great master, which with the smallest and least perceptible of bodies performs the most divine of acts [*theiotota erga apotelei*]."[52]

I would like to stress that beyond the ontology-logology difference, it is in fact, a moment of political invention: performance consists first of all in making a passage from the communion in the values of the community (including the communion in the values of language via the meaning of words and metaphors, as Nietzsche emphasized[53]) to the creation of new values.

The first two paragraphs of the *Encomium of Helen* attest to this passage and begin to produce it. I don't wish to resume the entire analysis, just sketch it out by citing the paragraphs:

> Order, for a city, is the excellence of its men, for a body, beauty, for a soul, wisdom, for an action, value, for a speech, truth. Their opposite is disorder. Man, woman, speech, deed, city, thing, should be honored with praise if praiseworthy, and incur blame if blameworthy; for to blame the praisable or to praise the blamable is of equal error and ignorance.
>
> It is to the same man that it befalls to say with rectitude what must be said, and to contradict those who blame Helen, a woman who brought together, in one voice and in one soul, the credence of the poets' auditors, as well as the sound of a name which bears the memory of misfortunes. *I* want, giving logic to discourse, to have brought to an end the accusation against her of whom we hear so much abuse, demonstrate that those who blame her are wrong, show the truth, and put an end to ignorance. (§1–2, emphasis added)

As such, via the manner in which a "self" gives *logismon* to *logos*—"come and pass from the one to the other in my discourse"[54]—the liturgy (*kosmos, kallos, sophia, aretê, alêtheia*) opens onto a happening that performs another world.

It seems to me that here we are closest to the labile frontier between the "perlocutionary" and the "illocutionary": the perlocutionary, with its rhetorical effect on the other *by saying*—subjective, one might say—(Austin talks here, it will be recalled, of "what we bring about or achieve *by* saying something, such as convincing, persuading, deterring, and even, say, surprising or misleading" [*How to Do Things with Words*, 109]), and the illocutionary, the most active of speech acts, capable of directly changing the state of the world *in saying* and exceeding the perlocutionary with something like an immediate and objective world effect. It wouldn't be absurd to call this "force," but whatever the case may be, from Euripides to Offenbach or Hofmannsthal, I wouldn't want to say whether henceforth the innocence of Helen is a fact or a value.

Working Perspectives

A GENEALOGY OF THE PERFORMATIVE: "I CLASP YOUR KNEES" /

"THIS IS MY BODY" / "THE SESSION IS OPEN"

To conclude I would like to indicate the two directions that I have started to explore by making use of this Austinian "tangle" as a trampoline.

The first is a genealogy of the performative in relation to performance and the total speech act. Drawing on Jespersen's highly debatable notion of a "primitive language," Austin suggests that, "historically, from the point of view of the evolution of language, the explicit performative must be a later development than certain more primary utterances" in the form, notably, of "implicit performatives, which are included in most or many explicit performatives as parts of a whole. For example, 'I will . . .' is earlier than 'I promise that I will . . .'" (*How to Do Things with Words*, 71). With the constative and the performative, it is a matter no so much of "two poles" than of a "historical evolution." For my part, I propose to distinguish three ages or three models of the performative in the restricted sense, which can evidently overlap. A poetic and political pagan performative, a religious and sacramental Christian performative, and a secularized, socialized, or sociologized performative. These three models can be exemplified thus: "I clasp your knees" / "this is my body" / "the session is open."

The first is evidently the least well known, and that is why I will dwell on it a little. It is the *kerdaleon muthos*, on *kerdos*, "gain, profit, advantage," this "winning discourse" that Ulysses addresses to Nausicaa when he sees her: "I clasp your knees," he says instead of clasping her knees, by conforming to the gesture of the supplicant, because, he says, "I am terribly frightened of clasping your knees." To say it is the only way of clasping her knees without frightening the young girl, naked as he is, with only a leafy branch (which he might drop . . .) covering his sexual organs. Is not this *kerdaleon muthos* that Ulysses has just proffered, a speech act that strongly resembles the performative? All in all, this act would even fall under the category of *behabitives*: " 'I salute you' may become a substitute for the salute and thus a pure performative utterance. To say 'I salute you' now *is* to salute you" (81) on the condition, however, that we specify that Ulysses appears as its "inventor." It is not so much that he invents the first "salute" that does without saluting, the first supplication without the gesture of supplicating, but because he (Ulysses/Homer) draws attention to the substitution of the speech act for the real act, the act of the thing, and to the advantage constituted by this substitution.

With Ulysses and Homer it is a matter of a "pagan" performative. "Pagan" refers here to conditions of felicity that could be sketched out in the following way: the cosmos is needed for this invention; in any case, this invention is made in a cosmic structure of communication and analogy, and—the entire passage testifies unceasingly—in the permeability of the boundary between man and god. Ulysses the divine is a mountain lion, a naked, virile man, a foamy wreck; Nausicaa is a young girl, a goddess or a mortal, more precisely, the stem of a palm tree. The *kerdaleon muthos*, let's be sensitive to this, is the invention of a man for a woman: the least frightening way of clasping her knees with this gesture of the supplicant, which, according to the "hazardous considerations of Onians,"[55] is addressed to the power of engendering (*gignomai*) to the knee (*gonu*) as center of vital power. But above all the pagan is authorized only by himself; he is his own authority. Why? Because far from monotheism, there is nothing to say that he is not himself a god: a pagan is someone who supposes that whoever comes toward you might be a god. He says to her: "I clasp your knees," "whether you are goddess or mortal," and she says to herself, "Now he resembles the gods of the sky" (V243). Jean-François Lyotard is right to affirm that "a pagan god is an effective narrator, for instance,"[56] just as Ulysses and Nausicaa are authors, authorized by themselves only, in the sense that they are authorized by their power to be a god/goddess.

It is to be understood by its difference from the originary *fiat lux* of the religions of the book and by its ersatz sacraments such as "this is my body." This is only my body because God, the sole God says so and authorizes me to say it, with the guarantee of God's institution, the church. It is also to be understood by its difference from the modern "I declare this session open," whose conditions of felicity derive from the authority of the judiciary conferred on me and from the organization of society in its entirety.[57] It is thus a history with a long duration, which would be traced out in broad strokes.

ENUNCIATION AND SIGNIFIER

"That one speaks stays forgotten behind what is said in what is heard." Jacques Lacan wrote this formula on the blackboard to serve as a starting point for "L'étourdit."[58] "That one speaks": it is simultaneously a question of a speech act and an utterance, two entities that entertain a relation that is at least as complex and little theorized by Austin as that between performance and the performative. The other major site for work for me is to understand how the Austinian categories and their way of calling into question the two fetishes to the profit of "happiness" clarify the linguistic practice that is psychoanalysis.[59]

One can set off again from Benveniste, taking together his definition of the performative: the statement is the act, and his astonishment regarding the singularity of psychoanalysis, praised by Lacan as a good diagnostic: "just what is this 'language' which acts as much as it expresses something?"[60] This astonishment has as its starting point Freud's 1910 article "The Antithetical Sense of Primal Words": consciousness of the performative thus finds itself linked to what I would call "motivated homonymy." Benveniste concludes that "the unconscious uses a veritable 'rhetoric' which, like style, has its 'figures,' and the old catalogue of tropes would supply an inventory appropriate to the two types of expression."[61] Language as act, homonymy, rhetoric, metaphor, metonymy: pulling on a thread brings the distaff.

Evidently it is this thread that Lacan performs—fabricating it at the same time as he describes it. One of the most consequential quilting points knots together enunciation and signifier in the scansion of interpretation. The singular tangling of "L'étourdit," which renders this text so unreadable for an Aristotelian, refers to the place of homonymy, which is not just uttered but inscribed (the title, "L'étourdit," says and writes it) under the aegis of the speech act. In return, "a language, amongst others," Lacan says, regarding the languages of the unconscious, "is nothing more than the integral of equivocations that its history has allowed to persist in it."[62] The Aristotelians know that here one is touching on the principle of noncontradiction and its defeat by the *legein logou karin*—"speaking for the pleasure of speaking" or "speaking at a loss [*en pure perte*]," which relates to the Lacanian part of psychoanalysis.

Linked to the sophistic perception of language, such is the ensemble of what the Austinian categories, in all the force of their bricolage, can help us think.

Translated by Andrew Goffey

ELEVEN

The Performative Without Condition: A University *sans appel*

"Take your time but be quick about it, because you don't know what awaits you," said Jacques Derrida in 1998 at Stanford.[1] Indeed. He himself would not have expected to be cited like this by Valérie Pécresse, French minister for higher education and research, in January 2009:

> We are taking all measures to ensure that a new ethic founds the autonomy gained by the university community in the conduct of its own destiny. . . . "*To profess is to pledge oneself,*" writes Jacques Derrida in *The University Without Condition*. The hour has come to fully recognize this engagement, which is at once individual and collective, to have confidence in the university and in academics.[2]

One can truncate a citation, distort a claim, pervert the spirit of a text.[3] But perhaps one should in the first place rejoice that a French government minister knows her Jacques Derrida—unlike a president of the republic who hadn't heard of Anne of Clèves and seems to be at pains to master his mother tongue.[4]

Derrida said that something awaited us. In 1998, one could not have known what. Now we know. The law that was supposed to institute the "autonomy" of the universities in France is titled "The Freedoms and Responsibilities of the Universities":[5] a vocabulary and a political symptom at once. "Ethic," "autonomy," "community," "destiny," "engagement," "confidence." These are the words of Minister Valérie Pécresse.

One can read some of them in Derrida, too, the same and with similar undertones: "and what matters here is this promise, this pledge of responsibility."[6]

"I am thus referring here to a university that would be what it always should have been or always should have represented, that is, from its inception and in principle: autonomous, unconditionally free in its institution, in its speech, in its writing, in its thinking."[7]

Nothing is easier, but nothing is more tempting than to draw a parallel between Sarkozy's "autonomy" and Derrida's "without condition." Both are grasped in an ethic of responsibility. It is the ethic of responsibility that strikes, in a really Petainist fashion today, when candidates for professorial positions are evaluated for their competence to "act as a civil servant [*fonctionnaire d'état*] and in an ethical and responsible fashion."[8] Not, however, the same responsibility. Because the "without condition" of Derrida is grasped in the ethic of *dessaisissement*, of nonmastery, of the always excessive event,[9] in short, of masculine hysteria.

On the other hand, "autonomy" (that of our ministers, in any case) is grasped in the ethics of performance—in other words, the culture of results. "Autonomy is essential for the university because autonomy is the culture of the result. If the minister decides, it is irresponsibility"; "it is necessary for us today to admit that the culture of results be a part of the university."[10] As the icing on the cake, Pécresse added: "for the first time, a government will judge the universities, finance them, equip them as a function of their real performances." Autonomy, then, is a "culture of results" insofar as that culture is judged heteronomically. The university is autonomous when it suits the government, in itself the only judge of "real performances." The university is quite literally "irresponsible" (dependant on the minister) where it is said to be autonomous.

Today and in itself, then, autonomy is the mask behind which everything that we do not want progresses, that is to say, the *evaluation of performance*. And if we have begun with Derrida and Pécresse, it is because it is very difficult, *hic et nunc*, to call into doubt the ethics of responsibility even when it results in the requirement of evaluation. Do you refuse to be evaluated? Do you want to be inefficient (*nonperformants*), or as the French Agency for the Evaluation of Research and Higher Education says, "nonproductive"?

A knot to be untied then: responsibility, evaluation, performance.

Derrida unties it in advance by speaking not of performance but of the performative. The performative intervenes three times in the "University Without Condition."

The first time, in the principle of an unconditioned university, frank/free, that is to say, set free of everything, and in particular of all "territorial (thus national) rootedness."[11] It performs itself in affirming itself in "the place of the self-presentation of unconditionality that will go by the name 'Humanities.'"[12] Affirmation, "self-presentation"—one might be tempted to say *Selbstbehauptung*, but for the difference of nationality, which is no small thing. *Ecce* Heidegger:

> Battle alone keeps this opposition open and implants in the entire body of teachers and students that basic mood which lets self-limiting self-assertion empower resolute self-examination to genuine self-governance.[13]

The second time, in the declaration of principles of the professor. "To profess or to be professor" is to "promise to take a responsibility that is not exhausted in the act of knowing or teaching"; the "affirmation" of the declaration of principles "in effect closely *resembles a performative speech act*."[14] As we know, "to profess is to pledge oneself," say the minister and our two philosophers, Derrida and Heidegger, calm, uneasy.

The final, contemporary time: "at the moment that one takes into account not only the performative value of the 'profession,' but where one accepts that a professor produces 'oeuvres.'" That is to say, when, at the heart of the "transformed humanities,"[15] between literature and philosophy, one thinks as a poet, as Heidegger—once again—would say.

After Derrida-and-Pécresse, Derrida-and-Heidegger? An old cliché, one that is evidently false. One can dismantle its falsity in more than one philosophical language: Kantian, Austinian, Levinasian, too.

In Kantian language: Derrida—a child of the republic with the Crémieux decree—is Kantian when he speaks of autonomy. He is moral and a universalist where Heidegger, speaking of *Selbstverwaltung*, is a national bureaucrat. Besides, a Kantian thinking of the autonomy of universities exists. It is neither moral nor bureaucratic but rather industrial and commercial and is expressed in the first pages of the *Conflict of the Faculties*, those pages that Derrida precisely doesn't comment on:

> Whoever it was that first hit on the notion of a university and proposed that a public institution of this kind be established, it was not a bad idea to handle the entire content of learning . . . by *mass production*, so to speak—by a division of labor, so that [for] every branch of the sciences there would be a public teacher or *professor* appointed as its trustee, and all of these together would form a kind of learned community called a *university* (or higher school). The university would have a certain autonomy (since only scholars can pass judgment on scholars as such).[16]

In Austinian language: almost all the way. The distinction between performative *speech acts* and constative *speech acts*, in play from the start of the profession of the professor "will have been a great event in this century—and it will first have been an academic event" "*in* the University," and it will have been "the Humanities that made it come about and that explored its resources."[17] Evidently, it is not the same thing "when, performatively, one professes"[18] like Derrida and when one responds to the call of Being like Heidegger.

In Levinasian language: "In the face of what arrives to me, what happens to me, even in what I decide . . . in the face of the other who arrives and arrives to me, all performative force is overrun, exceeded, exposed."[19] It is the Other, in (the) place of Being, which, for Derrida, makes the "event" (*Ereignis* all the same—Levinas as a Jewish Heidegger?). A motive for finally abandoning the performative. We will come back to this.

We are moving too fast, and in play. But through these caustic remarks we have wanted to show that, once predicated of the university—in the trembling Heidegger/Kant—autonomy is a fundamentally homonymic notion.

We now want to show that the performative is a good way to outsmart the performance imperative and the "culture of results" on condition that one thinks it to the very end—without stopping, like Derrida, at the doubtful ethics of the "event."

"Ethics" and the Homonymy of Performance

After the homonymy of autonomy, we will take as our new point of departure the homonymy of performance. New European politics *evaluates* the university. It evaluates it on its "real performances." Such is the "culture of results" into which the university is invited to enter. This is to say, very officially, that those who evaluate the university are external, foreign to it, and intend to remain so. The ex-president of the French republic, Nicolas Sarkozy, is not a university type. On the other hand, he is a big theorist of the link between evaluation, performance, and the culture of results. The university served as a privileged example for him for a while.[20] He barely altered his formulae as a result of the global economic crisis. He may even have toughened them up.[21]

As for us, less speculatively, we already know what "performance" really means.[22] So, as a consequence, let us continue with our definitions. In the language of received—and thus *uncontroversial*—opinion (that is, Wikipedia): "evaluation is a method that allows a result to be evaluated and thus the value of a result that can't be measured to be known. It is applied in numerous domains where results are expected but not measurable." Neither research nor health can be measured, and that is precisely what evaluation says when it talks of the "performance" of a hospital or a system of research. The challenge of quantifying the unquantifiable is supposed to be met thanks to performance.

What is magical about performance is that it is enough to transform more into better, quantity into quality, cardinal into ordinal. It comes at the right moment then: it is the synthesis of quality and quantity. The tension internal to the concept derives from its designating at the same time the most objectively measurable (the performance indicators of a machine) and what is most singular about the individual act, the performance of a horse, a champion, an artist—that which is unrepeatable. Not only does performance measure the unquantifiable and make the most singular enter into the most objective, but it gives it the democratic *look* of a numerical figure without being arbitrary. "To exit a purely mechanical, legal, egalitarian, anonymous approach" so as to promote genuine equality, genuine equality and not egalitarianism, says Sarkozy.[23] What does that mean? "Genuine equality" for Sarkozy is not equality of opportunity; it is equality of compensation for equal performance. When we perform well, we are each and every one of us like a racing car, a superb athlete, even a champion in bed. Visible and thus profitable.

If now we get closer to performance evaluation in the university sector, we come across two things: the search engine and the evaluation form. Do you think that we would exaggerate? Look at how we work already, with Google onscreen, and how one wants us to work when we apply for research funding or evaluate research projects.

Research and the Search Engine

Google, then, as a model of evaluation by performance. With Google, basic research and the research of a search engine no longer have anything homonymic about them. The PageRank algorithm, which ranks the page responses to a query and is one of the things that gives Google its great superiority, functions—if Brin and Page are to be believed—according to the academic model of the citation: pages that are click-cited the most are ranked first. It is even a question here of a *doxa* raised to the power of two: at the top of the page ranking are the sites that are most cited by the sites that are most cited—a "cultural democracy," according to Google, with a balancing mechanism, however, which gives this democracy a star system: a link from a Web site that does not cite much is worth more than one from one that cites a great deal.[24]

Now, this ranking mechanism is precisely that put into operation by Hirsch's famous H-index or *impact factor*, more or less amended to avoid absolute ridicule (no matter what neo-Nazi negationist is evidently ranked higher than Lévi-Strauss). It determines the admissibility of the applications for "senior researcher" submitted to the European Research Council in Brussels.[25] It classifies researchers, for example, by the number of publications they have in journals that are themselves classified and rated by balancing them with the number of citations that are made of these publications in journals that are themselves classified and rated. The classification of journals is evidently the object of a fierce national and international battle since it forms part of the barometer. "Tell us how many articles you have published in A-rated journals and how many times these articles have themselves been cited in A-rated journals, and we will tell you what you are worth!" Of course, we will not take into account the linguistic bias, which means that you may not necessarily be publishing in English—or rather in *Globish*—and that maybe it is necessary to be sure that continuing to speak in French or German (thus maintaining them as languages and not simple dialects) doesn't penalize you. Of course, we will also not take into account the disciplinary bias, which means that the human and social sciences can require publications that are lengthier and take longer to write (did you say "books"?). And of course we will not concern ourselves with the fact that evaluation might be a matter of reading and of thinking instead of citing one's own little clique or accounting for the impact that is forgotten tomorrow.

That such a treasure may make Google's fortune—which subordinates everything, including so-called cultural democracy, to "legitimate commercial goals"—is the name of the game, of a certain game. But for this kind of "research"—such as it is practiced by a "search engine"—to become the regulatory norm for the evaluation of basic research is something that must be opposed by every possible means and to the end because it evidently contradicts the very idea of emerging research. By definition, the (too singular) base of a Gaussian curve is invisible. Performance and the H-factor are incapable of measuring originality as such. As Lindon said apropos of Beckett: one doesn't notice the absence of an unknown. Now innovation would like researchers to produce prototypes, not stereotypes: there is no H-factor that could ensure either its rating or its conformity.

Language and the Ethic of Forms

Let us now come to the form.[26] Performance has its calculus, as we have just seen. But it also has its ethics, the "responsible" ethics of "autonomous" universities. It is interesting that this ethic has to pass through the sections of a *form*. What is it a question of? Phenomenologically, the form is the primary perception of evaluation. The project leader, the leader of the research team being evaluated completes an "evaluation form." The evaluator of the project or of the research team completes another form. What is called "evaluation" may be described—phenomenologically again—as the passage from one form to another. Why the form? We propose two answers.[27]

First, the form is the point of contact between *language* and evaluation. It is composed of sections that must be completed one after the other. The first function of the form is to sequence: it transforms the object evaluated— the illness and treatment of a patient, for example—into analogous portions that can be determined on a cost-per-action basis according to a preestablished protocol. The "personal appreciation" or *statement* of the evaluator is itself a section—generally the last one—because it is the least important. After evaluation, as the passage from one form to another, a closer description makes evaluation appear as the passage from one section to another. What do we do when we pass from one section to another? It is difficult to say, but in any case we do know what we don't do or don't do any more: we don't write or write up any longer. We progress in the form by separating, segmenting, and sequencing. Unlike the *topoi* of Ancient Greek rhetoric, which—although decried—constituted a reservoir of arguments for invention that one was free to assemble in the most appropriate and singular manner each time, the form is a fixed sequence.

Second, the form is the point of contact between evaluation and *morality*. From the point of view of the evaluated, more and more frequently, it contains the moment of *self-evaluation*, with the previous noting and identification of one's "strong points" and "weak points." In the laboratories and research centers one frequently ironizes the similarity between self-evaluation and the confession of sins (or Maoist self-criticism, depending on one's preferences). That sort of irony is easy. What is happening in reality is very serious. If you can find only "weak points," it is because you really must have a problem, but if you credit yourself only with "strong points," in a sense, this is even worse. What self-evaluation tests is your ability to acquire the Anglo-Saxon and Protestant virtue of *fairness*. What is *fairness*? It is exactly that which remains of the subjectivity of the researcher who puts his work through the grid of the form: just enough subjectivity not to be confused with a computer.

It is the same for both evaluator and evaluated. The form is what assures me that no-matter-what evaluator would have made the same decision as me. Here once again is *fair play* and something to soothe my conscience: the idea that I might have shown judgment, even taste, was in fact a source of deep insecurity. Who am I to judge when I am no longer elected by my colleagues and my task consists only of returning my correctly completed form before the deadline? The form, with its neatly ordered sections, gives at least a momentary response to my anxiety until the moment when I have to compare my form to those of peer evaluators with as little legitimacy as me. But even at this stage, that of the so-called update meeting, the comparison of forms will not require any more than the minimum of subjectivity that was required of those being evaluated. There will be trouble for me if I talk beyond the confines of the sections on the form: I will have come close to insider trading or—as the evaluation agencies call it—a "conflict of interest."

The language of forms is thus transparent and honest, consensual, euphemistic, and gentle. Its transparency is guaranteed by the procedure: the justice of evaluation is a procedural justice, à la Habermas. *Fairness* is ensured by *process*. That is why those in charge of the national and European evaluation agencies are generally decent, competent, and above all profoundly cooperative people: they will always encourage you to sit down next to them in order to "refine the criteria," as they say, to multiply them if necessary. The essential point is that this refinement of criteria does nothing but lead to a longer form. Just try getting away from forms: you will find yourself talking into thin air for your own amusement.[28] You will be considered "irresponsible."

The Performative Versus Performance

To finish, let us posit—delicately, provisionally, because it is where all the difficulty lies—an academic "we," a university thought of as (a) "we." There are two ways to call "ourselves" to "responsibility." Either by designating for ourselves the historical mission of the university—that is the old formula, born with Humboldt, continued-deformed by Heidegger and the incantation of *Selbstbehauptung*. Or by summoning ourselves—at last—to "perform" efficiently, to publish, to be "productive," and, even more so, to be "evaluated." That is the call that is coming from our government ministries, our evaluation agencies, our states today. In one case, we will have to *answer for* the university, like one answers for an idea that is greater than oneself. In the second, it will be necessary for us to "defend" our university (each one his or her own university, different from and in competition with all the others, "co-petitive," as Google says), in the way that one defends one's team, one's business, one's country: our responsibility will be to *respond to* calls for tenders. Always responding.

Those are the two current discourses on the university. Sometimes they seem to be opposed. Most often, as with Valérie Pécresse, they reinforce each other. What the present moment of the university shows us is that the ethics of responsibility has been unable to do anything against the culture of results; quite the contrary, in fact.

Here, we rediscover our initial knot: responsibility, evaluation, performance.

In 1998, Jacques Derrida's "University Without Condition" was barely touched by the fever of evaluation. Performance was not yet completely the university's business. Derrida placed the performative in the face of responsibility.

In our knot, then, one of the threads splits in two: performance and performative. That is without doubt the strangest thing that we discovered in the "University Without Condition." But how the devil did we pass from the performative university to the performances of the university as judged by the criteria of a "culture of results"?

One can answer in two ways. The first is the simpler. It consists of two toponyms and some slogans: the "Bologna process," the "Lisbon strategy."

Both make the university the primary motor in the transformation of Europe into a "knowledge-based economy." A chronology may be sketched out here. Bologna (June 1999) and Lisbon (March 2000) separate us from Derrida's lecture at Stanford (April 1998). Thus we have 1998–2010: two universities separated by a world.

But other evolutions have taken place. From the performative to performance, the journey sums up two centuries of the European university.

In Derrida, for a time at least, the performative saves the "university without condition" from *Selbsbehauptung* and the pathos of "destining." For Derrida, the unconditioned and the absolute are said performatively so as to avoid repeating Humboldt's lesson and even more so its being led astray by Heidegger. In affirming itself without any condition, the university fabricates or *performs itself*—is constituted as university—in anticipation of any merely transmitted knowledge.

The very idea of the university becomes a language act, that of the professor who knows that his or her freedom is not exhausted by the "pure technoscientific knowledge" that it accompanies.[29] In short: the performative university is no longer the essence that one contemplates and that one endeavors to realize. It is the act that one performs, the university that starts all over again with each lecture course.

The performative as a support for and vector of knowledge—that of the university: we must hold this to be something the topicality of which is still and always established. To tell the truth, we must maintain it for much longer than Derrida. Because, for Derrida, the performative is rapidly directed toward a "place where it fails."[30] Derrida designates this "place" as "event." The event "disregards the performative." It has to "dissociate" the humanities from "every phantasm of *indivisible sovereignty* and of sovereign mastery" shortly after the same humanities have been associated with "engagement" and the "promise" of a profession of faith characterized as performative.[31] That is what we called "masculine hysteria": an apology for impotence through fear of the counterperformance ("without power" or "without defense"; Derrida's quotation marks[32]); the poetry of *désœuvrement* versus the "masterable possible," with a definition of the event—in a dialectico-phenomenological patois—that is evidently oxymoronic as "impossible possible" ("only the impossible *can* happen"); the normative exacerbation of this impossible possible as the only "event worthy of the name"; and the final choice of the event as the antonym of the performative.[33] The whole argument is summarized in the superbly forged formulation: "the force of an event is always stronger than the force of a performative."[34]

The performative obliges us here to judge things by effects. The effect is that, eight years after its appearance, "The University without Condition" finds itself cited by a French government minister who has the whole of the university against her.

Certainly what is at stake here, as usual, is an appropriation of the other, not for the fundamentals of what the other says but for the emblem, self-designated as "opening"—whether it is a matter of "Jaurès," of the signifier "Mitterrand," or of "Derrida." What is at stake is a governmental ventriloquism in which no word, no idea, comes out unscathed.

However, we find a real convergence where the philosopher is most philosophical and the minister most political. Valérie Pécresse paraphrases: *"to profess is to pledge oneself,* wrote Jacques Derrida."[35] For his part, Derrida wanted to "exceed pure techno-scientific knowledge in the pledge of responsibility."[36] On the one hand, there is engagement[37] thought of as motivation in the horizon of an "ethics" (the word the minister uses) of responsibility; on the other hand, for the philosopher, there is an "ethico-political responsibility," the principle of the "unconditional resistance of the university."[38] Two concepts of responsibility, doubtless, and two ethics also. But in both cases, an *appeal,* an exhortation, a paraenesis.

The university without condition that, for our part, we are demanding is a university *without appeal* [*sans appel*]. Without appeal covers without ethics, without responsibility, but also without the dilemma between an autonomy desirable for every corporation and a heteronomy that is necessary to bring the university out of itself.

Is it worth specifying here that to reject the injunction to responsibility is not to vindicate irresponsibility—or immorality—for oneself? (Should one say "nonethics"?) In fact, our response, like Derrida's in his time, is strategically determined. It has nothing to do with a perennial, timeless—that is to say "essential"—definition of "the" university. In this sense, it is not "responsible" (ethico-ontologically responsible), or responsibility must be understood as the strength to respond "no." As it happens, we say "no" to the responsibility that is ideologically hammered out as the responsibility of the citizen professor and citizen student of a techno-scientific neoliberal state concerned with performance. And we protest—that is what we are maintaining, or: here we stand—that this performance is radically counter-productive on all levels, but first of all on that of knowledge and invention, including the invention that belongs intrinsically to the very notion of the transmission of knowledge.[39]

Just as the performative utterance—the university thought of in the form of an enlarged perlocutory—has been able to get the university out of an autonomy reduced to *Selbstbehauptung*, so—thought all the way through—it will serve us as a provisional arm for subtracting us from an autonomy confused with the performance of a manager. Its other name is: "let us continue the combat."

A "veritable" autonomy, then? Of course, it is this "ethic" that we will begin by breaking with.

Translated by Andrew Goffey

TWELVE

Genres and Genders.
Woman/Philosopher: Identity as Strategy

Local and Global—Identity as a Counterreply

The mission of UNESCO, the United Nations Educational, Scientific, and Cultural Organization, is "to construct peace in the minds of men," and it defines "peace" as "the determination to act in a way that is based on respect for difference and for dialogue." This is the heart of the matter: respect for difference. In creating a network of women-philosophers, are we respecting difference? And if the answer is "yes," what difference are we trying to respect? We are probably not trying to respect the man/woman difference—or if we are, not as such and not as it is usually understood, and probably not the philosopher/nonphilosopher difference, either—or again, not as such and not as it is usually understood. This is because we question these differences, stand them on their heads, deconstruct and reconstruct them. What differences, then, are we seeking to respect? Which ones do we want to take back to the drawing board, the better to construct peace in the minds of men? How should we go about it? UNESCO sees us as women of influence, and this is how I see us, too, especially in contrast to women of power. But what do we want to influence? What, precisely, do we want to change? This is a key question.

It seems to me that this question can be answered on two different levels: on one level, the answer is a general, global one that has to do with the relationship between men, women, and philosophy; on the other level, the answer is more localized in nature and is connected with the status of women as a class and in a particular country under a particular regime and in a particular culture. We need to coordinate these two levels, use each to support the other, and join them up in order to make them more effective. And since "we" are "philosophers" I want to try to join them up conceptually.

I think I know, roughly, what a concept is or at least what it means to talk-and-think (the old, Greek *logos*). But I am not at all certain that I know what the predicate "philosopher" means (hence the quotation marks), nor am I at all certain what is meant when I use, or when someone else uses, the word "woman." And finally, I know least of all whether the male-female distinction is relevant to philosophy, and if it is, to what extent and at what juncture. This is what we, Houria Benis, Geneviève Fraisse, and I, have tried to emphasize from the beginning of this venture in "Fundamental Problems, Founding Problems,"[1] especially with the provocative question: "Can a man be a woman-philosopher?" This question has prompted the theme of our first symposium: "What do men-philosophers think of women-philosophers?" The first issue of the *Women Philosophers' Journal* reflects this very preoccupation since it reproduces two replies by two men.[2] As I see it, the elements of provocation and irony contained in this question are as much a necessity as a luxury. In fact, I think it is only by using provocation and irony that we should, or even can, take pleasure in what we are doing. Men/women/philosophers: what does this mean, locally and generally?

Let us start with the local level, which under no circumstances should be put to one side. Although I may not know what it is to be a woman-philosopher, I do know that being a woman-philosopher in Afghanistan is not the same thing as being a woman-philosopher in Iran or Senegal (we learn about this from Tanella Boni) or China or France (a subject Catherine Malabou has recently written about)[3] or the United States . . . Sometimes because being a woman is not the same thing, sometimes because being a philosopher is not the same thing (always assuming that the word "philosophy" has a meaning—like François Jullien, we may well wonder, for instance, whether it has any meaning in China); at other times because the overlap between these two categories is not the same or perhaps because there is no overlap at all. It is not the same thing to be denied the right to go to school, to start by studying the history of philosophy when one studies philosophy, to be in a university that has a department of gender studies and where the history of philosophy comes under comparative literature. At this level, the network is fundamental: we must use it to create an identity as a counterreply, an identity based on all the other "woman-philosopher" entities throughout the world, not to standardize things or to construct a model but as a point of reference, a defense, a support, and a way of achieving strength through unity. I want to emphasize that the identity of woman-philosopher is primarily a strategic one designed for a particular purpose and as a means of resistance, an identity that has much in common with "affirmative action," which is tied to a particular situation, to a set of circumstances specific to a given time and place. This is the sense in which we can say: we are all women-philosophers even if we do not know what this means.

The "Best For" Notion of Relativism: A Strategic Universal

I now want to explore more deeply this identity we have created as a counterreply for a particular opportunity and as a form of resistance by linking it to the values of relativism. What is relativism? It is not the rejection of values, nor is it the idea that everything is of equal worth but rather the rejection of values that will remain exactly and eternally the same for all places and for all times. Since the time of Plato and throughout the entire history of philosophy, the maxim of Protagoras has been emblematic of the relativist position. "Man is the measure of all things" (*pantōn khrēmatōn anthrōpos metron*): probably more has been written about this little sentence than any other. When Plato's Socrates recalls this maxim in the *Theaetetus*, a dialogue "on science," he suggests an alternative version: "a pig or a baboon is the measure of all things." He immediately regrets saying it and thinks: "Protagoras would have said to me: 'Are you not ashamed of yourself, Socrates?'" And so he then presents "Protagoras's apology,"[4] allowing Protagoras to speak through him as if he were there in person to mount his own defense. Protagoras changes the parameters quite radically: he switches from the binary opposition between true and false to the comparative "better." We learn that there is no such thing as Truth with a capital "T," the Platonic idea that allows the philosopher-king to reign supreme over all men (and women, too, for sure), but rather that some things are "truer" than others. There is no absolute, only a comparative and, more specifically still, what I would call a "dedicated comparative": the "truer" is a "better for" since the "better" is defined as "the more useful," the better adapted to (the person, the situation, all that makes up the moment in question, the moment the Greeks call *kairos*, "the opportune moment"). This brings us back to the precise meaning of the *khrêmata*, of which man is said to be the measure, not "things" which are and are "there" as Beings, substances, essences, or ideas but things we make use of, *khrêmata*, objects which serve a purpose, which are there to be used and used up, "riches," which obviously include language and linguistic behavior.

This dedicated comparative, which takes into account the individual in context, defines, for me, the mission of culture and politics, not a politics that is good in absolute terms but a cultural politics that is "better." The best cultural politics does not consist in imposing truth universally or imposing universal truth. It consists in helping choose differentially what is best, and this is, for me, what a culture of peace means: to help choose differentially what is best. To put it another way, for me as a woman-philosopher, the universal is a strategy rather than a value per se, definitive and ultimate; or, even, the best universal is complex, many sided, and relative. Its nature is such that we rely on truth conceived as universal only to better resist, and I would even say that we rely on the universal only to better resist. This is how I make the transition from the local to the global level: I rely on the universal only to better resist.

The Philosophical Universal Crossed by Genre and Gender

And so we come to the general level, to the concept of "woman-philosopher," simply. What does it mean for the True, the Beautiful, and the Good to be crossed by the difference of genre and gender? What relevance does this have, and what effect?

I shall refer to the "Elles" exhibition at the Pompidou Center, which opened in May 2009 and ran until February 2011.[5] It is a remarkable exhibition, for which its organizer, Camille Morineau, the center's curator, has chosen only works by women artists that are part of the center's own collection. In the exhibition catalogue, she begins her introduction with the question used by an American art historian, Linda Nochlin, as the provocative title (like irony, provocation is also a weapon) of the essay she wrote in 1970, "Why Have There Been No Great Women Artists?" Her essay is one of the foundational texts of feminist critical theory in art.[6] You immediately hear: "Why have there been no great women-philosophers?" Obviously, the answer depends in part on how the question is asked: there are no great women-artists/great women-philosophers because, historically, women have never enjoyed the conditions needed for producing, presenting, and promoting their work, and this is clearly still the case today at a local level, if not generally. But, that said, how do we move on?

Let me quote what Camille Morineau says in the first issue of this journal: "The main criterion for the choice of the exhibited works of art is intended to remain in the background. The Museum is exhibiting exclusively women and yet the objective is neither to demonstrate the existence of a feminine art, nor to produce a feminist object. The objective is to lead the audience to consider this exhibition as a lovely history of twentieth-century art."[7] In other words, the universal has to be reinforced by difference, the same universal, with or without women, with or without difference.

I am not certain this is true of art, and both the catalogue and the exhibition itself make important qualifications to this view, but in any event I do not think it is true of philosophy. The universal in philosophy, or what passes for such, does not emerge unscathed from gender difference. It isn't simply modernized or dusted down, "twentiethcenturied." Even if we accept that the paintings in "Elles" resemble a wonderful history of twentieth-century art, I do not think that the publications by "elles" (women-philosophers) add up to something resembling a good history of contemporary philosophy but to something that would be much more akin to another (hi)story of, (hi)story for, or (hi)story involving philosophy.

Here are a few obvious areas in which gender difference has influenced the philosophical universal. I would like to arrange them in order, as Gorgias taught me to do in his treatise *On Non-Being, or on Nature*:

1. Historically speaking, there are no philosopher-women (from Hypatia to Hannah Arendt, their numbers in the history of philosophy are negligible compared to the number of philosophers, i.e., philosopher-men).
2. But, second, if there are, those there are, if we focus on them today, here and now, make the history of philosophy read differently.

As far as Western philosophy in the twentieth and twenty-first centuries is concerned, I shall take just a few examples. When Monique David Ménard writes about madness and pure reason in Kant, we read Kant through new eyes. When Catherine Malabou talks about plasticity in Hegel, we read Hegel through new eyes, and I hope that through my work on sophistic logology, we read the Greeks themselves (the basis for the history of contemporary philosophy for Heidegger, for example) through new eyes. We could say that "they/elles" focus on marginal objects and bring them from the margin toward the center, objects that are problem objects, unsettling, not only for our perception of history but also for our perception of concepts. Let me quote Catherine Malabou: "It may be true that women do not invent any philosophical question, but they create problems. Wherever they can, they put a spoke in the wheel of philosophers and philosophical systems. Thereby, the impossibility of being a woman becomes the impossibility of philosophy itself."[8] What we are to understand by the "impossibility of being a woman" is the "philosophical impossibility of being a woman-philosopher" linked to the rejection of a female essence, to a refusal to be naturalized.

The Permeability of Genres/Genders

For my part, I would like to offer a few comments on this displacement of impossibility and not simply register it.

So let me start with the comments. The impossibility—is it, in any case, the impossibility of being a woman (period) or that of being a woman-philosopher?[9]—becomes the impossibility of philosophy first and foremost in the sense that it "loosens up" philosophy, makes it a more fluid concept; it turns it into something which, in itself, no longer has an essence, no longer can have an essence. This is what I call in French the "*perméabilité des genres*," the "permeability of genres/genders."[10] Philosophy as practiced by women is decompartmentalized. Women-philosophers decompartmentalize genres (this is precisely what sophistry does, too, in its own way, which is something I'll come back to).[11] It will no longer be said that "literature is for women, philosophy for men," and it will be said less categorically that "this is literature, that is philosophy." While looking for a publisher for *L'effet sophistique*, which is a book of "pure philosophy" (in the way that we talk of "pure science"), about Greek philosophy in its relation to the contemporary world, I tried, at the same time, to publish a collection of short stories that, to my mind, said exactly the same thing. They were stories about what can be done with words and even about "how to do things with words," to borrow the title of one of Austin's books. For me, this is what Greek philosophy and sophistic logology are about, just as this is what our own lives are about at many points. For the title of the collection, I used a sentence that Gorgias applies to *logos*, to discourse: *With the smallest and most invisible of bodies*. But I found it completely impossible to get both books published together because every publisher rejected it, rejected the idea that a woman-philosopher, who was already finding it difficult enough to be recognized as a philosopher, should dare to publish simultaneously a collection of short stories, in other words, to mix different genres, philosophy and literature. But it seems to me this mixing and this permeability of genres, more than anything else, constitute "our territory." That is why it seemed to me imperative and symbolic to ask Giulia Sissa to talk to us about Nicole Loraux. Nicole Loraux is a historian; as a woman historian, she is a woman-philosopher. In other words, our relationship to our discipline and our relationship to our social identity are fuzzy.[12]

Can a man be a woman-philosopher? For me, as my answer would be "yes," it is simply a complementary way of approaching the permeability of genres/genders.

"*Ne Pas Vaincre, Con Ou Pas*": The Græcia Capta *Model*

So: the permeability of genres/genders in every sense of the expression. The Network of Women Philosophers implies that we do not relate to the universal, to essence, to genre/gender in quite the same way: all this, I think, adds up to the fact that we do not relate to being controlled in quite the same way. Control, as I see it—through the eyes of a woman-philosopher (let me say it once again, as far as I am capable of knowing what that means)—is not a value as such. At this point, I would like to draw on the words of Jacques Lacan, a man, a psychoanalyst (can a psychoanalyst be a woman-philosopher? Quite probably, yes). This is what he says: "What is proper to psychoanalysis is not to vanquish (*vaincre*), whether by strength of conviction or not" or "regardless of whether people are [idiots] [*con*] or not."[13] It is neither a mater of victory not even a matter of conviction. I do not think it is any more a case of "vincing," "con" or not: as with psychoanalysis in relation to current discourse, we need, instead, to find a different model.

We don't have to vanquish, we have to change the model, with which I contented myself for a very long time, and which I would sum up with a quotation from Horace, concerning Greece and Rome: *Græcia capta ferum victorem cepit*, "Captured Greece captivated the ferocious victor."[14] *Græcia capta*—listen to all those *a*'s—is quite unmistakably female, and the Roman Empire, *ferum victorem*, male. It seems to me that for a long time women have thought, in accordance with this model, that they need only vanquish—and even that they would always succeed in vanquishing. Vanquish by being vanquished and by captivating their conqueror, as if their handsome victory—definitely more guileful and beguiling, than dialectical—depended on their own submission but transcended it as well. For my own part, I am far less sure about all this today and not only because an age-old ideology is at work, one that justifies conquests of the worst kind. I prefer to believe that we do not have to vanquish at all and that we must really adopt a different model and put a stop to war altogether—or, to return to the UNESCO theme, that we can construct peace by means other than war.

Possible Areas of Influence

I would like to end with two kinds of conclusions, albeit tentative ones. The first are suggestions for action of a practical nature. The second are observations addressed to me, as a woman-philosopher, and which bring us back to the relationship between the impossibility of being a woman and the impossibility of philosophy.

The practical forms of action I want to suggest cast us in the role of women who wield influence rather than power—it remains to be seen whether this lays to rest the *Græcia capta* model. I would like the Network of Women Philosophers, on the strength of its UNESCO connection, to have within its ranks observers who are accredited, like journalists, for example, in their capacity as women-philosophers. They should be recognized by the courts, for instance, particularly by special courts such as international criminal tribunals (ICTs) and truth and reconciliation commissions. Hannah Arendt, as a journalist/philosopher covering the Eichmann trial, described herself not as a "woman philosopher" but as a "Jewish individual *femini generis*." I would like women-philosophers to be accredited as "philosopher" individuals *femini generis*. I once had the experience of serving on a jury in a French court of law, and what I saw there, significantly, was women—women judges, women lawyers, and women prosecutors—all of them white, judging men who were either black or of North African descent; this was true in about 80 percent of cases. It seems to me that a woman-philosopher who witnessed and reflected on what she saw would be as useful as Hannah Arendt as a Jewish woman at the Eichmann trial. We must use to full advantage the fact that we are women-philosophers, both with and against a certain kind of feminine domination and against a certain kind of masculine domination. I would also like us to be philosopher-observers *femini generis* in the world of economics. I cannot help feeling that, had there been a woman-philosopher observer at the meeting, a few months ago, of women heads of the world's biggest companies, we would have learned a few things and taught a few others. In short, we must use our position as women-philosophers to give a new direction to the increasingly important role of women.

A second possible area of influence would involve looking at the connection between language and philosophy. I have done a lot of work in this area myself, through the *Dictionnaire des intraduisibles*. I feel that, as philosophers, we have the opportunity and probably the duty to work on cultural diversity from the viewpoint of languages. This would mean, on a country-by-country basis and on a very practical level, giving priority to translations and bilingual editions of the major "philosophical" works—philosophical in the wider sense implied by the permeability of genres—the foundational texts of language and thought, so that these particular works are available to each and every one of us in what Derrida referred to as "more than one language," thus defining "deconstruction" in quite a rude way.[15]

But why, one may ask, is this influence the prerogative of women-philosophers rather than of philosophy in general? Or rather than the result of a more random experience or an attraction on the part of an individual?

"As a Philosopher" / "As a Woman"

As a reply, I would like to draw a little more on my own experience and investigate further the relationship between the impossibility of being a woman and the impossibility of philosophy.

I would like to spend a few moments on the little book I recently coauthored with Alain Badiou after twenty years of collaborative projects and of friendship. The book is called *There's No Such Thing as a Sexual Relationship*. A sentence in the jointly written introduction reads: "So, with regard to Lacan's 'L'étourdit,' to the modern theory of sexuation, and to the paradoxes of language and the unconscious, the philosopher at least will be able to say that a new confrontation between, or a new distribution of, the masculinity of Plato and the femininity of sophistics, is occurring."[16] This sentence should be segmented as follows: "the masculinity of Plato" (else-where: "speculative masculinity") and "the femininity of sophistry" (else-where: "critical and performative femininity") are two phrases that a philosopher-man would write, and they were, indeed, written by Badiou. "The philosopher at least will be able to say" is a discourse marker that I added. It takes account of the fact that a philosopher-man thinks that the philosopher, that is to say, the man, is Plato. Certainly, I recognize myself in sophistry, its critical approach, its attention to language, performance, and performativity. But the point is this: am I doing so as a woman or as a philos-opher? Are we really dealing with sophistic "femininity" or with sophistry as a modification of the philosophical universal? When I am working on sophistry, its relationship to language, criticism, and performance, should I look upon what I am doing as the work of a woman or as the work of a philosopher?

But that is just it; I neither want nor am able to answer such a question put to me in those terms. Or rather, I want to reply to it only in the follow-ing way: when someone says to me (that someone being a philosopher-man), "you're speaking as a woman, from a female standpoint," I shall reply: "No, I am speaking as a philosopher." The fact of the matter is that I am not interested in linguistic performance and in its destabilization of the universal, truth, and fact not because I am a woman but because I am a phi-losopher. But when someone says to me: "You are speaking as a philoso-pher," I shall reply: "No, I am speaking as a woman." It is from a woman's position that I am interested in *play[ing] old Harry with the true/false fetish and the value/fact one*,"[17] as the philosopher Austin (a man, by the way) says and does. It is my way of refusing to be assigned an essence: the only attribu-tion I accept is that of resistance. It is with this "Yes, but not like that" that I try to complicate the universal using the difference between genres and genders as well.

I now come back to the impossibilities Catherine Malabou refers to. Women "put a spoke in the wheel of philosophers and philosophical sys-tems," and "the impossibility of being a woman" becomes "the impossibil-ity of philosophy." If we do not get past that point, I fear that there is nothing easier or more convenient for "philosophy" than to manage the man/woman difference by applying it to the philosophy/antiphilosophy difference. This is precisely the Platonic operation effected by Badiou as a man-philosopher. "Those who subscribe to antiphilosophy, like Wittgenstein, Lacan and, ultimately, under the label 'sophistry,' Barbara Cassin, are only issuing a challenge to philosophy, the unusual challenge involving a new object, which, they claim, will strip philosophy of its old pretensions, because philosophy has either 'forgotten' or refused to examine it."[18] Throwing sophistry in the face of a latter-day Plato, bringing an object from the margin toward the center are of no interest apart from reinforcing the centrality of the center and reviving the Universal and Truth by criticizing them, which would be totally counterproductive for a woman-philosopher. Badiou's Platonic strength as a man-philosopher consists in putting in sequence: sophistry (or any other blunt instrument)-woman-antiphilosophy (and immediately it is as clear as day that a certain number of men-philosophers are actually women-philosophers—Nietzsche, Wittgenstein, and, of course, Derrida), and women can make waves, stick their oars (and their spokes) in for all they are worth, but it will be to no avail. And yet, if a spoke should be put into the wheels of any machine, then it is surely this particular juggernaut. This is precisely what the change of attribution (as a woman/no: as a philosopher/no: as a woman) is strategically undermining or at least seeking to undermine.

An identity based on resistance and not on essence. Does philosophy become impossible as a result, or transformed? If the answer is "transformed," and this is what my own answer would be, then I cannot go along with Catherine Malabou's conclusion that "I am absolute, isolated, absolutely isolated. I traverse the space of philosophy in absolute solitude."[19] Instead, my message would be: philosophy not dead, but universal badly shaken. Deep in no-woman's land, a unique network of woman-philosophers is growing. As Isabelle Stengers and Vinciane Desprets put it, "the awkward squad."[20]

THIRTEEN

Philosophizing in Tongues

As a preamble to this chapter and to pay homage to Jacques Derrida, I would like to quote a long extract taken from Derrida's last interviews with Jean Birnbaum, *Learning to Live Finally*, a pragmatic oxymoron in that the work is from the outset presented as a posthumous real-life experience:

> [J]ust as I love life, and my life, I love what made me what I am, the very element of which is language, this French language that is the only language I was ever taught to cultivate, the only one also for which I can say I am more or less responsible. That is why there is in my writing a certain, I wouldn't say perverse but somewhat violent, way of treating this language. Out of love. Love in general passes by way of the love of language, which is neither nationalistic nor conservative, but which demands testimonials—and trials. You don't just go and do anything with language; it preexists us and survives us. When you introduce something into language, you have to do it in a refined manner, by respecting through disrespect its secret law. That's what

might be called unfaithful fidelity: when I do violence to the French language, I do so with the refined respect of what I believe to be an injunction of this language, in its life and in its evolution. I always have to laugh, though sometimes with contempt, when I read those who think they are violating, precisely without love, the classic "spelling" or syntax of a certain French Language; they always look like virgin boys given to premature ejaculation, while the great French language, more untouchable than ever, watches on and awaits the next in line . . . I have only one language, and, at the same time, in an at once singular and exemplary fashion, this language does not belong to me . . . A singular history has exacerbated in me this universal law: a language is not something that belongs.[1]

It is from the basis of the deeply nonviolent premise of this sentence—"a language is not something that belongs"—that I would like to lay out what we attempted to achieve with the *Dictionary of Untranslatables* and hence reflect on translation in philosophy.[2]

I neither can nor wish to speak of the "untranslatable" in the singular because, to my ear, this would refer to what Derrida in "Freud and the Scene of Writing" calls the untranslatable "materiality" or "body" of languages:[3] in essence what literary translators are confronted with, the Untranslatable with a capital "U," the signifier itself, tones, rhythms, languages as we hear them and speak them, languages as they exist.

But what really suits us philosophers is the plural: to translate the "untranslatables," understood not as a destinal challenge to Babel but as an obviously deceptive and ironic commitment. The *Dictionary of Untranslatables* does not pretend to offer "the" perfect translation to any untranslatable; rather, it clarifies the contradictions and places them face to face and in reflection; it is a pluralist and comparative work in its nonenclosing gesture, rather more Borgesian or Oulipian—"the modern form of fantasy is erudition"—than destinal and Heideggerian.

One of the first characteristics of the dictionary is effectively its "multiplicity." This represents our starting point and for that matter our arrival point. We start from the primary and unavoidable fact of the plurality of languages. From this follows a second definition: untranslatables are the semantic and/or syntactic symptoms of the differences of languages. More precisely, the *Dictionary of Untranslatables* has set itself the ambition of capitalizing on the translators' expertise by moving the whole apparatus of footnotes and parentheses into the main text.

I would like to put this aim into perspective by using a certain type of philosophical work or, to be more precise, from the point of view of my own first encounter with Greek philosophy, namely sophistry and its critique of ontology. We know that the Greeks blissfully ignored the plurality of languages—they were, to use Momigliano's expression, "proudly monolingual"[4]—so much so that *hellenizein* means "to speak Greek" as well as "to speak correctly" and "to think and act as a civilized man," in contrast to *barbarizein*, which violently conflates the stranger, the unintelligible, and the inhuman. How, then, can a work about the Greeks give us any sort of apprehension of the differences among languages? It is very simple—or at least I think I can make it simple: either we start off with things or we start off with words.

On the one hand, we have ontology, as far back as Parmenides's poem *On Nature* and the position of *esti*, "is," and even "there is," "there is being," *es gibt*. In the poem, magnificently interpreted by Heidegger, Being, Thought, and Speech are intertwined. Man is the "shepherd of being": he has the responsibility of faithfully and accurately expressing Being. And when we leave thought in order to enter metaphysics—with Plato and Aristotle therefore—we can describe things in this way: language is an *organon*, a tool, a means of communication, and languages, as Socrates says in the *Cratylus*, are simply different materials that can be employed in making this tool,[5] mere costumes of the idea. This is why we must start from things, from what is, and not from words.[6] From this perspective, to translate is to communicate as quickly as possible the thing underlying the words, to reveal the unity of being under the difference of languages, to reduce multiplicity to the singular: translation is then what Schleiermacher calls *dolmetschen*, interpretation, a "go-between."[7]

On the other hand, we have "logology," that is to say, as far back as the *Treatise On Non-Being* by the sophist Gorgias, a critique of ontology that shows how being is nothing more than a result of saying. Being is not always already present. It is rather Parmenides's *Poem*, this time interpreted not by Heidegger but by Gorgias, that creates being as a result of combined semantic and syntactic effects. It produces a series based on the "word of the path," "is," *esti*, third-person singular of the present indicative, in such a way that this series ("is," "to be," "it is in being that it is") culminates in the nomination-creation of the subject, as if secreted by the verb, with the article substantiating the present participle: *l'étant* ["the being"], *to eon*, and its description in a well-rounded sphere—like Ulysses skirting the Sirens, it stays there, firmly planted in the limits of powerful bonds.[8]

The world that leads off from words is a completely different world: we are no longer in the realm of onto-logy and phenomeno-logy, which must tell us what is and how it is, but in the realm of the performative, which brings into being what is said. So much so that language is no longer considered in the first instance as a means but as an end and a force: "Whoever finds language interesting in itself is different from whoever only recognizes in it the means for interesting thoughts,"[9] and as Gorgias observes in his *Encomium of Helen* (§8): "Speech is a great master, which with the smallest and least perceptible of bodies performs the most divine of acts."[10]

This mode also governs the *Dictionary of Untranslatables*: it is essentially sophistic logology immersed in the plurality of languages. Because the only "there is" is the Humboldtian one of the plurality of languages, "language manifests itself in reality only as multiplicity."[11] Language is and is only the difference between languages. From this perspective, translating is no longer *dolmetschen* but *übersetzen*, understanding that different languages produce different worlds, making these worlds communicate and enabling languages to trouble each other in such a way that the reader's language reaches out to the writer's language;[12] our common world is at most a regulating principle, an aim, and not a starting point. The aptest metaphor is perhaps that of Troubetzkoy, who sees in each language an "iridescent net" so that each, according to the size of his mesh, pulls up other fish.

It is also by starting off with plurality that we philosophers manage to find a trace of the signifier, of the untranslatable "materiality" and "body" of languages. What is at stake, then, is not only the plurality of languages but also each language's internal diversity, the multiplicity of meanings of certain words. It is through equivocation that the signifier enters philosophy from Aristotle to Freud.

Indeed, Aristotle makes the refusal of homonymy a weapon of mass destruction against sophistry. He bases his refutation of the adversaries of the principle of noncontradiction (the only demonstration of the first principle that is possible without a petition) on the necessity of univocality: in order to speak one must say and signify a single thing, the same for oneself and others. A word cannot simultaneously have and not have the same meaning—"hello" cannot mean "go to hell"—the word is the first encountered entity to satisfy the principle of noncontradiction. The sense of a word, its definition, is the essence of the thing that the word names: "man" signifies a man and means "animal endowed with *logos*." Either one yields to the decision of meaning, or one does not even speak, and as speech is the definition of man, one must be either a plant or a god. Those who speak for the pleasure of speaking, *logou kharin*, find themselves drastically relegated beyond the limits of humanity, and the "sophists" are those who play on homonymy in order to shake the univocality of meaning, which the principle of all principles demands.[13]

The impossibility of (or ban on) contradiction is, *mutadis mutandis*, as structuring as the prohibition of incest. The work of the philosophers consists in preserving this univocality by dispelling homonymies, if necessary by creating new words.

But what happens when the homonyms, far from being accidental homophones or homographs, are historical signs of the internal fabric and genealogy of a language? Aristotle has great difficulty in finding even one good example of purely accidental homonymy: how can we not see that the shoulder bone resembles the long hooked key of great Greek doors, so much so that its paradigm, *kleis*, "key/clavicle" is not a case of accident but of image or metaphor just as much as the "foot" of mountains?

So, as good logologists, we have based our argument on Lacan. We have applied to languages what he wrote about the "lalangues" of each unconscious in "L'étourdit": "a language amongst others is nothing more than the integral of equivocations that its history has allowed to persist in it."[14] Homonymy, equivocation, instead of being—according to Aristotle—the radical evils of language, are not only the condition of witticism but also conditions inherent in a language. On reflection, the dictionary has never ceased to work on this principle.

I would like to make this perceptible by way of a few examples. Let us take the French word *sens*. More often than not it has several entries in the dictionary: *sens-sensation*, *sens-signification*, and sometimes *sens-direction*. If one thinks as a Hellenist, there is no overlapping zone between the aesthetic family (*aisthaneisthai*, to feel, to sense, to realize) and the semantic family (*sêmainein*, to signal, signify, to mean), and the French homonymy might be seen to be accidental. But when we consider the problem through the translation of Greek into the Latin of the church fathers, a different view emerges. The unity of meaning of *sens* operates under the aegis of *sensus*, which conveys, especially in the translations of the Bible, the Greek term *nous*. First, *nous* denotes the "flair" (Ulysses's dog, Argos, having "caught the scent of" his master, dies of joy on a dung heap), then "intuition," "spirit," "intellect," and in harmony with *sensus*, the articulation between man and the world, "signification," and the meaning [*sens*] of the letter. It is the passage from Greek to Latin that helped me to understand that what I took to be mere homonymy was in actual fact a semantic flux, a matter of convergence of meaning.

The choice of the symptoms which are the untranslatables also stems from an awareness of homonyms, for the homonyms of a language are generally perceived only from the viewpoint of or according to another language. Thus, in Russian: *pravda*, which we usually render as "truth," means in the first instance "justice" (it is the established translation of the Greek *dikaiosunê*) and is therefore a homonym from the perspective of the French. Conversely, the words *vérité* and "truth" are homonyms from a Slavonic viewpoint because the terms conflate *pravda*, which stems from "justice," and *istina*, which stems from "being" and "exactness." The same ambiguity (for us) appears in the root *svet*, "light/world," and also in the homonymic problem of *mir*, peace, world, and "peasant commune," on which Tolstoy continually plays in *War and Peace*. We could unravel a good part of the dictionary if we pulled on this thread because evidently it is not just a case of isolated terms but of networks: that which in German is indicated by *Geist* will sometimes be *mind* and sometimes be *spirit*, and the *Phänomenologie des Geistes* will be translated sometimes as *Phenomenology of Spirit* and sometimes as *Phenomenology of Mind*, making Hegel a religious spiritualist or the ancestor of the philosophy of mind. But this also applies to syntax and grammar, the framework of languages, with syntactic amphibologies or homonymies caused by word order, diglossias (a high and a low language in Russian, which one doesn't quite know how to convey), the subtleties of tense and aspect that certain languages, and not others, compress, right down to the Spanish couple *ser/estar*, which makes the French *être* and the English "to be" even more ambiguous.

Multiplicity is necessary for "deterritorialization," to use a Deleuzian term, which is the only way in which one becomes aware of one's "own" language. Two languages at least are needed to know that we speak one, in order to speak one. I became clearly aware of this when, as a pedagogue for psychotic adolescents at a day clinic, I started to write in Greek on the blackboard: a language that is stranger than many others, with letters that these young people, so challenged by words, could not—visibly and justifiably—understand at all. This therefore meant that they do have a mother tongue or at least a language more maternal than another, in comparative terms, and it was not Greek. And we read *Cratylus* as best we could, in Greek and in French, surfing on Socrates's passion for chancy, contradictory etymologies, until the moment when one of the youths raised his hand to tell me that he had understood and gave me his etymology for "concierge."[15] In short, we led from words and not from things, and it is through them that some sort of reality passed.

But this philosophical gesture is also, and perhaps above all, a political gesture. If we (and this "we" groups together 150 collaborators speaking among them fifteen or so languages) have worked together for more than a dozen years with the impression of having to invent or reinvent everything, it is because we had one question in our minds: what sort of linguistico-philosophical Europe (and world) do we want? Answer: there are two that we do not want, which I propose to characterize in this way: neither "all English" nor "ontological nationalism."

"All-English," "English all over." This worst-case scenario would leave room for only a single language, without author or oeuvre: Globish, "global English" and dialects. All European languages—French, German, and so on—are now no more than dialects, parochial, spoken at home, and to be preserved as endangered species through patrimonial policies. Shakespeare's and Joyce's varieties of English are among these dialects that no one understands anymore—even today, in international seminars where everyone speaks Globish, the only speaker that is not understood is the one who comes from Oxford. Globish is purely a language of communication that can be used to ask for a coffee in Tamanrasset or Beijing and to lobby in Brussels by proposing "issues" and "deliverables" in the frame of a program about *gouvernance*[16] in a "knowledge-based society." Obviously the difficulty lies in the relationship between Globish and the English language. This is in fact precisely what makes the threat so intense: the risk of collusion between a pragmatic Esperanto and a language of culture.

I would like to develop this point in the following way. English is obviously an imperial language, as was before it the *koinê*, Latin, and to a lesser extent French: it is the language of U.S. diplomacy and economy and has become the language of international transmission [Langue de Transmission Internationale] (Umberto Eco speaks of an "international auxiliary language," LIA, but in a somewhat less kind manner, I would prefer, in homage to Klemperer, the initials LTI).[17] However, there are also philosophical reasons behind the choice of English as Globish: the link between this imperial language and analytic philosophy, to my mind, constitutes the cultural foundation of the LTI.

On the one hand, effectively, a certain analytical philosophy supports universalist angelism: what counts is the concept, not the word—Aristotle is my colleague at Oxford. This is where we meet Plato again—languages clothe concepts, and the clothing is of little importance—and where Leibniz's universal characteristic comes into play: "*Quando orientur controversiae, non magis disputatione opus erit inter duos philosophos, quam inter duos Computistas. Sufficiet enim calamos in manus sumere sedereque ad abacos, et sibi mutuo (accito si placet amico) dicere: calculemus.*"[18] Actually, when controversies arise, the necessity of disputation between two philosophers would not be greater than that between two accountants. It would be enough for them to take their quills in hand, sit down at their abaci, and say (as if inviting each other in a friendly manner): "Let's calculate! [*Calculemus!*]"[19] Not to mention the project of the Enlightenment:

> Before the end of the eighteenth century, a philosopher who would like to educate himself thoroughly concerning the discoveries of his predecessors will be required to burden his memory with seven or eight different languages. And after having consumed the most precious time of his life in learning them, he will die before beginning to educate himself. The use of the Latin language,

which we have shown to be ridiculous in matters of taste, is of the greatest service in works of philosophy, whose merit is entirely determined by clarity and precision, and which urgently requires a universal and conventional language.[20]

We are here in truly wonderful philosophical company, which encourages us to consider English a credible ersatz for a universal language. Why not English?

Especially since universalist angelism is accompanied by a certain militancy of the ordinary, English, taken this time as an idiom, in the singularity of the oeuvres and authors who have expressed themselves in English in the philosophical tradition, is then par excellence the language of fact, the language of everyday conversation, attentive to itself. Whether it be a question of empiricism (Hume) or the philosophy of ordinary language deriving from a linguistic turn (Wittgenstein, Quine, Cavell), we deflate the windbags of metaphysics by being matter of fact and fact of the matter, mindful of what we say when we speak day-to-day English. It is no longer "Why not English?" but "Because English"!

Hence the exceptional force of Globish supported with or by "analytical English," which makes continental philosophy, ensnared in the history and the thickness of languages, appear amphigoric and which will have induced Jacques Derrida to teach only in faculties of comparative literature. Seen from this perspective, the very idea of the untranslatable is null and void, worse: it is of no use whatsoever.

The other worst-case scenario is from the outset philosophical, and it particularly concerns us, the French, who have worked on the history of philosophy using the tools of a relocated, even revamped Heidegger in our *classes préparatoires* and have therefore a firm hold on the most daring interlocutors from Char to Lacan. It is a shortcoming which is no longer analytic but hermeneutic and continental, whose modern starting point, linked to the cumbersome problem of the "genius" of languages, is German romanticism (Herder, for example, writes: "while the muse in Italy converses by singing, recounts and ratiocinates with preciosity in France, has knightly imagination in Spain, thinks with acuity and depth in England, what does it do in Germany? It imitates.").[21] There are "better" languages than others because some are more philosophical, with a finer grip on being and the discourse on being, and one must look after these superior languages just as one looks after superior races. I keep coming back to Heidegger's phrase, which makes this legible in a caricatural way:

> *The Greek language is philosophical*, i.e. not that Greek is loaded with philosophical terminology, but that it philosophizes in its basic structure and formation [*Sprachgestaltung*]. The same applies to every genuine language, in different degrees to be sure. The extent to which this is so depends on the depth and power of the people who speak the language and exist within it [*Der Grad bemisst sich nach der Tiefe und Gewalt der Existenz des Volkes und Stammes, der die Sprache spricht und in ihr existiert*]. Only our German language has a deep and a creative philosophical character to compare with the Greek.[22]

The Greek language therefore and, more Greek than Greek, German. I have suggested naming this second worst-case scenario "ontological nationalism," drawing on a diagnosis made by Jean-Pierre Lefebvre, to which I wholeheartedly subscribe:

> [W]hat starts with Fichte, in parallel with a cultural movement where poetry and politics play a major role, is a deliberate attempt by German thought to reappropriate its mode of expression in its most specific, original and irreducible nature. The untranslatable becomes the criteria for truth, and this ontological nationalism, strengthened by the stunned admiration which it triggers across the Rhine more than anywhere else, culminates in Heidegger, who nonetheless remains one of the greatest philosophers of his time.[23]

All our work runs counter to this tendency to "regard the untranslatable as sacred," a shortcoming which runs parallel to universalist contempt. But, if this tendency persists, it is because, on the one hand, Greek and German are two idioms that are full of philosophical oeuvres crucial to philosophy and its history and, on the other, Heidegger is the contemporary who has taught or reminded us that "to speak language is totally different from employing language"[24] and that to translate is a "deployment of one's own language through dialogue with a foreign language."[25]

We evidently escape analytic philosophy whenever we support the idea that our entries in the *Dictionary of Untranslatables* are words, rooted in languages and not concepts: the untranslatable does not amount to just contextual opacity. And we evidently avoid the historical hierarchy of languages whenever we retranslate the untranslatable instead of making it sacred, just as we avoid the historical whenever we depart from the misunderstandings of today by taking seriously the heterogeneous diversity of distinctions (for example, the legal vocabulary of common law and roman law, with *droit/loi* and "right/law"). All-English and the hierarchy of languages are two manifestations of the articulation between univocity and multiplicity, which seem to us to be detrimental to the Europe that is being formed at the moment.

What is left? Deterritorializing in order to produce a Europe, if not a world, that is neither closed nor immobile but in motion. One must uphold, in line with Humboldt in his "Fragments of the Monograph on the Basque," that "the plurality of languages is far from reducible to a plurality of designations of a thing; they are different perspectives on the same thing, and when the thing is not the object of the external senses, one is often dealing with as many different things fashioned differently by each language."[26] Being is a result of saying; we are not only perspectivists and relativists but also logologists. Humboldt adds: "the diversity of languages is the immediate condition for us of a growth in the richness of the world and the diversity of what we know about it. At the same time, this is how the region of human existence expands, and new ways of thinking and feeling are offered to us with determinate and real characteristics."[27] Such is the ambition of a work like our *Dictionary*, for which Humboldt, striving to translate Aeschylus's *Agamemnon* and despairing of ever succeeding, prefigures the intention (and also the sketch, *disegno*): "Such a synonymy of the major languages . . . has never been undertaken, although fragments of such attempts can be found in the works of many writers; yet such a work, if prepared with intelligence, would undoubtedly be a most fascinating study."[28] The "synonymy of principle languages" refers to the fact that words which correspond in each language are considered to express the same concept. But they do so only with a "difference," a "connotation," a "degree on the scale of feelings," which is precisely what creates the division between words and concepts:

> A word is more than just the sign of a concept, for the concept could not come into existence, let alone be grasped, without the word; the indeterminate force

of a thought forms itself into a word just as soft clouds form out of a clear blue sky. It should not be forgotten that the word has its own individual nature with its own specific character and specific shape, with its own power to affect the spirit, and that it is not without the ability to recreate itself.[29]

To deterritorialize, transplant, translate, retranslate: a language does not belong. When Umberto Eco, quoted in good ministerial speeches, suggests that "the language of Europe is translation," he confers upon Europe the dignity and gentleness of being *energeia* rather than *ergon*: in motion, unfinished, wavering.

I would like to conclude with a long quotation, just as long as the one I began with and which echoes it. Hannah Arendt wrote her *Denktagebuch* in several languages, which was a way of dealing with both her exile—"It was not the German language that went crazy,"[30] she said in her interview with Günter Gaus—and her philosophical culture "speaking not only Plato in Greek, Augustine in Latin, Pascal in French, Machiavelli in Italian, Kant, Hegel, Marx or Heidegger in German, but also in the American years, in English, when she only has translations to hand."[31] Significantly, she characterizes this practice of the plurality of languages as a philosophical gesture:

> *Plurality of languages*: if there were only one language, we would perhaps be more assured about the essence of things. What is crucial is that 1) there are many languages and they are distinguished not only by their vocabulary but equally by their grammar, that is to say, essentially by their manner of thinking, and that 2) all languages can be learned.
>
> Given that the object, which is there to support the presentation of things, can be called "*Tisch*" as well as "table," this indicates that something of the genuine essence of things that we make and name escapes us. It is not the senses and the possibilities for illusion that they contain that renders the world uncertain, any more than it is the imaginable possibility or lived fear that everything is a dream. It is rather the equivocity of meaning within language and, above all, with languages. At the heart of a homogeneous human community, the essence of the table is unequivocally indicated by the word "table," and yet from the moment that it arrives at the frontier of the community, it falters.
>
> This wavering equivocity of the world and the insecurity of the human that inhabits it would naturally not exist if it was not possible to learn foreign

languages, a possibility which demonstrates that "correspondences" other than ours exist in view of a common and identical world or even if only one language were to exist. Hence the absurdity of the universal language—against the "human condition," the artificial and all-powerful uniformization of equivocity.[32]

Trapeza is also a bank in Modern Greek; *mesa* is also a plateau in Castilla or in the Andes. One can well say that the signifier returns in the semantic halo or in the angle of view, like *Brot* and *bread*, according to Walter Benjamin. Equivocity is therefore internal and external; it unsettles the object in its own language, thanks to the tremor of other languages. This "wavering equivocity of the world," linked to the plurality of languages inasmuch as it is possible for us to learn them, seems to me to be the least violent of human conditions. A plurality of languages of culture that astound each other, this is what I wish for Europe. To be uncertain of the essence of things, uncertain of the essence of Europe, would be the best outcome for Europe and for us all.

Translated by Yves Gilonne

Part V "Enough of the Truth For . . ."

FOURTEEN

"Enough of the Truth For. . .": On the Truth and Reconciliation Commission

To open this chapter I would like to use two phrases concerning the truth, mirroring each other at the ends of the chain of time. The first, close to us, is from Gilles Deleuze: "the notions of importance, of necessity, of interest, are a thousand times more determining than the notion of truth. Not as substitutes for truth but because they measure the truth of what I am saying."[1] The second, which is more distant, is a phrase from Protagoras, who speaks through Socrates in Plato's *Theaetetus*. Socrates is remorseful and wishes to explain, but in the most Protagorean manner possible, the statement on man, the measure of all things, which he had first caricatured too much: "when a man's soul is in a pernicious state, he judges things akin to it, but giving him a sound state of the soul causes him to think different things, things that are good. In the latter event, the things that appear to him are what some people, who are still at a primitive stage, called 'true'; my position, however, is that the one kind is better than the others but in no way truer."[2]

My starting point is a remark of Desmond Tutu's, Anglican archbishop of Cape Town, winner of the Nobel Prize for peace, and president of the Truth and Reconciliation Commission (TRC) in South Africa. It is a remark that is to be found in §70 of the preface of the commission's report, presented to Nelson Mandela in 1998 and completed in 2003: "We believe we have provided enough of the truth about our past for there to be a consensus about it."[3]

"Enough of the truth for": it is this expression that stops me in my tracks. It goes against the idea that there is one unique and absolute truth, *the* truth: rather, there is some truth, a bit, bits of truth. It is a partitive—some bread, some water, some truth. And there is enough of it for it to serve and be useful: it is instrumentalized truth. Instead of our oath in court, "truth, the whole truth, and nothing but the truth," here is the commission, a court which is not a court, advocating the efficacy of a sufficient quantum of truth.

To make the sense of this injunction comprehensible, we must proceed first of all to a reminder of the facts, to explain the original political moment that the TRC constitutes and to understand how the conjuncture determines a politics of the truth. In the light of philosophy and the relation between ontology and sophistry, one can then analyze and evaluate this opportune conception, this "opportunism" of the truth, explicitly put to work in one of the rare encouraging moments of the twentieth century.

The TRC is the key to the apparatus (the *"dispositif,"* as Foucault might have said) invented by South Africa so as to avoid the bloodbath that was foreseen at the end of apartheid and to promote what Tutu calls the "miracle of the negotiated solution." It had to contribute to producing a new nation, a *rainbow people*. Two texts allow the length of the path taken to be measured: the fundamental law of apartheid, the Population Registration Act of 1950, and the epilogue to the provisional Constitution of 1993. Here is the first, signed de facto by the king of Great Britain:

> Be it enacted by the King's Most Excellent Majesty, the Senate and the House of Assembly of the Union of South Africa as follows:
>   1. . . . (iii) "coloured person" means a person who is not a white person or a native;

. . . (x) "native" means a person who in fact is or is generally accepted as a member of any aboriginal race or tribe of Africa; . . . (xv) "white person" means a person who in appearance obviously is, or who is generally accepted as a white person, but does not include a person who, although in appearance obviously a white person, is generally accepted as a coloured person". . . .

    5. . . . (2) The Governor-General may by proclamation in the Gazette prescribe and define the ethnic or other groups into which coloured persons and natives shall be classified in terms of sub-section (1), and may in like manner amend or withdraw any such proclamation.

And here is the second, that is, the "sunset clauses" of 1993, which constitute the act of the birth of the commission:

This Constitution provides a historic bridge between the past of a deeply divided society characterized by strife, conflict, untold suffering and injustice, and a future founded on the recognition of human rights, democracy and peaceful co-existence and development opportunities for all South Africans, irrespective of colour, race, class, belief or sex.

    The pursuit of national unity, the well-being of all South African citizens and peace require reconciliation between the people of South Africa and the reconstruction of society.

    The adoption of this Constitution lays the secure foundation for the people of South Africa to transcend the divisions and strife of the past, which generated gross violations of human rights, the transgression of humanitarian principles in violent conflicts and a legacy of hatred, fear, guilt and revenge.

    These can now be addressed on the basis that there is a need for understanding but not for vengeance, a need for reparation but not for retaliation, a need for *ubuntu* but not for victimization.

    In order to advance such reconciliation and reconstruction, amnesty shall be granted in respect of acts, omissions and offences associated with political objectives and committed in the course of the conflicts of the past. . . .

    With this Constitution and these commitments we, the people of South Africa, open a new chapter in the history of our country.

    May God bless our country.

Declared a crime against humanity by the United Nations in 1973, apartheid was abolished twenty years later, in 1993, one year before the election of Nelson Mandela. It was the TRC that, in the harsh words of Philippe-Joseph

Salazar, allowed for the "amnestying of apartheid."[4] The option chosen was explicitly contrary to that of the Nuremberg trials, if only in this respect: it was not a court of law but a commission. It was not presided over by a judge but by a Nobel Peace Prize winner. It did not pass sentence but recommended, or didn't recommend, amnesties to an amnesty committee.

What made this ensemble of differences possible was the choice of the *kairos*: to establish the commission it would have been necessary to grasp (Jacques Derrida never stopped saying that the temporality of South Africa is the future anterior) the "instant *t*," when there are neither winners nor losers. It would have been necessary to decide on a nonpunitive justice, a transitional justice, linked to this temporal opportunity, which allowed one to pass from a less good to a better state. It was a restorative justice, no less, which restored community, and even a foundational justice, as it established the new community, without apartheid, of the rainbow people. So: choosing amnesty for these crimes that, following Arendt, "one can neither punish nor pardon."

But it would simultaneously also have been necessary to utilize to its fullest extent—and this utilization interests me—the very small margin for maneuver that subsisted: that of the conditions for amnesty. They found themselves defined by the Promotion of National Unity and Reconciliation Act 34 of 1995, of which chapter 2 stipulates that "There is hereby established a juristic person to be known as the Truth and Reconciliation Commission." This name itself is enough to make us aware not only that it is a matter of a commission and not a trial (as already mentioned, all it does is propose amnesties to the Amnesty Committee) but also and above all that, if "Truth" defines it, it is nevertheless "Reconciliation" that is the goal, or, at least, the consequence of the Truth. "Truth *and* Reconciliation": amnesty is certainly linked to the truth, but one does not seek the truth for truth's sake; one seeks the truth for reconciliation. In other words, *alêtheia* aims at *homonoia*, *koinônia*, and *koinon*, something on the order of consensus, community, and the common.

Chapter 4 stipulates the three necessary and sufficient conditions for a demand for amnesty to be admissible and thus allowed. Let's remind ourselves what they are:

First condition: a *firm cutoff date* was necessary—the act took place during the period concerned, between March 1, 1960 (the Sharpesville massacre, which provoked the outlawing of the ANC), and May 10, 1994 (the taking of the presidential oath by Mandela).

Second condition: it had to be an act, an omission, or an infraction *"associated with a political objective."* In effect, one had to be able to make the division between what was common crime (the requests for amnesty coming from common criminals, who were quick to "apply" for it en masse) and what arose from politics. Eichmann would at once have been "amnestiable" since, in his banal status as bureaucrat, as "specialist," he only carried out orders: one meets the highly controversial "law of due obedience," which quite rightly agitated Argentina. The same action may or may not be amnestied depending on whether it is politically linked: if one authorized oneself, then no, but if one was obeying one's superior, then yes. I believe this moral scandal has a highly political, Aristotelo-Arendtian signification: one is not political by oneself, there is no political "idiocy," no political autonomy. Politics is and can only be shared and common, or, even, politics is not ethics; autonomy and the moral law have no political status. Amnesties and pardons do not come from the same genre.

Third and final condition: *full disclosure*. It is necessary for the person requesting amnesty to make a full disclosure of all the relevant facts: this time, we are at the heart of the question of the truth.

Some details are necessary so as to underline the controversies. The TRC amnesty is not a *blanket amnesty*, which would cover an indistinct group. On the contrary, it is an amnesty action by action, which goes into the particular, the concrete; it is linked to the exhaustive narrating of facts, of actions: what is not said cannot be amnestied and can, in fact, be judged. This publicness of the account is linked to the only sanction possible in spite of the amnesty, that is to say, *shame*, as the becoming conscious of the other's gaze. Under its Greek name of *aidôs*, linked then to *dikê* "justice," this affect already constituted the political sentiment par excellence in Protagoras's myth.[5]

On the other hand, the criminal act—and thus the act that can be amnestied—can consist not only in an "infraction" but also in an "omission": thus there will not be any passers-by of apartheid. The last days before the *cutoff date* saw the mushrooming of submissions for criminal "omissions."

Finally, a criminal act is criminal, whatever the intention, the political orientation, the soundness or justice of the cause: the end never justifies the means; the ANC and the death squads were equal before the commission. One will appreciate that each of these rules was bitterly debated.

The ensemble of these conditions produced the apparatus that allowed the deal with the past: "dealing with the past means knowing what happened" (§28). One is thus referred to a politics of memory: despite the cloak of silence, the unfindable bodies, and tons of destroyed archives, this is how the construction of a common past, such that no one can say "we didn't know," becomes possible. And this sharing constitutes the basis for the rainbow people. The truth thus appears a first time as a Mallarmean "beyond forgetting"—*disclosure, alêtheia, Unverborgenheit*, maybe, but politically and pragmatically oriented. One thus ends up with this singular and grandiose definition of amnesty from Bishop Tutu: "Freedom was granted in exchange for truth" (§29). The individual freedom of the perpetrator was granted in exchange for the truth shared in the fabrication of the new community. So much so that the perpetrator became a founding "father" of the rainbow people.

One has here an essential characteristic of this truth: its ironic nature, in the most Greek sense of the term, which refers to the exchange of roles in the jousting of dialectics, at the heart of Socratic dialogues such as Euthydemus or in Aristotle's *Sophistic Refutations*, when the interrogator starts to respond, or vice versa. This time, the person who ought to hide, from whom one ought to extract an "admission," now willingly starts to divulge the facts that incriminate him, thus becoming a claimant, an *applicant*. Such is the *ironic truth* that Tutu often speaks of: those who would block the truth are the very people through whom it comes to light. One of the rare counterexamples was Winnie Mandela, whom the commission had to call on and of whom journalist Antje Krog rightly says that only Winnie didn't ask for amnesty—so, she didn't have to tell the truth.[6]

In this way the apparatus constitutes a double procedure of transformation that gives all its sense to the expression "transitional justice." One passes from wrong to right, according to the untranslatable graffiti painted on the wall of the house in which Desmond Tutu then lived in Cape Town: *"How to turn human wrongs into human rights."* One transforms the sufferings, evils, errors, and wrongs into rights and justice rendered. In so doing one passes from the singular to the collective, from the criminal act committed each time by some "one" to a shared past and to common memory. Through the simple application of the legal apparatus, there is a radical transformation of an individual moral evil into a political good. That is why the *metabolê*, the conversion (in the sense of the "transformation," the "passage" from a less good to a better state, advocated by Protagoras, whom I cited earlier) doubtless constitutes one of the best possible descriptions of the TRC effect.

Let us try to understand more precisely the modalities according to which this "passage" implies the truth (in any case, it is said that *The Truth* was the name of the treatise of Protagoras), both for the individual and for the community of citizens. With regard to this question of the truth, I would like to cite at much greater length the second phrase mentioned at the beginning of this chapter, immersing it in its context:

> I take my stand on the truth being as I have written it. Each one of us is the measure both of what is and of what is not; but there are countless differences between men for just this very reason, that different things both are and appear to be to different subjects. I certainly do not deny the existence of both wisdom and wise men: far from it. But the man whom I call wise is the man who can change [*metaballôn*] the appearances—the man who, in any case where bad things both appear and are for one of us, works a change and makes good things appear and be for him . . . I would remind you of what we were saying before, namely, that to the sick man the things he eats both appear and are bitter, while to the healthy man they both appear and are the opposite. Now what we have to do is not to make one of these two wiser than the other—that is not even a possibility—nor is it our business to make accusations, calling the sick man ignorant for judging as he does, and the healthy man wise because he judges differently. What we have to do is to make a change from one state to the other [*metablêteon d'epi thatera*] because one of the states is better than the other [*ameinôn gar hê hetera hexis*].
>
> In education [*en têi paideiai*], too, what we have to do is to change a worse state into a better state [*epi tên ameinôi*]; only whereas the doctor brings about the change by the use of drugs [*pharmakois*], the sophist does it by the use of

words [*logois*]. What never happens is that a man who judges false [*pseudê doxazonta*] is made to judge true [*alêthê epoiese doxazein*]. For it is impossible to judge what is not or to judge anything other than what one is immediately experiencing; and what one is immediately experiencing is always true. This, in my opinion, is what really happens: when a man's soul is in a pernicious state, he judges things akin to it, but giving him a useful [*khrêstêi*] state of the soul causes him to think different things, things that are good. In the latter event, the things that appear to him [*phantasmata*] are what some people, who are still at a primitive stage, call "true"; my position, however, is that the one kind is better than the others but in no way truer [*beltiô men hetera tôn heterôn, alêthestera de ouden*].

. . . [M]y dear, Socrates . . . I look for wisdom, as regards animal bodies, in doctors; as regards plant-life, in gardeners—for I am quite prepared to maintain that gardeners, too, when they find a plant sickly, proceed by causing it to have good and healthy, that is, "true," perceptions instead of bad ones. Similarly, the wise and efficient politician is the man who makes useful things seem just to a city instead of pernicious ones [*ta khrêsta anti tôn ponêrôn dikaia dokein einai poiein*]. Whatever in any city is regarded as just and admirable is just and admirable in that city and for so long as that convention [*nomizêi*] maintains itself; but the wise man replaces each pernicious convention by a useful one, making this both be and seem just. Similarly, the sophist who is able to educate his pupils along these lines is a wise man and is worth his large fees [*pollôn khrêmatôn*] from them. In this way we are enabled to hold both that some men are wiser than others and also that no man judges what is false. And you, too, whether you like it or not, must put up with being a measure.[7]

"Relativism" is first of all an "ultraphenomenologism": there is no difference, no distance, between being and appearing—*einai* and *phainesthai*, *phainesthai* and *einai* manifestly constitute a single locution. But, for all that, not everything goes, or, if you wish, relativism is not a subjectivism. In effect, if there just is no truth and thus no bivalence "true/false," there is, in the comparative, a "better" [*beltiô*]. And this "better" is defined as a "useful for" or a "useful to" [*ta khrêsta*]. In the place of "true," the sage, that is to say, the "more sage," thus proposes the more useful, the more utilizable (*khrêsta*, from *kraomai*, "make use of," is from the same family as *kheir*, "the hand," and *khrêmata*, the "riches," with which the sophist is remunerated), adapted to the *kairos* of circumstances and person. Even if health remains to be defined, it is objectively preferable for an individual, a plant, or a city to feel better, to pass from a less good to a better state.

So one sees that the commission plays the role of the doctor-sophist. It was effectively a matter of "Healing our land," as the banner for this great "magic circus," on tour throughout the country, showed. "Healing our land" through catharsis on the scale of the individual and the nation at the same time ("personal and national healing," V §12). To cure apartheid, thought of as an illness of individuals, the social body, and the state, through nothing but speech, recounting ("tell your story"; "it is your turn," said the judges at the beginning of the hearings), by telling the truth: "healing through truth-telling" (V, §5). That is how one rediscovers the truth as a modality of the historical narrative in the nation's therapy: "truth is the essential ingredient of the social antiseptic" (V §12). A useful, minimalist definition—in terms of the useful—if ever there was . . .

"Enough of the truth for": to finish I would like to gather together the characteristics of this truth, which are legible in the apparatus of the TRC.

The essential characteristic: it is not an origin-truth, it is a result-truth. Nothing is already there, always already there, in the mode of Heideggerian *alêtheia*: one doesn't proceed from being to the saying of being in conformity with the faithful, destinal ontology put to work since Parmenides's poem *On Nature*. On the contrary, truth is produced by the process of speech as a provisional and sufficient endpoint, linked, as it happens, to the instant of reversal, which is the *kairos* of the commission. In the place of ontology then, is a construction procedure that is a performative procedure, such that being is an effect of saying.

In fact, according to the report itself, the TRC worked with four connected notions of truth, which are explicitly rhetorical notions, defined each time by a speech situation. The first is "factual" or "forensic" truth, that is to say, the truth of a tribunal, referring in particular to the decisions argued for by the Amnesty Committee. The second is "personal and narrative": it is the truth put to work by everyone during the hearings and in their stories. The third is called "social": it is the truth of a dialogue, obtained via the processes of confrontation, of sharing of language between victims and assailants. Finally, the fourth is the truth that "cures" and "restores": the truth at which one decides to stop, that which is *enough for* producing a consensus on which, with which, to construct the *rainbow nation*. Such are the steps of the discursive construction that establishes an effective truth by suspending the difference between true, objective truth and false, and subjective truths. Not only does the TRC not pretend to be in possession of something like the true Truth, but it even rejects the idea that its task would be to fix the historical truth (*"It is not our Commission's task to write the history of this country*," II, §62) or to produce a truth of a scientific and epistemological type: it vindicates a multidimensional, plural, differentiated truth.

The privilege of the performative dimension is cashed out according to three components.

The first and most global component refers to the construction of the world, to the "world effect" of the performance. One passes from Gorgias to Desmond Tutu via J. L. Austin simply with this idea that discourse produces the real. Allow me to establish a rapprochement between a passage from the *Encomium of Helen* and a statement made by the Commission: "Speech is a powerful master, which by means of the smallest and most invisible body performs most divine deeds. For it can put an end to fear, remove grief, instil joy, and increase pity."[8]

And here is this no less sovereign statement taken from the commission's report:

> It is a commonplace to treat language as mere words, not deeds, therefore language is taken to play a minimal role against violence. The Commission wishes to take a different view here. Language, discourse and rhetoric, *does* things: it constructs social categories, it gives orders, it persuades us, it justifies, explains, gives reasons, excuses. It constructs reality. It moves certain people against other people. (TRC 1998, III, "Perpetrators," §124)

One sees language in operation here, "doing things," "constructing the real" by acting on whoever listens and, doubtless, also on whoever speaks.

The second component, from the Sophists and Aristotle to Tutu via Arendt, is linked to the construction of man, no longer as a psychological other, but in his/her humanity itself, that is to say, in his/her politicalness. The commission is Aristotelo-Arendtian in that it rehumanizes all those who appear before it by allowing them to speak. It makes of them all, victims as much perpetrators, animals endowed with *logos*, discourse-reason, and thereby political animals "more political than the others," Aristotle specifies. What is most proper to man becomes fitting once again. They are no longer either "baboons" or passers-by mired in their silence, nor are the tormentors rendered mute by the horror of the crimes that they have to deny in order to continue to exist. One can assess here all the difference separating the Truth and Reconciliation Commission from a commission such as that recently established in Morocco, the "Equity and Reconciliation Commission," which allows only victims to speak and which forbids them from naming their tormentors. This congruent portion of truth is perhaps "enough of the truth for" the Moroccan monarchy to progress but not enough of the truth for everyone to become human or political again. One understands all the better, in comparison, that the conditions for amnesty in South Africa are a brilliant political invention.

Finally, the third component leads us back to our cathartic and therapeutic point of departure: from Protagoras to Tutu via Freud. I would simply like to underline the importance of this theme of the *logos-pharmakon* throughout antiquity and relate discursive therapy to its expression matrix, which, once again, one evidently finds linked to the "world effect" of rhetoric in Gorgias's *Encomium of Helen*:

> There is the same relation [*logos*] between the power of discourse [*hê tou logou dunamis*] and the disposition of the soul [*tên tês psukhês taxin*], the disposition of drugs [*hê tôn pharmakôn taxis*] and the nature of bodies [*tên tôn sômatôn phusin*]: just as one drug expels a humour from the body, and some stop illness, and others life, so amongst discourses, some distress, some charm, cause fear, make the hearers bold, and some, by some wicked persuasion, drug the soul and bewitch it.[9]

Producing a common world, making humans political animals, and curing by instituting a sharing of speech: making a city or state pass from a less good to a better city or state is all of that.

This discursive *deal* is linked to a politics of attention to language, which one could characterize as semantic responsibility. Wars, crimes, all the violations are also violations of language and render it a stranger to itself.

It is striking to see how this observation has been repeated time and again through the ages, irrespective of context. Analyzing the civil war in Corcyra with words he used to describe the plague in Athens, Thucydides demonstrates how the anomie of *stasis* completely alters the very use of words: "And people altered, at their pleasure, the customary significance of words to suit their deeds."[10] In *Eichmann in Jerusalem*, Hannah Arendt in turn describes Eichmann's heroic fight with the German language, which invariably defeats him. He apologized, she continues, "saying, 'Officialese [*Amtssprache*] is my only language.' But officialese became his language because he was genuinely incapable of uttering a single sentence that was not a cliché"[11]—this is precisely the "banality of evil." And that also resonates with the distressingly sober testimonies collected by Jean Hatzfeld for *Into the Quick of Life: The Rwandan Genocide—The Survivors Speak*: "There is something important I must point out: the genocide changed the meaning of certain words in the survivor's language; and it completely lifted the meaning out of other words, and so the person listening must be alert to such changes in meaning."[12]

The commission also vigorously collared the civil war of words. Thus, the security forces "failed to exercise proper care in the words they used" (TRC, vol. 6, paragraph 99); thus those who were guilty of terrorist acts and those who struggled by legal and peaceful means were called "terrorists" without distinction, confusing them all in the single category of "persons to be killed" (TRC, vol. 6, paragraph 90). That is why the young military recruits complained to the psychologist that "the present has destroyed the foundations of meaning that would allow them to recover from their traumatic experience" (TRC, vol. 6, paragraph 90). Antjie Krog, the remarkable Afrikaans journalist and writer who followed the commission's work, quotes a letter dated January 1986, addressed by the magnate Anton Rupert to President Botha: "I am appealing to you in person. Reaffirm your rejection of Apartheid. It is crucifying us; it is destroying our language"; with this, in the guise of a reply from the president: "I am sick and tired of the hollow parrot's cry: *Apartheid*. I have said many times that the word 'apartheid' means good neighbourliness."[13] And for her part, Krog begins with this question: "how easily and naturally the story shifts from politics to language . . . What do we do with the language of the Boere?"[14]

"Enough of the truth for": the syntagm ultimately contributes to clarifying the relationship between truth and politics. *Either* there is effectively a heteronomy of politics, and it is truth, ontological truth, which determines politics, in a gesture that goes from Plato's philosopher-king to Heidegger, a philosophical lineage that Arendt firmly refuses to belong to. Emblematic of this is, to my eyes, the text *Parmenides*, in which Heidegger, reetymologizing the *polis*, the city, as the "pole of *pelein*" (the archaic verb for *einai*, "to be"), affirms that "it is only because the Greeks are an absolutely nonpolitical people" that they could and had to come to found it, so much so that the essence of politics has nothing political about it but is ontology itself. *Or* one opts for the autonomy of politics. As Arendt says in "Truth and Politics": "to consider politics from the perspective of truth means to set foot outside the political domain."[15] Politics, then, is no longer linked to the Truth but, it seems to me, to something like "enough of the truth for," to a "true" that is "more true" because it is "better," "better for." No longer *the* truth but *some* truth—comparative, partial, constructed, and finalized. Other dangers announce themselves: who decides on the "better for" and how? But one of the great attractions of this other lineage is the kind of performative attention given to language, to what Lyotard called the "strength of the weak," as a means of removing from hate its eternity.

Translated by Andrew Goffey

FIFTEEN

Politics of Memory: On the Treatment of Hate

In his *Life of Solon* (21) Plutarch notes: "And it is political to remove from hate its eternity." The treatment of hate, which goes with civil war, is one of the most acute current problems in deliberative politics. Why is it that deliberating and shedding light on events and past actions may lead a political community, in its very attempt to achieve a reconstruction, to implode?

The management of the relation between past and future, which is decisive for a political present, has historically followed some very different models. I would like to compare three radically heterogeneous models: two procedures of exception (in Athens, after the civil war, the decree of 403 B.C.—it is as far as we know the first procedure of amnesty) and, in yesterday's South Africa, the Truth and Reconciliation Commission (TRC) after the collapse of apartheid. And a third, "normal" procedure, that of the French management of sensitive archives (like those of World War II).[1] I believe these three models help shed light on certain relations between politics, discursive practice, and deliberation and enable us to gain insights into the ways in which truth and deliberative politics are linked.

Athens: Amnesty-Amnesia

There is, at least in some languages, an immediate connection between "amnesty" and "amnesia." It has nothing to do with chance, as it is an etymological doublet. But a decree of amnesia is quite different from a decree of amnesty. The former goes against everything that we today regard as the duty of memory within the sphere of public deliberation.

The scene is in Athens at the end of the fifth century B.C. The Peloponnesian War, between Athens and Sparta, ends in the defeat of Athens. The city must demolish the Long Walls between the Acropolis and Piraeus. Democracy is rendered powerless. The Thirty seize power. They are not "oligarchs" but well and truly tyrants. (Fifteen hundred Athenians, which is a considerable proportion of the citizens, perish.) The Thirty are Spartophiles, they are collaborators, and the enemy occupies the Acropolis. Civil war breaks out, bloody and brief (one year). It is from Piraeus that democratic reconquest starts. As soon as the democrats, led by Thrasybulus, regain power in 403 B.C., they promulgate a decree of amnesty.

Stasis *and Discursive Troubles*

In order for the facts to make sense, it is necessary to explain how Greek and the Greeks represent *stasis*, or "civil war," and the content of the amnesty decree invented to put an end to it.

Stasis clearly is one of those Greek words that have become Freudian terms. It means an act that corresponds to the root *estên* (to hold straight, to be standing up), signifying at once "the fact of standing up," hence site, position, stability, firmness (*stasimos* is used to describe all that is calm and well planted, just like *stasimon* in a tragedy is the piece that the choir sings without moving), *and* "the fact of getting up," hence uprising, rebellion (*stasiôdes* qualifies the seditious). In political terminology the word came to signify at the public level the "state"[2] and at the individual level, the "position" of a person in the society[3]—*stasis* refers therefore to state, estate, government, establishment, standing and sometimes the "party," sometimes the "faction,"[4] and, more generally, the "civil war" itself,[5] as if the state found itself necessarily linked to insurrection, as to its shadow or its condition of possibility.

As for civil war, *stasis* is described as an "illness." Thucydides gives the tone with an analysis of the *stasis* of Corcyra (3, 69–86) with the words of the pest of Athens (2, 47–54). The "illness" (*nosêma*) produces "disorder," "illegality" (*anomia*) (2, 53), and in the civil war this anomie would go to changing the normal use of language. Remember: "And people altered, at their pleasure, the customary significance of words to suit their deeds" (3, 82).

When Philippe-Joseph Salazar evokes the South African apartheid legislation, the Population Registration Act 30 of 1950, he rightly pitches his analysis at the level of language itself: "One could admire the linguistic feats of the Lycurgus of Southern Africa."[6] The South African Act is well and truly that of a "nomothete," which transforms the meaning of words:

> In the name of his Very Excellent Majesty the King, the Senate and the
> Parliament of the Union of South Africa, it is promulgated that: . . . A "person
> of color" designates a person which is neither white nor native. . . . A "native"
> designates a person who is in fact or commonly considered from one of the
> aboriginal races or tribes of Africa. . . . A "white person" designates a person
> who is evidently such or commonly accepted as a white person, with the
> exclusion of any person, even in appearance being evidently white, who is
> commonly accepted as a person of color.

Thus the founding law of apartheid shows, among other things, *stasis* as discursive anomie. Inversely, consider how the president of Algeria, when newly elected, appealed to "civil harmony": "We must . . . *reinvent semantics*, find the words which are not injuring neither for the one nor for the other. Civil harmony is neither national reconciliation, nor eradication. It is simply to ask the Algerians: do you have a spare country? No, therefore admit that you are different. Accept it."[7]

Greek *stasis* is a public illness that, in its extreme phase, can be translated as "language trouble," akin to what the French call *la langue de bois*, a totalitarian speech artifact. In the new South Africa it was employed very scrupulously at this level by the TRC, which acknowledged seeking recourse to everyday words, to storytelling, as an integral part of a "process of national healing."

"And I Would Not Recall . . ."

Aristotle gives the full text of the amnesty decree in the *Constitution of Athens* (39).[8] The decree begins with a regulation of emigration, proper to ensuring civil peace. Those who had remained in Athens and collaborated with the Thirty could, if they wished to, emigrate to Eleusis and keep their citizenship rights, their full and entire freedom, and "the pleasure of their goods" on the condition that they enlist within ten days and leave Athens within twenty days. However, the last paragraph of the decree treats a radical regulation of memory: "The past events, it is not permitted to anyone to recall them against anyone." The verb used, *mnêsikakein*, glues together "memory" (*mnêmê*) and "evils" (*kaka*). It is a linguistic construct made of the genitive case of the thing and the dative case of the person: when one recalls the evils, one always recalls them "against," one reproaches them, one exerts the reprisals.[9] However, the decree does not aim to forbid reprisals but to censure their memory and recall. A proof of it is provided by Plutarch when he cites, as two *exempla* of the same attitude, susceptible of "forging a character [*êthopoiein*] and a wisdom [*sôphronizein*]" for those of today, the decree of 403 B.C. and the fine imposed on tragic poet Phrynicos in 493 B.C. for having represented the taking of Miletus. The audience in the theater broke out in tears, and Phrynicos paid a thousand drachmas for "the remembering of national evils [*anamnêsanta oikia kaka*]"[10]—recalling public evils.

The decree's modalities of application were by themselves drastic enough. Archinos, says Aristotle, *kalôs politheuesthai*, "practiced well and true politics," or, to make up a literal neologism, he "citizenized" beautifully.[11] The elements of this practice are a ruse, a summary execution, or lots of realism. The ruse concerns extension for enlisting ("Many dreamt of emigrating but postponed their inscription until the last day"). Archinos, having noticed their high number, wanted to retain them and revoked the last days of the extension for enlisting. Many people were then forced to stay, in spite of themselves, until they were reassured. The exemplary execution:

> One of those who came back began to recall the past [*mnêsikakein*]. Archinos dragged him in front of the council and persuaded them to put him to death without a hearing: it is now that we must show it if we want to maintain democracy and respect the oaths; to discharge them is to encourage the others to act like him, to execute him is an example for all. It is that which took place: after the execution, no one ever again recalled the past [*emnêsikakêsen*].[12]

Finally the decree was redoubled by an oath taken in the first person. Andocides cites the letter of this oath "which you all took after the reconciliation": "And I would not recall the evils against any of the citizens [*kai ou mnêsikakêsô tôn politôn oudeni*]."[13] Moreover, this oath is constantly renewed because it is this oath, falling within the obligations of his task, that each Athenian judge must take regularly before taking his seat.

Amnesty is there to construct a community and its institutions on a shared amnesia. Is endless memory an aporia?

Using Evil Politically

Aristotle's judgment on this historical decree is revealing. The Athenians, he says, "thus made use of [*khrêsasthai*] the preceding evils in private and in public [*kai idiai kai koinêi*] in the most beautiful and the most political way; not only, in effect, did they erase the accusations bearing on the past, but they also rendered joint [*koinôs*] the loans [*ta khrêmata*] made to the Lacedemonians by the Thirty, although the existing conventions stipulated that the two parties (those from the town and those from Piraeus) would repay the debt separately. They indeed considered that this would be the way to initiate consensus [*tês homonoias*]."[14] In fact, amnesty worked as an "eraser"—names were erased, memory was erased—which is the main consequence of the prescription of amnesia. But I would like to dwell on two more words.

The first refers to the method adopted by the Athenians: they make use of from *khrêsasthai*, "to use", the key word of relativism, which evokes the substantive coming from the same root, *ta khrêmata* (things of use, wealth)—in this particular case the "loans." Whatever the translation may be, the wording underscores what Protagoras means in his well-known phrase: "Man is the measure of all things [*panton khrêmaton*]." The Athenians use evil to make beautiful politics out of it, and this transformation or transmutation (as the adverbial adjective *kalôs* signifies in "a beautiful way") is lifted from political art to a major work of art: aesthetic politics.

The second term defines the aim: to initiate "consensus," "concord," *homonoia*, literally the sameness (*homo-*) of minds and sensitivities (*-noia*). This takes place through a convergence of the private (*idiai*) and the public (*koinêi*), as the public, the common good, prevails in the decision to enact financial solidarity and to treat loans taken out by adversarial parties as a jointly liable public debt.

Isocrates confirms the intelligence and political beauty of this use of evil in a passage in *Against Callimachus*. He says: "Since, converging toward the same, we have mutually given each other the marks of confidence, we politicize [*politeuometha*, we "citizenize"] with so much beauty and so much community that it is as if no evil ever struck us. Before, everyone judged us to be the most foolish and the most unhappy; at present it well seems that we are the happiest and wisest of the Greeks."[15] Which leads us to the following question:

What Is a Political Act? And What Is a Political Speech?

What do we learn from this first Athenian model?

We can define political action as a seesaw point that "utilizes" (*khrêsthai*) an old state to evolve into a new state. Here, the old state is the *stasis*, the civil war, and the new state is the *homonoia*, consensus. To produce the transformation one has to see the "opportunity," the "occasion," the "right moment" (or *kairos*) at the moment of *krisis* by an act of distinction and judgment that marks the crisis, the critical moment, like in medicine, when the turn toward either a fatal outcome or healing occurs. This *krisis* is in the event the decree of amnesty, a dated text which, as it is stipulated with regard to the TRC, proposes "a firm cutoff date"—a before and an after (*Report*). A political act par excellence is the one which knows to devastate the devastation and to make the evil irreversibly become a greater good.[16]

Such a political act is in one way or another an act of speaking. Not only is the decree written and promulgated, but it also curbs the characteristic words of the *stasis* (the "resemantization" of Bouteflika in Algeria) and gives them back their performative power: "I would not recall the evils." This reassurance of speech on its semantic and pragmatic bases produces a common language, and this permits the passage from the "I" to the "we," the constitution of a "with," of a "together," of a consensus.

What is then the exact place of the truth in such a context? The reply is to be sought, once again, in the *khrêsthai*, in use and utility. Let us return to Protagoras and to the apology that Socrates proposes for him, explaining, as if he were Protagoras himself, the phrase on the "man the measure" in Plato's *Theaetetus*: "From a false opinion, we have never let a person pass to a true opinion . . . Some opinions are better [*beltiô*] than others, but not any truer [*alêthestera*]."[17] This manifestation of relativism, which collapses the sphere of being and that of appearance, refuses to allow that truth could be the supreme moment.[18] Simultaneously it questions the oneness and unity of good (something like the Idea of the Good, which could provide a Platonic guarantee to the oneness and unity of truth) to the profit of "the better." Yet "the better" is not a superlative but a relative comparative or a "dedicated" one—a better is "better for" someone or some city in such a circumstance and not in another.

In my opinion there exist two grand philosophical gestures, and two only, to articulate truth with public deliberative politics.[19] The position just mentioned I call "the autonomy of the political." It denies that truth and good are identical or respective inferences. The second option, quite popular among philosophers, could be called "the heteronomy of the political." Here ontology determines politics. Being and truth are the key criteria in assigning value. This paradigmatic position is Plato's with his philosopher-king, for whom *theôria*, the contemplation of ideas and dialectical science, is the only condition for good government. This option, *stricto sensu* metaphysical, runs from Plato to Heidegger. In this regard Heidegger's perception of the Greeks and of their "grandeur," including political grandeur, is revealing: in *Parmenides*, as Heidegger utters the word "*polis*," he lets resound at once the old Greek verb *pelein*, which signifies *einai*, "being." He then implies that the *polis* in itself is but the pole of the *pelein* and, consequently, that "it is only because the Greeks are an absolutely nonpolitical people" that they were enabled to and did in fact bring politics into being.[20] In other words, the essence of "the political" has nothing to do with politics, and the Greeks invented "the political" to the extent that they had first conceived the thought of Being.

The second option may be called the "autonomy of the political." It has another lineage in the philosophical tradition, beginning at the Sophists. At that initial and radical stage, the Sophists held that the orders of being and truth do not command the order of action but are commanded by it, more exactly created by it. The Sophists proposed something like "the heteronomy of ontology," a logology. With the Sophists, in effect and in action (in particular, discursive action) "rhetoric" indeed produces Being, produces reality, and, notably, produces *this* reality, now and here—until now unheard of, paralyzed by discourse, and continuously performed— which is the *polis* and its consensual deliberation. If Aristotle carefully distinguished between ontology and logology in order to keep open a place for a science of being as being, at the same time he proposed, in utilizing the Sophists against Plato, a practical hierarchy: "The political is the supreme architectonic science . . . The end is not knowledge but action."[21] Among contemporary philosophers, Hannah Arendt, in opposing Heidegger, explicitly sides with the Sophistic-Aristotelian tradition when she stipulates that "to consider the political in the perspective of the truth means to set foot outside the domain of the political,"[22] or when she refuses, for herself, to let her work be subsumed under the term *political philosophy*: "The difference, you see, belongs to the thing itself. The expression 'political philosophy,' which I avoid, is already extraordinarily charged by the tradition. . . . He [the philosopher] does not maintain himself in a neutral way facing the political: since Plato this is no longer possible."[23]

The South African TRC and Full Public Disclosure

How do these few remarks on Greek tradition allow us to better apprehend, even partially, the intelligence of the original *dispositif* called the Truth and Reconciliation Commission?

At a first glance the contrast with the Athenian decree of amnesty is stark. Whereas in Athens one must "not remember" or "recall," in South Africa the imperative is one of "full disclosure." Only that which forms the object of such a move is able to receive "amnesty." We are then confronted with two opposite politics of deliberative memory: foreclosure or anamnesis, silence or story, closure of the past in the present, with an outdated past (in German, *Vergangenheit*), or the construction of the future by means of a living and active past faced with the present (a *Gewesenheit* faced with a *Gegenwart*). But let me attempt to reconcile both models.

The very order of the words "truth" and "reconciliation" is by itself a first strong indication of a possible synthesis of opposing models. As we saw in the previous chapter, the finality is in effect not the truth but the reconciliation. We do not seek truth—disclosure, *alêtheia*—for truth but with a view to reconciliation—*homonoia, koinon*. The "true" here has no other definition and, in any case, no other objectifiable status than that of the "best for." This "for," in turn, is explicitly a "for us," *koinônia* or *we-ness*. The TRC is the political act which, like the decree of 403 B.C., makes a cut (*a firm cutoff date*) and charges itself with using evil to transform the misfortunes, mistakes, and sufferings into good, a past on which to construct the "we" of a "rainbow nation."

This passage from a less good to a better state is analogous to the treatment of an illness: what is therefore envisaged is reconciliation through a process of national healing. It thus comes close to the discourse as remedy—it is there, said Protagoras, we remember it, the *pharmakon* of the Sophist. At the same time,[24] it shows discourse as performance in all the senses of the term, from the pragmatic to the theatrical. It is thus, theatrically, that one must interpret the spectacular character of this commission, deliberating *urbi et orbi* from city to city, for one and all, with a televised rebroadcast every Sunday evening. It is pragmatically that one must understand the repeated and nearly "incantatory" exigency to "*tell* the truth," "*tell*" their story." Just as the discourses, deliberations, epideictic, and judicial speeches performed the Greek city—this "most talkative of all worlds" (for Burkhardt), the act of storytelling performs the as yet unheard history of the South African community, which constitutes itself through "history-history" unraveled from the "history-stories."

Truth Is a Debt due to Narrative

I would like to reflect for a moment on the meaning that the injunction to speak the truth could have in this perspective. "Who says that which is [*legei ta eonta*] always recounts a story, and in this story the particular facts lose their contingency and acquire a meaning that is humanly comprehensible":[25] Arendt is very close, in a certain way, to tying together Africa and Greece. She does not deal here with philosophical truth, that of the *epistêmê*, the dialectics or science of being, but rather with the truth of narrative. Again at work is the *mimêsis*, which allows us to bring Aristotle's *Poetics* and Karen Blixen's *Out of Africa* together. Think of the famous Aristotelian motto: "Poetry is more philosophical than history," meaning that poetry makes the singular pass better to the plural and brings about its verification through the success of the *catharsis*. It is attuned to what the novelist says: "Me, I am a storyteller and nothing but a storyteller," and "All travails can be borne if we transform them into story, if we tell a story about them." Under Arendt's pen, the term *reconciliation* comes naturally to relay, to suppress and overcome, a statement about truth: "To the extent that the teller of factual truth is also a storyteller, he brings about that 'reconciliation with reality' which Hegel, the philosopher of history *par excellence*, understood as the ultimate goal of all philosophical thought and which indeed has been the secret motor of all historiography that transcends mere learnedness."[26]

Truth is certainly, for Arendt, of the order of good faith, in line with Kantian judgment: "The political function of the story-teller is to teach the acceptance of things as they are. From this acceptance, which we can also call good faith, the faculty of judgment appears."[27] Yet this benevolence and this way of collapsing reconciliation into acceptance (that is, resignation) do not appear to be either the only possible or the most appropriate

connotations. A decisively more Sophistic and less Judeo-Christian ap-
proach would be to accept the violence of having fiction constitute such
narrative or to resort to a Lacanian orthography, to talk of the "fix(at)ion"
of fiction—the decided, desired, and accepted fabrication of the past and of
a common history. This is also what Gorgias says in his own way: "He that
deludes (*hô aptaêsas*, on *apatê*, a Greek word, more Lacanian than Freudian,
which we could attempt to render by the sequence 'deception, illusion,
cheating, ruse, artifice, pastime, pleasure') is more just than he who does not
delude, and he who is deluded is more just than he who is not deluded."[28]
Fiction is in this sense the trope by which the best citizens among us, in
the sense of the "most useful" ones, make us take something as true; or
more, it is the point of impact on the truth of that "pretty politicizing."

The civil war of Athens lasted nine months. Apartheid lasted some
thirty years. It is without doubt appropriate to also measure the two treat-
ments of memory with this yardstick. In the first case, with no past to bring
to light, everything is immediately known by everyone; thus it is forgetting
that must be constructed. In the second case, on the contrary, the past is a
hole or a series of distortions which cannot be shared. *Full disclosure* and *to
tell the story* are the instruments of its common construction to such an ex-
tent that "not having to answer to" is first the ruse and the plot requested,
so that indeed accounts can finally be settled and the accounting report fi-
nalized (*logon didonai*, for Athenian magistrates; *accountability*, for the TRC).

Here are two opposed prescriptions, posited centuries apart from each
other but both on the base of a common horizon of speech, of delibera-
tion—of *parole publique*—and on the autonomy of the political leading up to
an analogous finality. The political proximity of these two extreme treat-
ments of memory appears even clearer when we confront them with a third
figure, the ordinary French rules concerning archives and of their dovetail-
ing with public deliberation.

Latency in French Memory Archives

The memory archive which preserves traces, classifies, and is there to con-
sult is the normal and general memory of historical events, regulated by

laws which are by and large similar around the world, at least in Europe and the United States.

The regulatory structure of archiving follows a simple pattern: a latency period is imposed, during which the archives may not be consulted. Let's call it, in contrast to historical time, "time of latency." The duration of this time of latency depends on the nature of the archives, themselves dependent on classification, and there is always room for infringements. This regulation is not a mere administrative act; it is a political act and as such subject to change. Changes generally happen under the pressure of crises (like in the case of sensitive archives in the United States, the Pentagon archives and those of the Vietnam War). There is a trend toward reducing the time of latency and making archives public sooner than before—Clinton ordered declassification after ten years.

Some recent changes in French regulation are worth looking at.[29] Before 1979, a fifty-year rule applied. Documents concerning the war period of 1939–40 have been open for consultation by the public since 1990. A 1979 decree (executive order), still in force, "liberalized" the rule down to thirty years. But simultaneously it instituted "special delays" in regard to documents listed in another executive order of December 1979. De facto, the orders increase to sixty years or sometimes one hundred years everything which concerns the Second World War and is deemed "exceptional," in particular judicial records (it was thus not possible to consult these documents before 2000 or 2010). To sum up: the norm is thirty years, but for medical files the latency time is 150 years (counting from the date of birth), for personal files 120 years (counting from the date of birth), down to one hundred years for notary records, registry files, and records of census and intelligence; also one hundred years (counting from the date of the last document, that is, from the date of closure of a given file) for all justice files, including pardons; finally sixty years for everything concerning private life, the security of the state, and national defense.

The 1979 executive orders were supplemented but not repealed by a 1998 decree under the Jospin administration that concerns procedures of declassification. It establishes that preference must be given to a short "delay" rather than a long "delay"; it thus makes the exception (asking for access within a latency period) the rule. As a result researchers' access has significantly improved. The status quo (1979) nevertheless remains in force: (a) clauses of secrecy or restrictive dispositions *ad actum* remain (interest of the state, private life, industrial and commercial secrets); (b) partial lifting of restrictions is given on personal request or *ad personam* (in effect a researcher can gain access to a specific document for statistical purposes, whereas a member of the public who wants to know "who did what in my village" will be refused access to the same document); and (c) the request procedure is rather complex (the request must be made jointly to the Archives of France and to the specific administration concerned). Today, 90 percent of requests are approved. The remaining 10 percent relates to unilateral archiving (the archives of the defense and foreign affairs ministries, the contested archives of the Paris police prefecture), practices of obstruction (slowness, default of inventory), questioning of living persons, and, in particular, persons at once "amnestied and living" (*amnistiées et vivantes*).

In the latter case the documents are *never* communicated.[30] This concerns all of the postbellum "purification" files, which are not accessible until the next generation, so that children cannot have access to information about their amnestied parents as long as the latter are alive. In a general sense this remains the status quo of the programmed time of latency. This delay of access functions like a suppression by keeping the "hot" information in limbo. The past never arrives directly in the present: it is a differed, disinfected, dead past. Deliberation is stifled. To put it crudely: a past so regulated is a past for historians and statisticians, never a past for the citizen.

This is why the Athenian imperative of "I would not remember" and the South African *full disclosure*—the silence and the story—fall on the same side of a divide, that of a memory politically alive, while the memory archive is staring at them from the other side, that of the written treatment of the written, which aims to "disinterest," to depoliticize memory. To rephrase this: the Athenian *stasis* is in the past tense, a past definitively closed yet achieved in its present; South Africa's apartheid is in the future perfect (*futur antérieur*) tense inasmuch as its future is constructed at present in the past; the Second World War is, in the perfect tense, programmed in order to never be anything other than a *has-been*. The time of the public, of the citizen, is one with the community's time (I keep silent before "us"), the time of the historian is one with a dichotomized they/us, "they," the specialists, the decision makers, those who have access to the files, and "we," the generation kept in ignorance and denial by forbidding the forgetting and the recollection to the profit of commemoration only.

Arendt emphasizes, with reference to the Pentagon archives and the McNamara Report, the double danger of such a policy of specialists. On the one hand, to paraphrase Arendt, the public or its elected representatives are denied the possibility of knowing what they need to know in order to make an informed decision: The "we" is disabled. On the other hand, those in charge, who have access, remain in ignorance.[31] Without "us" and with none of "them" being informed (because their knowledge or ignorance escapes control), a politics on nonfacts is put in place, performed as a historical narrative by singular rather than public agents. As Arendt cruelly emphasizes it, France, thanks to De Gaulle, is one of the Second World War victors, whereas, thanks to Adenauer, National Socialist barbarism has affected only a small part of the German population. In this world of specialists, let us evoke of Braumann's film on the archives of Eichmann trial: *The Specialist.*"

Reconciliation, Pardoning, and the Public "We"

In conclusion, let us consider a couple of points regarding reconciliation and the relationship between reconciliation and pardoning, which would allow us to come back to the question of the autonomy of the political in relation to what deliberation may be. At the beginning of a memorandum on the report of the TRC we read the following:

> It is based on the principle that a reconciliation depends on forgiveness and that forgiveness can only take place if gross violations of human rights are fully disclosed. What is therefore envisaged is reconciliation through a process of national healing. The promotion of [the] National Unity and Reconciliation Bill, 1995, seeks to find a balance between the process of national healing and forgiveness, as well as the granting of amnesty as required by the interim Constitution.

Reconciliation and pardoning, *forgiveness*, are presented as closely allied through *full disclosure*. An equilibrium is to be found between national health and pardoning on the one hand and amnesty on the other. However, when we look at the three conditions of the Amnesty Committee with which an amnesty application must comply before it can at all be considered, the term *pardoning* does not appear. The necessary and sufficient conditions are, as we saw in the previous chapter, that: (1) the deed be associated with a political motive; (2) the deed took place between March 1, 1960, and the cutoff date; (3) *full disclosure* has been made. But *full disclosure* itself apparently does not require pardoning or repenting. In effect: "Full disclosure . . . demands an inquiry into the state of mind of the person responsible for the act." One of the most controversial issues faced by the TRC had to do with this question of pardoning: faced with his victims or their families, was the perpetrator *required* to ask for pardon? Could anyone request that a perpetrator ask for pardon?

As far as I am concerned, I would like to plead for the practical wisdom and the political beauty of a nonrequisition of repenting and pardoning. Here we again find the autonomy of the political without any reference to ontology but with reference to religion and ethics, enacting the difference between Plato and Aristotle. Consider this: there is only one Platonic *Republic*, but there are two clearly distinct works of Aristotle, *The Nicomachean Ethics* and the *Politics*. In my opinion, reconciliation—effectively the production of a "we"—is not an ethical affair but a political affair. A clear distinction must be made between the recognition of a fact—*full disclosure*—and contrition. The recognition of a fact is in itself a sign of belonging to a political community, while repenting and pardoning form part of an entirely different sphere, ethical or religious. This is where Protagoras's myth comes in handy, as told by Plato in *Protagoras*. The myth relates how the human species, badly equipped on the day of its birth by Epimetheus the Improvident, was going to disappear from the face of the earth when Prometheus gave it the *enteknos sophia sun puri* (artistic— technological— wisdom and fire); how humans, now equipped to produce and manufacture, proceeded to kill each other as they lacked "political wisdom"; how Zeus then gave the human species a "supplement": *aidôs* and *dikê* ("scruple" or "respect"—the feeling of what one must do toward one self and under the gaze of the other—and "justice"—the public norm of conduct); how Hermes asked whether *aidôs* and *dikê* should be shared among all humans or given to experts, like medicine or the art of making shoes.[32]

As a reply, Zeus ordered that these things be given "to all and that all [shall] share them" and added: "[T]hose who do not share them [shall] be put to death as an illness of the city."[33] A paradox indeed: if everyone has these things, what exceptions could there still be? Protagoras, in the ensuing speech, explains and interprets his myth:

> It is about justice and, more generally, about political virtue, if a man that we know to be unjust publicly comes to state the truth on his own account, that which we previously judged to be common sense (to tell the truth) we now judge to be mad, and we affirm that everyone has to confirm being just, whether they are or not, or even more that *the one who does not infringe justice is a fool*—in the idea that there is necessarily nobody who does not in a certain way [*pôs*] have justice in common without which he does not count among the number of men.[34]

The key to this Protagorean paradox (everyone has justice and those who do not have it must be killed) is the following: *Everyone is just, even those who are not.* They only need to pretend to be just to be so "in a certain way." In affirming that they are just, they recognize justice as constitutive of the human community, and, in doing so, they themselves become part of the city—it is in some way the praise of virtue by vice that universalizes virtue.

The background of the myth and of the whole dialogue between Protagoras and Socrates is the question of knowing "whether virtue can be taught." Protagoras maintains that everyone is naturally virtuous *and* that virtue is taught according to the exact model of the mother tongue. Everyone has it, and *yet* we do not stop teaching it, from the nanny to the teacher. This is why Athenian democracy is properly founded, as it gives everyone *isêgôria*, equality of speech, freedom for everyone to speak in front of the assembly. Everyone speaks, everyone is just, everyone is a citizen. Public deliberation, *parole publique* at its best. But the fact is that some are better at it than others—for Protagoras they are the Sophists or politicians, under whose tutoring it is better, at least temporarily, to place oneself. Protagoras's analysis goes beyond being applicable to the TRC's practice and the TRC as a model for deliberation within reconciliatory politics.

It shows two things: first, that repenting, the apology, or the request for pardon is that much less necessary since "the one who does not infringe justice is a fool." The perpetrator who speaks in front of the TRC could well argue that his past acts, even barbaric ones, show justice, that consistency is still interpretable *ad majorem communautatis gloriam* as an indication that the perpetrator never ceased acting as member of the community, passing from a worse to a better state.

A solid further argument could be made that what counts in *full disclosure* is not that one declares one's *injustice*; it is that one *declares* one's injustice.

Translated by Johann Rossouw

SIXTEEN

Google and Cultural Democracy

Google, like the United States, thinks of itself and poses as a champion of democracy. Everyone will know, or try to know, how to view the United States in this regard. As for Google, one has to recognize the genius, perfectly honed for the Web, which consists in making a maximum of information available to a maximum number of people, and the genius, perfectly honed for the spirit of capitalism, which consists in making money, piles of money, from this "mission."

The democratic pretention of Google has two dimensions, according to Google itself: democracy upstream and democracy downstream.

Upstream, each one of "us," in equal measure or weighted aristocratically, constitutes a portion of the information that appears on the Web: "you are the web,"[1] its content. Above all, with the same immanentist gesture, each one us, in equal measure or weighted aristocratically, produces the order in which the Web presents information: "you are the web," its organization, this time via PageRank and the democracy of links and clicks.

Downstream, everyone has (or will or would have) free and equal access to the Web in terms of the sharing of knowledge. And all these aspects are connected, as what is upstream of the link and the click produces the figure that is taken downstream.

However, in relation to the idea of cultural democracy, more modesty is needed, both with democracy and with culture.

With regard to culture—and it really is of the order of an observation, even if it isn't often made—the missing dimension is that of the work, in the sense of a work of art, *œuvre d'art*, however open and performed it might be, which is necessary to think languages as much as books. Once again, like knowledge, culture can no more be reduced to a sum of information than information itself can be reduced to a sum of chunks of information.

With regard to democracy, that is a different kettle of fish. What exact concept of "democracy" is in play here?

One can leave to one side the swipes at the model even if they are very revealing. The Tiananmen affair[2] signals the tension, indeed the incompatibility, between a universal, virtually realist technique (everyone has or will have equal access, the digital divide notwithstanding), and a globally nonrealist politics (the Chinese, members of this or that nation, do not and will not have the same access to an identical content): a private politics is not a public politics, and a public politics of state or nation, is not world politics.

It is, I believe, the model itself that must be interrogated, and it is to a reflection on the very notion of democracy and of politics and on the status of the universal that one must turn. To understand what doesn't seem to me to be democratic in Google's "democracy," I would like to pass one more time through Greece.

There is a great deal of resemblance between Google and sophistic. From the very beginning of the success story, the common features struck me. We know the sophists are, to borrow Hegel's expression, the "masters of Greece," those who taught it both politics (and precisely "democracy") and culture. Yet Google, as it seems now, is a long way from being a master of politics or a master of culture. It is the contrast in this comparison that I would like to explore so as to clarify the relationship between Google and democracy.

Google is certainly on the side of Promethean invention: a crafty intelligence and tricky craft linked to a simple and effective technical know-how, which is, additionally, proteiform and quick to grasp the occasion. This complex description would be much more eloquent in Greek. It would be given (and that can help gain a better understanding of the process) in terms of *mêtis*, "plan, cunning plan, clever and efficacious wisdom, ruse," which characterizes the divine Ulysses, the aim of Zeus, and the tentacular mobility of the octopus; *tekhnê*, "know-how, craft, technique, art, competence, expertise, way of doing, means, system, artifice"; *mêkhanê*, "means, finding, ingenious invention, machine (of war), (theatrical) machinery, machination, expedient, thing, thingamajig, talent, cleverness, art, resources"; *kairos*, "critical point, opportune moment, propitious instant, appropriateness, occasion, advantage, profit," *kerdos*, "gain, profit, advantage, love of gain, profitable designs." It would arise also from the vocabulary of rhetoric, in terms of *prepon*, "what is distinguished, shows itself, announces itself by its exterior, what has the air of, what is related with and is suitable to, what is fitting, adapted to the auditorium as to the subject treated"; and above all in terms of *doxa*, *dokounta*, *endoxa*, "opinion, reputation, appearance, semblant, belief."

In fact, it is the world of sophistic, which is susceptible to the most extreme valorization/devalorization, that is sketched out in this way. Plato was the first to make it the "bad other" of philosophy: a pseudo omnicompetence with a hold on the real and the everyday, but at a distance from what truly counts, which is the idea and the truth, and a know-how, a know-how concerned above all to sell itself and to generate profit—a scandalous profit in the eyes of the Plato, who sleeps in each of us.

By diagnosing in its claim to the totality of knowledge a symptom of the inanity and vacuity of such a knowledge, one would find oneself—like Plato, I would find myself—accusing "Google the sophist" of pretending to be all knowing. One would reproach it, I would reproach it, for making available to anyone techniques that are catastrophic for knowledge and the truth. To which Google-Gorgias would have no difficulty in responding, as Gorgias does in the *Gorgias* of Plato (it's still Plato who is pulling the strings), that the master is not to blame, nor is the technique that he teaches to his pupils, whether it is a matter of rhetoric or of the art of combat, but the pupils themselves when they use it badly: "It's the misuser whom it is just to hate and exile or put to death, not the teacher."[3]

Information is not damaging to the truth—what is damaging is taking information for something that it is not and using it badly. The ball is in the user's court. Why the devil not make use of Google for what it is and not for what it is not? All the world's information does not pretend to be the truth of the world—and, anyway, what is the truth?

One thus arrives at a second line of attack and a second line of defense that are philosophically more serious: the truth is what one has to search for, not all opinions are equal, there are true opinions, there are even truths as in mathematics and "the" Truth as in philosophy. The second major reproach made by Plato to the Google-sophist would be that of concerning itself only with opinions and of placing all opinions on the same level: as a consequential relativist, Protagoras—who claims that man is the measure of all things—really ought to say that the pig or the cynocephalus is the measure of all things. To which Protagoras (in Plato's *Theaetetus*, where Protagoras speaks through the mouth of Socrates because yet again it is Plato pulling the strings) has no difficulty in responding: "You have no shame, Socrates!" and, arguing, at the greatest distance from the Truth contemplated and then imposed by the philosopher-king on the obscure crowd of those who don't see clearly that "what never happens is that a man who judges false is made to judge true." On the other hand, the doctor, the sophist, the orator, and the professional teacher know how to "change a worse state into a better state," and they know how to do it such that "wholesome things seem just to a city instead of pernicious ones."[4] Not all opinions valid; that is why, pedagogically and politically, one must render people capable of preferring the better (a comparative, not an absolute superlative)[5], that is to say, better "for" (in taking into consideration the contextualized singularity of the individual, as, too, of the city). Politics does not consist in universally imposing truth or in imposing universal Truth—as Hannah Arendt would say, that is "political philosophy," but not politics. It consists in differentially helping to choose the better. In fact, with the sophistic response, it is the dimension of politics and of a certain politics at a distance from the universal, which makes its appearance at the same time as that of *paideia* (from *pais*, "child"), "education" and "culture" as a sharing of language, apprenticeship to letters, exchange of discourse, agonistics of persuasion, that some masters, in any case, teach better than others.

That is precisely the dimension that doesn't exist with Google and which forms the limit of the comparison with sophistic. "Mass personalization" (an old fantasy of the marketing professionals!) is not democracy. One plus one plus one makes neither a community nor an assembly nor a *dêmos*, a "people," any more than a "multitude" (a nomadic and differentiated antipeople) but a load of "idiots" in the strict sense of the word, that is to say, private persons, deprived of the public dimension, reduced to the singularity of their simple particularity, to their "own" unknown and ignorant dimension. And clicking is not a political exercise of government (*-cracy*). There is no power in play, or, more precisely, there is nothing, no intermediary body, that might allow it to be exercised. To believe that the sum of singulars constitutes the universal, and, doubtless more radically, to believe that it is a matter of constituting the universal, this double equivalence signals the elision or the omission of politics. It has the omission of *paideia* as its effect, and the foundation of this "apolitical democracy" is an equality between users with unequal knowledge, such that the ignorant person has as much weight as the scholar with regard to the structuring of what he doesn't know.

Put brutally, Google is a champion of a cultural democracy with neither culture nor democracy because it is a master neither of culture (information is not *paideia*) nor of politics (the democracy of clicks is not a democracy).

It is not because Google elides the dimension of politics that it doesn't exist politically, but quite the contrary. One can even say that Google is antidemocratic because it is profoundly American without giving us the means to know it, to call into question its universality, such that the universal as American goes without saying. We are Aristotelians when we speak, regardless of whether we want it or know it; we are American when we google regardless of whether we want it or know it.

One symptom of this, to my mind, is the atrocious conclusion of John Batelle's otherwise good book, *The Search*: he looks up "immortality" (he had just had another child, so it's the word that comes to him), and he describes his search on Google. After disappointing results of the type "Immortality Institute," he comes across an ad for the epic *Gilgamesh*, which he doesn't buy because he wants to read the thing right away; then, via a professor in Washington, he finds "the oldest known named author," Shin-eqi-unninni, who, he says, "now lived in my own mind." He immediately thinks of Ulysses, who prefers the immortality of renown to the deathless life of Calypso. "Doesn't search offer the same immortal imprint: is not existing forever in the indexes of Google and others the modern-day equivalent of carving our stories into stone? For anyone who has written his own name into a search box and anxiously awaited the results, I believe the answer is *yes*."[6] This is appalling not because it is stupid but because it is the paradigm of information culture as such, of the "I google (myself)/I google for me" (the middle voice in Greek), with the basically subjective and quasi-onanist solitude of the googler. What one perceives here is the total absence of an intermediary reality: me/me/me, the fabric of the world, and a search engine make neither a common world nor worlds assembled with sophistication. Yet the Web is a continuous collective creation. It is even capable of giving rise to a space of confrontation, *agôn* and *dissensus*, surpassing the conquering of frontiers and warrior confrontations, as recently between the Lebanese and the Israelis or with the "Arab springs." It is in this sense, at once both collective and performative, that it is eminently sensible politically. But instead of politics, one finds with Google the transcendence of the denial of guarantees, a philosopher-king but with this difference, that it is not a philosopher—the worst.

Immanence of the Web and transcendence of Google: Google, the current name for the transcendence of the Web?

Or, more drily: we, Google of America?

Translated by Andrew Goffey

SEVENTEEN

The Relativity of Translation and Relativism

My starting point is going to be the core concern of my profession: a Greek sentence by the one whom Plato called "father Parmenides," a sentence that is so important that it can serve as an *exemplum*. I would like to show that this sentence is the product of a series of interpretive operations whose ultimate achievement or crowning is, and is nothing but, translation. The most appropriate name for this series of operations is *fixion*, spelled with the Lacanian *x* in order to emphasize, through Bentham and Nietzsche, that the fact is a fabrication, the *factum* is a *fictum* one decides to *fix*. I will show, therefore, that translation—in this case, the translation of this sentence by Parmenides—regularly (as a rule and every time) violates the principle of noncontradiction to a degree that it must account for ambiguities and homonymies. Finally, I will show that this violation, according to Aristotle himself, who formulates the principle in book *Gamma* of the *Metaphysics*, amounts to a return to Protagoras's position, that is, to what we call "relativism." Translation, too, could be described as a "dedicated comparative" and play the role of a good—a better—paradigm for the human sciences. This will be my way of posing the question of the very complex relationship between interpretative plurality and truth.

Fixion and the Relativity of Translation

Parmenides (fifth century B.C.) is the "first to." He inspires "respect and awe" in everyone from Plato (whose *Theaetetus* I quote here[1]) to Heidegger, who in the twentieth century said the following about his poem *On Nature*: "These few words stand there like archaic Greek statues. What we still possess of Parmenides' didactic poem fits into one slim volume, one that discredits the presumed necessity of entire libraries of philosophical literature. Anyone today who is acquainted with the standards of such a thinking discourse must lose all desire to write books."[2] Be that as it may, the question for us is, how does a fragment by Parmenides reach us at all?

Editors, Quoters, Copyists: Trafficking in Letters

What is at stake here is a series of operations that emerges from the trafficking of the letter—"Erudition is the modern form of the fantastic," says Borges. A fragment is the result of an arborescent series all aiming to produce the One. The "authentic text" is in fact traditionally produced from a multiplicity of sources that all cite or can cite the fragment multiple times, each time from multiple manuscripts, each in turn susceptible to a multiplicity of readings and corrections. Translators, editors, quoters, and scribes contribute to the production of the naturally lost original text according to the following schema:

In fact, this is how the great German philology of the nineteenth century operated. Through the publication of *Die Fragmente der Vorsokratiker*, it provided itself and us with the possibility of an upstream return to the source, seeking to identify what Hermann Diels called in the *Doxographi græci* the "first lips." This group represents an impressive construction of

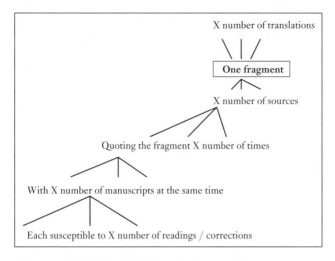

Figure 5. Production of the naturally lost original text.

knowledge and competence which I would like to call, through a suggestive play of multilingual etymologies, the *building of Bildung*. Its foundation is the work of one particular person, Hermann Diels, who intervened at every link of the chain. He is the author of the following works:

- *Doxographi græci* (1879) identifies antique transmitters and modalities of transmission (doxo-graphy: "writing of opinions").
- *Simplicii in Aristotelis physicorum libros quatuor priores commentaria* (1882) is an edition of Simplicius's commentary on Aristotle's *Physics*, which provides a gold mine of quotations from the Presocratics and in particular from Parmenides.
- *Parmenides Lehrgedicht* (1897) proposes an edition of Parmenides based on these foundations.
- *Poetarum philosophorum fragmenta* (1901) presents the first edition of the "philosopher-poets," whom he henceforth calls the "Presocratics"
- The latter edition served as the matrix for *Die Fragmente der Vorsokratiker* (the first edition was published in 1903 and revised by Walther Kranz in 1934), which edits these "Presocratics" by distinguishing these texts from their contexts and apocryphal

fragments with such reliability that even contemporary editions rely on it as an *editio princeps* and merely amend or augment it.

The fundamental principle of this enterprise is formidably simple: one must try to "un-deform" in order to find the authentic (the true, the one) version. At the foundation of this method, we find the idea that the closer a text is temporally (the more recent a manuscript is), the less likely it is to be reliable since it has passed through a series of suspicious transmitters that, deliberately or not, introduce errors, deformations, and, to put it briefly, a certain amount of obscurity and thus hinder understanding.

The Meaning of a Spoonerism: Thumos Hodoio/Muthos Hodoio

Let us turn to my textbook example, Parmenides's expression transmitted twice in very different forms.

A. Thumos Hodoio: *Yet Another Effort to Be a Skeptic*

First, the expression is transmitted by Sextus Empiricus, a skeptical doctor from the second century A.D., to whom we owe a great number of fragments. He is the only one to transmit one of the two longest fragments, what we consider to be a "proemium," a little bit more than thirty verses of an introduction edited as Fragment I by Diels. By Sextus Empiricus (in his *Adversus mathematicos*), the proemium ends with the following version of our expression: *monos d'eti thumos hodoio leipetai*, which we could render in a provisional and approximate manner as something like this: "all by itself, the heart still loses the way."[3] Therefore, and this is obvious in Sextus's commentary, Parmenides is a milestone on the road to skepticism: just like Plato, Parmenides already believed that neither the senses nor the heart (the two primary "faculties" of the soul) can attain real knowledge. Parmenides says that another effort is necessary (the soul or *nous*) in order to become a rationalist, to which Sextus adds that in order to become a skeptic, yet another effort is necessary to cast doubt not only on the senses and the heart but also on reason itself.

Fragment I:

χρέω δέ σε πάντα πυθέσθαι
ἠμὲν ἀληθείης **εὐπειθέος** ἀτρεμὲς ἦτορ
[30] ἠδὲ βροτῶν δόξας, ταῖς οὐκ ἔνι πίστις ἀληθής.
ἀλλὰ σὺ τῆσδ' ἀφ' ὁδοῦ διζήσιος εἶργε νόημα
μηδέ σ' ἔθος πολύπειρον ὁδὸν κατὰ τήνδε βιάσθω,
νωμᾶν ἄσκοπον ὄμμα καὶ ἠχήεσσαν ἀκουήν
καὶ γλῶσσαν, κρῖναι δὲ λόγῳ πολύπειρον ἔλεγχον
[35] ἐξ ἐμέθεν ῥηθέντα. **μόνος δ' ἔτι θυμὸς ὁδοῖο
λείπεται.**

Il faut que tu sois instruit de tout,
et du cœur sans tremblement de la vérité bien persuasive,
et de ce qui paraît aux mortels, où n'est pas de croyance vraie.
Toi, écarte donc ta pensée de cette voie de recherche,
Et qu'une habitude aux nombreuses expériences ne te force pas le long de
    cette voie
à agiter un regard sans but, une ouïe bruyante d'échos
[35] et une langue, mais juge par le dire de cette épreuve aux nombreux
    combats
telle que je l'ai énoncée. **Le cœur à lui seul manque encore
la voie.**

It is necessary that you be taught everything,
the unshaken heart of persuasive truth,
as well as what appears to mortals when there is no true belief.
So turn your thoughts away from this path of pursuit,
so that the habit of frequent experiences does not force you along this way
to excite an aimless look, a hearing loud with echoes,
[35] and a tongue, but by saying it judge this ordeal of many battles
that I have uttered myself. **All by itself, the heart still loses
its way.**

B. Muthos Hodoio: *The Affirmation of Being*

Four centuries later, the expression is transmitted a second time in a differ-
ent way by Simplicius, a neo-Platonist from the sixth century A.D., in his
commentary on Aristotle's treatise *On the Heavens*. Simplicius does not

transmit the "proemium." He places our sentence (or at least almost the same sentence) at the heart of the poem, immediately after a fragment identified in those days as Fragment VII. This time the sentence signifies the affirmation of Being.

But it is not exactly the same sentence. An inversion of consonants has taken place, as in a spoonerism: *muthos* replaces *thumos*, "speech, story," in place of "heart, drive, will, desire." At the same time, a clause consisting of two words is also added: the story is *hôs estin*, "that is." Parmenides changes his nature: he is no longer already a Platonist but not yet a skeptic philosopher who has been dragged into the predetermined course of the history of philosophy but, as Plato put it, the father at the origin of ontology. Here is the verse and its new context in the second version:

Fragment VII:
οὐ γὰρ μήποτε τοῦτο δαμῇ εἶναι μὴ ἐόντα
ἀλλὰ σὺ τῆσδ' ἀφ' ὁδοῦ διζήσιος εἶργε νόημα
μηδέ σ' ἔθος πολύπειρον ὁδὸν κατὰ τήνδε βιάσθω,
νωμᾶν ἄσκοπον ὄμμα καὶ ἠχήεσσαν ἀκουήν
[5] καὶ γλῶσσαν, κρῖναι δὲ λόγῳ πολύπειρον ἔλεγχον
ἐξ ἐμέθεν ῥηθέντα.
VIII μόνος δ' ἔτι **μῦθος** ὁδοῖο
λείπεται **ὡς ἔστιν**· ταύτῃ δ' ἐπὶ σήματ' ἔασι
πολλὰ μάλ', ὡς ἀγένητον ἐὸν καὶ ἀνώλεθρόν ἐστιν,
οὖλον, μουνογενές τε καὶ ἀτρεμὲς οὐδ' ἀτέλεστον·

VII. Car jamais ceci ne sera dompté: être des non-étants.

Toi, écarte donc ta pensée de cette voie de recherche,
Et qu'une habitude aux nombreuses expériences ne te force pas le long de
    cette voie
à agiter un regard sans but, une ouïe bruyante d'échos
[5] et une langue, mais juge par le dire de cette épreuve aux nombreux combats
telle que je l'ai énoncée.
VIII **Seul reste donc le récit de la voie**
"est." Sur elle, les marques sont
très nombreuses: en étant sans naissance et sans trépas il est,
entier, seul de sa race, sans tremblement et non dépourvu de fin.
VII. Because this will never be mastered: being of nonbeings.

So turn your thoughts away from this path of pursuit,
so that the habit of frequent experiences does not force you along this way
to excite an aimless look, a hearing loud with echoes,
[5] and a language, but judge by discourse this ordeal of many battles
as I have uttered it myself.
VIII. **Thus, sole remains the story of the way "is."**
On this path, the marks are
quite numerous: having no birth or demise, it is
complete, one of its kind, unshaken, and not deprived of an end.

This is, therefore, the sequence and the lesson that all the editors and interpreters retain today, and thereby they simply conform to the fifth edition, produced by Diels himself (in 1934), and follow it *ne varietur* in all subsequent reconsiderations and discussions.[4]

Translation as Multiplicity: The Flowering of Possibilities

As I have said, translation is the ultimate achievement of fixion. When I was editing and translating *On Nature*, I wanted to draw up for every linguistic unit an apparatus of semantic and syntactic alternatives that imbricate each other—but I never managed to do so without, among other things, an adequate model that could be proposed on paper.[5] This opening up of possibilities would have to be realized as a calculus with its compossibilities (in a Leibnizian sense) and its avenues, which close themselves off as soon as certain interpretations, which were still possible at the previous stage of the temporally enunciated discursive sequence, are rendered impracticable by the word that follows. Accordingly, translation would be of the order of arborescence rather than that of the line.

In order to raise a few questions, let us briefly highlight some of the major semantic and syntactic bifurcations that can be imagined for this sequence, which now exists only in its edited form, and then list a few examples of the actually retained translations along with their descriptions in terms of the choices that they represent from this list of bifurcations:

VIII 1 *Monos d'eti muthos hodoio leipetai hôs estin*:

- Syntactic and semantic bifurcations:
  The meaning of *muthos*: a. word, or b. story?
  Hôs estin completes a. *muthos* or b. *odoio*, the road?
  The meaning of *estin*: a. existence; b. copula; c. veritative meaning;
    d. possibility?
  Structure of the sentence : a´. without ellipsis of the grammatical
    subject; b´. with ellipsis of the grammatical subject
  The meaning of *hôs*: a. that (shortened as ":"); b. how?
- Examples of bifurcations of translation:
  ○ Taran: "There is a solitary word (1a) still left to say of a way: exists
    (2 a + 3 a a´ + 4a)";
  ○ Mourelatos: "Only the account (1b) still remains of the route, that
    is (2 b + 3 a a´ + 4a)";
  ○ Collobert: "Une seule parole (1a) demeure: celle du chemin est
    (2 b + 3a a´ + 4a)";
  ○ Heitsch: "Allein also noch übrig bleibt die Beschreibung (1 b) des
    Weges 'es ist' (2 b + 3 ab´ + 4a)";
  ○ Barnes: "A single story (1b) of a road is left—that it is
    (2 a + 3 a b´ + 4a)"

I shall refrain from presenting a syntactic-propositional calculus here. Rather, let us examine the sometimes "stylistically" grandiose, sometimes minimalist invention that it makes possible, which once again refers us to the differences among languages:

- Diels-Kranz: "Aber nur noch eine Weg—Kunde bleibt dann, dass IST ist."
- Heidegger: "Die Sage des Weges . . . (auf dem sich eröffnet), wie es um sein steht"; in Gilbert Kahn's French translation: "mais seule reste encore la légende du chemin (sur lequel s'ouvre) ce qu'il en est d'être."
- Beaufret and Rinieri: "Il ne reste plus qu'une seule voie dont on puisse parler, à savoir qu'il est."
- O'Brien: "Il ne reste plus qu'une seule parole, celle de la voie énonçant: 'est'"; "The only tale still left is [that] of the way [which] tells us that 'is.'"

- Cordero: "Il ne reste qu'une proposition du chemin: (il) 'est.'"
- Conche: "De voie pour la parole ne reste que: 'il y a.'"
- Bollack: "Seul reste encore en lice le récit du chemin que 'est.'"

The Reasons for a Choice

It is on the basis of this philologically and linguistically more or less controllable plurality that I have personally chosen to privilege two translations in a simultaneously arbitrary and motivated fashion (as Gerard Genette put it, playing with the expression *rira bien qui rira le dernier,* "the last one to read is the one who reads well," *lira bien qui lira le dernier*). The fact that I have decided to hold on to two translations, however, is unusual. Here are the two translations that I find important to maintain simultaneously:

- First translation: "Reste à faire le récit de la route du 'est'" / "What remains is to tell the story of the road of 'is'" (where *muthos*=story; *hôs estin* completes *odoio*; *estin*, the "total" meaning is "complete" without a subject; *hôs*, that; that is to say, it could be written like this: 1b + 2b + 3abcd a' + 4a);
- Second translation: "Seul demeure le mot du chemin: 'Est'" / "Sole remains the word of the path: 'Is'" (where *muthos*=word; *hôs estin* completes *muthos*; *estin*, "total" meaning is "complete" without a subject; *hôs*, that; that is: 1a + 2a +3abcd a' + 4 a).

We witness here once again the force of "style," which based on an identical analysis or something very close to it through the play on the upper- and the lowercase and through different connotations, hallow for transformations that are as profound and violent as the change of horizons. Let us explore the two worlds opened up by these translations.

A. "THE STORY OF THE ROAD OF 'IS'" OR, THE HEROISM OF BEING
AND THE HOMERIC PALIMPSEST

In the case of "the story of the road of 'is,'" we are in the world of Kerouac or *Easy Rider*: more precisely, we are in the world of Homer and Ulysses's odyssey. This world presents a contrast to us vulgar readers, who are used to quotation marks since, for the Greeks, "quotation is something that hides itself": "the hand and the index finger must find themselves somewhere. Often an isolated particle is a sign of a hidden quotation. But first we must transpose ourselves into the same sphere as the one who speaks" (Schleiermacher 1987, 97).[6] The paradigmatic mode of writing of the ancients is the palimpsest. It is what they call "culture," *paideia*, "formation." Parmenides's *On Nature*, written in the dactylic hexameter of epic poetry, describes the voyage of a man who is guided by the gods and who risks getting lost, falling into error, and losing himself. Parmenides makes use of all the earlier grand stories, including their sovereign matrix, the Homeric epic, and rearticulates them in order to turn them into philosophy. The key moment that points toward all the others is the appearance in the middle of the poem of *to eon*, "the Being," described by the same words that are used in the *Odyssey* to describe Ulysses when in the midst of his men, who are rowing with their ears plugged with wax. He is tied to the mast so that he won't give in to the lure of the song and jump overboard and perish like all the other sailors; in this manner he sails by the Sirens, who start singing about him as the "renowned Odysseus, great glory of the Achaeans." Listen to the merciless cross-reference:

Fragment VIII: the Being as it is in itself
Αὐτὰρ ἀκίνητον μεγάλων ἐν πείρασι δεσμῶν
ἔστιν ἄναρχον ἄπαυστον, ἐπεὶ γένεσις καὶ ὄλεθρος
τῆλε μάλ' ἐπλάχθησαν, ἀπῶσε δὲ πίστις ἀληθής.
Ταὐτόν τ' ἐν ταὐτῷ τε μένον καθ' ἑαυτό τε κεῖται
[30] χοὖτως ἔμπεδον αὖθι μένει· κρατερὴ γὰρ Ἀνάγκη
πείρατος ἐν δεσμοῖσιν ἔχει, τό μιν ἀμφὶς ἐέργει,
οὕνεκεν οὐκ ἀτελεύτητον τὸ ἐὸν θέμις εἶναι·

Alors, immobile **dans les limites de larges liens,**
il est sans commencement, sans fin, puisque naissance et perte

sont bel et bien dans **l'errance** au loin, la croyance vraie les a repoussées.
Le même et restant dans le même, il se tient soi-même
[30] **et c'est ainsi qu'il reste planté là au sol,** car la nécessité puissante
le tient **dans les liens** de la limite qui l'enclôt tout autour;
c'est pourquoi il est de règle que l'étant ne soit pas dépourvu de fin

Then, immovable **within the limits of mighty bonds,**
without beginning, without end, since birth and ruin
are very much **wandering** afar, and true belief has cast them away.
It is the same and stays in the same, it remains itself
[30] **and thus it remains there rooted to the spot** since hard necessity
keeps it **in the bonds** of the limit that surrounds it on all sides.
This is why as a rule what exists is not deprived of an end

Homer: *Odyssey*, XII, 158–64: Ulysses sails by the Sirens
Σειρήνων μὲν πρῶτον ἀνώγει θεσπεσιάων
φθόγγον ἀλεύασθαι καὶ λειμῶν' ἀνθεμόεντα.
οἶον ἔμ' ἠνώγει ὄπ' ἀκουέμεν· ἀλλά με **δεσμῷ**
δήσατ' ἐν ἀργαλέῳ, ὄφρ' ἔμπεδον αὐτόθι μίμνω,
ὀρθὸν ἐν ἱστοπέδῃ, ἐκ δ' αὐτοῦ πείρατ' ἀνήφθω.
εἰ δέ κε λίσσωμαι ὑμέας λῦσαί τε κελεύω,
ὑμεῖς δὲ πλεόνεσσι τότ' ἐν **δεσμοῖσι** πιέζειν.

[Circé] commande d'abord de fuir les accents des Sirènes
au chant divin et le pré en fleurs
pendant qu'elle ordonne que moi j'entende leur voix;
mais **liez-moi, dans un lien douloureux, pour que je reste planté là au sol,**
droit sur l'emplanture, et que je sois maintenu en des limites qui partent
    d'elle.
Mais si je vous supplie et vous ordonne de délier,
Alors, vous, serrez **dans des liens** plus nombreux.
First [Circe] bids us avoid the voice of the Sirens,
their divine song and their flowery meadow
while she orders that I should listen to their voices;
but **bind me with painful bonds so that I remain rooted to the spot,**
upright at the foot of the mast, and so that I am kept within the limits
    set by it;
But if I implore and bid you to free me,
then tie me with even more **bonds.**

In this tradition, which is our own tradition, Being becomes forever the hero of philosophy, the same way Ulysses is forever the hero of the epic. It is in order to open up this world that I hold on to the translation "the story of the road of 'is'" and to the notion of the poem (and the philosophy) that it induces.

B. "THE WORD OF THE PATH: 'IS,'" OR, THE ONTOLOGY OF GRAMMAR

The second translation takes us back to the way the Greek language is deployed throughout the *On Nature*, that is to say, to the specific modality of this writing. As Schleiermacher notes, "the relation of the one who speaks to language: he is its organ and it is his" (Schleiermacher 1987, 75)[7]: this time, what is at stake is this distance, which turns the poem into a singular work. The Greek language exists, and it exists prior to the poem even if this language has a history and is subject to evolution (like the evolution of the article, which is primarily a deictic or demonstrative element, and the poem simultaneously plays on it and has an effect on it). At the same time, the poem marks and calls attention to the way language is made, the way it constructs itself, and the way syntax and semantics mutually intervene. As the poem unfolds, the verb exudes the subject through a series of clearly legible stages: "is" (*estin*, fragment II, 3, the third-person singular of the present indicative, which, from the very beginning, names the path of research that should be followed, and the word of the path clearly constitutes its internal echo), "to be" (*einai*, infinitive, VI, 1), "being" (*eon*, participle, VI, 1), and finally "the Being" (*to eon*, substantive participle, VIII, 32), named as such immediately after the Homeric palimpsest. Thus, the Being that has finally become identifiable, like "Ulysses," passes on to eternity.

And here are the most important traces or pieces of evidence:

Fragment II, 3: "is" (third-person singular):
Εἰ δ' ἄγ' ἐγὼν ἐρέω, κόμισαι δὲ σὺ μῦθον ἀκούσας,
αἵπερ ὁδοὶ μοῦναι διζήσιός εἰσι νοῆσαι·
ἡ μὲν ὅπως ἔστιν τε καὶ ὡς οὐκ ἔστι μὴ εἶναι

Viens que j'énonce—mais toi, charge-toi du récit que tu auras entendu—
quelles voies de recherche seules sont à penser:
l'une que **est** et que n'est pas ne pas être

Come and I will proclaim—but you decide what to do with the story you will hear—
which are the only paths of research worth thinking:
the one that **is** and that is not not to be

Fr. VI, 1. "to be" (infinitive) and "being" (participle):
Χρὴ τὸ λέγειν τε νοεῖν τ' ἐὸν ἔμμεναι ἔστι γὰρ εἶναι

Voici ce qu'il est besoin de dire et de penser: **est en étant, car est être.**
Mais rien n'est pas: c'est ainsi que je te pousse à t'exprimer,
Car c'est en premier de cette voie de recherche-là que je t'écarte.

Here is what need be said and thought: **"is" in being, because "is" is to be.**
But nothing is not: this is how I urge you to express yourself,
Because this is the first path of inquiry that I divert you from.

Fr. VIII, 32: "the Being" (substantive participle):
κρατερὴ γὰρ Ἀνάγκη
πείρατος ἐν δεσμοῖσιν ἔχει, τό μιν ἀμφὶς ἐέργει,
οὕνεκεν οὐκ ἀτελεύτητον τὸ ἐὸν θέμις εἶναι·

car la nécessité puissante
le tient dans les liens de la limite qui l'enclôt tout autour;
c'est pourquoi il est de règle que **l'Étant** ne soit pas dépourvu de fin
car il n'est pas en manque, alors que n'étant pas il manquerait de tout.

for hard necessity
keeps it in the bonds of the limit that surrounds it on all sides;
this is why as a rule **the Being** is not deprived of an end
for it lacks nothing, while not being it would lack everything.

I do not want to choose between these two translations, nor can I choose.
But why even stop at these two translations? The only answer is that
they interest me. They make more sense to me than the others. They present a meaning to which it is necessary to be sensible. This choice, which
presents itself as a choice, is much crueler than a description in terms of
hermeneutic circle, horizon of expectation, and interpretation. It highlights
the type of consistence that characterizes normal interpretive operations:
cultural construction, textual fixion, trafficking in the letter, and translation as the terminal point of interpretation. These can be described correctly only in the plural since they are measured by the interest that they

arouse. We are back to Deleuze, when he opens his discussion of relativism by defining the exact position of truth: " the notions of importance, of necessity, of interest, are a thousand times more determining than the notion of truth. Not as substitutes for truth but because they measure the truth of what I am saying."[8]

Noncontradiction, Measure, and Relativism

I maintain that translation regularly violates the principle of noncontradiction if only to the extent that there exists more than one (possible/good/correct/true) translation since this is already enough to contravene the principle in its Aristotelian form. In fact, it proves that a sentence, a sequence of words, an expression, a word (all of which are expressed by *logos* in Greek) has more than one meaning in the original. Before defending this extreme and paradoxical thesis by revisiting the Aristotelian thesis and its demonstration, I would like to point out the magnitude of the problem.

Translation and Ambiguity

I shall leave aside the plurality of languages as such, which is nevertheless a feature of the real (Wilhelm von Humboldt: "Language manifests itself in reality exclusively as multiplicity"[9]). It is tied to the syntactic and semantic discordance of linguistic networks, and it is manifested through its symptoms, which are the "untranslatables."[10] In the case of Parmenides, the most appropriate example would obviously be the verb "to be." Thus, in contrast to the French translation, the Spanish translation of the poem imposes a supplementary choice between the couple *ser/estar*, which is at first sight completely foreign to the original language.

But it is enough to simply examine the relation between two languages, Greek and French. Translation, as a putting into relation of sets that do not overlap, is directly connected to the ambiguities of each language. We have seen that I needed at least two sentences to express what I believe needed to be expressed so that we can understand something of the expression *monos leipetai muthos hodoio*, the story of the road and the word of the path. This is enough to reveal syntactic ambiguities (or amphibolies), equivocations, or even the homonyms of the source language and, for that matter, without doubt also those of the target language. We could say it with Lacan, generalizing what he applies exclusively to the languages of the unconscious: "A language, amongst others, is nothing more than the integral of the equivocations that its history has allowed to persist in it."[11]

In an extreme case, however, one language can also be sufficient to reveal its own ambiguities through something like an intralinguistic translation. Thus, in his treatise *On Non-Being*, Gorgias operates an intralinguistic translation of Parmenides's *Poem*, whose objective is to make visible the ambiguous usage Parmenides makes of *esti* ("is"), an ambiguity in which Gorgias diagnoses the condition of possibility of ontology. He starts from a sentence that he uses successively in three different ways: *ouk estin oute einai oute mê einai*. In strict obedience to Greek language's orthodoxy, this sequence simultaneously means "it is not possible to be, nor not to be" (no verb); "neither being, nor nonbeing exist" (no subject); and "it is neither being, nor nonbeing" (no predicate). Gorgias, therefore, shows that only ambiguity—the ambiguity between modality, copula, and existence and the ambiguity of subject and predicate—allows us to make ontology work. Moreover, this is why I, in turn, have just proposed, in an attempt at a literal formalization of my own translation of the Parmenidean *hôs esti*, to maintain 3 abcd, all the meanings of *esti* captured for better or worse in my "est" ("is"). In any case, Gorgias utilizes this ambiguity in order to prove that being is an effect of language and speech, and far from being always already there, it is the product of Parmenides's poem.[12]

But ambiguity is a banal diagnosis, especially easy in Greek in the case of being, which reconciles clever philosophical enemies from Heidegger to Benveniste. Heidegger: "the *Greek language is philosophical*, i.e. not that Greek is loaded with philosophical terminology, but that it philosophizes in its basic structure and formation [*Sprachgestaltung*]."[13] Benveniste: "All we wish to show here is that the linguistic structure of Greek predisposed the notion of 'being' to a philosophical vocation. By comparison, the Ewe language offers us only a narrow notion and particularized uses."[14]

There is more than one translation because words—not merely taken one by one but as they appear forming a set within a sentence, a text, and a context—present ambiguities that enter into meaningful combinations.

I am not speaking about Quine's "Gavagai" and the inscrutability of reference.[15] I am also not speaking of the signifier and the untranslatable body of languages. I am simply speaking of the intimacy of each language in its not strictly communicative usage, to the degree that it does not reduce itself either to *Globish* (low version) or to a universal trait (high version). It is this usage that Francis Ponge has described as the optimum of writing:

> Every word has many habits and possibilities; all of them should be always used and cultivated. This would be the height of "propriety in terms". . . .
>
> In a sentence, compound words must be situated in such a way that the sentence has a meaning for each meaning of each one of its terms. This would be the height of the "logical depth of the sentence" and truly of "life" through the infinite multiplicity and necessity of relations.
>
> In other words, this would be the height of the pleasure of reading for a metaphysician.
>
> And, in her own way, the cook could find it pleasant. Or she could understand it.
>
> The rule of liking would be then obeyed as much as possible, and the desire of liking would be satisfied.[16]

Noncontradiction and Univocity

Translation—even more inevitably than writing since it involves two ambiguities that cannot be superimposed—regularly violates the principle of noncontradiction because the principle of noncontradiction is based on the requirement of strict univocity: one word, one meaning—or, in any case, no two meanings at a time, no two meanings at the same time.

In order to understand this, it is necessary and sufficient to revisit the formulation of the principle and its demonstration by Aristotle in book *Gamma* of his *Metaphysics*: "It is impossible that the same simultaneously belong and not belong to the same and in the same respect."[17] Aristotle's proof is quite remarkable. This demonstration cannot be a direct proof structured according to predicative logic (often presumed without consulting the text) since, as Aristotle puts it, in that case it would fall prey to a *petitio principii*. Thus, the proof has to proceed by "refutation," that is, by demanding that the adversary say something in order to prove to the adversary from then on that he has always already followed the very principle that he believes he has rejected. As a result, the demonstration plays on what we could justly call the transcendental conditions or the conditions of possibility of language itself.[18] We remember the beginning, but I wish now to complete the chain of equivalences with a last sentence:

> But even this can be demonstrated to be impossible, in the manner of a refutation, if only the disputant *says something*. If he says nothing, it is ridiculous to look for a statement in response to one who has a statement of nothing, insofar as he has not; such a person, insofar as he is such, is *similar to a plant* . . . In response to every case of that kind the original [step] is not to ask him to state something either to be or not to be (for that might well be believed to raise what was originally at issue), but at least *to signify something both to himself and to someone else*; for that is necessary if he is to say anything. For if he does not, there would be no statement for such a person, either in response to himself or to anyone else. But if he does offer this, there will be demonstration, for there will already be something definite . . .
>
>   *For not to signify one thing is to signify nothing*, and if names do not signify, discussion is eliminated with others; and, in truth, even with oneself . . .
> (8–10)[19]

As we can see, the demonstration proceeds by establishing a chain of equivalences: "to speak" = "to say something" = "to signify something" = "to signify one thing," "the same thing both to himself and to someone else." Meaning is the first entity that we encounter and the first entity that can be encountered which does not tolerate contradictions: beings are constructed like meaning. The requirement of univocity is as much a structuring force as the prohibition of incest. Essentially, there are two possibilities: either the adversary says something that has a meaning and only one meaning, and thus he speaks like Aristotle and submits himself to the principle, or he refuses to do so, but in that case he does not speak, and he does not satisfy the definition of the human being as an animal endowed with *logos*: he is a plant. We already know that the principle of noncontradiction is founded, from Aristotle to Apel and Habermas, on an injunction to communicate: speak (like I do and with me) if you are human!

Protagoras and the Proper Name of the Plant

For Aristotle, Protagoras is the eponym of extremist resistance. The whole work of the philanthropist philosopher is to humanize humankind. Thus, he does everything so that the universal principle will be universally accepted. But he encounters two quite distinct fronts of refusal. The first is represented by physicians like Heraclitus, who, observing the changing world, believe that the same does not exist. But it is not too difficult to persuade them otherwise through the vast machine of the categories and the distinctions of the meaning of being. The counterpunch is provided by the word anchored in the definition of the thing: "the same wine might be thought sweet at one time and not sweet at another, if there is an alteration either in it or in the body; but the sweet such as it is, when it is, has never yet altered" (20–21). The meaning of a word is by definition anchored in the essence of the thing named by this word.

The others, led by the Sophist Protagoras, remain intractable since they do not speak to say something but "for the pleasure of speaking [*legei logou kharin*]" (16).[20] They reject meaning and its univocal regulation, and they stick with *is* when they say *is*. If we maintain that the identity of the signifier is a manifestation of the identity of the signified, so that homonymy or equivocation become the norms of language, we strike a mortal blow to the principle of noncontradiction. Supposedly, the remedy is "to refute the statement which is in their speech and in their words [*tou en têi phônêi logou kai tou en tois onomasin*]" (16), but this is precisely what is impossible: "those who seek only to be defeated in the argument seek the impossible" (22).

As Nietzsche says in *Homer and Classical Philology*, "those who find language interesting in itself are different from those who see in language nothing but the medium of interesting ideas[21]": the sophistic tradition— which is certainly Greek but in this respect not philosophical—refuses to see in language an *organon*, a medium of communication. Thus, we can connect in series the multiplicity of translations, the feeling that equivocations and homonyms are constitutive and irreducible, and the attack on the principle of non-contradiction. You are never sure where to stop in and between languages —back to the *Dictionary of Untranslatables!*"

Relativism as Dedicated Comparative

To be positioned in *logos* and in homonymy, to speak *logou kharin* ("for the pleasure of speaking") does not mean speaking in any old way. On the contrary, it means: *not to* aim for the One, be it in the form of a definition, essence, or truth. But is there another model, another type of linguistic regulation that might work? The answer is yes. It is the relativist model. But we must be very careful with what that actually means.

Since Plato, Protagoras's sentence is the emblem of the relativist position for the whole history of philosophy. "Man is the measure of all things" (*pantôn khrêmatôn anthrôpos metron*) is without doubt one of the most often-discussed short sentences. In Protagoras, via Plato and Aristotle, relativism and the resistance to the principle of noncontradiction are joined together, and this conjunction mostly still remains to be described. When Plato's Socrates recalls this sentence in *Theaetetus*, a dialogue "on the sciences," he puts forth the following statement as its equivalent: "The measure of all things is the pig, or the baboon."[22] Then he repents and tells himself that "You have no shame, Socrates, Protagoras would say." So he proposes "Protagoras's apology," thereby lending his voice to Protagoras as if the latter were present to defend himself. I believe that this is the strongest interpretation of relativism that one can in fact offer. I have just used it to think transitional justice and cultural democracy. I wish to conclude now by means of it in favor of anti-anti-relativism:

> For I do indeed assert that the truth is as I have written . . . By reason of a useful [*khrêstêi*] state of mind one is moved to useful opinions, representations that some people ignorantly call true, whereas I should say that one set of thoughts is better than the other, but not in any way truer. . . . In this way it is true that some men are wiser than others without anyone possessing falsely opinions, and you like it or not, must put up with being a measure . . . [23]

I will simply underline once again the manner in which Protagoras changes the terms of the discussion: he moves from the binary opposition of true/false to the comparative "better" and, more precisely, to what I call "dedicated comparative": "better for." What is "better" is defined as "the most useful," the best adapted to the person, the situation, all the components of *kairos*: we find here the precise meaning of these *khrêmata*, whose measure is man, not the "things," "existing beings" (*pragmata, onta*), but what one uses, the *khrêmata*, objects of use, the resources that language and discursive performances obviously form a part of. From this perspective, there is no being to be sought beneath appearance. There is no One to be sought beneath or beyond the multiple. Unlike in Leibniz, there is no divine point of view that could unify all the perceptions of the monads.

And yet—and this is what all our contemporaries who vilify relativism fail to see, from Alan Sokal and Jean Bricmont to Jean-Paul II and Ratzinger—not all opinions have the same value. The reason for this is that it is necessary, pedagogically and politically, for individuals as well as for communities to be capable of preferring what is better, that is to say, what is "better for." Politics does not consist of the universal imposition of Truth (or the imposition of universal truth). It consists of the differential aid to choose the better. Such is the immense subtlety but also the immense objectivity of relativism. It obviously denies the dominant diagnosis: "May '68 imposed on us an intellectual and moral relativism. The heirs of May '68 have imposed the idea that everything is worth the same, that there is no difference whatsoever between good and evil, between the true and the false, between the beautiful and the ugly."[24] In reality, however, it is relativism—also as a historical doctrine—that allows us to understand the notion of plurality itself.

Translated by Roland Végső

INTRODUCTION: TOWARD A NEW TOPOLOGY OF PHILOSOPHY

1. *On Feminine Sexuality, the Limits of Love and Knowledge, 1972–1973: Encore, The Seminar of Jacques Lacan, Book XX* (New York: Norton, 1999), 120.

2. Cassin, *L'effet sophistique* (Paris: Gallimard), 1995.

3. See my books *There's No Such Thing as a Sexual Relationship* with Alain Badiou (New York: Columbia University Press, 2013) and *Jacques le Sophiste: Lacan, logos et psychanalyse* (Paris: Epel, 2012).

4. Aristotle, *Topics*, book 1, 11: 105a (cf. *The Complete Works of Aristotle*, ed. Jonathan Barnes, 2 vols. [Princeton, N.J.: Princeton University Press, 1984]). In this book, all translations from the Greek are, with stated exceptions, my own. These have in turn been rendered as directly as possible from French into English to minimize the risk of giving quotations at a double remove from the original. Various translations could sometimes be given for one and the same passage. References are given directly in the text when no ambiguity is possible.

5. The dictionary is currently being translated into many languages: Arabic, Ukrainian, Romanian, Russian, Spanish, Portuguese, and Persian, for example; three volumes in Ukrainian and one in Arabic have already been published (see http://intraduisibles.org). The English version, which has been edited by Emily Apter, Jacques Lezra, and Michael Wood, will be published in Spring 2014 under the title *Dictionary of Untranslatables: A Philosophical Lexicon* (Princeton, N.J.: Princeton University Press, 2014).

6. For a discussion of Globish, see Barbara Cassin, *Plus d'une langue* (Paris: Bayard, 2012).

7. Secondary or high school, which culminates with a baccalaureate. Philosophy is taught in the final year.

8. See "Noyade d'un poisson," in *Avec le plus petit et le plus inapparent des corps* (Paris: Fayard, 2007), as well as Cassin, *Jacques le Sophiste*.

9. A phrase often applied to certain nineteenth-century French poets such as Baudelaire, Rimbaud, and Verlaine because of their interest in socially marginal elements.

10. *How to Do Things with Words* (Cambridge, Mass.: Harvard University Press, 1975).

1. WHO'S AFRAID OF THE SOPHISTS? AGAINST ETHICAL CORRECTNESS

1. Parmenides (Winter semester 1942/43), ed. M. S. Frings, 1982, 2nd edn. 1992, XII, p. 142

2. Francis Ponge, "La cruche," in *Pièces* (Paris: Gallimard, 1961), 209–10.

3. Aristotle, *Topics*. See Introduction, note 4.

4. Novalis, *Philosophical Writings*, trans. M. Stoljar (Albany: State University of New York Press, 1997). I am referring here to the first paragraph of fragment 15, which begins, "*Philosophistieren ist dephlegmatisieren—Vivificiren.*" The paragraph has been omitted from Stoljar's English translation of fragment 15.

5. For a full translation of Parmenides in French, see *Sur la nature ou sur l'étant: Le grec, langue de l'être?* trans. Barbara Cassin (Paris: Seuil, Points-bilingues, 1998). For a full translation of Gorgias in French, see *L'effet sophistique*, 128–32. For an English translation, see, for example, Kathleen Freeman, *Ancilla to the Pre-Socratic Philosophers* (Oxford: Basil Blackwell, 1948): Parmenides, 41–46, and Gorgias, 127–38.

6. This is the first sentence of Gorgias's Treatise *On What Is Not, or On Nature*, as transmitted in ps. Aristotle, *On Melissus, Xenophanes, and Gorgias*, 979a12s. I have edited this text in *Si Parménide*, which is available online (http://www.centreleonrobin.fr/index.php/membres/9-cassin-barbara/3).

7. On translation problems in Parmenides, see part V, chap. 17, "The Relativity of Translation and Relativism."

8. Heidegger's translation appears in English in Krell and Capuzzi's partial translation of Heidegger's *Parmenides* as "For Thinking and Being Are the Same," in Heidegger, *Early Greek Thinking*, trans. David F. Krell and Frank A. Capuzzi (New York: Harper and Row, 1975), 79.

9. This sentence belongs to the other version of the same treatise by Gorgias transmitted by Sextus Empiricus, *Adversus mathematicos*, VII, 65–87 (here 79). See Freeman, *Ancilla*, 129.

10. *Catalogue des travaux de Jean Dubuffet. Fascicule XXIV: Tour aux figures, amoncellements, cabinet logologique* (Geneva: Weber, 1973), 115.

11. Novalis, "Monologue," in *German Aesthetic and Literary Criticism: The Romantic Ironists and Goethe*, ed. Kathleen Wheeler (Cambridge: Cambridge University Press, 1984), 92–93.

12. Gorgias in ps. Aristotle, *On Melissus . . .*, 980b4.

13. I am paraphrasing Francis Ponge's formidably dry statement. See *Pratiques d'écriture ou l'inachèvement perpétuel* (Paris: Hermann, 1984), 40. See part V, chap. 17, "The Relativity of Translation and Relativism," 330.

14. Arendt, "Philosophie et politique," *Cahiers du Grif* 33 (1986): 90. This lecture was originally given in 1954.

15. See "Truth and Politics," in Hannah Arendt, *Between Past and Future: Eight Exercises in Political Thought* (London: Penguin, 1993), 259.

16. See part I, chap. 2, "Speak If You Are a Man, or the Transcendental Exclusion."

17. *Metaphysics*, Gamma, 4 1006a 12–13, in *Books Gamma, Delta, and Epsilon*, 2nd ed., trans. Christopher Kirwan (Oxford: Clarendon, 1993). All subsequent in-text citations are based on modifications of this edition.

18. Ibid., 14–15.

19. Ibid., 5 ·1009a, 21–22.

20. *Jokes and Their Relation to the Unconscious*, trans. James Strachey (Harmondsworth: Penguin, 1976), 45.

21. *Feminine Sexuality: Jacques Lacan and the* école freudienne, ed. Juliet Mitchell and Jacqueline Rose (London: Macmillan, 1982), 157.

22. Apel, "The *A Priori* of the Communication Community and the Foundations of Ethics: The Problem of a Rational Foundation of Ethics in the Scientific Age," in *Towards a Transformation of Philosophy*, trans. Glyn Adey and David Frisby (London: Routledge and Kegan Paul, 1980), 225.

23. Apel, "Rekonstruktion der Vernunft durch Transformation der Transzendentalphilosophie." Interview. *Concordia* 10 (1987): 3.

24. Aristotle, *Metaphysics*, IV, 5, 1009a 21–22.

25. Aristotle, *De Interpretatione*, 1, 16a 16, in ibid.

26. Dio Chrysostom, *Discourses 37–60*, trans. H. Lamar Crosby, Loeb Classical Library (London: Heinemann and Macmillan, 1946), 53, sec. 7–8, p. 363.

27. Lucian, *A True Story*, in *Lucian in Eight Volumes*, vol. 1, trans. A. M. Harmon, Loeb Classical Library (London: Heinemann and Macmillan, 1925), 253, sec. 4; translation modified.

28. Nietzsche, *The Will to Power*, trans. Walter Kaufmann and R. J. Hollingdale (New York: Vintage, 1968), 231 (§427).

29. Plato, *Protagoras*, in *The Collected Dialogues of Plato*, ed. Edith Hamilton and Huntington Cairns (Princeton, N.J.: Princeton University Press, 2005), 323b.

30. Aristotle, *Metaphysics*, IV, 2, 1004b 17–18.
31. Ibid., 24–25.
32. Quintilian, XII, 3, 12, in *The Institutio Oratoria of Quintilian in Four Volumes*, vol. 4, trans. H. E. Butler, Loeb Classical Library (Cambridge, Mass.: Harvard University Press, 1922), 407.
33. Joseph Moreau, "Qu'est-ce qu'un sophiste?" in *Platon devant les sophistes* (Paris: Vrin-Reprise, 1987), 14.
34. Ibid., 16.
35. Ibid., 17.
36. François Furet, "L'utopie démocratique à l'américaine," *Le Débat* 69 (March–April 1982): 84.
37. Bloom, *Giants and Dwarfs: Essays 1960–1990* (New York: Touchstone, 1990), 18.
38. Badiou, *Conditions* (Paris: Le Seuil, 1992). See also Badiou, *Manifeste pour la philosophie* (Paris: Le Seuil, 1989).
39. Badiou, *Conditions*, 59. Further references are given in the text.
40. Badiou, *Manifeste pour la philosophie*, 85.
41. Ibid., 74.
42. Ibid., 86.

2. SPEAK IF YOU ARE A MAN, OR THE TRANSCENDENTAL EXCLUSION

1. In Barnes, *Complete Works of Aristotle*, vol. 1, 174.
2. Translator's note: The French word *sens*, used throughout Cassin's essay to resonate with the term *consensus*, is here translated variously as "meaning" and "sense."
3. Aristotle, *Metaphysics*, *Gamma* 3, 1005 b 13–14.
4. Ibid., translation modified.
5. Ibid., translation modified.
6. Nietzsche, quoted by Martin Heidegger in *Nietzsche*, ed. and rev. David Farrell Krell, trans. Joan Stambaugh (San Francisco: Harper, 1987), vol. 3, *The Will to Power as Knowledge and Metaphysics*, 111. Heidgger's emphasis.
7. Heidegger, ibid., 111–12.
8. Ibid., 112.
9. Martin Heidegger, *History of the Concept of Time: Prolegomena*, trans. Theodore Kisiel (Bloomington: Indiana University Press, 1985), 272–73.
10. Apel, "Rekonstruktion der Vernunft," 3.
11. Apel, "*A Priori* of the Communication Community," 260.
12. Karl-Otto Apel, "La question d'une formation ultime de la raison," trans. S. Foisy and J. Poulain, *Critique* 15 (October 1981): 899.
13. Ibid., 903.

14. Ibid., 926–27.
15. Translations modified.
16. Apel, *"A Priori* of the Communication Community," 261–62.
17. Translations modified.
18. Apel, "La question d'une formation ultime de la raison," 926.
19. Gilles Deleuze, *The Logic of Sense*, trans. Mark Lester with Charles Stivale (New York: Columbia University Press, 1990), 68.
20. Jürgen Habermas, *Moral Consciousness and Communicative Action*, trans. Christian Lenhardt and Shierry Weber Nicholsen (Cambridge, Mass.: MIT Press, 1990), 99–100.
21. Ibid.
22. Richard Rorty, "Pragmatism, Relativism, Irrationalism," in *Consequences of Pragmatism* (Minneapolis: University of Minnesota Press, 1982), 165.
23. Ibid., 166–67.
24. Ibid., 170.
25. Jacques Poulain, "Richard Rorty ou la boîte blanche de la communication," *Critique* 417 (February 1982): 149.
26. Rorty, "Pragmatism, Relativism, Irrationalism," 167.
27. Gorgias, 82B23D.K.
28. Rorty, "Pragmatism, Relativism, Irrationalism," 172.

3. SEEING HELEN IN EVERY WOMAN: WOMAN AND WORD

1. Goethe, *Faust I*, v. 2604.
2. Nietzsche, *Fragments posthumes*, 7 [27], end 1870–April 1871, " 'Sieht Helen in jedem Weibe,' die Gier zum Dasein verbirgt das Unschöne," *Œuvres philosophiques complètes*, *La naissance de la tragédie*, Fragments posthumes, Gallimard, I, 1, p. 266s.
3. Letter from Freud to Jung, April 16, 1909, in *The Freud/Jung Letters*, ed. William McGuire, trans. Ralph Mannheim and R. F. C. Hull (London: Picador, 1979), 145.
4. To translate Jacques Lacan's *"La / une femme."* See *On Feminine Sexuality, the Limits of Love and Knowledge*, op. cit., 72–73.
5. Hofmannstahl-Strauss's *Helen in Egypt* and Offenbach's *Beautiful Helen*, for example.
6. Nietzsche, *The Gay Science*, trans. Walter Kauffman (New York: Vintage, 1974), 38.
7. Goethe, *Faust II*, v.9952s, in *Œuvres philosophiques complètes*, and Jean Giraudoux, *The Trojan War Will Not Take Place*, 3rd ed., trans. C. Fry (London: Methuen, 1983), 11.

8. Pierre Chantraine, *Dictionnaire étymologique de la langue grecque: Histoire des mots* (Paris: Klincksieck, 1968–1970); Giraudoux, *Trojan War*, 10.

9. Ronsard, *Sonnets for Helen, with English renderings by Humbert Wolfe* (London: Allen and Unwin, 1934), II, 9.

10. Ibid., I, 3.

11. Christopher Marlow, *Doctor Faustus*, V, 1, 89.

12. Isocrates testifies to this in *Encomium to Helen*, 4–5. My translation.

13. Raymond Queneau stages it thus: "LN in two letters. I am of cruciverbal origin." See Queneau, *The Flight of Icarus*, rev. ed., trans. B. Wright (Richmond, UK: OneWorld, 2009), 19.

14. Lucian, *A True Story* in *Lucian in Eight Volumes*, vol. 1, trans. A. M. Harmon, Loeb Classical Library (London: Heinemann and Macmillan, 1925), II, 20.

15. The brackets contain what editors take out. From this, one can infer that English editors and translators are less prudish than French ones. See, for example, Samuel Butler's *The Odyssey, rendered into English prose for the use of those who cannot read the original* (London: A. C. Fifield), c. 1900.

16. Homère, *L'Odyssée*, trad. Philippe Jacottet, La Découverte, 1992.

17. Euripides, *Helen*, v.593, quoted in Ernst Bloch, *The Principle of Hope*, vol. 1, trans. N. Plaice, S. Plaice, and P. Knight (Cambridge, Mass.: MIT Press, 1995), 185.

18. Euripide, vol. V, trans. Grégoire (Paris: Les Belles Lettres), 1973, "Je suis Hélène," v.22, 50.

19. 31ss, my translation.

20. I have retranslated it in Barbara Cassin and Maurice Mathieu, *Voir Hélène en toute femme: D'Homère à Lacan* (Paris: Les Empêcheurs de penser en rond, 2000), 78–82.

21. *Encomium of Helen*, 82 B11 DK, §8–9, vol. II, 290. I am quoting directly from the Greek text; all translations are my own.

22. Ibid., §14, 292–93.

23. Ibid., §21, 294.

24. Giraudoux, *Trojan War*, act 1, scene 4.

25. Jacques Lacan, *On Feminine Sexuality: The Limits of Love and Knowledge*, trans. B. Fink (New York: Norton, 1998). This is the title given to the English language translation of Lacan's *Seminaire XX. Encore*.

26. Ibid., 60.

27. Ibid., 74.

28. Ibid., 75.

29. Ibid., 7.

30. Ibid., 73.

31. Ibid., 10.

32. Ibid., 52.

4. RHETORICAL TURNS IN ANCIENT GREECE

1. Roland Barthes, "The Old Rhetoric: An Aide-Mémoire," in *The Semiotic Challenge*, trans. R. Howard (Berkeley: University of California Press, 1994), p. 11–94; George Alexander Kennedy, *The Art of Persuasion in Greece* (Princeton, N.J.: Princeton University Press, 1963); John Poulakos, *Sophistical Rhetoric in Classical Greece* (Columbia, S.C.: University of South Carolina Press, 2008).

2. Aristotle, *On Sophistical Refutations*, trans. E. S. Forster and D. J. Furley, Loeb Classical Library (London: Heinemann and Macmillan, 1955), XXXIV, 184 a 2–10.

3. Edward Schiappa, "Did Plato Coin *Rhêtorikê*?" *American Journal of Philology* 111 (1990): 457–70. See also "*Rhêtorikê*: What's in a Name? Toward a Revised History of Early Greek Rhetorical Theory," *Quarterly Journal of Speech* 78 (February 1992): 1–15, and *The Beginnings of Rhetorical Theory in Classical Greece* (New Haven, Conn.: Yale University Press, 1999).

4. Werner Pilz, *Der Rhetor im attischen Staat* (Weida, Germany: Thomas und Hubert, 1934); also quoted by Edward Schiappa.

5. *Encomium of Helen*, 82 B11 DK, §8, vol. II, 290.

6. Ibid.

7. Ibid., §1, vol. II, 288.

8. "Order" and "disorder," but one would like to render *kosmos* by the Baudlerian syntagm "*ordre et beauté*," maybe combined in the modern "structure."

9. *Encomium of Helen*, 82 B11 DK, §2, vol. II, 288.

10. *Agamemnon*, v. 687–90. I am quoting directly from the Greek text; all translations are my own.

11. Ronsard, *Sonnets for Helen, with English Renderings by Humbert Wolfe* (London: Allen and Unwin, 1934), 12, 9.

12. See part I, chap. 3, "Seeing Helen in Every Woman: Woman and Word."

13. Hannah Arendt, "'What Remains? The Language Remains': A Conversation with Günter Gaus," (1965) in *The Portable Hannah Arendt*, ed. Peter Baehr (New York: Harcourt, Penguin, 2000), 3–24.

14. Badiou, *Magazine Littéraire* 447 (November 2005): 34.

15. Trans. W. R. M. Lamb, Loeb Classical Library (Cambridge, Mass.: Harvard University Press and Heinemann, 1924, repr. 2006); in general, I have followed this translation, although I have made some modifications of my own. Further references are given in the text.

16. "Respect" is nevertheless perhaps the best way of expressing the reciprocity of sight: watch and be—"and they saw that they were naked," as it says in the Bible.

17. *Arêtê* means "excellency," beginning with the quality of the Homeric hero, something closer to Italian *virtu* than to the French *vertu*, but the meaning has, of course, been "ethicized" from Plato on.

18. See part V, chap. 15, "Politics of Memory."

19. There is a frequent mistranslation of 327 E-328 A: *hôsper an zêtois tis didaskalostou hellenizein, oud'an heis phaneie* does not mean "you might as well ask who is a teacher of Greek; you will find none anywhere" (trans. Lamb), but "you will find more than one."

20. *Pros Platôna huper rhêtorikês*: "Against Plato," and not "To Plato," as in C. A. Behr's translation in *Aristides in Four Volumes*, Loeb Classical Library (Cambridge, Mass.: Harvard University Press, 1973), vol. I. But there exists no French translation except the fragment I have included in the *Effet sophistique* (Paris: Gallimard, 1995), 309–24). I quote Behr's translation with some modifications.

21. *Problêma poiêsamenos anti allou phulaktêriou ton logon*: discourse, speech is the unique and sufficient phylactery. Behr chooses to translate *logos* as "reason" in the whole passage, and it is impossible then not to get lost, confused, and bored.

5. *TOPOS/KAIROS*: TWO MODES OF INVENTION

1. Diogenes Laertius, IX, 56 (=80 A 1 DK). For the set of preserved testimonies, see A. Capizzi, *Protagora: Le testimonianze e i frammenti* (Florence: Sansoni, 1955), 154–58 (Diogenes) and 164–68 (Quintilius, and especially Apuleius and Aulus Gellius). Diogenes has just said (52) that Protagoras is "the first to have distinguished *merê kronou*," the "parts of time" (which is always understood as "the tense of verbs"), "and to have exposed the dynamic of the *kairos*."

2. *Rhetoric*, III, 9, 1409b1.

3. Philostratus and Eunapius, *Lives of the Sophists*, trans. Wilmer Cave Wright, Loeb Classical Library (Cambridge, Mass.: Harvard University Press, 1968): "Agathon . . . often gorgianized in iambic feet" (493), and when Proclus of Naucratis embarked upon an exordium, "it was a Hippias or a Gorgias that he resembled [*hippiazonti te . . . kai gorgiazonti*]" (604); "to gorgianize" is also, according to Plato, what the Thessalian cities do (501). My translation.

4. Echoed in the third sophistic: "gongorism." The adjective *gorgieios* can be found in Xenophon (*Smp.*, 2, 26) and in Dionysus of Halicarnassus (*Dem.*, 5).

5. *Rhetoric*, III, 1, 1404 a24–29; cf. 1406 b9, 1408 b20. Aristotle specifies that "the form of the style [*to skhêma tês lexeôs*] must be neither metrical [*emmetron*] nor arrhythmic" (b21s.)

6. Souda = 82 A2 DK (II, 272); Diodorus, *Historical Library*, XII, 53 = 82 A4 DK (273). To perceive the specificity of Gorgias's prose, in particular its rhythm, one can scrape something together out of E. Norden's consistent work in *Die antike Kunstprosa vom VI Jahrhundert v. Chr. bis in die Zeit der Renaissance* (Leipzig: Teubner, 1898), part I, 15–79. Baldwin concludes his overview of the *Lives* by expanding space and time still further: "The same 'Gorgian figures' are learnt by St Augustine in Latin Africa, by St Gregory of Nazianzus in the Greek East, and by the pagan Libanius. Greco-roman rhetoric was as pervasive as Roman law and almost as constant" (*Medieval Rhetoric and Poetics to 1400*, Gloucester, Mass.: Peter Smith, 1959, 9).

7. See *Encomium of Helen*, 82 B11 DK, §8.

8. What is as yet unclear is what should be thought of Prodicos's fable as sophistics. Jean-Paul Dumont poses this problem in "Prodicos: De la méthode au système," in *Positions de la sophistique*, ed. Barbara Cassin, 221–32 (Paris: Vrin, 1986). Should this fable be considered by relating it to other testimony, specifically Platonic, essentially from the point of view of onomastics and synonymy (the beautiful lady, for example, is named *Eudaimonia/Kakia*, depending on who is calling her)? (*Prodikos von Keos und die Anfänge der Synonymik bei den Griechen* is the title of H. Mayer's dissertation, which was published in 1913 by the University of Michigan Library.) Should one attempt to think the consensual constitution of the gnomic and ask just which tasks Hercules will have to complete in order to become, like Helen, Palamedes, or Prometheus, a "sophistical" hero?

9. Here Bernard Gallet's work is essential; see *Recherches sur* kairos *et l'ambiguïté dans la poésie de Pindare* (Bordeaux: Presses Universitaires de Bordeaux, 1990). I repeatedly refer to this work as well as to Monique Trédé's doctoral dissertation, Kairos: *L'à-propos et l'occasion: Le mot et la notion d'Homère à la fin du IVe siècle avant J.C.* (Paris: Klinsieck, 1992), which analyzes in particular, via Alcidamas and Isocrates, "the *kairos* of the orators" (247–82). Gallet was wise enough to depart from Richard Broxton Onians's work, *The Origins of European Thought* (Cambridge: Cambridge University Press, 1951), which poses the *kair'os/kaîros* relationship (343–49).

10. Onians, *Origins of European Thought*, 344.

11. On the possible etymologies, see Trédé, *Kairos*, chap. 1.

12. For example, *Iliad*, IV, 185–87; see Gallet's commentary, which rightly corrects J.R. Wilson ("KAIROS as 'Due Measure,'" *Glotta* 58 (1980), 177–204) and Trédé, *Kairos*, 51s, and all of chap. 2.

13. Onians, *Origins of European Thought*, 346; Pierre Chantraine, *Diction-naire étymologique de la langue grecque: Histoire des mots* (Paris: Klincksieck, 1968–1970).

14. Gallet, *Recherches sur* kairos, 22.

15. Ibid., 93s. Gallet identifies and then verifies, in an admirable fashion, the four technical functions that produce a semantic descendance: as "guiding or main thread," *kairos* is a "take," an "influence," a "control"; as the "regulating thread," which limits the breadth of the loom determining the zone of weaving, it is a "rule," a "good order," a "precise measure," a "brevity," and an "advantage"; as an "interwoven thread," encountering each of the warp's threads at a right angle, it is a "conjunction," a "conjuncture," an "occasion," a "propitious moment"; as a "separating thread" between the lap of odd threads and that of even threads, it is a "choice," a "separation," a "judgment," and a "decision" (65).

16. Ibid., 94, 357.

17. Pindar, *Pythians*, I, 81 = Str.5, 157.

18. Aristotle, *Topiques*, tome 1, livres I–IV, trans. J. Brunschwig (Paris: Belles Lettres, 2003), xxxix. My emphasis.

19. *Rhetoric*, II, 26, 1403a17.

20. Aristotle, *Topiques*, tome 1, livres I–IV, xl.

21. Ibid., livres I–IV, note 3, xxxix; Roland Barthes, *The Semiotic Challenge*, trans. R. Howard (Berkeley: University of California Press, 1994), 64–65.

22. Heidegger, "Logos Heraklit Fragment B50," in *Early Greek Thinking*, trans. D. F. Krell, (New York: HarperCollins, 1985), 61; my emphasis. It is a 1951 text based on the 1944 summer semester course. Evidently Heidegger's interpretation of Heracleitus via Parmenides and of *logos* as a "gathering process" is of fundamental importance here. As for the interpretation of Protagoras's phrase, which again derives from Parmenidean *alêtheia* and *sophia* via a series of equivalences (i.e., *khrêmata-pragmata-phainomena-onta*), see the eighth appendix to "The Age of the World Picture," in *The Question Concerning Technology and Other Essays*, trans. William Lovitt (New York: Harper and Row, 1977), 143–47, which is taken up with a few modifications in "The Statement of Protagoras," in *Nietzsche*, vols. III and IV (New York: HarperOne, 1991), 91–95. See also my critique in "Peut-on être autrement présocratique? Remarques sur l'interprétation heideggérienne de la sophistique," *Revue de Philosophie Ancienne* IV, no. 2 (1986), 211–229.

23. *Against Plato, in Defense of Rhetoric*, in *Aristides in Four Volumes*, Loeb Classical Library (Cambridge, Mass.: Harvard University Press, 1973), vol. I, 408. The original reads *"Hoi logoi tôi khronôi sumprobainousin,"* but Charles Allison Behr translates it as "Reason increases with time."

24. Without a doubt, this is the correct perspective for understanding Protagoras's famous phrase on humankind as a measure in regard to its sophistical implications: the phrase concerns the *khrêmata*. One can find an echo of this relation between the *khrêmata* and the circulation of goods in Aristotle's fine-tuning of the determination of the virtues in the *Nicomachean Ethics*. After having defined without ambiguity (but certainly not without an allusion to Protagoras) *khrêmata* as "everything which is measured by money" (IV, 1, 1119b, 26–27), Aristotle drives the etymological nail home with a syllogism:

> Whatever has a use [*khreia*] can be used [*khrêsthai*] either well or badly. Riches [*ho ploutos*] are something useful [*tôn khrêsimôn*]; and the best user of something [*arista khrêsetai*] is the person who has the virtue [*aretên*] concerned with it. Hence the best user of riches will be the person who has the virtue concerned with wealth. Using wealth [*khrêsis . . . khrêmatôn*] seems to consist in spending and giving [*dapanê*—"consumption"—*kai dosis*], whereas taking and keeping seem to be possessing rather than using [*hê de lêpsis kai hê phulakê ktêsis*]. (1120 a5–10)

The point of this entire passage is to oppose expenditure to accumulation and to insistently tie the good use of *khrêmata* to expense and gifts, that is, to putting into circulation.

25. G. Bataille, "Preface," in *The Accursed Share*, vol. 1, *Consumption*, trans. R. Hurley (New York: Zone, 1989), 12.

26. Ibid., 89 n1.

27. The difference between the two sophistics is certainly at work in the composition of the treatise since the second section of the first book deals with the old sophistic, from Gorgias (chap. 9) to Isocrates (chap. 17), while the third section and all of the third book deal with the second sophistic. But the sophists of the second sophistic do not stop imitating Gorgias (Proclus of Naucratis, *VS*, 604; Scopelian, 518; cf. Norden, *Die antike Kunstprosa*, in particular 379–86). Besides, the place of Æschine (chap. 18) clearly demonstrates the ambiguity of the classification. He follows Isocrates, who is chronologically the last of the ancients. He precedes Nicetes of Smyrna, who flowers at the end of the first century A.D; logically, the latter is the first of these "moderns" who go up to Claudius Ælianus at the end of the third century. One can see how chronologically twisted the sequence is: it resembles a collage, a precipitate of the ancient and the modern, which skips four centuries without leaving a trace and ignores those who elsewhere count among the greats. It does so to the point that, along with Kayser, in his introduction to the Teubner edition of Philostratus, one would prefer to

believe that part of the treatise was lost and that originally it was a question of Demetrius of Phalerum, of Hegesias and Fronto, without speaking of the case of Lucien. But Pierre Vidal-Naquet is right when he remarks that "the Greek intellectuals of that epoch, historians, sophists, novelists, directly unite, via a singular collage, Sparta's and Athens's political past with their aesthetic present. The Hellenistic epoch is the evident victim of this perilous leap" (in "Flavius Arrien entre deux mondes," postface to the translation by Pierre Savinel of Arrien, *Histoire d'Alexandre* [Paris: Minuit, 1984], 327). On the construction of the *Lives*, see Graham Anderson, *Philostratus: Biography and Belles Lettres in the Second Century* A.D. (London: Croom Helm, 1986), chap. 5, and on the past-present relation see Graham Anderson, *The Second Sophistic: Cultural Phenomenon in the Roman Empire* (Oxford: Routledge, 1993), chap. 3.

28. The most complete description of this proliferation, including the forms specific to Christian literature, can be found in B. P. Reardon's summa, *Courants littéraires grecs des IIème et IIIème siècles après J.C.* (Paris: Les Belles Lettres, 1971). This is a remarkable work even if the erudition and common sense are sometimes, from my point of view, trapped within the traditional opposition between literature and philosophy to the point that some of the resulting evaluations end up being as detrimental to philosophy as they are to literature. This is the case for Aristides, for example: "The parallelism *homonoein-homou*, which hardly even makes a jingle, constitutes the structure of this phrase. The rest is mere verbiage. This indeed is the spirit of most of Aristides's œuvre" (129). A phrase like "Quite simply, Lucien was not a thinker, and there's hardly any point in going further into the question" (157) is no less symptomatic.

29. The year 1759 saw the publication of Lessing's *Briefe, die neueste Literatur betreffend*, and 1800 saw that of Madame de Staël's *De la littérature*. See R. Escarpit, "La définition du terme 'littérature,'" Third Congress of the International Association of Comparative Literature, Utrecht, 1961, cited by Philippe Lacoue-Labarthe and Jean-Luc Nancy in "Le dialogue des genres," *Poétique* 21 (1975): 149.

30. Barthes, *Semiotic Challenge*, 21.

31. Bompaire, *Lucien écrivain* (Paris: De Boccard, 1958), 26. See E. Stemplinger, *Das Plagiat in der griechischen Literatur* (Leipzig, 1912). If I thus subscribe to the thesis according to which "in truth originality and imitation are only incompatible for a modern sensibility" (Bompaire, *Lucien écrivain*, 75)—although I feel like adding that this modern sensibility would thus have misunderstood a large part of the Renaissance, classicism, and even modernity—I believe, on the contrary, that it is not "false" but true or, at the very

least, operative to "think that these two imitations of opposite origins, philosophical for one, and sophistical for the other . . . are thus fundamentally opposite" (this is note 7 on page 26 of Bompaire, which further comments on the phrase cited earlier on the "imitation of books" and the "imitation of the world"). Let's say that Don Quixote's madness is the novelistic "emblem" of this opposition.

32. Bompaire, *Lucien écrivain*, 91.

33. Ibid., 47.

34. *Rhetoric*, III, 3, 1406b15–19.

35. *Poetics*, 4, 1448 b 6–19, with Lallot and Dupont-Roc's always extremely accurate commentary: "One would be mistaken to see here the beginning of an aesthetic of the sublime which would account for the transmutation of the ugly into the beautiful via the alchemy of art. Aristotle's perspective is not aesthetic (in the modern sense of the word), but rather intellectual, cognitive" See *La poétique*, trans. Roselyne Dupont-Roc and Jean Lallot (Paris, Éditions du Seuil, 2011), 164.

6. TIME OF DELIBERATION AND SPACE OF POWER:
ATHENS AND ROME, THE FIRST CONFLICT

1. Kindly refer to my chapter on discourse as *pharmakon* in Barbara Cassin, Maurice Mathieu, and François Boissonnet, *Voir Hélène en toute femme: D'Homère à Lacan* (Paris: Les Empêcheurs de penser en rond, 2000), 110–13.

2. I follow the most recent edition of this text, namely, Charles Allison Behr's. All references made here are based on the Lenz-Behr edition of *Ælius Aristides: Opera quae exstant omnia*, vols. 1–2 (Leiden: Brill, 1976–78). The 1978 edition, short of the critical apparatus, is nearly identical to the one published in 1973 and served as the basis for the first translation into English, suggested by Behr, of which only the first volume has been published. A revised translation of a text that was barely modified but comprises more extensive notes can be found in Behr, *Ælius Aristides: The Complete Works* (Leiden: Brill, 1986).

3. The *Roman Oration* and the *Panathenaic Oration* have been translated and commented by James Henry Oliver; see, respectively, "The Ruling Power: A Study of the Roman Empire in the Second Century after Christ through the Roman Oration of Ælius Aristides" (in *Transactions of the American Philosophical Society*, 1953, vol. 43, Part IV, 869–1003) and *The Civilizing Power: a Study of the Panathenaic Discourse of Ælius Aristides Against the Background of Literature and Cultural Conflict* (Philadelphia: American Philosophical Society, 1968). Each was given a splendid title, "The Ruling Power" and

"The Civilizing Power," respectively, before being translated more recently by Behr in *Ælius Aristides: The Complete Works* (Leiden: Brill, 1981 [1st ed.], 1986 [2nd ed.]). It is important to point out that interpreters do not agree on the date: were the two speeches delivered at the same time (in 155 A.D., during the second of Aristides's journeys to Rome), or do they mark the beginning and the end of his career—in short, was Aristides playing a double game: was he a hypocrite, or was he smitten with patriotic remorse? I refer to the *Panathenaic Oration* as *A.*, followed by the paragraph, and the *Roman Oration* as *R.*, also followed by the paragraph. I am quoting directly from the Greek text; all translations are my own.

4. Pierre Vidal-Naquet, "Flavius Arrien entre deux mondes," afterword to the translation by Pierre Savinel of Arrien, *Histoire d'Alexandre* (Paris: Minuit, 1984).

5. André Boulanger, *Ælius Aristide et la sophistique dans la province d'Asie au IIème s. de notre ère* (Paris: De Boccard, 1923 [1st ed.], 1968 [2nd ed.]), 340. For a more recent and comprehensive view, see G. W. Bowersock, *Greek Sophists in the Roman Empire* (Oxford: Clarendon, 1969).

6. Quintilian, *The Institutio Oratoria of Quintilian in Four Volumes*, vol. 4, trans. H. E. Butler, Loeb Classical Library (Cambridge, Mass.: Harvard University Press, 1922), III, 7, 2.

7. Boulanger, *Ælius Aristide et la sophistique*, 347.

8. Ibid., 369–72.

9. I will touch on some conclusions drawn from Nicole Loraux's reflections in *The Invention of Athens: The Funeral Oration in the Classical City*, trans. Alan Sheridan (Cambridge, Mass.: Harvard University Press, 1986), on at least two levels: first, on eulogy in general, as it can be found at the heart of the dialectic between history and fiction—"a certain idea that the city wishes to have of itself emerges, beyond the needs of the present: within this orthodoxy of an official speech, there is a certain gap between Athens and Athens" (14); second, on the perception of Aristides's *Panathenaic* as the achievement of such a movement toward fictionalization, which ousts what remains of history, spatial-temporal limitation in the funeral oratory given by Pericles, and produced our common place of Hellenism (323–30).

10. Ibid., 348.

7. FROM ORGANISM TO PICNIC: WHICH CONSENSUS FOR WHICH CITY?

1. André Franquin, Greg (Michel Régnier), and Jidéhem (Jean de Mesmaeker), *Le prisonnier du bouddha* [1960] (Marcinelle: Les Éditions Dupuis, 1986), 18.

2. Gorgias, *Encomium of Helen*, 82 B11 DK, §11, vol. II, 291.

3. Ibid., §2, vol. II, 288.

4. See part I, chap. 3, "Seeing Helen in Every Woman: Woman and Word."

5. Plutarch, quoted in Gorgias, *Encomium of Helen*, 82 B8a DK, vol. II, 287.

6. Philostratus, quoted in ibid., 82, A1, DK, §4–5, vol. II, 272.

7. From now on, it is necessary to quote from the edition by Fernanda Decleva-Caizzi and Guido Bastianini, *Corpus dei papiri filosofici greci e latini*, I, 1, 176–236 (Florence: Leo S. Olschki, 1989). The fragment that I am interpreting here, fragment B (*Poxy* 1364 and 3647), corresponds to fragment A of *Die Fragmente der Vorsokratiker*, ed. Hermann Diels and Walter Kranz (Berlin: Weidmann, 1952; 1st ed., 1903), 87B44 DK, vol. II, 346–52.

8. Ibid., col. I, 9–10.

9. Ibid., col. II, 5, 9f., 23.

10. Ibid., col. I, 23–26.

11. Ibid., col. I, 29f., 33f., and col. II, 6.

12. Ibid., col. I, 32f.

13. Antiphon, *Peri Homonoias*, 87 B44a DK, vol. II, 356–66.

14. Xenophon, *Memorabilia*, IV, 4 12. I am quoting directly from the Greek text; all translations are my own.

15. Ibid.

16. Hesiod, *Theogony*, 775–805: when *eris* and *neikos* are about, the gods take the great oath to find out who is lying. The one who swears falsely on the waters of the Styx remains "without breath for" a whole year and then for a period of nine years takes no part either in the council or in the banquets of the gods.

   In the following part of the Xenophon's *Memorabilia*, Socrates goes on to examine the "unwritten laws," those that are everywhere the same and which, since men do not all assemble together or "speak the same language," can have been established only by the gods (19). Let us note the strict equivalence of these to "nature" in Antiphon: they are in fact characterized as that "lawfulness" from which there is no escape and which includes within itself the punishment for its transgression; thus, when Hippias asks: "What trouble is incurred when one commits incest?" Socrates replies, "one begets badly" (22–25).

17. Xenophon, *Memorabilia* 87 44aDK, pg. 356, line 16.

18. The line is all the more difficult for the textual problem that it poses: *hê homonoia . . . sunagôgên homoiou tou nou* (*homoiou* Halm, *ho monou* cod.) *koinônian te kai henôsin en heautêi suneilêphen.*

19. The French quotation is taken from an expression by Callicles, following the translation of Alfred Croiset, with Louis Bodin, of Plato's *Gorgias*

(Paris: Les Belles Lettres, 1955): "mais ce qui fait l'agrément de la vie, c'est de verser le plus possible" (494b). In W. R. M. Lamb's translation of *Plato: Lysis. Symposium. Gorgias*, Loeb Classical Library (Cambridge, Mass.: Harvard University Press, 1991; 1st ed., 1925), the line reads: "But a pleasant life consists rather in the largest possible inflow." But this and other English versions do not allow the dual application of the phrase that is possible in the French. The verb *verser*, the literal act of pouring, extends to financial payment and so here, by opposition, to the situation of the miser (translator's note).

20. *De Divinatione*, II, 70, 144 = B80 DK.

21. Cf., for example, E. R. Dodds, *The Greeks and the Irrational* (chap. 1), or Pierre Chantraine, *Dictionnaire étymologique de la langue grecque: Histoire des mots* (Paris: Klincksieck, 1968–1970), s.v. *aidomai*. For details of a rhetorical as opposed to an ethical analysis of the myth of Protagoras, from Ælius Aristides to modernity, one can refer to the collected essays in *Philosophie* 28 (Autumn 1990), "Rhétorique et politique: Les métamorphoses de Protagoras."

22. Antiphon's *On Truth*, fr. B, col. I, p. 192f.

23. The English title of this speech is perhaps better known, in the 1973 Loeb translation of C. A. Behr, as "To Plato: In Defence of Oratory" (translator's note). (Carolus Allison Behr, *P. Ælius Aristides. Opera quæ exstant omnia*, vol. 1, fasc. 2, 269–289, Leiden, Brill, 1978).

24. Auguste Diès, introduction to *Platon, Oeuvres complètes*, vol. VI, *La République*, books I–III, ed. and trans. Emile Chambry (Paris: Les Belles Lettres, 1932), xii.

25. For all this, cf., in particular, ibid., 440e–41a.

26. Here is the Greek phrase in its entirety: *tautên tên homonoian dophrôsunên einai, kheironos te kai ameinonos kata phusin xumphônian hopoteron dei arkhein kai en polei kai en heni hekastôi* (432a). The term *homonoia* is sometimes replaced by *homodoxia*, the agreement of opinion between the rulers and the ruled for the better part to rule (ibid., 433c, 442d).

27. Cf., for example, ibid., 433b, 433d, 441e: *to ta hautou prattein . . . to hautou hekastos heis ôn epratten kai ouk epolupragmonei.*

28. H. G. Liddell and R. Scott, *A Greek-English Lexicon*, rev. H. S. Jones (Oxford: Clarendon, 1940).

29. Cf., in relation to the philosophers, Plato's *Republic*, 519e.

30. *Politics*, II, 1264b19–22.

31. Ibid., VII, 13, 1332a36–8.

32. Here is the Greek: *hôsper kan ei tis tên sumphônian poiêseien homophônian ê ton rhuthmon basin mian* (ibid., II, 1263b34–5).

33. Ibid., 1274b38–41.

34. Ibid., 1276b32f.

35. Ibid., III, 4, 1277a5–12.

36. This is to say that it does not strike me as necessary to attach two different meanings to *plêthos*—good "plurality" and perhaps "majority," when it is a question of the city, and, conversely, bad "mass," when it is a question of democratic deviation; indeed, quite the contrary is true. The use of *plêthos* up to chap. 11 constantly gives the lie to this opposition, as *plêthos*, in contrast to *oligoi*, is the equivalent of *hoi polloi* (ibid., 1281a40, 42, b8, 11), and Aristotle questions whether it is "every *plêthos*" or just "a determinate *plêthos*" that is likely to behave as a good mixture (ibid., 1281b15–21).

37. Ibid., 1281a42–b10. The lines immediately following pose a double problem. "For all that (*alla*), it is in this way that those men who are politically virtuous differ from each one of those who make up the plurality, just as it is said that those who are not beautiful differ from those who are beautiful, and the objects painted by an artist from real objects: they differ through the gathering up of distinct and separate traits into a unity, for in any case, taken separately, it is the eye of such and such a person, found in the painted object, and some other part of someone else, that has the greatest beauty [*epei kekhôrismenôn ge kallion ekhein tou gegrammenou toudi men ton ophthalmon, heterou de tinos heteron morion*]" (1281b13–15). The first problem concerns the way in which the value of the crowd connects with that of politically virtuous individuals. The argument needs to be situated in its context: is it better to give power to the mass or to a small number of excellent men—democracy or aristocracy (1281a39–41)? The *alla* brings the argument of the aristocrats into alignment with that of the democrats: the crowd holds on to what is best in those who make it up, just as the virtuous in politics bring together the disparate qualities to be found in them individually. The second problem is that of the relation between the painted object and the plurality of its models. Tricot translates as follows: "*les éléments disséminés çà et là ont été réunis sur une seule tête, puisque, considérés du moins à part, l'oeil d'une personne en chair et en os, ou quelque autre organe d'une autre personne, sont plus beaux que l'oeil ou l'organe dessiné* [the elements scattered here and there have been reunited in a single head, for, considered apart at least, the eye of a person who is of flesh and bone, or some other organ of some other person, is more beautiful than the eye or organ painted]." The part that serves as the model is in this instance superior to the resulting part, which is to say that something gets lost in the process of gathering up and therefore that the qualities of the crowd or of the virtuous person are inferior to the qualities, taken one by one, in individuals. But it is the opposite that needs to be brought out: on each occasion, the gathering up gathers only what is best, in the crowd, in the virtuous person, or in the painting. For Plato, the part does not have to be

optimal; it is even the case that in itself it must not be, in order for the whole to be so. For Aristotle, the whole retains only the optimum: moreover, as his notes *ad loc.* attest, Tricot lapses here into Platonism. The area of contention is sharply defined: it concerns the function of *tou gegrammenou* (14). If this is the complement of the comparative, *kallion*, then the eye of the model is indeed "more beautiful than the eye painted." If it is a subjective genitive, then the eye of so and so has been chosen for its beauty and reproduced in the painting. Let us acknowledge that the construction proposed by Tricot is the one that most immediately comes to mind.

38. The image is again taken up in III, 16, 1287b25–31, in relation to the benefit of having several magistrates: "For each magistrate judges well when he has been well trained by the law, and it is doubtless absurd that someone should see with two eyes, judge with two ears, or act with two hands and feet better than many would with many. In actual fact, monarchs make many eyes for themselves, many ears, hands, and feet: they bring into positions of power those who are friendly toward their power and toward their person." It would be interesting to ask how this image of a body with a plethora of organs becomes that of tyranny.

39. I will leave aside the argument that follows this in Aristotle, according to which the user (of a house, of a helm) and even the consumer (of a meal) is a better judge of the quality of the product than the producer and refer the reader to an article by Pierre Aubenque, "Aristotle and Democracy," in *Individu et société: L'influence d'Aristote dans le monde méditerranéen, Proceedings of the Conference in Istanbul, January 5–9, 1986,* ed. Thierry Zarcone (Istanbul: Editions Isis, 1988), in particular 36. It only remains to be noted that the argument makes of the city a fabricated object and an object of use—which might perhaps save a certain number of misinterpretations of the famous *phusei* (Aristotle, *Politics,* I, 1, 1253a2).

40. We find *homonoêtikon* only in the critique of the *Republic*: if everyone says together, "It's mine," this does not produce concord (II, 3, 1261b32). Then—and we will come back to this—*homonoousa,* in V, 6, 1306a9, is used to describe an oligarchy that is hard to bring down from within.

41. *Nicomachean Ethics,* IX, 6, 1167b5.

42. *Houtoi gar kai heautois homonoousi kai allêlois* (1167b5–6); cf. IX, 4, where, as in the testimony of Iamblichus, the *homonoia/stasis* opposition serves to describe the individual and, in this instance, to differentiate between the *epieikeis* and the *phauloi* (*homognômonei,* 1166a13; *stasiazei,* 1166b19).

43. *Politics,* IV, 7, 1293b5f.

44. *Nicomachean Ethics,,* VIII, 13, 1161b8–10.

45. Ibid., IX, 7, 1167b9f.

46. Plutarch, *Concerning Chattering* 511b (context in Heraclitus, B 125 DK), cited, with flawless commentary, by Nicole Loraux, whose terms I take up here, in "Le lien de la division," *Le Cahier du Collège International de Philosophie* 4 (Dec. 1987): 101–24, in particular 111–12. But it is with the whole article that I am in grateful *homonoia*.

47. Aristotle, *Politics*, I, 2, 1253a7–10.

48. Ibid., VII, 15, 1334b15.

49. *Nicomachean Ethics*, I, 1, 1094a26–28.

50. Ibid., 1094b11.

51. Here I am exploiting, in the light of the two models of consensus, certain arguments better backed up in Part III, Chapter 9.

52. Here, of course, there could be more than one translation. The corresponding translation of Hugh Lloyd-Jones reads: "Many things are formidable, and none more formidable than man . . . Skilful beyond hope is the contrivance of his art, and he advances sometimes to evil, at other times to good. When he applies the laws of the earth and the justice the gods have sworn to uphold he is high in the city; outcast from the city is he with whom the ignoble consorts for the sake of gain" (Sophocles, *Antigone*, vol. 2, ed. and trans. Hugh Lloyd-Jones (Cambridge and London: Loeb Classical Library, 1994), 35.

53. Martin Heidegger, *An Introduction to Metaphysics*, trans. Ralph Manheim (New Haven, Conn.: Yale University Press, 2000), 152. The text dates from 1935.

54. *Republic*, IV, 421a.

55. *Parmenides, Gesamtausgabe*, Band vol. 54, trans. André Schuwer and Richard Rojcewicz (Frankfurt am Main: Vittorio Klostermann), 1982), 133–42. The lectures date back to 1942 and 1943.

56. "Only a God Can Save Us," *Der Spiegel*'s interview with Martin Heidegger, trans. Maria P. Alter and John D. Caputo, in *The Heidegger Controversy: A Critical Reader*, ed. Richard Wollin (Cambridge, Mass.: MIT Press, 1993), 104; translation first published in *Philosophy Today* 20 (April 1976): 267–85. This English title is a quotation from the text of the interview (following the German: "Nur ein Gott kann uns noch retten," *Der Spiegel*, May 31, 1976). See, in French, "Réponses et questions sur l'histoire et la politique," trans. Jean Launay (Paris: Mercure de France, 1988), 42.

57. "Martin Heidegger at Eighty," in *Heidegger and Modern Philosophy: Critical Essays*, ed. Michael Murray (New Haven, Conn.: Yale University Press, 1978), 303; Hannah Arendt, *Vies politiques*, trans. Barbara Cassin and Patrick Lévy (Paris: Gallimard, 1974), 320.

58. Arendt, "What Is Freedom?" in Hannah Arendt, *Between Past and Future: Eight Exercises in Political Thought* (London: Penguin, 1993), 157.

59. Arendt, in *The Human Condition*, for example (Chicago: University of Chicago Press, 1998; 1st ed., 1958), 198), takes up an expression from the *Nicomachean Ethics* (IV, 12, 1126b11f.), which in Aristotle serves to define neither the city nor sociability but "affability" and indeed even "servility," the flaw that is the opposite of "ill humor" or "pettifoggery" but just as far removed from the medial virtue, a certain sort of friendship. Arendt erases the pejorative connotation in favor of a political interpretation of the term *suzên*, "live together," which appears throughout the *Politics*. I interpret this infidelity or inaccuracy as a consequence of the independence of the political in relation to the ethical.

60. Taminiaux, "Heidegger et Arendt, lecteurs d'Aristote," *Les Cahiers de Philosophie* 4 (Autumn 1987): Hannah Arendt. Confrontations 41–52.

61. Arendt, "Philosophy and Politics," *Social Research* 57, no. 1 (Spring 1990), "Philosophy and Politics II" (quotations taken from 84–85); compare with "The Concept of History" in her *Between Past and Future*, 51.

62. Arendt, *Human Condition*, 3.

63. Ibid., 26–27. In this particular text, Arendt's own English version of the Aristotelian definition of man is "a living being capable of speech" (translator's note).

64. Arendt, "Philosophy and Politics," 90.

65. Arendt, "Truth and Politics," in her *Between Past and Future*, 259.

8. ARISTOTLE WITH AND AGAINST KANT ON THE IDEA OF HUMAN NATURE

1. Aristotle, *Politics*, ed. R. F. Stalley and trans. Ernest Baker (Oxford: Oxford University Press, 1995), VII, 15, 1334b 15. I prefer of course the Latin translation of *logos: ratio et oratio*.

2. Kant, *Groundwork to the Metaphysic of Morals*, trans. Mary Gregor (Cambridge: Cambridge University Press, 1998), II, 37, 14:429.

3. This is very much the case with the following collections: M. Riedel, *Rehabilitierung der praktischen Philosophie*, 2 vols. (Freiburg: Rombach, 1972–74), and W. Kuhlmann, *Moralität und Sittlichkeit: Das Problem Hegels und die Diskursethik* (Frankfurt: Suhrkamp, 1986).

4. Here are some of the most useful of these appraisals: Enrico Berti, *Aristotele nel Novocento* (Rome-Ban: Laterza, 1992); "Les stratégies contempo-raines d'interprétation d'Aristote," *Rue Descartes* 1–2 (1991): 33–55; "Strategie di interpretazione dei filosofi antichi: Platone e Aristotele," *Elenchos* X, fasc. 2 (1989): 289–315; Carlo Natali, "Recenti interpretazioni dalla etiche aristoteli-che," *Elenchos* VIII, fasc. 1 (1987): 129–39; Franco Volpi, "Réhabilitation de la

philosophie pratique et néo-aristotélisme," in *Aristote politique: Etudes sur la politique d'Aristote*, ed. Pierre Aubenque, 461–84 (Paris: Presses Universitaires de France, 1993).

5. Pierre Aubenque, *La prudence chez Aristote*, 3rd rev. ed. (Paris: Presses Universitaires de France, 1986), 125. The subject of Kantian readings of Aristotle and the fate of prudence in the face of practical reason are treated in the third appendix, "La prudence chez Kant" (186–212), from which I have drawn extensively in the course of the present discussion.

6. I am thinking of the trend-setting article by Jan Lukasiewicz, "O zasadzie sprzecznosci u Arystotelesa" (*Über den Sat: Des Widerspruchs bei Aristoteles*), *Bulletin international de l'Académie des sciences de Cracovie* (Classe d'histoire et de philosophie, 1910): 15–38. This article was translated into French by B. Cassin and M. Narcy and published in *Rue Descartes* 1–2 (1991): 9–32. Also see Christopher Kirwan's translation with notes of Aristotle's *Metaphysics, Books Gamma, Delta, and Epsilon*, 2nd ed. (Oxford: Clarendon, 1993).

7. As Berti and Volpi (see note 4) have clearly demonstrated, the return to Aristotle's practical philosophy was initiated by both Hannah Arendt, *The Human Condition* (Chicago: University of Chicago Press, 1958, translated into German in 1960), and Hans-Georg Gadamer, *Wahrheit und Methode: Grunzüge einer philosophischen Hermeneutik* (Tübingen: Mohr, 1960).

8. Alasdair MacIntyre, *After Virtue: A Study in Moral Theory*, 2nd ed. (London: Duckworth, 1985); Martha Nussbaum, *The Fragility of Goodness: Luck and Ethics in Greek Tragedy and Philosophy* (Cambridge: Cambridge University Press, 1986). I have chosen to discuss these two, more recent works in order to illustrate my argument here. Similar issues are addressed in Giovanni Giorgini, "Esiste un neoaristotelismo anglosassone?" in *Etica, Politica, Retorica: Studi su Aristotele e la sua presenza nell'eta moderna*, ed. Enrico Berti and L. M. Napolitano Valditara, 271–97 (Rome: L. U. Japadre Editore, 1989), which appraises the work of Bernard Crick, Stuart Hampshire, and Alasdair MacIntyre.

9. I am borrowing Ferry's terminology here and summarizing his argument in *Homo Æstheticus: The Invention of Taste in the Democratic Age*, trans. Robert de Loaiza (Chicago: University of Chicago Press, 1993), chap. 7, "The Problem of Ethics in an Age of Aesthetics," 246–262.

10. Ibid., 252.

11. Ibid., 253.

12. Ibid., 258.

13. Ibid., 260.

14. Aubenque, *La prudence chez Aristote*, 334.

15. Ferry, *Homo Aestheticus*, 251.

16. See *Metaphysics*, A, 1075 a 17–23. This passage is quoted by Ferry (*Homo Æstheticus*, 249), who discusses Brunschwig's article, "L'esclavage chez Aristote," *Cahiers philosophiques* 1 (September 1979): 20–31. According to the commentators, the stars correspond to free men, the sublunary beings to slaves and domesticated animals; the actions of the free men are "orderly" (*tetaktai*), and they are not allowed—unlike the others—to act randomly. This passage, which occurs within a very specific context (is the good immanent in the structure of the whole, or transcendent, or both at once, as in an army?), is perhaps rather more difficult to interpret than it at first appears. For this passage is not, in fact, concerned with action (*prattein*) but rather with manufacture, with the work (*poiein*); nor are these domestic animals (*hêmera*) but rather wild, untamed beasts (*thêria*; cf. Aristotle, *Politics*, I, 3, 1254 a 10–26).

17. Brunschwig, "L'esclavage chez Aristote," 30.

18. Aristotle, *Politics*, I, 5, 1254 b–55 a 1.

19. Brunschwig, "L'esclavage chez Aristote," 26, cited in Ferry, *Homo Aestheticus*, 250.

20. Aristotle, *Politics*, I, 2, 1252 a 32.

21. Nussbaum, "Shame, Separateness, and Political Unity: Aristotle's Criticism of Plato," in *Essays on Aristotle's Ethics*, ed. A. O. Rorty, 395–435 and especially 420 (Berkeley: University of California Press, 1980); W. W. Fortenbaugh, "Aristotle on Slaves and Women," in *Articles on Aristotle*, vol. 2, *Ethics and Politics*, ed. Jonathan Barnes, Malcolm Schofield, and Richard Sorabji, 135–39 (London: Duckworth, 1977).

22. Ferry, *Homo Aestheticus*, 251.

23. Ibid.

24. Aristotle, *Politics*, I, 2, 1253 a 9 s; VII, 13, 1332 b 4 s.

25. Ferry, *Homo Aestheticus*, 251.

26. Aristotle, *Politics*, 2, 1252 b 12.

27. Ibid., 4, 1253 b 32.

28. Ibid., 2, 1252, a 32–34.

29. Fortenbaugh's bibliography of work on this question is recommended. See Fortenbaugh, "Aristotle on Slaves and Women," 136, n3.

30. Aristotle, *Politics*, 6, 1255 b 11 s.

31. Ibid., 13, 1259 b 21–8; cf. 5, 1254 b 16. I have modified Baker's translation slightly, replacing "goodness" with "excellence" and restoring *logos* for the sake of continuity with my article and the work of the other French philosophers whom I cite.

32. Ibid., 1260 a 7.

33. Ibid., 1260 a 10–12.

34. The slave does not possess the finished form of the logical part of the soul—the faculty of deliberation (*to bouleutikon*)—which characterizes the male, the father, but he does possess *logos* in the minimal sense in which the appetitive or desiring part possesses it, which is deprived of *logos* but nonetheless, in a sense, shares in it. Cf. *The Nicomachean Ethics*, trans. David Ross (Oxford: Oxford University Press, 1998), 1, 13, 1102 b 13 s. See also Fortenbaugh, "Aristotle on Slaves and Women," which is particularly strong on this question of the bipartite division of the soul in Aristotle, how it differs from Plato's tripartite division, and the relationship between the bipartite soul and the soul of the slave, the child, and the woman.

35. Aristotle, *Politics*, 1260 b 5–7.

36. Ibid., 13, 1260 a 31–3.

37. On the admonition of the child by the father and more generally of the citizen by the lawmaker, cf. the entirety of the closing section of *Nicomachean Ethics*, IX (in particular, 1180 a s.) and chap. 13 of book VII of Aristotle's *Politics*. Some of the terms used are the same as those applied to the slave at the end of book I of the *Politics*.

38. *Nicomachean Ethics*, 12, 1161 b 5–8. The difficulty involved in establishing precisely what this part of the slave consists in has occasioned a rather hasty reading of this same passage from Martha Nussbaum: "This is probably a reference to the conventional slave, for he is assumed to have capacities that Aristotle denies to the natural slave" ("Shame, Separateness, and Political Unity," 434, n54). This is clearly not the case, as the following passage from the *Politics* will, if need be, demonstrate: "There is thus a community of interest, and a relation of friendship, between master and slave, when both of them naturally merit the position in which they stand. But the reverse is true, when matters are otherwise and slavery rests merely on legal sanction and superior power" (Aristotle, *Politics*, 1, 6, 1255 b 12–15).

39. Ferry, *Homo Aestheticus*, 251.

40. It is worth noting that Aristotle inserts here a line from Sophocles: "'Women should be seen and not heard'—the old, old story!" (Ajax, 1.293), trans. E. F. Watling, in *Electra and Other Plays* (London: Penguin, 1953), 28.

41. Nussbaum, "Shame, Separateness, and Political Unity," 283–87. For a discussion of T. H. Irwin, see "Reason and Responsibility in Aristotle," in Rorty, *Essays on Aristotle's Ethics*, 117–55. The relevant passages on the comparative "morality" of animals and children are, in *The Nicomachean Ethics*, essentially 1, 10, 1099 b 32–1100 a 4—the child, who takes no part in politics, is no "happier" than an ox; III, 3, 1111 a 25 s. and 4, 1111 b 8–10—the child

resembles an animal in that he acts voluntarily (*hekousiôs*) but not through a deliberate choice (*proairesis*); VI, 13, 1144 b 8–17—the child resembles an animal in that he possess "natural virtue" (*phusikê*) but not "virtue in the proper sense" (*kuriôs*), which presupposes *nous* and is to the natural disposition what prudence is to skill. Yet all these passages also show that if the child, like the slave, resembles an animal, unlike an animal (but like the slave?), he can come to acquire *nous*.

42. See, in particular, *The Life of the Mind* (New York: Harcourt, 1971), part II, chap. 2, section 7.

43. Ibid., 57.

44. Ibid., 61.

45. Ibid., 62.

46. Aubenque, *La prudence chez Aristote*, 138.

47. *Nicomachean Ethics*, VI, 2, 1139 a 22 s.

48. Ibid., III, 4, 1112 a 15.

49. Aubenque, *La prudence chez Aristote*, 119–24.

50. Aristote, *Ethique à Nicomaque*, 2nd ed., trans. Jules Tricot (Paris: Vrin, 1967), 309n2.

51. *Nicomachean Ethics*, II, 3, 1105 a 28–33.

52. Ibid., 1105 b 7–9.

53. Ibid., VI, 13, 1144 a 13–20.

54. Kant, "First Introduction to the *Critique of the Power of Judgment*," in *Critique of the Power of Judgment* (*The Cambridge Edition of the Works of Immanuel Kant*), trans. Paul Guyer and Eric Matthews and ed. Paul Guyer (Cambridge: Cambridge University Press, 2000), 1–52.

55. Kant, *Education*, trans. Annette Churchton (Ann Arbor: University of Michigan Press, 1960), 108.

56. Kant, *Religion Within the Boundaries of Mere Reason*, trans. Allen Wood and George di Giovanni (Cambridge: Cambridge University Press, 1998), 47. The italics are Kant's.

57. Ibid., 47/6:21. The italics are mine.

58. Ibid.

59. Ibid.

60. Cf. Kant, *Religion*, 50–52/6:26–29.

61. Alexis Philonenko, ed., *L'oeuvre de Kant* (Paris: Vrin, 1969–1972), II, 1131.

62. Kant, *Religion*, 55–56, 6:32. The first and second italics are Kant's; the third and fourth italics are mine.

63. *Critique of Practical Reason*, part II. See Kant's *Critique of Practical Reason and Other Works on the Theory of Ethics*, trans. T. K. Abbott (London:

Longmans, 1883), 249–62. See also *Groundwork*, II; *Religion*, III; "On the Common Saying: That May Be Correct in Theory, but It Is of No Use in Practice," in *Practical Philosophy (The Cambridge Edition of the Works of Immanuel Kant)*, trans. and ed. Mary J. Gregor (Cambridge: Cambridge University Press, 1996), 273–310. On the relationship between education and nature, cf. Paul Moreau, *L'éducation morale chez Kant* (Paris: Editions du Cerf, 1988).

 64. Kant, *Education*, 7.

 65. Ibid., 2–3. (Translater's note: I have modified Churchton's translation slightly, restoring Kant's "humankind" for her "mankind.")

 66. Kant, *Groundwork*, 37.

 67. Aristotle, *Politics*, VII, 15, 1334 b 15.

 68. Compare Pierre Aubenque's conclusion concerning the ban on a moral doctrine of prudence—"What is in question here is not the coherence of the Kantian system, but its truth" (Aubenque, *La prudence chez Aristote*, 211)— with Luc Ferry's remark: "The extraordinary power of Kantian ethics stems from the fact that none of us is quite capable of thinking in different terms. I have never yet met, among those who call themselves anti-Kantians . . . , a modern who could completely do without the concept of merit (except in words, and even there)" (Ferry, *Homo Aestheticus*, 255).

 69. Nussbaum, *Fragility of Goodness*, 286.

 70. Ibid., 287.

 71. Nussbaum, "Shame, Separateness, and Political Unity," 397.

 72. Ibid., 404.

 73. Aristotle, *Politics*, 1261 b 16s, quoted in ibid., 417.

 74. Nussbaum, "Shame, Separateness, and Political Unity," 422.

 75. Ibid., 423.

 76. Nussbaum, *Fragility of Goodness*, 20.

 77. Nussbaum, "Shame, Separateness, and Political Unity," 361.

 78. On this point, it seems to me that Nussbaum is in agreement with Irwin, who writes that, against the background of an agreement between Aristotle and Kant on "the conditions of human responsibility," Aristotle offers an alternative response to Kant's question, one that avoids the metaphysics of Kantian freedom ("Reason and Responsibility in Aristotle," 143).

 79. Alasdair MacIntyre, *After Virtue: A Study in Moral Theory*, 2nd ed. (London: Duckworth, 1985). I shall only be discussing this work here and not the broader sweep of MacIntyre's intellectual trajectory, of which this book is both typical and atypical in more ways than one.

 80. Ibid., 110–11.

 81. Ibid., 114.

 82. Ibid., 259.

83. Ibid., 117–18.

84. This is particularly clear at the beginning of the last chapter, "After Virtue: Nietzsche *or* Aristotle, Trotsky *and* St. Benedict."

85. MacIntyre, *After Virtue*, 117.

86. See, in particular, chap. 16: "From the Virtues to Virtue and after Virtue." It is here that the difficulty inherent in the attempt to integrate Plato into a Greek tradition conceived along these lines becomes apparent.

87. MacIntyre, *After Virtue*, 149.

88. Ibid., 229.

89. Ibid., 259.

90. Kant, "Conjectures on the Beginning of Human History," in *Kant: Political Writings*, ed. H. S. Reiss (Cambridge: Cambridge University Press, 1990), 227.

91. *Nicomachean Ethics*, I, 1, 1094 a 1 s.

92. Ferry, *Homo Aestheticus*, 256–57.

9. GREEKS AND ROMANS: PARADIGMS OF THE PAST IN ARENDT AND HEIDEGGER

1. Hannah Arendt, "'What Remains? The Language Remains': A Conversation with Günter Gaus," in *The Portable Hannah Arendt*, ed. Peter Baehr (New York: Harcourt, Penguin, 2000), 3. It should be noted that in the original the language is the *Muttersprache*, namely, the mother tongue.

2. Ibid., 4. English translation modified.

3. Michael Murray, ed., *Heidegger and Modern Philosophy: Critical Essays* (New Haven, Conn.: Yale University Press, 1978), 303.

4. Hannah Arendt, *The Life of the Mind* (New York: Harcourt, 1971), vol. 1, 145.

5. Ibid., 156.

6. Ibid., 162.

7. Ibid., 157.

8. Ibid., vol. 2, 186.

9. Ibid., vol. 1, 179.

10. Ibid., vol. 2, 187. I pass over Arendt's difficult analysis of "Der Spruch des Anaximander," where she attempts to do justice to another reversal (which Heidegger, for his part, does not mark as such): here there would no longer be room for a History of Being but only for a sequence of ages of errancy broken by privileged moments of transition or crisis.

11. Hannah Arendt, "Preface: The Gap Between Past and Future," in *Between Past and Future* (New York: Viking, 1961), 13.

12. Ibid., 14.

13. Arendt, *Life of the Mind*, vol. 1, 211.

14. Ibid., 212.

15. Murray, *Heidegger and Modern Philosophy*, 297.

16. Arendt, *Life of the Mind*, vol. 1, 212.

17. Murray, *Heidegger and Modern Philosophy*, 295.

18. Arendt, "What Is Authority?" in Arendt, *Between Past and Future*, 94.

19. Arendt, "The Crisis in Culture," in Arendt, *Between Past and Future*, 204; cf. "Tradition and the Modern Age," ibid., 28.

20. "Preface: The Gap Between Past and Future," ibid., 15.

21. *Men in Dark Times* (New York: Harcourt, 1970), 204.

22. Hannah Arendt, *The Human Condition* (Chicago: University of Chicago Press, 1998; 1st ed. 1958), 3.

23. Arendt, *Life of the Mind*, vol. 1, 212.

24. *Partisan Review* 20 (1953): 388.

25. In Martin Heidegger, *Poetry, Language, Thought*, trans. A. Hofstadter (New York: Harper, 1971), 23.

26. Heidegger, *Parmenides, Gesamtausgabe*, vol. 54, trans. André Schuwer and Richard Rojcewicz (Frankfurt: Klostermann, 1982). See Eliane Escoubas, "La question romaine, la question imperiale: Autour du 'Tournant,'" in *Heidegger: Questions ouvertes*, ed. Eliane Escoubas (Paris: Osiris, 1988), 173–188.

27. Ibid., 67.

28. Ibid.

29. Arendt, *Life of the Mind*, vol. 1, 140; cf. 154n72.

30. Arendt, *Human Condition*, 23.

31. Ibid., 27.

32. Ibid.

33. Ibid., 100.

34. Arendt, *Life of the Mind*, vol. 1, 151.

35. Arendt, "Crisis in Culture," 212.

36. It was in order to defend the very life of the philosophers after the trial of Socrates that Plato invented the philosopher-king and substituted the Idea of the Good for that of the Beautiful. On this, see the odd analysis advanced in Arendt, "What Is Authority?" 107–15; see also *Life of the Mind*, vol. 1, 152.

37. Arendt, "What Is Authority?" 120.

38. Arendt, *Human Condition*, 195n21.

39. Ibid., 198.

40. Arendt, "What Is Authority?" 124.

41. See ibid., II, 212–14.

42. Arendt, "What Is Authority?,"136.

43. Arendt, "Tradition and the Modern Age," 28.

44. *Revue de philosophie ancienne* 1 (1986): 5–32; cf. Marlène Zarader, *Heidegger et les paroles de l'origine* (Paris: Vrin, 1986).

45. For the term *prephilosophic*, see *Life of the Mind*, vol. 1, 129ff. ("The Pre-Philosophic Assumptions of Greek Philosophy"), *Between Past and Future*, 165 ("What Is Freedom?"), and *Human Condition*, 207.

46. See Arendt, *Life of the Mind*, vol. 2, 187–94.

47. Arendt, "What Is Freedom?" 157.

48. "Du privé et du public," *Cahiers du Grif* 33 (1986): 63; cf. Arendt, *Life of the Mind*, vol. 1, 174.

49. Arendt, *Life of the Mind*, vol. 1, 166–79.

50. Hannah Arendt, "Philosophy and Politics," *Social Research* 57, no. 1 (Spring 1990): 85–94.

51. Arendt, *Life of the Mind*, vol. 1, 167.

52. Ibid., 168.

53. Arendt, "Philosophy and Politics": 90; cf. Arendt, *Life of the Mind*, vol. 1, 188.

54. Arendt, *Life of the Mind*, vol. 1, 187.

55. Note especially Philostratus's comments on Gorgias (82A1 DK, II, 27lf.) and the significance of Antiphon's title, *Peri homonoias* (esp. 87B44a DK, II, 356).

56. "Heidegger et Arendt, lecteurs d'Aristote," *Cahiers de Philosophie* 4 (1987): 41–52.

57. *Nicomachean Ethics*, IV 12, 1126b11f.; cf. Arendt, *Human Condition*, 197f.

58. See 87B44 DK—or, better, A. Battegazzore and M. Untersteiner, eds., *Sofisti: Testimonianze e frammenti*, vol. 4 (Florence: La Nuova Italia, 1962), 72–105.

59. Arendt, "Philosophy and Politics," 90.

60. Ibid., 89.

61. Arendt, "The Concept of History," in *Between Past and Future*, 51.

62. Gorgias, *Encomium of Helen*, 82B26 DK, II, 306; cf. Arendt, *Life of the Mind*, vol. 1, 25.

63. Arendt, *Human Condition*, 26.

64. Arendt, *Life of the Mind*, vol. 1, 172.

65. Arendt, "Philosophy and Politics," 90.

66. Aristotle, *Politics*, III, 11, 1281b2–3. See Part III, chapter 7.

67. In Plato's phrase: *Sophist*, 231b; cf. Arendt, *Life of the Mind*, vol. 1, 173.

68. Arendt, *Life of the Mind*, vol. 1, 174.

69. Ibid., 193.

70. Ibid., 15.

71. Ibid.

72. Arendt, *Human Condition*, 158.

73. 716d, quoted in ibid., 159.

74. See ibid., 166.

75. See "Zusatz 8" to "Die Zeit des Weltbildes," in *Holzwege* (Frankfurt: Klostermann, 1950), and "The Statement of Protagoras," in *Nietzsche*, vols. 3 and 4 (New York: HarperOne, 1991), 91–95.

76. The proposition, preserved both by Sextus and by Plato, runs like this: *pantôn khrêmatôn metron anthrôpos, tôn men ontôn hôs estin, tôn de ouk estin hôs ouk estin* (80Bl DK, II, 263).

77. See Part V, "Enough of the Truth For. . . ."

78. Arendt, "Crisis in Culture," 222.

79. Plato, *Protagoras*, in *The Collected Dialogues of Plato*, ed. Edith Hamilton and Huntington Cairns (Princeton, N.J.: Princeton University Press, 2005), 323bc.

80. Arendt, "Truth and Politics," in *Between Past and Future*, 250.

81. Sophocles, *Antigone*, 370. I am quoting directly from the Greek text.

82. Martin Heidegger, *An Introduction to Metaphysics*, trans. Ralph Manheim (New Haven, Conn.: Yale University Press, 2000), 162–63 (translation modified).

83. Heidegger, *Poetry, Language, Thought*, 42.

84. *Parmenides*, trans. André Schuwer and Richard Rojcewicz (Bloomington: Indiana University Press, 1992), 132.

85. Ibid., 134.

86. Ibid., 142.

87. Thucydides, *History*, II, 40; cf. Arendt, *Human Condition*, 197–99 and 204–6; Arendt, *Life of the Mind*, vol. 1, 133 and 178; Arendt, *Between Past and Future*, 7lf., and esp. 213–26. Compare Benjamin Jowett's translation: "We are lovers of the beautiful, yet simple in our tastes, and we cultivate the mind without loss of manliness" in

88. Arendt, "Crisis in Culture," 214.

89. Ibid.

90. Aristotle, *Parts of Animals*, 683a24. I am quoting directly from the Greek text; all translations are my own (emphasis addedd).

91. Aristotle, *Metaphysics*, I, 3, 984a4.

92. Aristotle, *Poetics*, 4, 1448b26.

93. Ibid., 22, 1458b22.

94. Arendt, "Crisis in Culture," 224.

95. In *The Human Condition*, Arendt translates as follows: "everywhere everlasting remembrance of [their] good and [their] evil deeds" (206).
96. *Human Condition*, 216–17.
97. Ibid., 218.
98. *Human Condition*, 174.
99. Ibid., 205.
100. Ibid., 188.

10. HOW TO REALLY DO THINGS WITH WORDS: PERFORMANCE BEFORE THE PERFORMATIVE

1. *Philosophy the Day After Tomorrow* (Cambridge, Mass.: Belknap Press/ Harvard University Press, 2005), 156.
2. *How to Do Things with Words* (Cambridge, Mass.: Harvard University Press, 1975), 114.
3. 82 DK 11 §8, vol. II, 290.
4. Pierre Chantraine, *Dictionnaire étymologique de la langue grecque: Histoire des mots* (Paris: Klincksieck, 1968–1970). I rely on Chantraine for everything that follows.
5. H. G. Liddell and R. Scott, *A Greek-English Lexicon*, rev. H. S. Jones (Oxford: Clarendon, 1940).
6. On the term *logology*, see Chapter 1, note 10, of this book.
7. J. Lacan, "The best that I can do is make an effort and show you how I write it: dit-mension," in "Conferences and Conversations at North American Universities," *Scilicet* 617 (1976): 42.
8. About this double reduction, see part III, chap. 7, "From Organism to Picnic: Which Consensus for Which City?"
9. See Edward Schiappa, "Did Plato Coin *Rhêtorikê*?" *American Journal of Philology* 111 (1990): 457–70.
10. *Rhetoric* I, 2, 1355b 10s: "*ou to peisai ergon autês, alla to idein ta huparkhonta pithana peri hekaston.*"
11. "*Dunamis peri hekaston tou theôrêsai to endekhomenon pithanon,*" ibid., 1355b 25s.
12. The first phrase of the *Rhetoric*, 1354 a1.
13. "*Khrêsimos de estin hê rhêtorikê dia te to phusei einai kreittô talêthê kai ta dikaia tôn enantiôn,*" ibid., 1355a 21–22, a part of the text that is not without problems (*te/ge*). This phrase is reminiscent of the title of a book by Václav Havel, *L'amour et la vérité doivent triompher de la haine et du mensonge* (Paris: Editions de l'Aube, 2007).
14. "*Hê tekhnê ta men epitelei ha hê phusis adunatei apergasasthai, ta de mimeitai.*" One will note the proximity to the vocabulary of Gorgias in the *Encomium* (*dunastês, apotelei, energasasthai*).

15. On this point, see Barbara Cassin and Michel Narcy, *La décision du sens* (Paris: Vrin, 1998); cf. part I, chap. 1 ("Who's Afraid of the Sophists? Against Ethical Correctness") and chap. 2 ("Speak If You Are a Man, or the Transcendental Exclusion").

16. Austin, *How To Do Things with Words*, 101. Further pages will be given in the text.

17. "Our interest in these lectures is essentially to fasten on the second, illocutionary act and contrast it with the others. There is a constant tendency in philosophy to elide this in favour of one or other of the other two. Yet it is distinct from both" (ibid., 103).

18. In French, we translate *statement* by "affirmation." However, an "affirmation" does not usually designate a negative phrase, a negation, although a *statement* can indeed be negative. "The cat is not on the mat" is a *statement*; it *states* a factual state and corresponds rather to an "énoncé," the term that certain translators reserve for *utterance* (see the introduction to Austin's *Ecrits philosophiques*, trans. L. Aubert and A.-L. Hacker [Paris: Seuil, 1994, 17–19]). One will note that (1) there is already an ambiguity of this kind in Greek: *apophansis*, "declaration," has as its double *apophasis*, at least as one of the two entries for *apophasis* in the dictionary, which also signifies "déclaration," although the other entry for *apophasis*, which is indiscernible from it, signifies "négation" (and that is not unproblematic for interpreting Aristotle's *De interpretatione*); and that (2) where *statement* is translated by "énoncé" and *utterance* by "énonciation," in particular in the last lectures, nothing guarantees that, in what Austin says, the *statement/utterance* distinction can be superimposed onto the "énoncé/énonciation" difference any more than the *language/speech* distinction is equivalent to the triplet "langue/langage/parole." Translation can't work miracles.

19. For a topology of Aristotelian sense that assigns a place to fiction, allow me to refer to Cassin and Narcy, *La décision du sens*, 58, and to its development in Cassin, *L'effet sophistique*, 333–36. It is evidently a nodal point of contemporary reflection.

20. Émile Benveniste, "Analytical Philosophy and Language," in *Problems in General Linguistics*, trans. Mary Elizabeth Meek (Miami: University of Miami Press, 1971), 236–37.

21. J. L. Austin, "Performatif-constatif," in *La philosophie analytique* (Paris: Minuit, 1962), 271–81. This article was translated by G. J. Warnock and appears under the title "Performative-Constative," in Charles E. Caton, ed., *Philosophy and Ordinary Language* (Urbana: University of Illinois Press, 1963), 22–63.

22. Benveniste, "Analytical Philosophy and Language," 309n10.

23. See part IV, chap. 11, "The Performative Without Condition: A University *sans appel*."

24. One doesn't find the terminological family in the French translation, in which "to perform an act" is rendered as "*produire un acte*" and the cited phrase as "*Nous appellerons un tel acte un acte* perlocutoire, *ou une* perlocution" in *Quand dire, c'est faire*, trans. G. Lane (Paris: Éd. du Seuil, 1970), 114. This nontranslation is not false in any way; it reveals that *performance* and *perform* are nonmarked.

25. "It was for too long the assumption of philosophers that the business of a 'statement' can only be to 'describe' some state of affairs, or to 'state some fact,' which it must do either truly or falsely" (Austin, *How To Do Things with Words*, 1). After the *sea-change*, referring to this same "descriptive fallacy," Austin notes: "It may be said that for too long philosophers have neglected this study, treating all problems as problems of 'locutionary usage'" (ibid., 100).

26. A first occurrence of the expression *sea-change* must be signaled, in relation to the parasitic use or the etiolation of language and in particular of the performative, in the iteration or citation (by an actor, in a poem, but also "generally"), evidently pointed out by Derrida. For Austin, "a performative utterance will, for example, be *in a peculiar way* hollow or void if said by an actor on the stage, or if introduced in a poem or spoken in soliloquy. This applies in a similar manner to any and every utterance—a sea-change in special circumstances" (ibid., 22). See, in particular, Stephen Mulhall, "Sous l'effet d'une transformation marine: Crise, catastrophe et convention dans la théorie des actes de parole," in *Revue de métaphysique et de morale* 2, no. 42 (2004): 305–23.

27. It is the movement of the "gap between past and future." See Arendt, "Preface: The Gap Between Past and Future," in *Between Past and Future* (New York: Viking, 1961), 3.

28. Let us note that the word "illocution" previously appeared once and once only, in a footnote to the first lecture obviously added to refer to the later elaboration: "to issue a constative utterance . . . is to make a statement. To issue a performative utterance is, for example, to make a bet. See further below on 'illocutions'" (ibid., 6n2). One will note that it is the "locutionary" that provides the eponym for the others ("il . . ." and "per . . ."). On the other hand, it is the notion of the "speech act" thought on the basis of the performative and not the constative that will provide the common genre.

29. The start of lecture 12. It is one of the *morals* to take from Austin's analyses (ibid., 148).

30. Cavell, "Performative and Passionate Utterance." In this article, Cavell devotes himself to reevaluating the perlocutionary. For him it is a question of thinking of it as an utterance that is "passionate," unlike the conventional, legal character of the performative. "A performative utterance is an offer of

participation in the order of law. And perhaps we can say: A passionate utterance is an invitation to improvisation in the disorders of desire" (ibid., 185). Evidently, of course, passion and rhetoric are linked, as the phrase from the *Encomium of Helen*, with which we started, should suffice to attest. So much so that Cavell says, "my idea of passionate utterance turns out to be a concern with performance after all" (ibid., 187). But Cavell is not interested in the performance/performative difference that concerns me here.

31. Austin, *How to Do Things with Words*, 45, cited in ibid., 166.

32. Ibid., 168.

33. Ibid.

34. Cavell also draws attention to this phrase.

35. *Oukh ho logos tou ektos parastatikos estin, alla to ektos tou logou mēnutikon ginetai*, quoted by Sextus Empiricus, *Adversus Mathematicos* VII, 85 (= 82 B 2 DK II, 282). I have commented on this phrase in *L'effet sophistique* (70ff.).

36. Austin himself blames the difficulties in maintaining his distinctions on the expression "use of language" and the notion of "use," which is as empty and polysemic as that of "meaning." Thus, for the locutionary/illocutionary distinction, with regard to the *eo ipso*, which is not at all mysterious, the problem is "the different uses of the expression 'use of language,' or 'use of a sentence,' etc.: 'use' is a hopelessly ambiguous or wide word, just as is the word 'meaning,' which it has become customary to deride" (*How to Do Things with Words*, 100). Similarly, for the illocutionary/perlocutionary distinction, "We have already seen how the expressions 'meaning' and 'use of sentence' can blur the distinction between locutionary and illocutionary acts. We now notice that to speak of the 'use' of language can likewise blur the distinction between the illocutionary and perlocutionary act" (ibid., 103). On use in its relation to sophistic, see part V, "Enough of the Truth For. . . ."

37. A comparative study would be required so as to draw a parallel between Aristotle's decomposition of the acts required for *legein* and Austin's decomposition of the acts required to *issue an utterance* (ibid., 92). Austin's vocabulary is explicitly Greek, but it displaces the meaning of the terms, as much in relation to their Aristotelian use as to their linguistic use ("we may say," "we may call" [ibid.]). For Austin, "to say something" (*legein ti*) is to accomplish three acts, which he calls phonetic, phatic, and rhetic. "Phonetic" designates the production of sounds (an animal can thus carry off this kind of act—a perfectly Aristotelian point); "phatic" designates the production of "sounds of a certain kind," that is to say, words belonging to a certain vocabulary and conforming to a certain grammar and thus production of phrases (there is here a conflation of several stages in Aristotle, with an aim

different from that of the stages in *De intepretatione.* A plausible example for Austin could, under the same heading as "the cat is on the mat," be grammaticalized nonsense (*sinloss*) such as the "present king of France is bald" or "colorless green ideas sleep furiously" but not agrammatical nonsense (*Unsinn*) such as "cat thoroughly the if"). Finally, the rhetic act, which he defines with the use of sense and reference: "the rhetic act is the performance of an act of using these vocables with a *certain more or less definite sense and reference*" (ibid., 95; my italics). It will be noted that the "rhetic" examples are restricted to indirect speech ("this is the so-called 'indirect speech'" [ibid., 96]): "he said that the cat was on the mat," such that, in order to understand the tripartite distinction, the "certain" must be emphasized: sense and reference, naming and referring are "ancillary acts performed in performing the rhetic act" (ibid., 97). Austin concludes that "though these matters are of much interest, they do not so far throw any light at all on our problem of the constative as opposed to the performative utterance" (ibid., 98). So why, then, does he make these considerations? For now, I will lend my tongue to the cat on the mat.

38. One puts one's finger here on the difficulty of translating *performance* by "execution," as the current French translation of Austin does.

39. Austin's commentary, which, following Gilles Lane (footnote p. 115), could be found in the 1958 manuscript, seems appropriate here: "(1) All this isn't clear! distinctions etc. (2) and in all senses relevant ((A) and (B) X (C)) won't all utterances be performative?" This cooking up of examples is even more suspect when one immerses it in the difference of languages. But the importance of the rheme, as indirect discourse, shows the tip of its nose. It is here that the analyses of perlocutionaries given by Cavell in his article should be placed. NB The Lane's french translation is quoted note 24. Lane translated in his footnote Austin's commentary.

40. Jean-François Lyotard, *The Differend* (Minnesota: Minnesota University Press, 1983), 84.

41. "So, here are three ways, securing uptake, taking effect, and inviting a response, in which illocutionary acts are *bound up* with effects; and these are all distinct from the *producing of effects* which is characteristic of the perlocutionary act" (Austin, *How to Do Things with Words*, 118); my italics. It will be taken up again at the start of the tenth lecture.

42. Ibid., 129.

43. Ibid., 117.

44. I leave to one side the discussion, which calls for an intervention by Benveniste and his astonishment that Austin doesn't stick to the only criterion that is certain in his eyes. "An utterance is performative in that it *denominates*

the act performed because Ego pronounces a formula containing the verb in the first-person present" (Benveniste, "Analytical Philosophy and Language," 237). Used with caution, this simple test gives us "a list of verbs of the order of the third power of 10," which is that of the "explicit performative verbs" (Austin, *How to Do Things with Words*, 149), always linked to illocutionary acts. The difficulty evidently derives from the fact that after the *sea-change* it is no longer a matter of statements but of situated acts.

45. " '*In* saying I would shoot him I was threatening him.' '*By* saying I would shoot him I alarmed him.' Will these linguistic formulas provide us with a test for distinguishing illocutionary from perlocutionary acts? They will not" (Austin, *How to Do Things with Words*, 122–23; italics added). "These formulas are at best very slippery tests" (ibid., 131).

46. For Parmenides, see *L'effet sophistique*, part one, section one, and Parménide, *Sur la nature ou l'étant: Le grec, langue de l'être?*; cf. part V, chap. 3. For Helen, see part I, chap. 3, "Seeing Helen in Every Woman."

47. Logology implies the rethinking of truth: "No one *knows* the essential thing about language, that it is concerned only with itself. That is why it is such a marvellous and fruitful mystery—for if someone merely speaks for the sake of speaking, he utters the most splendid, original truths," in Novalis, "Mono-logue," in Wheeler, ed., *German Aesthetic and Literary Criticism*, 93; italics added. Let us think of the striking Lacanian motto, "Moi, la vérité je parle. . . ."

48. "*Kai legei hô legôn . . . arkhên gar ou legei de khrôma, alla logon*," in *On Melissus, Xenophanes, and Gorgias* (this is the other version of the treatise, transmitted anonymously at the tail end of the Aristotelian corpus), §10 980b, ed. and trans. into French by Barbara Cassin as *Si Parménide* (Lille: PUL-MSH, 1980), 540–41.

49. One need only consult §7 of *Being and Time*.

50. Outside of (discussions of) rhetoric in Aristotle, one of the most instructive occurrences is from the grand ancestor Thales, who takes his revenge on his Thracian servant by inventing the monopoly on oil presses so as to play off supply and demand. "Wise," but not "prudent," he is said to "have given a striking proof of his wisdom" (Aristotle, *Politics*, in *Complete Works of Aristotle*, 1259a 20).

51. Ponge, "La cruche."

52. *Encomium of Helen* §8 = 82 B11, 8 DK, II, 290.

53. "[F]or as yet we have heard only of the obligation imposed by society that it should exist: to be truthful means using the customary metaphors—in moral terms: the obligation to lie according to a fixed convention, to lie herd-like in a style obligatory for all. Now man of course forgets that this is the way things stand for him. Thus he lies in the manner

indicated, unconsciously and in accordance with habits which are centuries old; and precisely *by means of this unconsciousness* and forgetfulness he arrives at his sense of truth. From the sense that one is obliged to designate one thing as red, another as cold, and a third as mute, there arises a moral impulse in regard to truth" ("On Truth and Lie in an Extra-Moral Sense," in *Friedrich Nietzsche on Rhetoric and Language*, ed. Sander Gilman, Carole Blair, and David J. Parent (Oxford: Oxford University Press, 1989), 250.

54. *"Phere dê pros allon ap'allou metastô logon,"* in *On Melissus, Xenophanes, and Gorgias,* §9 (82 B 11 DK, II, 290, 1. 25). This is how Gorgias punctuates his eulogy to poetry, by drawing attention to the act of language, which is operating and in the process of being accomplished.

55. This is how Chantraine, *Dictionnaire étymologique de la langue grecque,* refers to R. B. Onians's *Origins of European Thought: About the Body, the Mind, the Soul, the World, Time and Fate* (Cambridge: Cambridge University Press, 1951), 174–83.

56. *Instructions païennes* (Paris: Galilée, 1977), 43–49.

57. It remains to balance up the "performative virtue" of language and the "authority of the outside" in conformity with the critical injunction of Pierre Bourdieu. For him, the *vis performativa* is anchored not "in the intrinsic properties of discourse itself" but "in the social conditions of production and reproduction . . . of the recognition of legitimate language" ("Langage et pouvoir symbolique," in *Ce que parler veut dire: L'économie des échanges linguistiques* [Paris: Fayard, 1982], 113).

58. Lacan, "L'étourdit," *Scilicet* 4 (1973): 5–52, and epublished in *Autres écrits* (Paris: Seuil, 2001), 449–95.

59. Austin ends up speaking of truth as a supplementary dimension for the constative utterance: "so we have here a new dimension of criticism of the accomplished statement" (*How to Do Things with Words,* 144).

60. Benveniste, "Language in Freudian Theory," in *Problems in General Linguistics,* 66.

61. Ibid., 75.

62. Lacan, "L'étourdit," 47. Kindly refer to Cassin, *Jacques le Sophiste op. cit.*

11. THE PERFORMATIVE WITHOUT CONDITION: A UNIVERSITY *SANS APPEL*

This chapter was cowritten with Philippe Büttgen.

1. Jacques Derrida, "The University Without Condition," in *Without Alibi* (Stanford: Stanford University Press, 2002), 237.

2. Valérie Pécresse, "Ce que je veux dire aux enseignants-chercheurs," *Libération,* Jan. 27, 2009 (emphasis added).

3. It is worth noting that the original French of the expression that Pécresse cites is *"Professer, c'est s'engager."* The verb *s'engager* can mean "to take a stand," "to commit oneself (to something)." Derrida plays on the verbal form *engager* and the nominal expression *en gage*, "pledge" (translator's note).

4. See "Sarkozy m'à tuer" [*sic*], *Le Monde*, Mar. 1, 2009, 14.

5. See the *Journal officiel de la République française*, Aug. 11, 2007, and Law 2007–1199, dated Aug. 10, 2007, relative to the freedoms and responsibilities of universities.

6. Derrida, "University Without Condition," 215.

7. Ibid., 213–14.

8. New modes of organization relative to the *concours* (competitive exam) for the recruitment of high school teachers (the *agrégation*, CAPES, CAPET, etc.), contained in the decrees of Dec. 28, 2009. See the *Journal officiel de la République française*, Jan. 6, 2010.

9. Derrida, "University Without Condition," 234–37.

10. Valérie Pécresse on "Dimanche soir politique," *France Inter*, Jan. 12, 2009.

11. Derrida, "University Without Condition," 213.

12. Ibid., 208.

13. Martin Heidegger, "The Self-Assertion of the German University and the Rectorate 1993/34: Facts and Thoughts," *Review of Metaphysics* 38, no. 3 (March 1985): 479. In the German original: *"Der Kampf allein hält den Gegensatz offen und pflanzt in die ganze Körperschaft von Lehrern und Schülern jene Grundbestimmung, aus der heraus die sich begrenzende Selbstbehauptung die entschlossene Selbstbesinnung zur echten Selbstverwaltung ermächtigt."*

14. Derrida, "University Without Condition," 217 (emphasis added).

15. When Derrida ultimately interrogates himself about the nature of his discourse, in "The University Without Condition," this gives: "is it philosophy or literature? Or theatre? Is it an œuvre or a course, or a sort of seminar?" (ibid., 237).

16. Immanuel Kant, *Der Streit der Fakultäten* (1798), Einführung, AK VII, 17:

Es war kein übeler Einfall desjenigen, der zuerst den Gedanken faßte und ihn zur öffentlichen Ausführung vorschlug, den ganzen Inbegriff der Gelehrsamkeit ... gleichsam fabrikenmäßig, durch Vertheilung der Arbeiten, zu behandeln, wo, so viel es Fächer der Wissenschaften giebt, so viel öffentliche Lehrer, Professoren, als Depositeure derselben angestellt würden, die zusammen eine Art von gelehrtem gemeinen Wesen, Universität (auch hohe Schule) genannt, ausmachten, die ihre Autonomie hätte (denn über Gelehrte als solche können nur Gelehrte urtheilen)." Quoted in translation from *The Conflict of the Faculties*, trans. Mary J. Gregor (Lincoln: University of Nebraska Press, 1979), 23 (emphasis added).

354 *Notes to pages 224–27*

17. Derrida, "University Without Condition," 209; emphasis in the original.

18. Ibid.

19. Ibid., 235.

20. Thus, "Personally, I see in evaluation the compensation for performance. If there is no evaluation, there is no performance" (speech given by the president of the republic on the occasion of the launch of the reflection on the National Strategy for Research and Innovation at the Palais de l'Élysée, Jan. 22, 2009). Or: "the culture of results and of performance has always been at the centre of my action. We should not have any taboo with regard to figures, and I have always advocated the greatest transparency" (speech given by the president of the republic at a meeting with the main [actors] in security, prisons, and national education, May 28, 2009). All of Nicolas Sarkozy's speeches could be read online during his term at www.elysee.fr.

21. "I have a deep conviction: we will not change our behaviour if we don't change the measure of our performance. And our behaviour absolutely must change" (speech of the president of the republic at the International Conference for the Presentation of the Conclusions of the Commission for the Measurement of Economic Performance and Social Progress, given at the Sorbonne, Paris, Sept. 14, 2009). The measure changes, perhaps. However, it remains a measurement of performance. See on this point Barbara Cassin, "L'état schizophrène, Dieu et le nous raisonnable," in *L'appel des appels: Pour une insurrection des consciences*, ed. Roland Gori, Barbara Cassin, and Christian Laval (Paris: Éditions Mille et une nuits, 2009), 351–74 (especially 373–74), and Philippe Büttgen, "D'ailleurs toute activité sans évaluation pose un problème," a paper presented at the "La valeur de la science. Pourquoi évaluer la recherche?" conférence, Université de Liège, December 10 2009.

22. See part IV, chap. 10, "How to Really Do Things with Words: Performance Before the Performative."

23. Speech by the president of the republic during a visit to the Institut Régional d'Administration in Nantes, Sept. 19, 2007.

24. See Sergey Brin and Lawrence Page, "The Anatomy of a Large-Scale Hypertextual Web Search Engine," part V, section 3, http://infolab.stanford.edu/~backrub/google.html.

25. Eugene Garfield created the "journal impact factor" in 1960 to support the "Garfield impact factor" in selecting reviews for the Canadian Medical Association. We insist on the fact that the H-factor constitutes the unwarranted extension, even the uncontrolled importing of a practice that has its place in bibliometry, introduced in Canada for the well-controlled and numerically significant collections of medical publications.

26. The term that we use is *grille*, which in this context can be translated as "form" or "grid" or "questionnaire" (translator's note).

27. On this and the previous aspects, see Philippe Büttgen and Barbara Cassin, "'J'en ai 22 sur 30 au vert.' Six thèses sur l'évaluation," *Cités* 37 (2009): 27–41.

28. The expression that the authors use is *pour le plaisir*. It is an oblique reference to Cassin's work on sophistic and the *plaisir de parler* (translator's note).

29. Derrida, "University Without Condition," 215.

30. Ibid., 209. For the rest (of the argument) one would have to measure the exact impact of the debate between Searle and Derrida: the mention of "Signature, Event, Context" and of *Limited Inc* has an important part to play in Derrida's destitution of the performative (ibid., 301, footnote).

31. *Limited Inc*, 235 (Derrida's italics).

32. Ibid., 206.

33. Ibid., 234–35 (emphasis added).

34. Ibid., 236.

35. See note 14 of this chapter.

36. Derrida, *Limited Inc*, 215.

37. See footnote 6 in this chapter (translator's note).

38. *Limited Inc*, 218.

39. On performance as the principle of an economic thought bankrupt since 2008, see Cassin, "L'état schizophrène." This "appeal of appeals" has for its first function an appeal to say no from the heart of each of our *métiers* and, in particular, to say no to performance: in its own way it, too, is without appeal.

12. GENRES AND GENDERS. WOMAN/PHILOSOPHER: IDENTITY AS STRATEGY

The original title, "La perméabilité des genres," plays on the ambiguity of *genre* in French, which means both "genre" and "gender" (translator's note).

1. See the "Philosophical Tribune" in *Women Philosophers' Journal* 1 (November 2011), http://www.unesco.org/new/en/social-and-human-sciences /resources/periodicals/women-philosophers-journal/past-issues/.

2. Of course, this question did not stand alone, and we created a context (a contratext) for women-philosophers to ask "what do women-philosophers think of men-philosophers and think of what men-philosophers think of them?"

3. See Boni Tanella, *Que vivent les femmes d'Afrique?* (Paris: Karthala, 2011), and Catherine Malabou, *Changer de différence: Le féminin et la question philosophique* (Paris: Galilée, 2009).

4. What we have to do is to make a change from the one to the other because the other state is *better*. In education, too, what we have to do is to change a worse state into a better state; only whereas the doctor brings about the change by the use of drugs, the professional teacher does it by the use of words. What never happens is that a man who judges what is false is made to judge what is true. . . . But giving him a sound state of the soul causes him to think different things, things that are good. In the latter event, the things which appear to him are what some people who are still at a primitive stage call "true"; my position, however, is that the one kind is *better* than the others but in no way *truer*. . . . I look for wisdom, my dear Socrates, as regards animal bodies, in doctors; as regards plant-life, in gardeners—for I am quite prepared to maintain that gardeners too, when they find a plant sickly, proceed by causing it to have good and healthy perceptions, instead of bad ones. Similarly, the wise and efficient politician is the man who makes wholesome things seem just to a city instead of pernicious ones. . . . In this way, we are enabled to hold both that some men are wiser than others, and also that no man judges what is false. And you, too, whether you like it or not, must put up with being a "measure." (in Plato, *Theaetetus*, trans. M. J. Levett and rev. Myles Burnyeat [Indianapolis: Hackett, 1990], 166–67).

5. Women-philosophers were invited, and a visit was planned but had to be called off because of a strike.

6. "'Elles@centrepompidou': An Appeal to Difference," in *Elles@ centrepompidou—Femmes artistes dans les collections du Musée national d'art moderne* (Paris: Editions du Centre Pompidou), 15.

7. Ibid., 16.

8. Malabou, *Changer de différence*, 128.

9. As for the impossibility of being a woman, I would find it difficult not to refer to Lacan's "There Is No Sexual Relationship" (see *Il n'y a pas de rapport sexuel: Deux leçons sur "L'étourdit" de Lacan*, op. cit.).

10. "Perméabilité des genres" is to be taken in all its senses, and we see in the editorial of the journal titled "Fundamental Problems, Founding Problems" how they are interrelated: "a man can be a woman philosopher" (gender), "we are not precluding universal reporting or conversation" (genre).

11. Here is the conclusion of *L'effet sophistique* (op. cit.): "to consider as our primary world not nature but culture, the world as product." In a posthumous fragment of 1888, Nietzsche also writes that Parmenides said: "we cannot think of what does not exist"—we are at the other extreme and say: "what can be thought of must certainly be a fiction." I would sum up all of this with: the demystification of the ontological act of giving decompartmentalizes the genres of the *logos*.

12. Giulia Sissa, "A Woman, a Style of Thinking: The Craft of Nicole Loraux," *Women Philosophers' Journal* 1 (November 2011): 91–108.

13. Lacan, *On Feminine Sexuality, the Limits of Love and Knowledge, 1972–1973: Encore, The Seminar of Jacques Lacan, Book XX* (New York: Norton, 1999), 53. Lacan plays on the word *vaincre* (vanquish, Lat. *vincere*) and *convaincre* (convince, Lat. *convincere*) by separating the verbal prefix *con* (Lat. *cum*), a signifier that, in French, designates the female genitals and currently means "an idiot," "a jerk."

14. *Epistles*, 2, 1, 156. The line continues: *et artis intulit agresti Latio*, "and brought the arts into rustic Latium": it is through the cultivation of the soul and politeness that the female makes the naturally rustic and boorish male more mellow, whence so many (aptly named?) "common"-places.

15. Jacques Derrida, *Memoires: For Paul de Man*, trans. Cecile Lindsay, Jonathan Culler, and Eduardo Cadava (New York: Columbia University Press, 1989), 14–15.

16. Badiou and Cassin, *There's No Such Thing as a Sexual Relationship*, forthcoming.

17. *How to Do Things with Words*, 150; italics added.

18. Malabou, *Changer de différence*, 106.

19. This is the last paragraph of Catherine Malabou's book.

20. See *Les faiseuses d'histoires: Que font les femmes à la pensée?* (Paris: Les Empêcheurs de penser en rond, 2011). The expression "les faiseuses d'histoires" plays on more than one meaning: "faire des histoires" is a colloquial expression meaning "to make a fuss" or "to make a to-do about nothing," but one could hear also something like "to tell stories" and, then, "to make history."

13. PHILOSOPHIZING IN TONGUES

1. Jacques Derrida, *Learning to Live Finally: The Last Interview*, trans. P.-A. Brault and M. Naas (Basingstoke: Palgrave Macmillan, 2007), 36–38. Jacques Derrida's "singular history" refers here to his book *Monolingualism of the Other*.

2. I still regret the inversion of the title (*Vocabulaire européen des philosophies*) and the subtitle (*Dictionnaire des intraduisibles*) imposed by the French publishing house. Fortunately, it will be corrected in the English adaptation, directed by Emily Apter, Jacques Lezra, and Michael Wood, op. cit.

3. "The materiality of a word cannot be translated or carried over into another language. Materiality is precisely that which translation relinquishes. To relinquish materiality: such is the driving force of translation," in Jacques Derrida, *Writing and Difference*, trans. Alan Bass (London: Routledge, 2001), 264.

4. Arnaldo Momigliano, "The Fault of the Greeks," in *Essays in Ancient and Modern Historiography* (Middletown, Conn.: Wesleyan University Press, 1977), 11.

5. "If different rule-setters do not make each name out of the same syllables, we must not forget that different blacksmiths who are making the same tool for the same type of work don't all make it out of the same iron. But, as long as they give it the same form, even if that form is embodied in different iron, the tool will be correct, whether it is made here or abroad," in Plato, *"Cratylus," Complete Works,* ed. J. M. Cooper and D. S. Hutchinson (Indianapolis: Hackett, 1997), 108 (389 e1–390 a2).

6. "It is not from the words that we ought to start, but rather we should seek and learn from the things themselves rather than from the words," ibid., 154 (439b) (translator's note: translation modified according to Cassin's French version).

7. Friedrich Schleiermacher, "On the Different Methods of Translating," in *The Translation Studies Reader,* ed. Lawrence Venuti and trans. Susan Bernovsky (London: Routledge, 2004), 34–35. Please also refer to C. Berner's glossary in the French version of the text: Friedrich Schleiermacher, *Des différentes méthodes de traduire et autre texte,* trans. A. Berman and C. Berner (Paris: Seuil, 1999), 135–38.

8. See part I, chap. 1 ("Who's Afraid of the Sophists? Against Ethical Correctness"), and part IV, chap. 10 ("How to Really Do Things with Words: Performance Before the Performative"); for *to eon,* see part V, chap. 17, "The Relativity of Translation and Relativism."

9. Friedrich Nietzsche, *"Fragments sur le langage"* (*note de travail pour Homère et la philologie classique*), trans. into French by J.-L. Nancy and P. Lacoue-Labarthe in *Poétique* 5 (1971): 134. (This note does not appear in the English translation of *Homer and Classical Philology,* translated here from the French by Y. Gilonne.)

10. Gorgias, *Encomium of Helen* (translation from Cassin's French version by Y. Gilonne).

11. Wilhelm Von Humboldt, *Über die Verschiedenheiten des menschlichen Sprachbaues,* in *Gesammelte Schriften,* vol. VI, ed. A. Leitzmann (Berlin: Behr, 1907), 240 (*"Die Sprache erscheint in der Wirklichkeit nur als ein Vielfaches"*).

12. I am paraphrasing the well-known alternative: "Either the translator leaves the writer in peace as much as possible and moves the reader toward him, or he leaves the reader in peace as much as possible and moves the writer toward him" (Schleiermacher, "On the Different Methods of Translating," 49). I am choosing with Schleiermacher the uneasiness of the first possibility.

13. See part I, chap. 2 ("Speak If You Are a Man, or the Transcendental Exclusion"), and part V, chap. 17 ("The Relativity of Translation and Relativism").

14. Jacques Lacan, "L'étourdit," *Scilicet* 4 (1973): 5–52, 47 (trans. Y. Gilonne).

15. His etymology was a simple cut: con/cierge. I have told the story in "Noyade d'un poisson," in Cassin, *Avec le plus petit et le plus inapparent des corps*, and commented on it in Cassin, *Jacques le Sophiste*.

16. We are transposing the English *governance* into the French *gouvernance*, or, rather, we are operating a resemanticization since the French word, which appeared in 1679, referred to a child under the care of a governess and is "employed today in Senegal in the philological and political action of President Senghor to designate the administrative services of a region" (in *Dictionnaire historique de la langue française*, ed. Alain Rey and trans. Y. Gilonne [Paris: Robert, 2000]). In Brussels, the word *gouvernance* "owes nothing to its Senegalese counterpart: the 'gouvernement,'" and therefore the political dimension disappears. When France speaks of *gouvernance*, not only does it speak in pidgin English, but it also thinks in Anglo-Saxon.

17. Victor Kemperer, *The Language of the Third Reich: LTI, Lingua Tertii Imperii: A Philologist's Notebook*, trans. Martin Brady (London : Continuum, 2006).

18. Gottfried Leibniz, *Philosophische Schriften* (Berlin: Gerhardt, 1980), vol. VII, 200.

19. Translation Yves Gilonne.

20. Jean Le Rond d'Alembert, *Preliminary Discourse to the Encyclopedia of Diderot*, trans. R. N. Schwab (Chicago: University of Chicago Press, 1995), 92–93.

21. Johann Gottfried von Herder, "Briefe zur Beförderung der Humanität," no. 100, in *Werke*, vol. 7, ed. Dietrich Irmscher and trans. Y. Gilonne (Frankfurt: Deutscher Klassiker Verlag, 1991). The French translation appears in P. Caussat, D. Adamski, and M. Crépon, *La langue source de la nation*, trans. Y. Gilonne (Paris: Mardaga, 1996), 105. Imitation becomes the genius characteristic of a language which would lack genius, much like the hand in Aristotle is the "tool of all tools," capable of utilizing them all and therefore worthy of them all.

22. Martin Heidegger, *The Essence of Human Freedom: An Introduction to Philosophy*, trans. Ted Sadler (London: Continuum, 2002), 35–36; italics in the original.

23. Jean-Pierre Lefebvre, "*Philosophie et philologie: Les traductions des philosophes allemands*," in *Encyclopaedia Universalis: Symposium, les Enjeux*, vol. 1, trans. Y. Gilonne (Paris: Encyclopaedia Universalis, 1990), 170.

24. Martin Heidegger, *What Is Called Thinking?* trans. J. G. Gray (New York: Harper and Row, 1968), 128.

25. Martin Heidegger, "Hölderlin's Hymne 'Der Ister,'" in *Gesamtausgabe*, vol. 53, trans. Y. Gilonne (Frankfurt: Klostermann, 1984), 79–80.

26. Wilhelm von Humboldt, "Fragment de monographie sur les Basques," in Caussat, Adamski, and Crépon, *La langue source de la nation*, 433.

27. Ibid.

28. Wilhelm von Humboldt, "From His Introduction to the Translation of Agamemnon," trans. Sharon Sloan, in *Theories of Translation: An Anthology of Essays from Dryden to Derrida*, ed. Rainer Schulte and John Biguenet (Chicago: University of Chicago Press, 1992), 55.

29. Ibid.

30. Hannah Arendt, "'What Remains? The Language Remains': A Conversation with Günter Gaus," in *The Portable Hannah Arendt*, ed. Peter Baehr (New York: Harcourt, Penguin, 2000), 13.

31. Sylvie Courtine-Denamy, "Postface," in *Hannah Arendt, journal de pensée: 1950–1973*, vol. 2, trans. Y. Gilonne (Paris: Seuil, 2005), 1062–67.

32. Ibid., 56–57.

14. "ENOUGH OF THE TRUTH FOR . . .": ON THE TRUTH AND
RECONCILIATION COMMISSION

1. Gilles Deleuze, *Negotiations*, trans. M. Joughin (New York: Columbia University Press, 1995), 131 (translation slightly modified).

2. Plato, *Theaetetus*, 167b.

3. The report of the Truth and Reconciliation Commission (1998) is available, with related documents, at http://www.justice.gov.za/trc/report/.

4. Philippe-Joseph Salazar, *Amnistier l'apartheid: Travaux de la Commission Vérité et Réconciliation*, ed. Desmond Tutu (Paris: Seuil, 2004).

5. See part III, chap. 7: "From Organism to Picnic: Which Consensus for Which City?"

6. Antje Krog, *Country of My Skull* (Johannesburg: Random House, 1998).

7. Plato, *Theaetetus*, 166d–67.

8. *Encomium of Helen*, 82 B 11 DK §8.

9. Ibid., §14.

10. Thucydides, *History*, 3, 82.

11. Hannah Arendt, *Eichmann in Jerusalem: A Report on the Banality of Evil* (New York: Viking, 1963), 48.

12. Jean Hatzfeld, *Into the Quick of Life: The Rwandan Genocide—The Survivors Speak*, trans. Gerry Feehily (London: Serpent's Tail, 2005), 159.

13. Krog, *Country of My Skull*, 266–70.

14. Ibid., 99.

15. See part III, chap. 9: "Paradigms of the Past in Arendt and Heidegger," and Arendt's *Between Past and Future*, 259.

15. POLITICS OF MEMORY: ON THE TREATMENT OF HATE

1. For Athens, I draw on a remarkable article by Nicole Loraux, "De l'amnistie et de son contraire," in *Usages de l'oubli*, ed. Yosef Yerushalmi, Nicole Loraux, Hans Mommsen, Jean-Claude Milner, and Gianni Vattimo (Paris: Seuil, 1988), 22–47. For South Africa, see Philippe-Joseph Salazar's books, *Afrique du Sud: La révolution fraternelle* (Paris: Hermann, 1988), and *An African Athens: The Rhetorical Shaping of Democracy in Post-Apartheid South Africa* (Mahwah, N.J.: Erlbaum, 2002). For the use of archives I drew a lot from "Transparence et secret: L'accès aux archives contemporaines," *La Gazette des Archives* (1997), 177–78.

2. Polybus, 16, 34, 11.

3. Ibid., 10, 33, 6.

4. Herodotus, 1, 59.

5. Thucydides, *History*, 3, 68–86. Further references are given in the text.

6. Salazar, *Afrique du Sud*, 27.

7. Printed in *Le Monde*, Sept. 15, 1999.

8. See also Isocrates, *Against Callimachus*, 25, and Andocides, *Mysteries*, 90, 31. The decree (*hai suntêkai*, "the conventions") is sometimes designated (by Aristotle) as *hai dialuseis*, "the decollation, the solution, the outcome," as if the *stasis* were too fusional to link, sometimes (Isocrates, Andocides) as *hai diallagai*, "the exchanges, the circulation" (which we translate as "the reconciliation"), as if it were about reestablishing a circuit.

9. See Plato, *Letters* 7, 336 e–337 a: "a city in *stasis* does not know the end of its evils [*kaka*]" except when its conquerors cease to *mnêsikakein* [cease reprisals] by expulsions or by cutting throats.

10. Plutarch, *Political Precepts* (17); to be completed by Herodotus (6, 21). I would voluntarily like to deduce from this that Phrynicos was a bad poet, one who presented instead of "re-presenting." Without *mimêsis*, that is to say, in the distance of the "as if," which the imitation-representation introduced, there is no *catharsis* possible. The passions of hate and terror are summoned, they clutter up like nonexorcised phantoms, but they are not "purged." This question relates directly to the inherent theatralization of the TRC, as well as to the symbolic consistency of the staging of the general elections.

11. Aristotle, *Constitution of Athens*, 40.

12. Ibid.

13. Andocides, "On the Mysteries," 90–91.

14. *Constitution of Athens*, 40.

15. Isocrates, *Against Callimachus*, 46.

16. We could propose several versions of this. The "ontotheological" version is represented by the following phrase, constantly cited by Heidegger: "There where the danger is, that which saves also grows." But I much rather prefer the graffiti that I read on the walls of Desmond Tutu's house in Cape Town: "How to turn human wrongs into human rights."

17. Plato, *Theaetetus*, 167.

18. See part V, chap. 14: "'Enough of the Truth For . . .': On the Truth and Reconciliation Commission."

19. See part III, chap. 7 ("From Organism to Picnic: Which Consensus for Which City?") and chap. 9 ("Paradigms of the Past in Arendt and Heidegger").

20. Heidegger, *Parmenides, Gesamtausgabe*, vol. 54, trans. André Schuwer and Richard Rojcewicz (Frankfurt am Main: Vittorio Klostermann, 1982), 142.

21. *Nicomachean Ethics*, I, 1, 1094a 25–30.

22. Hannah Arendt, "The Crisis in Culture," in Hannah Arendt, *Between Past and Future* (New York: Viking, 1961), 259.

23. Hannah Arendt, "'What Remains? The Language Remains': A Conversation with Günter Gaus," in *The Portable Hannah Arendt*, 4.

24. The idea that discourse is essentially performative (the Sophistical *epideixis*) is related to its *pharmakon* status, "poison-remedy," by its difference from the *organon* status of "instrument" of Platonic-Aristotelian orthodoxy. See "Du pharmakon," in Barbara Cassin, Maurice Mathieu, and François Boissonnet, *Voir Hélène en toute femme: D'Homère à Lacan* (Paris: Les Empêcheurs de penser en rond, 2000).

25. Hannah Arendt, "Truth and Politics," in Hannah Arendt, *Between Past and Future: Eight Exercises in Political Thought* (London: Penguin, 1993), 229.

26. Ibid., 262.

27. Ibid.

28. 82 B23 DK (Plutarch, *De Glor. Athen*.5, p.348C), which is often quoted by Arendt.

29. Law 79–18 passed on Jan. 3, 1979, and was followed by the implementing decree on Mar. 12, 1979. I thank Jean Pouëssel from the French National Archives, who facilitated access to documents and explained to me the regulations and their perverse effects.

30. There is a case of a legal journalist, amnestied and living, who wins all of his court cases on the basis of this regulatory clause.

31. Hannah Arendt, "Lying in Politics," in *Crises of the Republic* (New York: Mariner Books, 1972), 1–47.

32. See part II, chap. 4, "Rhetorical Turns in Ancient Greece."

33. *Protagoras*, 320c–22d.

34. Ibid., 323b–c.

16. GOOGLE AND CULTURAL DEMOCRACY

1. Larry Page, quoted in Jason Kottke, "Playboy Interview: Google Guys," *Playboy* (Sept. 24, 2004).

2. For the purposes of comparison, *Libération* published the photographs for "Tiananmen Google Images" from France (with tanks) and "Tiananmen Google Images" from China (with celebrating crowds, magnificent parades). Google admitted to having censored prohibited sites in February 2004, notably those concerning Tibet, Taiwan, and the Tiananmen demonstrations and their suppression. The sites disappeared, Google stated, so that users would not end up clicking on error messages. As with the Patriot Act, one doesn't even know that one doesn't know.

3. *Gorgias*, op. cit., 457d.

4. *Theaetetus*, op. cit., 167a–c.

5. In French *le/la meilleur/e* (with the definite article) becomes a superlative. Without the definite article, it has a comparative value (translator's note).

6. John Batelle, *The Search: How Google and Its Rivals Rewrote the Rules of Business and Transformed Our Culture* (New York: Penguin, 2005), 234; emphasis added.

17. THE RELATIVITY OF TRANSLATION AND RELATIVISM

1. Plato, *Theaetetus*, 888.

2. Heidegger, *Introduction to Metaphysics*, 102.

3. Sextus, *Against the Logicians*, trans. Richard Bett (Cambridge: Cambridge University Press, 2005), 24. Translation modified.

4. The formal and substantive reasons for preferring the text transmitted by Simplicius are clearly summarized by Denis O'Brien in *Le Poème de Parménide: Texte, traduction, essai critique* (Paris: Vrin, 1987), 239–42.

5. See my translation of the poem in *Sur la nature ou sur l'étant. Le grec, langue de l'être?*, 70–117. (In the present chapter, I rely on the central theses of this work with regard to the interpretation of the poem.

6. French Edition, FDE Schleiermacher, *L'Herméneutique générale, 1809–1810*, trad. C. Berner, Paris, Cerf, 1987.

7. Ibid., 75.

8. Gilles Deleuze, *Negotiations*, trans. M. Joughin (New York: Columbia University Press, 1995), 131 (translation slightly modified).

9. *Über die Verschiedenheiten des menschlichen Sprachbaues*, 240.

10. See part IV, chap. 13, "Philosophizing in Languages."

11. Lacan, "L'Étourdit," 47. See also part IV, chap. 13, "Philosophizing in Languages."

12. See part I, chap. 1, "Who's Afraid of the Sophists? Against Ethical Correctness."

13. *The Essence of Human Freedom: An Introduction to Philosophy*, trans. Ted Sadler (New York: Continuum, 2008), 36.

14. "Language in Freudian Theory," 63.

15. *Word and Object* (Boston: MIT Press, 1975), 52.

16. Ponge, *Pratiques d'écriture ou l'inachèvement perpétuel*, 40.

17. Aristotle, *Metaphysics*, IV, 3, 1005 b 19–20.

18. See part I, chap. 2, "Speak If You Are a Man, or the Transcendantal Exclusion."

19. Aristotle, book *Gamma, Metaphysics*; translation slightly modified; emphasis added.

20. Translation modified.

21. "Fragments sur le langage", trad. J.-L. Nancy et P. Lacoue-Labarthe, *Poétique*, 5, 1971, p. 134 (note de travail pour H*omère et la philologie classique* datant de 1868–1869).

22. Plato, *Theaetetus*, 867.

23. Ibid., 872–73.

24. These sentences are taken from a speech by Nicolas Sarkozy given at Bercy on April 29, 2007.